Elizabeth Warnock Fernea is a lecturer in Middle Eastern studies and English at the University of Texas at Austin. She is the author of a number of books dealing with the Middle East and co-editor of *Middle Eastern Muslim Women Speak* (University of Texas Press, 1977). The research for *Women and the Family in the Middle East* was conducted with the assistance of a grant from the National Endowment for the Humanities.

Women and the Family in the Middle East

Women and the Family in the Middle East
NEW VOICES OF CHANGE

Edited by Elizabeth Warnock Fernea

 University of Texas Press, Austin

First Edition, 1985

Requests for permission to reproduce material from this work
should be sent to Permissions, University of Texas Press,
Box 7819, Austin, Texas 78713.

*The National Endowment for the Humanities provided partial
support for the publication of this work. The views expressed
throughout the work do not necessarily represent the views of
the Endowment.*

LIBRARY OF CONGRESS CATALOGING IN PUBLICATION DATA
Main entry under title:
Women and the family in the Middle East.
   1. Women—Arab countries—Addresses, essays, lectures.
2. Family—Arab countries—Addresses, essays, lectures.
3. Arab countries—Social life and customs—Addresses,
essays, lectures. 4. Women—Iran—Addresses, essays,
lectures. I. Fernea, Elizabeth Warnock.
HQ1784.W65 1984 305.4'2'09174927 84-11944
ISBN 0-292-75528-7
ISBN 0-292-75529-5 (pbk.)

Contents

Preface

In January 1981, after an absence of five years, I went back to the Arab world. I had been awarded a grant from the National Endowment for the Humanities to make a classroom film and a study guide for teachers on social change in the Arab world from the woman's perspective. Everywhere I went, from January to July, old friends and new presented me with manuscripts. "Look at this poem," they would say. "Read this essay. You see how things are going and how everyone is questioning?" When I returned home and looked through the materials, it seemed that many new issues were being discussed and new insights offered. Above all, many new voices were being raised, most of which had not been heard in the West before. Here was a book, the book that follows. No collection, however, can be totally representative and this one is no exception. Turkey, Israel, and the Gulf States, which are not included, obviously deserve volumes of their own, edited by scholars more conversant than I with those specific regions.

I would like to thank the translators who worked out of concern that the materials be made available in English: Basima Bezirgan, Tura Campanella, Adele Fath, Salah-dine Hammoud, Mohammad Khazali, J. Michael McDougal, Fedwa Malti-Douglas, Christopher Middleton, and Tim Mitchell. Dr. Alex Baramki, professor at Beirut University College, reviewed the translation of *Those Memories* by Emily Nasrallah. Robert Fernea encouraged me to finish the work. Daniel Goodwin aided greatly in the editing of the volume, and I want to express special appreciation for his counsel and assistance. I owe a special debt of thanks to Jenny Morter for her help with the final editing. Cora Boyett, Joy Lough, James Taylor, and Diane Watts typed various versions. I thank them all.

ELIZABETH FERNEA

Poem

SALMA KHADRA JAYYUSI
Translated from the Arabic by Patricia Alanah with the
author and Christopher Middleton

To Usama

I am a woman of April
December fires that burn to ash frighten me.

 Hide me, my son, you who rocket to the stars
 You who spread over the earth like grass.

Ominous December thunder will overwhelm
My river rippling with secrets of love.
It will stifle the music on whose echoing
Waves you were born.

You shrug:
 This woman is rooted in time.
 She spans the air like a dove
 In flight for a thousand years.

 I know her.

 She is a willow, a supple reed, I know her.
 Twisted or bent, she returns to her old self.

 A palm tree, I know her.
 Pick her fruits and she sprouts more,
 More fruits, and their honey.

 A cypress tree, I know her.
 Never shedding leaves, why should she care about
 December winds?

Son, the winds blow stronger.
My longing to hear your voice burns low, bitten off
By the iron edge that echo in your voice has;
It is wise, cruel, innocent, selfish.

Without your presence
All times of day and night are void.

We both permeate the wind, the air, the rains,
But like different galaxies we drink
Our own heart's wine,
We are poured, each, in our own glass.
Yet you were born of my elements,
I gave you my impetuosity,
That constant flitting in the public world,
That private elusiveness,
Chronic dizziness,
Rocklike will
And the fixity of faithful stars
In the valleys of the sky.

And I gave you
That spark of conquest, the rapture of love,
The intensity
And absorption of your being, all of it,
In the presence of holy fire.

Should I blame you?

And you offered me the promise, a pledge of calm,
A love like a tide that comes ashore
Only to recede.

Should you blame me?

I am a wild gazelle; you are rock, and
The blood is on my head.

PART I
Introduction

A generation has grown up in the Middle East since the fifties, when almost every nation in the area gained its independence from some form of foreign rule. And in every national charter and constitution, proclaimed in triumph on the day of independence, one of the cited goals was the improvement of women's status. To achieve this end, and to improve and equalize the lives of all of the new citizens, laws were passed regulating what was seen as an inequity in the courts between men's rights and women's rights. Both men and women were to benefit equally from changes ranging from agrarian reform and industrialization to free public education and health care. Thus, much was promised.

But after the idealism of the revolutionary and independence period has been tempered by the realities of managing new nations and attempting to right economic and political imbalances, what has happened to the status of women?

The book that follows is in part a progress report, seen not through the prism of ideology but through women's and men's own statements about their lives and their experiences. Of the "new voices," the majority are Middle Easterners themselves, many translated here for the first time into English from Arabic, French, and Persian sources. The statements are offered in different forms: short stories, essays, interviews, poems, social analyses, and life histories.

Throughout the materials, one senses an enormous urgency, an anxiety about the future, a disap-

pointment that many of the revolutionary promises have not been kept, and a feeling that the
pace of change has slowed. An immense creativity is also present, a resourcefulness in grappling
with the difficult economic, social, and emotional pressures, a willingness to struggle against
that narrowness of spirit that is the essence of reaction. Survival is basic, but the idealism of the
fifties has left its mark, and these women and
men wish to survive with honor.

The ways in which the aspirations of men and
women are expressed vary. No longer is the example of the West seen as the answer to the problems of the Middle East. This is one of the great
shifts evident in the volume. People are attempting to improve their lives through indigenous traditions and customs; through the dominant religion of the area, Islam; and through their own
kinship and family patterns. They are improvis-
ing and combining the new and the old, adapting,
changing, and building, trying to create their own
form of independence.

The West is generally unaware of the current out-
pouring of concern, criticism, and self-reflection
evidenced in these documents, documents that
represent only a small sampling of such activities
throughout Middle Eastern cultures today and in
many countries not represented in this volume.
Thus, it is not surprising that Western writers,
ignorant of the range of such self-expression,
often present a narrower, less well-informed view
of Middle Eastern peoples in general and women
in particular.

If one tries to pinpoint the most striking contrast between the Middle Eastern women writing
here and much similar material from the pens of
Western women, it seems to be that Middle Eastern women do not see the existing problems as
exclusive to themselves. Over and over again,
they say in different ways that the "feminine condition" cannot be separated from that of men, the
family, and the wider society. Self-identity is becoming important, but identity is still contextual.

The documents represent a wide variety of women from different parts of the Middle East. They voice anxiety, optimism, fear, hope, bitterness. But they continue to ask questions and to conscientiously struggle to improve not only their situation but that of their societies as a whole. The article by Fatiha Akeb and Malika Abdelaziz, taken from *Algerie actualité*, includes interviews with more than sixty women who articulate concern about the accomplishment of the past generation and the failure of the state to keep the promises of the revolution, while Mustafa O. Attir, a well-known Libyan sociologist, gives an account of government policies and ideologies relating to women in the new revolutionary period in Libya since 1969.

The rising rate of inflation, the costs of industrialization and of providing public education, plus the population explosion in many countries of the area have made it difficult for families to survive on one salary—the man's. More and more, the traditional pattern of woman at home and man in the workplace is breaking up, primarily out of necessity. The new problems faced by women working outside the home, once considered shameful, are raised in the short story "The Shoes" by the Egyptian short story writer Iqbal Barakah, in Safia Mohsen's account of middle-class Egyptian women, in the five life histories of factory women in Cairo by Barbara Lethem Ibrahim, and in Andrea Rugh's account of poorer women in Cairo.

But Algerian women also talk about "the *right* to work," as do Egyptians, Moroccans, and Lebanese. Women are beginning to see a virtue in the necessity and are insisting on their freedom to choose that right. Egyptian women are campaigning like Algerian women for more state support to make their working easier. They want day-care centers in the factories, better bus service, more labor-saving appliances.

Family planning is related to the economic situation but touches on other areas of society, particularly women's right to decide on the number of children and then use or not use contraceptives, and the basic belief in the family as the central unit to which allegiance is still required. Family planning is part of every nation's health care efforts, and the progress in this area is reflected in Donna Lee Bowen's account of a young Moroccan woman's journey through the complex labyrinth of the new national health care system. Ann Bragdon al-Kadhi's brief research report indicates the strong relationship between fertility and education. The problem of female circumcision, which occurs in Islamic countries along the Nile Valley, is discussed by Nahid Toubia, a Sudanese woman doctor.

Another basic promise of the revolutions and of the new nationalist governments all across the Arab world and North Africa (the Meshriq and the Maghreb) was free compulsory public education. A great effort has been made to fulfill that promise for both men and women in many countries, but women are saying that the promise has not been completely fulfilled. Nagat al-Sanabary of Egypt asks, "Education where and for what?" in her survey of women's education throughout the area. Figures from both the Sudan and Algeria tell the same story: a beginning, but not yet enough.

Religious revival, discussed frequently in the media, is here given some depth in Shireen Mahdavi's analysis of the position of women in Iran as interpreted in Shi'a Islam and in Valerie Hoffman's translation of a section of Zaynab al-Ghazali's autobiography and her interview with Hagga Zaynab conducted in 1981.

Zaynab al-Ghazali's life, here presented in English for the first time, provides a new insight into the development of the women's movement in Egypt. Huda al-Sha'rawi, pioneer Egyptian feminist, is seen in the West as the leader of the major movement. But as we read Zaynab's autobiography, it is clear that the movement took two directions. Hagga Zaynab, who was part of Huda al-Sha'rawi's Feminist Union, split off in the thirties and formed another women's union, the Muslim Women's Association, dedicated to reinterpretation and reconstitution of Islam among women. Familiarity with this part of the movement would have made recent religious movements in the area much more understandable and less surprising to scholars. That the split continues today is clear from Farzaneh Milani's study of two Iranian women poets.

Political revolution has taken its toll on women in the area as well as men. Rosemary Sayigh's account of Palestinian women on the West Bank makes this all too clear, and the disturbing article from Beirut, "The Kalashnikov Generation," is evidence from a whole generation of alienated youth in Lebanon who have been raised on war and strife and whose lives have been irremediably changed.

The Koran and Shariʿa law are still the basis for the legal system across the area, particularly in the realm of family law, the law that affects women's lives and covers marriage, divorce and child custody, and inheritance. The *Algerie actualité* article was prompted by the current reappraisal of the secular personal status code, which had been passed after the Algerian revolution in 1962 but which, the women say, has never been properly implemented. Efforts to reform the family law in Egypt resulted in a new law of 1979, and the law's strengths and weaknesses are discussed by Aziza Hussein, former Egyptian delegate to the UN and for many years a member of the UN committee on the status of women. Eric Mueller summarizes important influences on new family laws.

However complex and varied the new social position of women is, it has served as a catalyst for a burst of creativity that has resulted in much new artistic and literary experimentation, both with new forms (short stories) and with traditional forms (poetry). Hoda al-Namani, born in Damascus and now living in Lebanon, cites the influence of Muslim mystic poetry on her own new work, which is briefly discussed by Amin al-

Rihani, the Lebanese critic. The Palestinian poet Fadwa Tuqan writes with passion in the style of the "new poetry," as does Lamiᶜa Abbas ᶜImarah of Iraq. Salma Khadra Jayyusi, another Palestinian poet, combines both new and old in her attempt to articulate poetically some of the new problems and new situations that women face. Such new situations are also dealt with in the short stories: Fathiyyah ᶜAwada of Egypt tells the story of an affair between a single woman and a married man, an affair that is ending because the woman refuses to become a second wife, polygamy being allowed still in most Muslim countries. Such a situation would scarcely have arisen, much less been delineated in fiction, a generation ago. Nawal al-Saᶜdawi uses the novel form to depict the socialization of girls in Egypt during her own lifetime. Leila Abouzeid of Morocco and Ilfat Idilbi of Syria take old themes that affect women—divorce, polygamy—and deal with them in new ways. Iqbal Barakah of Egypt discusses the petty conflicts of women office workers whose life choices are limited, and Daisy al-Amir of Iraq chronicles the tale of a young girl caught up in an unnamed political revolution who has lost her identity in the process. The excerpt from Emily Nasrallah's novel *Those Memories* deals with another new phenomenon: friendship between Lebanese women of different social classes and how that friendship is maintained across civil war and across years and miles of migration. Folk art is also changing in response to new social conditions, as Sabra Webber demonstrates in her account of the new types of folktales being told by women in Tunisia.

Identity is a word hardly mentioned a generation ago, a word that had little meaning then in the Western sense of individuality except among a few elitist women. But the word is discussed by many women today as they struggle to maintain a balance between the demands of their own traditional families (which they still feel are more or less justified and necessary) and the demands they believe in or state that they, as persons, are entitled to. Halim Barakat raises the whole complex issue of the modern family versus the individual in his essay. This is a thread that runs through all the documents offered here, from Evelyn Early's life history of a poor Egyptian woman ("Friends are the people I depend on! Even family is not always to be trusted") to Safia Mohsen's interviews with middle-class women who are trying to find their way along a difficult, tangled, and often inchoate route between tradition and the world of today.

Assia Djebar, one of Algeria's most well-known writers, poses today's conflict for Middle Eastern women in metaphors represented by Western views. Delacroix painted the *Femmes d'Alger dans leur appartement* in the 1830s "in a luminous light" but "at the end of a long dark hall"; in other words, as enigmatic prisoners in a world composed largely of women. Picasso painted the women of Algeria more than a hundred years later with the doors of the hall open and sunlight streaming in. Two views. Two periods. "Let us hope it is Picasso's vision that is the vision of the future," says Assia Djebar. If that is the case, the women of the Middle East will have helped fashion that future themselves. The text of this book articulates their efforts in the process of achieving their goal.

Algerian Women Discuss the Need for Change

FATIHA AKEB and MALIKA ABDELAZIZ
Translated from the French by Adele Fath

The following is an edited version of an article that appeared in a 1981 is-sue of Algerie actualité, *a major Algerian news weekly, at the time when the personal status code, a reform law governing the lives and conduct of men and women, was being considered for possible revision by the central government.*

The personal status code should not exist for women only, but should define and adjust the roles of men, women, and children in this country, which is ours by virtue of our own struggles. Its achievements, its op-tions, and its problems belong to us all.

As a reappraisal of the code approaches, we decided to explore women's views of social change. We interviewed women throughout the country, and found that in the family, on the job, and in the society as a whole women feel their lot is difficult and often unjust and that their contribu-tions are not fully recognized.

Our article examines those areas where the relationships and endeav-ors of the members of society are interwoven—family, work, social life. Working women, students, housewives speak for themselves. Our pur-pose was not to present an analysis of the status of women but, rather, to ask women to reflect, to summarize their experiences, their prob-lems, their points of view.

Work: A Right to Defend

A woman's voice has just called my name. A gesture at an office win-dow signals me to wait while a woman comes down two flights of stairs. She hands me a thick envelope. Intrigued, I draw out six long handwritten sheets. Incredible. These working women, whom we had interviewed for four hours the day before, have drawn up an official re-port of their discussions!

Yesterday some other working women we had interviewed came to see us at the newspaper. "Last night, after thinking it over, we realized that some things were missing, . . ." they announced. At the price of having to fill out the usual company questionnaire to get approval for their absence, they had come to make sure that their remarks about their work were strong and convincing enough. For it is through their professional lives that they feel themselves involved with the same problems that preoccupy everyone; at the same time they feel involved in a controversy about women's place that they see as mortifying and unjust. For despite the revolution and the constitution, women still constitute only 25 percent of the working population.

Louisa, forty-seven years old, staff member: "Society looks askance at the working woman. It sees her as a job thief, as a woman of easy virtue."

Dalila, thirty-eight, assistant instructor: "In the framework of her profession, a woman is never considered as a working individual. She is forever being reminded that she is a woman, from displays of gallantry to the obstacles that hinder her in the practice of her profession."

Fatouma, twenty-eight, worker: "I work eight hours a day just as a man does, plus I do my household tasks; I have double labor and on top of that my morals are disparaged!"

The women find it "inadmissible" that after "twenty years of independence and four national plans," women's professional activity still retains a "pejorative" or "privilege-granted" reputation. Akila, thirty, staff member, expresses a sense of profound injustice on the subject.

The undervaluation of her typist's job provoked twenty-five-year-old Yamina to say: "Why not follow our feelings to their logical conclusion? Supposing all of us were to resign, teachers, hospital employees, university women, company staff, doctors, workers, technicians. What would the country be reduced to, I ask you?"

Women's work is a reality that has proved women's capacity as validly as did the resistance movement, says Zohra, forty-four, former member of the resistance movement against the French and now a secretary.

Ouardia, thirty, secretary: "Work is a right recognized by the National Charter and the Constitution."

Malika, twenty-four, student: "Work allows a woman to make something of her life. She becomes a citizen, part of the whole."

Linda, twenty, student: "What use is someone who does not work? For a woman, work is a way to gain freedom, she acquires it little by little through her work."

Fadila, twenty-seven, lawyer: "Work is a right. The right to share in the development of one's country, an expression of one's patriotic sentiment."

Yamina, twenty-eight, accountant, and Soumia, twenty-five, clerk, said, "Life is so painfully demanding, you simply have to work."

Work is an "obligation," a "constraint," "bondage" for "a salary," "some money to help a couple make both ends meet."

All of the women passionately defend the right to work.

Dahbia: "The right to work is constantly postponed. Fathers, brothers, and husbands tend to intervene, even when a woman has a real career."

Zohra: "Our children refuse to understand why they have to go on wearing patched pants or carry a paper sack instead of a proper school bag. If the neighbor has cheese to eat we want to give our kids some. Life forces the right to work on a woman. Married, divorced, widowed, she has to work. No one is in a position to grant or refuse her the authorization to bring up the future men of Algeria."

The women with college degrees define the right to work as a logical extension of the right to education.

Fadila: "Even the male intellectuals have not yet digested the idea of a woman's right to work, though they cannot justify not putting our education to use."

Men and women in the public sector are also faced with the problems of equal opportunities for recruitment and advancement. The older women point out that strong sex discrimination still exists and keeps white-collar workers in subordinate positions.

Dahbia: "For management, given equal competence between men and women, a man is still preferred. A strong misogynist spirit still exists."

Yamina: "The problem should be posed in feminist terms. A supervisor can always say that a pregnant woman has no right to take on a job with greater responsibility. The heaviness of pregnancy will cut down the woman's efficiency at the typewriter!"

More than sixty women, employed at different jobs and with different training and qualifications, were interviewed. All agreed that women's role as mother and wife militates against the development of a career and the access to positions of responsibility.

Louisa, forty-seven, office worker: "Given the busy system, a working woman is generally away from home about ten hours per day. Exhausted from double responsibilities, how can she dedicate herself to an interesting career? Further, given the housing conditions, how can she find a private place where she can sit alone to study or prepare for competitive examinations?"

Assia, thirty, office worker: "A worker is obliged to travel, to go on business trips, to stay late for office staff meetings . . . these things influence a woman who must often choose between keeping her marriage and assuming greater job responsibility."

Still all the women graduates, on the strength of their education, share a clear sense of their just rights.

Yamina: "As for me, I am able to explain that I studied to improve my chances in the future. But what about those women in situations inferior to ours? Who have to work out of necessity? How can their rights be established?"

In constrast to women whose professional satisfaction may compensate for other difficulties, many women resent the burdens of jobs that are thankless, laborious, degrading, and ill paid. For them work is not emancipation if work is "a right to get nowhere." "Our work contributes to the national economy and women workers have certain rights." Promotion is basic, they say.

Lila, Farida, Wahiba, Leila, Nassima, Fatiha, Nadia, Souad, Mezzaka, Rabia, Farida, and Soumia write: "No effort has been made to assure us of promotion. We stagnate at the lowest level. There is not even any on-the-job training." The highest level is that of secretary. "So we spend our lives in front of typewriters just because we're women!"

The hope for professional training is rarely stated in terms of expanding the creative capacity of each individual, or even as a realistic response to the needs of the national economy. Women simply state they are trying to get what they can out of the system. Any training is viewed primarily as a means of escaping the "adverse working conditions at the bottom of the ladder."

The issue of working hours is hotly debated.

Louisa: "Considering our living conditions, forty-four hours is too long."

What do they propose?

Lila, Farida, Wahiba, Leila, Nassima, Fatiha, Nadia, Souad, Mezzaka, Rabia, Farida, and Soumia write: "By our right as mothers we demand that the SGT (labor law) be applied to part-time work."

Ludmilla, twenty-five, white-collar worker: "Part-time work diminishes a woman. Does an employee do effective work in four hours? No. Part-time work is just a facile solution."

Zohra, thirty-five, clerk: "Part-time work equals part-time pay, doesn't it? That's only good for those who consider their salary as pocket-money."

Fatouma, twenty-eight, worker: "Can the assembly line function part-time, or will they simply replace us with men at the machines?"

No satisfactory solution can be agreed upon that will diminish their anxiety "to insure greater harmony between job and family without detracting from either."

Ludmilla: "Many women crack under the strain. Their job, the housework, the education and care of the children. The husband does not share those tasks."

Fatima, forty-three years old, three children, housewife: "With the high cost of living I find myself thinking about taking a job. But when I consider the children, I change my mind."

Zakia, twenty-eight, secretary: "It's when the child gets to be six years old that everything is really done for. School hours create insuperable problems . . ."

Ouardia, thirty, secretary: "The woman bears all the social burdens. The State has done little to allow a woman to do her part as a worker. To relieve her of the transportation problem, of the children, to help her with domestic tasks."

Najet, forty, assistant instructor: "A great many people are displeased with the increasingly large number of women at work. Why? Because of the ensuing problems that arise within the family when women work." Such problems, she says, are used as reasons to block women's access to the work place.

Female students hope for gradual change in the public perspective. They propose equality of education at home, co-education in the schools, an objective knowledge of Islam, and the organization of young people's free time.

But women workers want changes quicker and sooner. They want enforcement of current laws dealing with the woman's right to fourteen weeks' maternity leave, respect for child-feeding schedules, the right to on-the-job training, to promotion, to equal salaries, enlargement of protection and fringe benefits, prohibition of night work, permanent jobs, overtime pay . . .

What will be the driving force for these transformations the women propose?

First, the State. Its power to initiate reform. Its responsibility to inform the public via education and the mass media—particularly television. The State, believes Akila, must enact "laws that recognize that work is a right, that promotion is a right, that recognize equal rights for men and women."

Sakina, thirty, white-collar worker: "The National Charter and the Constitution are clear. Algerians have equal rights regardless of the color of their hair or eyes, or of their sex."

Fadila, twenty-seven, lawyer: "All the documents subsequent to the

National Charter should be in conformity with the National Charter."

Fatiha, law student, quotes the Koran: "Work, God will see your work, as will His Prophet and the believers!" It is a commandment in Islam, she says, directed at both men and women.

Change must also come through the efforts of women themselves, they say. Dahbia muses: "We are five thousand to six thousand women working at the PTT as opposed to twenty thousand men. What claims do we have as a minority?" But all acknowledge and object to "the over-passivity of women."

"How," in Najet's words, "can we rouse women's consciousness? What catalyst will work?"

"There is no women's organization," claims Malika, student. "Each of us feels herself isolated and believes herself lost whenever there is a problem." "But," she continues, "if that women's organization does not exist, it is also because we go quietly home and do nothing to change anything."

There remains the trade union.

Louisa: "We must make them do their job. After all, we are workers."

Dahbia: "It is not always the most qualified workers who climb the ladder, but that is our own fault."

For Fadila, the need is for "closer ties between the institutions of the country, mass organization, and the substance of the National Charter."

Sakina, member of a trade union, is hopeful about the union's role. From her own experience, she says, the union does offer women an opportunity to mobilize the women workers. Certain unions, including the ATU, took part in the preparation of our article. The representative of the national union of postal employees spoke before a group of postal employees gathered together at our request. He spoke of "the considerable problems facing women, including those in professions. The trade union," he also said, "must profit by the personal status code. Some "like to pretend that it is a secondary document, whereas its implications are fundamental to social relations and the future of our children!"

Is his point of view an exception, or can it be found in other sectors and businesses in our society? The women postal employees react favorably to the proposals of their union in reference to women workers.

Najet, forty, assistant instructor, summarizes the women's views. Current laws about work must be implemented, she says, and "equality on the job will remain only an abstraction as long as support structures, such as day-care centers and transportation, do not follow."

MALIKA ABDELAZIZ

A Place in Society

The street is a hostile, occasionally forbidden zone, say the women. Everyone is quick to mention this to women and to remind them that woman's place is in the home.

Transparent dresses, slit up the sides, shoes with laces that snake up the leg—this is what private industry has provided to dress the "citizenesses" of Algeria. But the women who wear these garments, garments displayed in the shop windows of the national capital, receive disapproving glances and insulting remarks from men. And many people associate such women with a marked lowering of the standards of behavior and dress. But what about the display model? Does it confer decency? This is only one example from the complex world that Algerian women face today. How do they define "the feminine condition," or what they themselves call "the situation of the woman"?

Ouardia, secretary, married: "A woman has the role that the man is willing to confer on her, a role that is inferior, undervalued, without autonomy; she is constantly under guardianship."

Saida, translator, married: "A woman is always a minor who is refused the right to live her own life; any imposition on her is seen to be the normal 'state of affairs.'"

"The woman's aspirations are not recognized." Farida, psychology student: "Everything is geared to the man, around whom the women organize their lives." What, then, can be done about it? Zakia, secretary, proposes: "A woman has to believe in herself, she must learn to say 'I.'"

To Yamina, secretary, the problem is not so simple: "Women have to be seen not just in relation to men, but in relation to the State. I don't solve a thing by standing up for myself individually and saying to my husband, me, I want to work. The State must define how women can participate in the National Economy. The women who are at home must be considered, as well as the workers."

Saida, translator: "A woman's self-awareness does not necessarily rise with education. Country women who work in agriculture have no reason to envy intellectuals who after years of study rush home the minute the husband calls."

Yamina: "I recently heard a woman white-collar worker declare that a responsible job should not be given to a pregnant woman. So then I asked myself is there any use in trying to work if I will be sent home once I'm pregnant?"

The interviewees say that the traditional image of the woman in the home is so rooted in people's minds, so ingrained, that any status outside the home seems to be only provisory. Yamina adds: "And what will make the State act to protect my rights if I can't defend myself?" For the woman it is a question of struggling with herself and at the same time struggling to get the State to implement Article 39 of the Constitution: "All citizens are equal in their rights and in their duties."

Najet, mother of one child, assistant instructor, reads page seventy-one of the National Charter: "The condition of women, whom the feudal ethic and traditions contrary to the emancipatory spirit of Islam have for a long time reduced to an unjust rank in Algerian society, with, as its corollary, restriction of their rights and attitudes that discriminate against them, . . . has greatly improved since the war of liberation."

Zohra, secretary, mother of two, and former member of the resistance movement, speaks of that period. It was her brother, the freedom fighter, who urged her to join the fight for independence. "I went personally into the barracks, I issued orders to the militants, which they obeyed, and they liked me better than my husband because he was completely illiterate." At that time the word "independence" transcended any sacrifice, any taboo, any tradition. The women speak of that period today with nostalgia. "To whom can we cry out today?" they say. "Development concerns us just as much as independence!"

Zohra: "In the old days, in the country, the women were active, they ground the grain, worked in the fields, wove the burnouses, gathered wood, carried water. And the artisans, rug makers, who were they? The women, of course. But today women are still not accepted as equal citizens."

The right to education is not respected everywhere even at the most elementary level. Although 66 percent of all six-year-old girls are in school, percentages vary by region. Djelfa sends only 36 percent of its school-age girls to be educated; Mostaganem, 46 percent (Table 1). This even though Article 65 of the Constitution declares: "Education is free of charge, it is compulsory for the duration of literacy school." Women constitute only 25 percent of the working population. These few figures indicate the enormous gap between the actual status of women and their formal legal status.

In view of this, women are faced with the dilemma of "how to step into the future and still conform." Miriam, a biology student, confesses that it is hard for this generation between "tradition" and "modernity." "I feel torn between the past and what I learn daily . . . everything is subject to discussion because there are no longer any values that separate good from bad. It is all so mixed up that even the right to work is questioned."

Dalila, agronomy student: "In the old days maybe it was easier. He was a peasant, she was a peasant; he worked, so did she."

Djamila, inspector, mother of two: "Even repudiation of the wife was not as common in the past as it is today. The goal of Islam and the

Table 1. Women and Elementary Education

District	% Female	% Male
Djelfa	35.9	58.5
Tebessa	46.2	76.9
Medea	48.2	79.4
Mostaganem	45.7	74.2
Tizi-Ouzou	81.4	95.5
Annaba	85.8	90
Oran	84.5	86
Algerie	66.2	82.5

Hadith is to protect woman; among the rights of a woman conferred by Islam was the right to manage her own welfare. To the Prophet, a woman was not an inferior being. We can move forward in terms of this interpretation of Islam."

Fatiha, physics student, who wears the veil, agrees: "Islam does not cut women off from education or from work." The Prophet himself advised men "to take half their religion 'from that red-head,' pointing out his wife Aisha." Boudhiba, in *Islam and Sexuality*, writes, "Aisha typifies the Arab woman, militant feminist, who, secure in the power conferred on her by the devoted love of her masculine counterpart, manages to carve out a positive place for herself in the midst of an essentially masculine society. She tried until her dying day to play a political and even a military role in order to assure that Abu Bakr would succeed Muhammad."

"Who would dare," concludes Boudhiba, "not to acknowledge woman as friend, sister, companion, and consort?"

But, several centuries after the death of Muhammad, women who feel stifled by tradition and custom are asking themselves the same question and are uncertain of the answer. Not the slightest trace of misogyny can be found in the Koran. After fifteen centuries it is like a breath of fresh air to read: "The relationship of a couple is a complementary one."

The rare couples in harmony with this definition look like pioneers. Frightened by the very idea of marriage, many young Algerian girls have yet to find a believer who can say with real conviction: "Only with a woman does a man reach completion."

Amal, agronomy student: "You have to distinguish between true Islam and what it has been saddled with. People were deprived of cultural resources during colonization, and as they emerge from ignorance, they often have a superficial or distorted idea of Islam."

"For example, I heard a radio broadcast recently. The host of the show,

Table 2. Education at Age Sixteen

District	% Female	% Male
Adrar	25.64	67.44
Tebessa	37.86	68.38
Jijel	46.99	75.51
Djelfa	30.92	59.29
Oran	76.83	81.90
Alger	79.55	83.23
Algerie	56.84	77.44

a sort of marriage counselor, was asked by a listener if, as the father of six children, he could marry a second wife. Yes, said the host, there is nothing to prevent you even if you have fifteen or twenty children. Islam authorizes polygamy. That is a totally false interpretation of the Koran, almost an invention of the radio host."

If Islam, the National Charter, the Constitution, all recognize women's need to fulfill themselves, where does the image of woman whose only identity is her sexuality come from?

Djamila: "Separation of the sexes at an early age, token co-education in the universities, school textbooks, the mass media; all contribute to reinforcing the idea of the woman in the home."

Fadila, accountant: "In 'Egyptian'-type films like the *Dallas* series, the emphasis is on the woman as sex object." The street, the work place, relations in general between men and women respond to this conditioning. Even at the university, a woman does not escape such judgments.

Dalila, teacher at the university: "The working woman sees her occupation discredited at the least reproach, justified or not."

Najet, assistant instructor, also at the university: "A man is never looked upon as being part of a unit, whereas it is always a woman's private life that validates her professional life and not the reverse."

Zineb: "A woman's potential for action is limited by the constant fear of adverse criticism." "What's more," adds Najet, "when departmental meetings are called, even at an administrative level, the woman is never summoned unless the man is not available." Even at the center of the university she is quickly reminded that she is a woman.

Dalila considers herself fortunate because "social divisions are such that we do not have the same problems as secretaries or housewives. But the lower a woman stands on the professional ladder, the more aggressive and disrespectful the man's behavior." Why should that be?

Djamila, economics student: "Women have obtained a certain amount of liberty. They have not known what to do with it; they have not been able to make use of it." This is denied by Nedjma: "Girls' conduct that is labeled indecent is simply a deviation; society is just as much to blame as the girl herself." The model offered by the media (Western, wearing sexy clothes) contributes to the problem.

Zineb summarizes: "Women have evolved, but the environment has not followed suit."

Najet thinks that the present is also "a period of transition in which the man is insisting more and more on the presence of his wife, almost as though he had a bad conscience." That he should notice her absence without being convinced of her competence shows the immaturity of the relations between men and women. Women are initiating profound changes, and have at least begun the inevitable struggle for progress and for less hypocritical and more equitable relations between men and women in our society.

FATIHA AKEB

In the Family: Rethinking Relationships

"Society ignores family problems even though the family is its basic unit." A controversial opinion, at least. The women are unanimous on this point. "Society," they say, "does not exert a positive enough influence on the evolution of the family." One question arises, then; that of knowing what types of relationships animate this basic unit of the family and more precisely how women actually live within it.

Zahia, secretary, mother of two: "A woman is never responsible for herself, she always has a guardian, her father, her brother, her mother, an uncle . . ."

Ludmilla, white-collar worker, unmarried: "Advanced studies permit a certain autonomy, a certain confidence even if the girl is made to consult her relatives. But for one without any education, the family makes all the decisions regarding her."

Akila, white-collar worker, unmarried: "It would be dishonest to say that I am exploited, but it remains relative, partial. I am not altogether independent in my actions; I am obliged to consult my parents."

What is abnormal about that? Nassima, white-collar worker, married, argues: "I have the right to vote, then I must also have the right to divorce." She refuses to be a partial citizen to whom the right of control over her own life is denied.

Wahiba, teacher, married: "The wife has no support from society. She can be beaten within an inch of her life, no one intervenes, she belongs to her husband who therefore can do as he pleases with her." She continues, "How many women, married for the space of a week or a fortnight, have been deserted, sometimes without even being divorced? You get the impression that women are not human beings but some kind of consumer goods." Violent declaration? Harsh attitude? Not altogether! If the words are sometimes intense, and if they strike like whip lashes, it is because they spring from hearts that fear repudiation by an angry husband.

Zohra, secretary, mother of two: "In the man's mind he is conferring a favor on the woman by marrying her."

The women ask: "How many men consult the first wife when they are on the point of marrying a second one?"

Nassima adds: "Where is the respect for human dignity and what is happening to the homogeneity of the family" when a second wife is considered?

Nacera, superintendent, mother of three: "By what laws am I protected? When I married my husband he was a mere agent. Once promoted a step, he ordered me to quit my job or he would divorce me. Then he remarried! He has other children; me, I have three kids on my hands and no food allowance."

The abuses are such that to the question, "What does marriage mean to you?" a student answers, "Seeing the number of divorces, one ends up believing it's no longer anything but a pre-divorce stage."

Wahiba, political science student, on the rejection of the intellectual girl: "It is not easy," she says, "to find a husband when you've finished your studies." Fadila, lawyer, agrees: "Surprisingly enough it is the so-called intellectual men who turn down the educated young woman." Why? "Because she brings with her a different concept of life and of marital relations." The intellectual woman when it comes to marriage is like the working woman in regard to the street. "When she is molested," Nacera adds, it is by "a man who envisages a woman cloistered and meekly silent. By his act he is just reminding her that she should not be there—according to him—but in the kitchen."

Yamina: "We never insist on supplementary rights! But we will not let those we have already acquired be taken away."

Nedjma, a student at the University of Algiers: "We have no exact information about the situation of women, about claustration, compulsory marriage, interruption of studies against a woman's will, not only in the cities but in the interior of the country."

"In the popular parlance," says Rabia, housewife, "when the man is approached, he is usually asked, 'Do you want a wife?' rather than 'Do you wish to be married?'"

At birth a girl is rarely received with shouts of joy. The years that follow will be but an extension of that lackluster reception.

Luckily we don't have to get permission to come into the world, is what Akila, white-collar worker, unmarried, seems to be thinking, "because in the bosom of the family the problems are more crucial for the women. To get an education you have to struggle, and to get permission to work it is the same way. For each initiative the inevitable authorization is required." It is a continual struggle, a constant strain.

Has a woman's situation deteriorated? Today notions of modesty, of decent behavior, seem to be mixed up with the very different ones of seclusion, of submission, of inferiority. The leading women of the Islamic community appear to be "ardent feminists, though it seems they are mixing traditions." Najet, assistant instructor at the university, remarks, "We have to live with situations with which we are not necessarily in harmony. Traditional dress that is espoused by pious Muslims is more of an adaptation to reality than a voluntary act." What can be done to keep from upsetting a balance that is threatened at every step? Akila: "Use hypocrisy! Perform a dual role, one in the outside world and one at home. If I have to wear traditional dress at home to avoid conflict, I'll do it."

Zakia also recommends hypocrisy in order to avoid seeing relations deteriorate with illiterate relatives of another generation. "One tries desperately to take up two different attitudes at the same time." Fatma Zohra, history student: "A woman is not free to display the same demeanor at all times." Najet: "A woman makes great efforts to change, causing too much havoc. She changes roles accordingly. She puts down her pen, puts on her apron, dashes from one role to another."

To Zineb, assistant instructor at the university, it appears "necessary from this point on to rethink associations beyond the traditional family structure where everything is meticulously laid out." Najet proposes: "No longer envisaging tasks in terms of the sexes but in terms of work, the essential factor whatever Algerian society offers in the way of day-care centers, schooling, etc. . . . We need a new distribution or roles, inspired by a dynamic force that would put men and women to work."

A few families are evolving toward that system. Zineb talks about it: "Even when the husband agrees with the principle of distribution of tasks, there are still outside pressures on private life."

The balance needs readjusting even for those who, like Najet, have made marriages that were not arranged and where, as Zineb would say, "What is essential is never compromised." Najet takes herself as an example: "I have the agreement of my husband, but I'm harassed by the family, and not just my in-laws. My own mother finds it inconceivable that I let my husband do the housework."

There are also the social reflexes, the education the woman has received, that diminish her enthusiasm for the new approach to tasks. Najet confesses: "In reality I feel more responsible for the care of my child. Maybe that is a leftover from my education."

Zohra, secretary, mother of two, recommends "an education for the children that does not underrate the girl in relation to the boy." Zineb has been through it. "The children," she says, "who are shaped by an education without any discrimination, are victims when confronted with the real-life models they observe in the outside world. Imagine a schoolboy doing a composition in which Zina wanders off and Malik helps his mother! These children are shocked to discover that what they learned at home is not the rule." But Najet feels bound to say optimistically: "I hope for their sakes that there will be no going backward."

We all hope so.

Emancipation: A Vital Necessity

All the women we interviewed called for change, from the seventeen-year-old girl with her crown of dark curls to the oldest woman who gestured with her hands cracked by dishwashing and laundry.

Voices, some muffled, some passionate, some serene.

Fadila: "Still, society has evolved." Some examples: schooling, the university, work, marriage between freely-consenting couples with mutual understanding.

Dalila reckons: "When I look back on our mothers' situation I think things are moving fast. The young people today are striding along the streets with an assurance that is irreversible."

However, the women all reiterate: "Full emancipation is still a vital necessity, for women are still hobbled by all sorts of prejudices, by all sorts of social and family practices, and by the lack of the implementation of the law that is designed to protect them and guarantee their equality."

The women are saying yes to emancipation. Seeing the bright light at the end of the tunnel, some women blink, frightened by the glare. There is calm conviction among some, sighs of relief from some, a shrug of the shoulders from the skeptics who have heard it all too often.

So we have contrasting and occasionally contradictory outlooks.

"The word emancipation is difficult," blurts out Yamina. "Between women, it can be understood, but . . ." What does it mean to the average citizen? The Sue Ellens and bosomy fake blondes of the serials and the American and Egyptian films on our screens, like *Dallas*. "The spectacle of girls flitting about our streets plastered with makeup and sporting tight little pants cut off at the knee."

According to Najet, we all need to rediscover the true meaning of the word emancipation: "In my youth it was a watchword of all the progressive parties at the time, in particular the Islamic Oulema. It meant a reinstatement of women's rights, a freedom from bondage and slavery. The Oulema conducted campaigns to explain to parents and to society in general the woman's right to education, to job training, to work, and the need for abolition of the veil. But now the term "emancipation" has become suspect and is associated with renunciation of one's cultural and religious identity and is basically associated with the myth of Western influence; this usage obstructs women's aspirations."

Dalila: "The problem is not between men and women. Tendencies hostile to the evolution of women are found in the country today, particularly among those who call themselves 'Muslim brothers.' To deal with their rancor, with their contempt for women, we must be willing to fight back, to defend our character as Algerian women."

Salima: "The situation of women cannot evolve in isolation. Everyone's individual liberty in this society must be reinstated."

Akila: "Women may have evolved faster than men who try to hang onto their old privileges. But at what price? Misunderstanding, solitude, the bar . . ."

These are mature, considered statements about the need for true emancipation. Work and education are, they consider, "the two basic conditions" for the social advancement of women.

Maria: "The State contributed to our education. Our parents suffered privations. It is now up to us to do our duty toward the family unit; overcome our fear of conflict and explain what we are and what we want." This is an opinion shared by Dahbia, who talks about the responsibility of women workers toward others.

Dahbia: "We have to organize! Help other women who are not yet aware of their rights or who are far too suppressed." "Women workers in the private sector endure inadmissible inequalities," says Yamina. They must join with all workers. "We share the same problems, the same duties," declares Zohra. And presumably, also, the same aspirations.

Yamina sees the need for a radically transformed society, democratic, hard-working, and dignified. "We must reestablish the dignity of the trades. I am a stenographer and I never wanted to be. But each one contributes to the country's development. We have to recognize that, and get to like it. As far as I am concerned, emancipation means having the right to like your work."

Zohra, formerly in the resistance movement, says the nation must look ahead to meet the needs of all of its people. "The State," she notes, "did launch the 'green belt,' the 'United African Highway,' so why not schools in isolated villages? If, for example, motor-operated wells are sunk in distant areas, schools and villages and gardens for the children will spring up everywhere . . ."

Explains Louisa, "I want conditions that would take into account my work, my intelligence, and also my emotions." Emancipation is a totality.

PART II
The Family

If the Koran is the soul of Islam, then perhaps the institution of the Muslim family might be described as its body. In the past, individual men and women found their economic and emotional support within the traditional extended family structure; they were reassured as to their identity and their social position in the world and were encouraged to form new family units of their own. In exchange, the members of the family, both men and women, were expected to contribute to the support and maintenance of the unit and to behave according to traditional codes of family honor. Honor meant, for women, a chaste reputation, and for men, courage, religiosity, hospitality. Assumption of responsibility in the support and rearing of the family was expected of both men and women. At the time of marriage and in times of crisis, the individual man or woman was expected to view the family group's survival or improvement as being of more importance than individual fulfillment. Rebellion against the system was not unknown, but the system persisted. Today that old system is under severe strain through changed political and economic conditions, the transformation from a rural to an industrial society, war and conflict, and the influence and interference of the West.

However, though the extended family in its ideal, traditional form is currently under stress, for most Middle Eastern people kin remain the focus of everyday life, a means of survival. In times of change, the support of the family is needed more, not less, and women and men are struggling to adapt family ties to new conditions. In the West, as the family changed, institutions such as orphanages, mental hospitals, homes for the elderly, and child and family services gradually developed in response to the needs of individuals whose old kinship networks had become frayed or broken. Although the beginnings of such institutions can be seen in some Middle Eastern countries today (an orphanage in Turkey, a hospital for handicapped children in Morocco, an old people's home in Egypt), they still care for only a tiny minority. For the majority of people, nothing yet has replaced the family as a source of support and alliance.

But relations between kinfolk cannot be the same in an industrial urban environment where relationships are forced to become ever more impersonal. The face-to-face personal ties of the smaller urban neighborhoods and the rural towns and villages are disappearing. Halim Barakat analyzes recent work by both Western and Middle Eastern sociologists to give a more general overview of the transformation of the family system now in progress. Safia Mohsen's interviews with middle-class Egyptian women indicate that other women are also beginning to ask themselves whether the disadvantages of family ties outweigh the advantages. Even close family members must evaluate their relationships as Fatima, a poor woman of Cairo, does in Evelyn Early's record of her life history. Three short stories by Ilfat Idilbi of Syria, Leila Abouzeid of Morocco, and Fathiyyah ʿAwada of Egypt illuminate new and old family relationships, especially the women's fear of polygamy and divorce, which have always been part of the family system.

The Arab Family and the Challenge of Social Transformation

HALIM BARAKAT

The family is the basic unit of social organization in traditional and contemporary Arab society. At the center of social and economic activities, it remains a relatively cohesive social institution. Yet the Arab family has been undergoing significant changes and needs to be examined in the context of the transitional nature of Arab society, the ongoing confrontations, and the struggle for social transformation in response to formidable challenges. Successive disappointments (particularly 1948–49, June 1967, and the Israeli invasion of Lebanon in the summer of 1982, as well as the bitter experience of setbacks in achieving unity, building democratic institutions, establishing effective control and proper utilization of Arab wealth, and furthering the cause of women) ushered in a period of self-criticism and reflection perhaps unparalleled in Arab history.

Many different explanations for the plight of the Arab world have been proposed. Various Arab thinkers have put the blame on such diverse factors as the prevalence of a reactionary religious outlook (Sadiq Jalal al-ʿAzm),[1] the collapse of religious and moral traditions (Salah Eddin al-Munajjid),[2] the ideological divisions among Arab nationalists (Adib Anssour),[3] repressive family socialization and child-rearing practices (Hisham Sharabi),[4] the absence of a scientific tradition and rational thinking (Constantine Zuraiq),[5] the suppression of creativity throughout Arab history (Adonis),[6] the impact of alienating social conditions (Halim Barakat),[7] and a kind of disequilibrium in the Arab ego (Ali Zayʿour).[8]

Unlike most Western critiques of Arab culture, these writings emerged out of an intense and anguished identification with the Arab cause during a bleak period of its history. This essay attempts to follow these lines of internal critique in setting its analysis fully within the heterogeneity and the dynamic character of Arab society—its immersion in a state of perpetual struggle, confrontation, becoming, and transformation—and tries to explore human conduct as it manifests itself in everyday life rather than through its depiction in abstract norms, proverbs, sayings, and other cultural traditions.[9] To look at actual behavior is not to neglect culture but to perceive it in depth as an integral part of social and historical reality.

Basic Characteristic Features of the Arab Family

The Arab family (as an ideal type) may be described as the socioeconomic unit of production at the center of Arab social organization and socioeconomic activities. As such it is patriarchal, pyramidally hierarchical (particularly with respect to sex and age), and extended. The latter three characteristic features have been undergoing significant changes as a result of structural change at the level of socioeconomic production and social organization supported and reinforced by encounters with the West, education, discovery of new resources (such as oil), diffusion of science and technology, and the challenges of decolonization.

The Arab Family as a Central Socioeconomic Unit.   The traditional Arab family constitutes an economic and social unit in the sense that all members cooperate to secure its livelihood and improve its standing in the community. Enterprises (shops, factories, businesses, fields) are commonly owned and operated for the benefit of all. Until recently, when the state began to provide services for its citizens, the family undertook such diverse tasks and responsibilities as education, socialization, training, defense, welfare, securing jobs, and religious upbringing.

The family is at the center of social organization in all three Arab patterns of living (bedouin, rural, and urban) and particularly among tribespeople, peasants, and urban poor. The family constitutes the dominant social institution through which persons and groups inherit their religious, social class, and cultural identities. It also provides security and support in times of individual and societal stress.

The success or failure of an individual member becomes that of the family as a whole. Every member of the family is held responsible for the acts of every other member. The sexual misbehavior of a girl, for example, reflects not just upon herself but upon her father, her brother, her family as a whole. Thus the "crime of honor," which sometimes still occurs in tightly knit communities, is an attempt to restore the family's honor and place in the community.

One's commitment to the family may involve considerable self-denial. Parents, and particularly the mother, deny themselves for the sake of their children. The source of the mother's happiness is the happiness and prosperity of her children. Both children and parents ideally are totally committed to the family itself.

Recently I came across a tape sent by a youth from a Syrian Christian peasant village to his father and mother, who were on a two-month visit to their elder two sons studying in the United States. Since the tape sheds considerable light on family internal dynamics in Arab peasant communities, I will quote it at length. The Syrian youth addresses himself to his parents as follows:

> Hello father, hello mother . . . how is your health? How are my brothers Samir and Walid? . . . I can imagine how they met you at the airport. I am sure they were overwhelmed with joy at seeing you.
>
> I hope you will keep in contact and if you plan to stay longer I wish you would write often and send us your pictures. I miss you very, very much. I miss seeing my father. I miss seeing you coming home smiling . . . I don't know what to tell you, my father. I want you to rest assured. I remain an ideal model for the whole village. Don't worry at all . . . My time is totally devoted to the fields. I am taking good care of it. Don't worry . . . I'm working the land more than if you were here. . . .
>
> Now, mother, it's your turn, my mother. I don't know what to say to you. First, your hands and feet I kiss . . . I always, always miss you. I miss the times when I say, "Mother, give me my allowance," when I embrace you, I kiss you, I cause you trouble and suffering . . . My mother, I don't know my feelings toward you. When I say, "my mother," tears burn in my eyes. . . .
>
> Now I come to my eldest brother, Walid. How are you, my brother? How are you, my eyes, my soul, the one we are proud of wherever we go? We raise our head [notice he does not say "heads," because the family is one head] among people. You are a model for everybody. May God protect you from the eyes [evil eyes] of people. I'm sure you are very happy with my parents. . . .
>
> Now you, the love of my heart, you, Samir. You, my brother. There is nothing more beautiful than the word "brother." May you finish your studies and come back, and I can call again to my brother. Samir, I don't know what to say. By God, by God, I miss you very, very, very, much, my brother. . . . Please, tell me your feelings when your parents arrived at the airport, please. I miss my parents very much.
>
> My grandfather misses you very much. He cried a lot after you left and sobbed, "Would my son come back before I die?"
>
> Hello, father. How are you, father? There is one thing I forgot to tell you. I have sprayed the apple trees . . . Do not forget to bring back the camera and film. And you, mother, don't forget to get me what I asked for. Whether you bring it or not, I am always grateful to you. My mother, my mother. My God, I'm right now sitting in the room by myself and recording on the bed. I don't know, mother, my mother, how much I miss you. God damn separation. I hope you return safely. I don't know how, when I pronounce the word "mother," my heart inside contracts. . . .
>
> I conclude, my father, my mother, and my brothers, by kissing your hands, father, and asking for your blessing. The son realizes all his

dreams if he has the blessings of his parents. My mother, my eyes, my soul, you are my heart, you, my mother. My mother, when I say the word "mother" it rises from deep inside me. My mother, please don't cry when you hear this tape. Please don't cry; don't worry. My brothers, my father, my eyes, I will conclude by asking for your blessings and particularly the blessings of my father. Father, you can't imagine how happy I am for you. I'm happy for you, you cannot imagine how. . . . You have worked hard, and we want you to rest, my father. . . . My mother, I asked you to bring me some underwear, to put it frankly. I like American underwear. My brother, don't forget the camera and the bottle of perfume. My brother, when I say the word "brother" I almost collapse. You are two, but I am alone. I'm alone in the world, I'm alone in the world. But God is generous, I hope to be with you. I conclude by kissing your hands and feet, my father, and you, my mother, I kiss your hands and feet. I ask for your blessing. With your blessings, my father, I can face anything. My brother Walid, I kiss you, I kiss your cheeks. You Samir, how I miss your smile and your eyes. With regards . . .

This tape illustrates many aspects of Arab family life, including its interdependence, sentimentality, commitment, and self-denial. At the same time, the deep integration into the family verges on morbidity (this is particularly true for mother-son relationships) and results in a shunning of society. Both the individual and society are denied for the sake of the family.

Family loyalty is one reason why many parents still desire large numbers of children. Children in peasant communities and among the urban poor start to work and earn at a very early age. An extra child is seen not as another mouth to feed or another person to educate but as an extension of family power and prestige and an additional source of labor.

This centrality of the family as a basic socioeconomic unit is now being increasingly challenged by the state and other social institutions. State structures are in control of the economy and education and have already become the biggest if not the sole employers in most Arab countries. Young men and women are seeking education and careers away from their parents in towns and cities inside and outside Arab countries. Expanding economics, industrialization, and urbanization have contributed to the emergence of bourgeois classes and cultures.

These structural changes have already begun to undermine traditional relationships, roles, and value orientations within the Arab family. Old patterns of marriage and divorce are being slowly replaced by new ones. Different sets of relationships are developing between family and society. However, young men and women show less alienation from the family than from any other social institution, religious, political, or social.

The Patriarchal Tradition of the Arab Family. In the traditional Arab family the father holds the authority and the responsibility. The wife joins his kinship group (patrilocal) and the children take his surname (patrilineal). The father expects respect and unquestioning compliance with his instructions.

This image of the father is clearly reflected throughout contemporary Arabic literature. The famous novel *Midaq Alley* by the Egyptian novelist Naguib Mahfouz, for instance, describes Radwan al-Hussainy as a highly positive and moral character who is well known in the neighborhood for his goodness and piety (being a "true believer, a true lover, and truly generous"). Yet "it was remarkable that this gentle man was harsh and uncompromising in his own house . . . Hussainy imposed his influence on the only person who would submit to his will—his wife." He believes in "the necessity of treating a woman as a child for the sake of her own happiness before anything else." This belief is reinforced by his wife's lack of complaint and acceptance of her role; she considers herself "a happy woman proud of her husband and her life."[10] A similar relationship is portrayed in another work by Mahfouz that depicts life in Egypt in the 1930s through its impact on the family of Ahmed ʾAbd al-Jawwad. When the father departs on a business trip, "a strange atmosphere of release and relaxation enveloped the household . . . Each member began to think about how he or she might be able to spend this wonderful day, a day of freedom from the ever-present, ever-watchful eyes of the father."[11] The mother, Aminah (her name means "faithful"), feels that the limits her husband placed on her should be maintained, including his ban on her leaving home without his permission. Thus, she initially resists (but later accepts) a suggestion by one of her children that she visit the shrine of al-Hussayn, a saint for whom she has great devotion. The husband learns of the visit and upon his return orders her to leave his house for challenging his pride and authority. Despite her twenty-five years of marriage, she returns to her mother and anxiously awaits her husband's forgiveness for her terrible mistake.[12]

Though this incident is unusual even in the traditional setting, it can be said that according to the traditional norms a woman commits a grave mistake by challenging her husband's authority. This culturally imposed image of powerlessness explains why women are constantly depicted in Arab mythology as being masters of trickery and wit.

In everyday life, the father is in fact off-stage, spending most of his time outside the house. After work, he comes home for a short while and then departs to the village square or neighborhood café. Although cultural norms assign family power to the father, it is the wife who actually exercises power over the children. She is in effect entrusted with raising and disciplining them, though she may often use the father as a scare or threat. Both sons and daughters are consequently much closer to their mother than to their father.

The father traditionally maintained his hold over authority and responsibility mainly because he owned family property and provided the family's livelihood. However, recent changes in family structure (particularly in response to the emergence of competing socioeconomic units, the employment of women, and the immigration of children to the city seeking education and work) have contributed to the democratization of husband-wife and father-children relationships. In other words, the patriarchal tradition is passing trough a transitional period. Increasingly, fathers are tending to relinquish their grip over family life and to share authority and responsibility with other family members. Yet the family remains hierarchical in structure.

The Hierarchical Structure of the Arab Family. The traditional Arab family is stratified on the basis of sex and age. The fact that the young are subordinate to the old and females to males prompted Sharabi, in his important study of the Arab family, to conclude that the most repressed elements of Arab society are the poor, the women, and the children.[13]

Arab society has traditionally assigned women a subordinate status. Certain features of Arab society reflect this, although its expression varies according to class.

1. Women are secluded and segregated. Though an increasing number of women are receiving education (still seen as a man's priority) and are occupying important roles and positions in the public domain, the majority continue to occupy the private domain of the household.

2. The roles most available to women are those of daughter, sister, wife, mother, mother-in-law, etc. Few professional careers are available to women under the existing division of labor.

3. Veiling is still widespread in most of the Arab world.

4. Personal status codes discriminate against women, particularly in such areas as marriage, divorce, and inheritance.

5. Among certain classes, ownership of property is almost exclusively confined to men. Social, economic, and political organizations relegate women to marginality.

6. The prevailing standard of morality stresses those values and norms associated with traditional ideas of femininity, motherhood, wifehood, and sexuality.

7. The prevailing religious ideology considers women to be a source of evil, anarchy (*fitna*), and trickery or deception (*kaid*).

8. Women may still be exposed to such practices as forced marriage, honor crimes, clitoridectomy, etc.

Arab writings tend to agree that society assigns women a subordinate status, but strongly disagree on the extent of acceptance of this situation, its origin, and the nature of required reforms. Arab writers who concern themselves with women's isues tend to subscribe to one of the following easily discernible trends:

1. Followers of the traditionalist trend assert that women are subordinate by nature and/or by God's will and design. A prominent twentieth-century Egyptian writer, Abbas Mahmood al-Aqqad, states in his book *The Women in the Koran* that women are subordinate by nature. According to him, women are disposed to shyness and receptivity both by nature and because they receive their character (*ʿirf*) from men. This traditionalist view may be traced back to al-Imam al-Ghazzali (1050–1111), whose school of thought dominated the Islamic establishment and put an end to further reinterpretation of the Koran. In a special chapter on the manners of marriage in his famous book *Ihyaʾ ʿuloum ad-deen* (The revivification of the religious sciences), al-Ghazzali talks about woman's limited mind (*qusour ʿaqlihinna*) and insists on the right of man to be followed and not be a follower because the Koran described men as being superior to women.

That this traditional view has continued to dominate the Islamic establishment is evidenced in a 1975 special issue of the *Journal of Islamic Thought (Majallat al-fikr al-Islami)* published by Dar al-Iftaʾ in Lebanon. The editorial points out that Islam decreed equality between woman and man "where equality was possible . . . and preference was admissible where equality was impossible, for God said, 'men are superior to women,' made it the duty of man to struggle . . . and to provide for dependents, and relieved woman from such burdens on account of her physical potential, personal circumstances, and family responsibilities."[14] Another article in the same issue addresses itself to the question of inheritance and explains that Islam gave the male twice the share of the female because it "relieved the woman from financial responsibilities in the different stages of her life. The father carries out this responsibility before her marriage, the husband after marriage, and the sons carry it out in case the husband dies . . . consequently . . . the man is assigned twice the woman's share, for it is quite clear that five monetary notes without responsibilities are more valuable and lasting than ten monetary notes with immense responsibilities."[15]

2. A reconciliatory apologetic reformist trend attributes subordination of women to misinterpretation of Islam rather than to Islam itself. As we are told by the Egyptian author Aminah al-Saʿid, Islam in its time

> appeared as a great social revolution in the history of women's position, not only for us in the Arab nations but also for the whole world. Just before the rise of Islam . . . woman was scarcely a human being; she had

no rights . . . Islam restored to woman her total humanity; it . . . freed her from the domination of the male by giving her (a) the right to education, (b) the right to buy and sell property, and (c) the right to hold a job and go into business . . . Islam did not differentiate between men and women except in giving the woman half the man's share of inheritance, in return for the fact that the man was to be responsible for the woman's material needs. At the time this was a gain, but it is now considered a curse. For with the decay of Arab civilization, reactionary forces gained ascendancy, and these forces used inheritance as an excuse to lower the entire status of women to that of half the man or even, in some cases, less than half.[16]

3. More liberal and radical or progressive writings reject both the traditional and reconciliatory apologetic trends. The subordination of women became a significant issue in the writings of Boutros al-Boustani (1819–1893), who wrote a book in 1849 entitled *Taʿlim al-nisaʾ* (The education of women), Shibli Shmayyil (1860–1916), Farah Antoun (1874–1922), and others. Kassem Amin (1863–1908), however, is often considered the pioneering voice on behalf of the emancipation of women. He wrote two books on the subject, *Tahrir al-marʾa* (Liberation of women) (1899) and *Al-marʾa al-jadida* (The modern woman). In his first book, Amin based his defense of women's rights on religious texts and drew upon modern ideas and views. In his second book, Amin based his arguments on the social sciences and was influenced by the liberal concepts of individual freedom and the rights of free expression and belief. He linked the decline of woman to the decline of society, and saw her oppression as one of several other forms of oppression. In eastern countries, he pointed out, "you will find woman enslaved to man and man to the ruler. Man is an oppressor in his home, oppressed as soon as he leaves it."[17] As practical measures, Amin called for the removal of the veil, the granting to women of the right to divorce, the prevention of polygamy, specification of the conditions under which a man might be allowed to proclaim divorce, education of women as well as men, and women's participation in scientific, artistic, political, and social activities.

Since then, other writers, including Salama Moussa, [18] the Algerian feminist Fadela Mʾrabet,[19] the Lebanese novelist Layla Baʿalbaki,[20] the Syrian fiction writer Ghadah al-Samman,[21] the Syrian literary critic Khalida Saʿid,[22] the Egyptian physician-essayist-novelist Nawal al-Saʿdawi,[23] Fatima Mernissi,[24] and several others have contributed to a sophisticated and progressive understanding of the woman's rights issue.

It has become increasingly clear that socioeconomic conditions rather than some inherent nature are responsible for the woman's role as dependent on men (father, husband, and son); for her evaluation in terms of role (that is, feminist, mother, sister, daughter) rather than her personality; for her responsibility not only for her own sins but also for those of men because she is seen as a source of enticement, seduction, and evil; and for the expectation that she be totally faithful to her husband, who, while expected to provide her with material support, is not held to strong moral commitment toward her. Progressive elements in Arab society reject the legitimacy of this in diverse domains of Arab life, including education, work, politics, and social movements. Male-female relations have been significantly transformed within the context of liberation movements such as those of the Algerian revolution and the present-day Palestinian community.[25]

Yet despite the achievements of women in many fields, they continue to suffer from severe problems even on the most elementary level. The veil is still omnipresent in several Arab countries and is widespread in others. Moreover, as Khalida Saʿid observes, the fact that women wear miniskirts in some places (Beirut, for example) does not necessarily constitute a qualitative departure from the wearing of the veil. Both trends reinforce the image of the woman "as being essentially a body to be covered or exposed." Furthermore, Saʿid argues that "the woman continues in most instances to be a persecuted follower and a private property . . . if we are asked about the identity of a certain woman, we would say that this is the wife, the daughter, or the sister of so-and-so . . . What is the woman? She is the female of the man, the mother, the wife. In brief, she is defined relative to the man, for she has no independent existence. She is a being defined in terms of the other and not a being on her own."[26]

In a previous paper,[27] I have suggested that the prevailing general order and the nature of its division of labor, property ownership, degree and quality of involvement in social and economic activities, control over the production process and products, and the overall position in the social structure constitute the basic factors contributing to the subordination of women. If we consider woman's subordination to be the dependent variable, we may consider the prevailing socioeconomic conditions and structures to constitute the basic or independent variables while culture and psychological tendencies constitute intervening variables, as shown in the schematic model on the following page. The relationships between these variables on social, cultural, and psychological levels are not one-way influences. Rather, they are interactional as shown (the lined arrow indicates causal and direct influence and the dotted arrow indicates indirect or reinforcing and justifying influence). This model may help us explain what is actually at issue in discussing and attempting to change the status of woman in contemporary Arab society. Change toward emancipation of women must begin by transform-

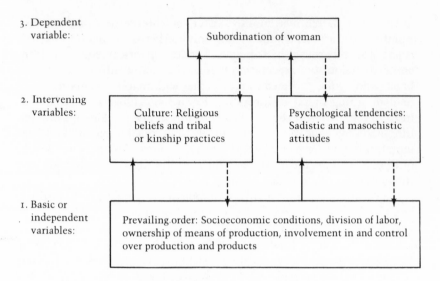

3. Dependent
   variable:

Subordination of woman

2. Intervening
   variables:

Culture: Religious
beliefs and tribal
or kinship practices

Psychological tendencies:
Sadistic and masochistic
attitudes

1. Basic or
   independent
   variables:

Prevailing order: Socioeconomic conditions, division of labor,
ownership of means of production, involvement in and control
over production and products

ing the prevailing socioeconomic structures in the context of eliminating all forms of exploitation and domination.

A recent work by Hisham Sharabi attempts to demonstrate that the child in the Arab family is socialized into dependence and escapism. According to Sharabi, children realize that they are loved and consequently experience guilt feelings whenever they annoy or fail to do their duties toward their parents. Their main commitment in later life is usually to the family (sometimes at the expense of society or of their own personal interests). My own data (*Lebanon in Strife*) showed that university students in Lebanon are least likely to be alienated from their families, while they are often alienated from religion, politics, and society. Nevertheless, some of Sharabi's comments are entirely valid. As I wrote in *Lebanon in Strife*,

> . . . parents are usually overprotective and restrictive, and children grow
> up to feel secure only on familiar ground. They avoid taking risks and
> trying new ways of doing things, for independence of mind, critical
> dissent, and adventure beyond the recognized limits are constantly and
> systematically discouraged by parents and other older members of the
> family. . . . While there is lack of individuality among Arabs, there is
> a great deal of individualism, selfishness, self-centeredness, and self-
> assertion. . . . In fact . . . individualism could be seen as a reaction to
> the constant attempts of the family and other institutions to crush in-
> dividuality.[28]

Children in villages, on the other hand, may become quite independent because parents (unalarmed by their immediate environment, with which they are highly familiar) may allow their children to explore their surroundings freely.

In general, however, the hierarchical structure of the Arab family based on sex and age traditionally requires the young to obey the old and adhere to their expectations. This hierarchy creates vertical rather than horizontal relationships between the young and the old. In such relationships downward communication often takes the form of orders, instructions, warnings, threats, reprehensions, shaming, etc. Upward communication, on the other hand, often takes the form of silence, pleas, appeals, apologies, explanations, inquiries, etc. Furthermore, while downward communication may be accompanied by anger and punishment, upward communication may be accompanied by crying, self-censorship, covering up, and deception.

The present-day Arab family is not usually extended in the strict sense; it is rare for three or more generations to live together in the same household. Urbanization, industrialization, education, exposure to the developed world, and the emergence of a middle class have had some impact, and recent studies show a continuing trend toward the nuclear family. According to the data on the Arab Middle East collected by Prothro and Diab,[29] the majority of wives interviewed who married in the 1960s never lived with their in-laws. A more recent study of family and kinship ties in Iraq showed that the percentage of extended families changed from 82 percent in the 1940s to 34 percent in 1975.[30]

Yet despite the reduced prevalence of the extended family, relatives generally remain closely interlocked in a web of intimate relationships that leaves limited room for independence and privacy. They continue to live in the same neighborhood, to intermarry, to group on a kinship basis, and to expect a great deal from one another. Such relationships and expectations are not severely damaged by emigration or by forced separation resulting from war or political upheavals. Palestinian refugees are a case in point; members of Palestinian families that have been dispersed as a result of the establishment of Israel and the subsequent wars continue to be interdependent and committed to one another. Special radio programs enable scattered Palestinian families to exchange greetings and information. A novel by Emile Habibi describes a striking encounter during the aftermath of the 1967 war among dispersed Palestinian family members. When one of the characters living under Israeli rule since 1949 meets his uncle and cousins who have lived under Jordanian rule, he feels that "he is no longer a stranger without roots."[31] His relatives are his roots.

The extended character of the Arab family is interrelated with its other three characteristic features and particularly its function as a socioeconomic unit. Such an arrangement renders family members symbiotically interdependent. Hence the dominance of the tribe among the bedouin in the desert, of the extended family in villages and urban working neighborhoods, and of the nuclear family in the city and among bourgeois classes.

Marriage and Divorce Patterns

Traditionally, marriage in the Arab world has been seen as a family and communal or societal rather than an individual affair. Officially, it has been perceived as a mechanism of reproduction, human survival, reinforcement of family ties and interests, perpetuation of private property through inheritance, socialization, and achievement of other goals that transcend the happiness of the individual to guarantee community interests. This principle is reflected in such aspects of marriage as arranged marriage, endogamy, polygamy, age of marriage, the *mahr*, and absence of civil marriage.

The system of arranged marriage is directly related to the seclusion of women and the conception of marriage as a family and/or communal affair. Consequently, it has declined as a result of social contact between the sexes at schools and in public life and of the newly emergent view of marriage as a strictly individual choice. Love is increasingly becoming a prerequisite for marriage in the minds of young Arabs.

Custom requires parents to seek the consent of their daughter before promising her in marriage, but this does not mean that they will abide by her expressed wishes. Traditionally, the daughter is expected to shy away from expressing her wish. According to the Egyptian religious scholar Ahmed Shalabi, "if the girl insists on her own choice without the consent of her father, Islam gives her this right as long as she makes a good choice and she is not deceived by false appearances. If she errs in her choice and marries a person who is not of her status [*kifʾ*] . . . then the father has the right of objection because of . . . the effect on the family and the future of the girl, who may be unaware due to the immunity of youth. In this case . . . the guardian . . . may object and prevent the marriage or nullify it if it has already taken place and the girl has abused her right."[32]

The dilemma of Arab girls who must choose between biding by their parents' will and making their own choices has been portrayed in several Arab works of fiction. The novel *Hunters in a Narrow Street*[33] (1960) by Jabra I. Jabra, a Palestinian writer residing in Iraq, narrates how the young Sulafa was forced by her father into marrying a son of a bedouin chief whom she had never met in order to reconcile the two families and to put an end to her father's financial decline. She feels angry and is terrified that sooner or later she may have to succumb to the harshness of a father whose "love can be as deadly as hate." A novel by the Sudanese writer Tayeb Salih, *Season of Migration to the North*,[34] tells how a young widow is ordered by her father to marry an old man who "changes wives like he changes donkeys." The woman threatens to kill herself but the father is not swayed; he worries that he would become the joke of the community if she were to get away with disobeying him. She is forced into the marriage but she carries out her threat and kills her husband and herself.

A more recent novel by the Palestinian woman writer Sahar Khalifa, *As-sabbar*,[35] depicts the lives of Palestinians under Israeli occupation. Though radicalized by her involvement in her people's struggle for independence, a young woman character, Nawwar, finds herself in an awkward situation. Her old father suddenly tells her that he intends to marry her to a doctor whose "material conditions are above the wind and whose clients gather in front of his clinic like flies." When Nawwar mentions to her father that she does not know this man, the father angrily answers. "For sure you don't know him. Did you assume the opposite?" Here again the girl cannot face the father. Her eyes avoid his and her heart starts to pound with horror. She dares not argue with him lest he suffer a stroke that might end his life. It is a younger brother who faces the father and tells him that Nawwar loves an imprisoned fighter, Salih, and that she is too afraid to confess. Suddenly the girl explodes in defiance, "Yes, I will not marry anyone except Salih. I will not see another man. . . . I will not marry anyone except Salih even if I have to wait a hundred years." Shocked by such defiance, the father has a stroke and has to be carried to the hospital. The author, wisely, does not have the father die; he may still be a threat.

Another aspect of traditional marriage that is undergoing change is the custom of endogamy—marriage within the same lineage, sect, community, group, village, and/or neighborhood. Like others, this custom reflects the fact that the family rather than the individual constitutes the fundamental social unit. The advantages of endogamy lie not only in the convenience of lower bride-price and the retention of family wealth and property within the clan, but in the strengthening of kinship solidarity and the avoidance of rupturing close relationships between the bride and her immediate kin.[36] The Lebanese sociologist Zuhair Hatab observed that traditionally those Arab tribes that were economically more self-sufficient and concerned about their solidarity preferred endogamy in contrast to trading tribes that sought to improve their relationships and alliances with other tribes through intermarriage (exogamy).[37]

The most over-studied aspect of endogamy has been the *bint ʿamm* (patrilineal parallel cousin) marriage; that is, marrying one's father's brother's daughter. It is repeatedly written that this type of marriage is the one traditionally preferred in tribes, villages, and closely knit communities. However, field studies conducted in diverse communities of Arab society during the present century reveal that the percentage of *bint ʿamm* marriages usually ranges on the average between only 3 and 8 percent,[38] although the percentage was found to be considerably higher in more traditional and isolated communities.

Endogamy is not limited to kinship ties. It extends to neighborhoods, villages, towns, cities, and, most particularly, sects. The Syrian sociologist Safouh al-Akhras found that in the case of 232 out of four hundred families living in Damascus in the early 1970s, the husband and wife were born in the same neighborhood of the city. He also found that the wives of 88 percent of husbands born in Damascus were also born in Damascus.[39]

The *mahr* is a dowry presented by the bridegroom to the bride on the date of the marriage. This amount is ideally paid to the bride although in reality it is often paid to her father or guardian. (Unfortunately, the father or guardian of the bride may expropriate all or part of it for himself instead of spending it on outfitting his daughter.) The amount and nature of the dowry are settled through bargaining between the parents, usually between the fathers of the bridegroom and the bride.

There is some disagreement on the meaning of the *mahr*. Some see it as practice intended to protect women, particularly against divorce, and to be used toward buying clothing and jewelry for the bride. Others see it as a bride-price, affirming male dominance. While the former view is mostly advanced by religious scholars, the latter is often made by Western observers. Still others see it as a mere symbolic gift.

The rising cost of the *mahr* is a topic of constant discussion and criticism. A study based on analysis of 3,398 marriage contracts in the court of the Druze sect in Beirut from 1931 through 1974 showed that there had been a consistent increase in the amount of *mahr* over the years (the average *mahr* negotiated more than doubled each decade) and that the level of the *mahr* was generally in proportion to the prestige of the families involved. Other considerations that affected the amount of the *mahr* included the "physical status" of the bride, her social class, the political division within the Druze community, the degree of endogamy (the closer the kin the less the *mahr*), the physical proximity and social distances (the further, the higher the *mahr*), and the age of the bride. The complaint is often made that the *mahr* has soared in oil-producing countries. Such mounting pressures and complaints have encouraged the media to expose and combat such abuses.

Traditionally, girls married at a significantly earlier age than boys (the acceptable age being at puberty or between twelve and thirteen. Ottoman law required a girl to be at least nine years old to marry. Presently, the officially required age in Arab countries ranges from fifteen to seventeen years for girls (fifteen in Morocco, sixteen in Algeria and People's Democratic Republic of Yemen, and seventeen in Tunisia) and between eighteen and twenty years for boys. More significant, however, is the steady narrowing of the average age gap between marrying partners. While the average age of marriage for women has risen, for men it has remained almost constant. For instance, the average husband-wife age difference in Sidon was about fourteen years in the 1920s, but declined to eight years in the 1960s. The results of Safouh al-Akhras' study of a representative sample of four hundred families of Damascus showed that the average age of husbands was about forty-four years while that of wives was about thirty-seven years. The lower the age of the husbands, the smaller the age gap between husbands and wives.

Another relevant set of findings supports the hypothesis that the higher the education of women the older their age of marriage.[40] In fact, one of the present women's issues, particularly in oil-producing countries, is the growing number of educated women who remain single.

Finally, it is worth mentioning that the trend toward lower husband-wife age difference represents a positive development in view of the problem inherent in the traditional great gap in age between marriage partners. Fatima Mernissi mentions in her book *Beyond the Veil* that boys quite often lost their girl friends to older men. Folktales from contemporary Arabia often tell of young wives married to old men who have secret boy friends (*sahib*).

Another tradition of Arab marrige is polygamy, which is restricted by Islam to four wives (whom the husband is required to treat equally) and any number of concubines. Though polygamy is not encouraged, it has been justified or rationalized by conservative Muslims. Some argue that polygamy serves as an anti-adultery mechanism: "we live in a society that allows for adultery . . . if a man does not marry another wife, what do you think of him if he commits adultery?"[41] Implicit here is the assumption that women are created for the convenience of men. As a spoiled person, the man is not willing to compromise his privileges: he insists on either adultery or polygamy. A related line of reasoning leads to a male-supremacist justification of prostitution. As one of Jabra's characters in *Hunters in a Narrow Street* puts it, "to preserve the honor of our wives and sisters we must create a whole class of honourless women."[42]

In reality, however, polygamy is now rare. It is almost entirely limited to some tribal chiefs, feudal lords, childless husbands, and a few peasants in need of labor. Official statistics show that in the 1960s it was practiced by less than 2 percent of married Muslim men in Lebanon, 4 percent in Syria, 8 percent in Jordan, 8 percent in Egypt (1951), and 2 percent in Algeria (1955). Research conducted in the 1930s showed that 5 percent of married Muslim men in Syria had more than one wife and that this phenomenon was more widespread in rural than in urban areas.[43] In the 1970s a field study conducted by Safouh al-Akhras showed that only 2 percent of married men in Damascus had more than one wife. Similarly, studies of the family in Baghdad showed that out of married men, 8 percent had more than one wife in the 1940s and that this percentage was reduced to 2 percent in the 1970s.[44]

Where secularism has not yet had an impact, the rules and traditions regulating divorce are essentially determined by religious affiliation. While divorce is almost impossible among some religious sects (for example, Maronites and Catholics), it is an accepted practice and *halal* (lawful) among others, though it may be described as *akrah al-halal* (the most hated of lawful practices).

While divorce was widespread in pre-Islamic Arabia, it was not exclusively a man's prerogative. In certain communities, we are told (as in Kitab al-Aghani), the wife could as easily divorce her husband. Islam ended such practices, maintaining the practice of divorce as almost entirely a man's right.

Currently, the divorce rate is high in the Arab countries, particularly in the urban centers, ranging during 1958 to 1967 between sixty-six and 105 per one thousand marriages in Syria (170 and 210 in Damascus), between 119 and 149 in Jordan (166 and 236 in Amman), and between sixty-one and seventy-four in Lebanon (103 and 129 in Beirut). Though overall divorce rates in the Arab world have varied a good deal during the century, it could be hypothesized that the divorce trend is likely to climb due to the same pressures of modernization that have affected family life in the West.

In the Arab world, divorce is most common during the early years of marriage. Prothro and Diab found that about one-third of divorces in Sidon and Tripoli took place before marriage; that is, after the marriage contract was signed but before the couple began to live together. From a Western point of view this is closer to breaking an engagement than a true divorce. Official statistics in Jordan and Syria show that in the early

1960s about 40 percent of all divorces took place during the first two years of marriage, especially when there was no pregnancy. According to Jordanian official statistics for 1973, about half of the cases of divorce occurred during the first two years of marriage. Furthermore, analysis showed that over half of these divorced women (56 percent) were childless.[45] The same trend was found in a similar study on the Egyptian family by Amira al-Bassiouni, who reported that 720 out of one thousand divorces occurred among childless parents.[46]

In many Arab countries, the husband can easily divorce his wife, while it is impossible for the wife to get a divorce against the will of her husband except in court in extreme cases of neglect, maltreatment, nonsupport, indefinite absence, and/or impotence. The feminist movement in Arab countries is struggling to establish women's right to divorce and to prevent divorce outside a court of law (as demanded by the Arab women's conference in Cairo, 1944). An increasing number of women insist that the marriage contract clearly states their right to ask for a divorce. Certain reforms have been achieved. Since 1960, an Egyptian husband seeking a divorce must state in court his reason for doing so. Some other Arab countries such as Algeria, Tunisia, Syria, the People's Democratic Republic of Yemen, and Iraq also require divorce proceedings to take place in court. Tunisian law decrees that the judge may not grant a divorce without considering the reasons given and counseling the husband and wife. Moroccan law (Articles 46 and 80 of the personal status laws), however, restricts the role of the judge to recording the husband's decision to seek a divorce.

The Family and Society

It has been a consistent theme of this discussion that the family has to be studied in the context of its relationship to all other social institutions. One peculiar aspect of such interrelationships is their complementary-contradictory nature. This can be demonstrated through allusion to specific aspects of the complex network of interconnections between family and social class, religion, and politics.

It was already pointed out that the family is at the center of socioeconomic activities in Arab society and that persons and groups inherit their social class through the family in the same way they inherit their religion, sociopolitical affiliations, and language. Islam has further reinforced this sort of interconnection between family and social class by making inheritance compulsory within the family circle, for individuals cannot dispense with more than one-third of their estate to anyone other than their legitimate inheritor. Social class in turn regulates several aspects of family life such as patterns of socialization, marriage, and divorce. Marriage across classes, for instance, is limited and religiously reinforced by the principle of *kafaʾah* (equality of marriage partners).

Persons and groups also inherit their religious affiliations and orientations from the family. Religion reciprocates by stressing the holiness of a family and its ties and the value of obedience to parents, hence such proverbs as *ridha al-ab min ridha ar-rabb* (father's satisfaction with his children is part of God's satisfaction) or *ghadhab al-ab min ghadhab ar-rabb* (father's anger is part of God's anger). There are striking similarities between religious conceptions of father and of God. Such similarities indicate that God is an extension or abstraction of the father. *Rabb al-ʿamal* (the lord of work, a concept that continues to refer to the employer) became *rabb-al-usra* (the lord of the family) and later *rabb al-kawn* (Lord of the universe or existence). Similarly, just as the mother plays the role of mediator between children and the father in Arab society, Mary in Christianity and ʿAʾisha (*umm al-muʾmineen*, or the mother of believers) or Fatima and Zainab in Islam also play the role of the mediator (*shafiʿ*) between the believers and God.

Interrelationships between family and politics may also be characterized as complementary-contradictory in several respects. While kinship loyalties may conflict with national loyalty and undermine national consciousness, much of the legitimacy of political orders and of rulers derives from the family and its value orientations. Besides political socialization, which takes place in the home (hence the congruency in political orientations among members of the family), rulers and political leaders are cast in the image of the father and citizens in the image of children. Thus, God, father, and the ruler have many characteristics in common. They are the shepherds and the people are the sheep. Citizens of Arab countries are referred to as *raʿiyyah* (the shepherded).

A consideration of societal complexity and its variations according to social class, life-style (bedouin, rural, or urban), political order, and encounters with other societies calls for a reexamination of some previously accepted generalizations. One such generalization is that the Arab family socializes its children into dependency. The dependency present in Arab society is only partly a product of the family. Much of it is due to political and economic repression, as the following incident illustrates. After a three-week study of a Palestinian refugee camp in Jordan immediately after the June 1967 war, I concluded that a few well-armed and well-organized persons might be able to invade and control this camp of more than three thousand people because the camp lacked organization. Every family lived on its own, totally occupied with immediate and personal problems and interests. Less than a year later, in the spring of 1968, I visited the same camp and found it to be totally transformed.

Palestinian resistance organizations had mobilized the people, trained them, engaged them in political dialogue, and involved them in preparation for surprise attacks. People were talking about principles, arguing about ideological issues, learning about themselves and their enemies, and proudly narrating stories of heroes and martyrs of the liberation struggle. I sought the explanation for this sudden transformation from a condition of dependency to a condition of autonomy not in the realm of the constant (that is, early childhood upbringing), but in the realm of the social variant.

Before 1967, Palestinians in Jordan and other Arab countries were not allowed to organize into political or even social movements. All significant organizations were dismantled and the people were watched, threatened, demoralized, and constantly pushed or bribed into their own private and secure shells. Communities were atomized into separate families that had to be preoccupied with their daily needs and concerns. Since the family is the basic economic unit and no other forms of social organization were allowed, communities were exposed and accessible. In short, people were disarmed and forced into dependency.

Sharabi tells how dependence can result from family socialization, but does not say much about its relationship to political and economic repression. Furthermore, it is becoming increasingly clear that socialization is an ongoing process that is not restricted to childhood. One continues to be desocialized (to unlearn what one has learned earlier) and resocialized as a result of new experiences and involvement in new situations. National crises can transform consciousness. The emergence of radical parties and movements in Arab countries has served as an agency of desocialization and resocialization. However, the Arab family continues to be the most significant agency of socialization of the young into functioning members of the society. Other such agencies include schools, mass media, religious institutions, political systems, ideological movements and parties, and peers. While some of these agencies (such as religious institutions) tend to reinforce family socialization, others such as ideological movements and peers may conflict with it.

The Arab family has served also as a mediator or link between the individual and community and society, in addition to socialization, by directly facilitating access by its members to positions, roles, and careers in public life and by protecting them. The Arab family has served as a society in miniature. As suggested earlier, similar sets of relationships prevail both within the family and the society as a whole as well as in the economic, religious, political, and educational institutions. Stratified and patriarchal relations are common to all. For instance, each political leader, employer, and teacher behaves and is conceived of as a father. The ruler refers to the citizens as "my children" and may even name the country after his family. The employer-employee relationship is another form of parent-child or father-son relationship. The educational system (even at the college level) is also patriarchal; students are constantly referred to as "my children" or treated in a paternalistic manner. Vertical relationships continue to prevail and are regulated and reinforced by a general overall repressive ideology based on *at-tarhib* (scaring) and/or *at-targhib* (enticement) rather than on discussion aimed at persuasion.

Arab society, then, is the family generalized or enlarged, and the family is society in miniature. Both act on and react to one another. The interconnection renders social institutions inseparable even for the purpose of abstract analysis. Within such a network of relationships, social phenomena develop and change in a manner dictated by their locations and affiliations with respect to the whole rather than by any internal individual laws.

NOTE: *This paper is a version of a chapter in a forthcoming book in Arabic by the author on contemporary Arab society to be published in Beirut by the Center for Arab Unity Studies.*

Notes

1. Sadiq Jalal al-ʿAzm, *An-naqd al-dhati baʿd al-hazima*(Self-criticism after the defeat) (Beirut: Dar at-Taliʿa, 1968) and *Naqd al-fikr ad-dini* (Criticism of religious thought) (Beirut: Dar at-Taliʿa, 1969).

2. Salah Eddin al-Munajjid, *Aʿmidat an-nakba* (Pillars of disaster) (Beirut: Dar al-Kitab al-Jadid, 1967).

3. Adib Anssour, *An-nakba wal-khataʾ* (The disaster and the mistake) (Beirut: Dar al-Katib al-Arabi, n.d. [1968?]).

4. Hisham Sharabi, *Muqaddamat li dirasat al-mujtamaʿ al-Arabi* (Introduction to the study of Arab society) (Jerusalem: Dar Salah Eddin, 1975).

5. Constantine Zuraiq, *Maʿna an-nakba* (The meaning of disaster) (Beirut: Dar al-ʿilm Lil-Malayin, 1948); *An-nakba mujaddadan* (The disaster revisited) (Beirut: Dar al-ʿilm Lil-Malayin, 1967); and *Nahnu wal-mustaqbal* (We and the future) (Beirut: Dar al-ʿilm Lil-Malayin, 1977).

6. Adonis, *Ath-thabit wal-mutahawwil* (Continuity and change) (Beirut: Dar al-ʿAwda, 1974).

7. Halim Barakat, "Ath-thawra wal-ightirab fi al-hayat al-ʿArabiyya al-muʿasira" (Revolution and alienation in contemporary Arab life), *Mawaqif* 1, no. 5 (1969): 18–44 and *Lebanon in Strife* (Austin: University of Texas Press, 1977).

8. Ali Zayʿour, *Tahlil al-dhat al-ʿArabiyya* (Analysis of the Arab ego) (Beirut: Dar at-Taliʿa, 1977).

9. Raphael Patai, *The Arab Mind* (New York: Charles Scribner's Sons, 1976).

10. Naguib Mahfouz, *Zuqaq al-Midaqq* (Midaq alley), 6th ed. (Cairo: Maktabat Misr, 1965), p. 58. See the translation by Trevor Le Gassick (Beirut: Khayats, 1966; also by Heinemann and Three Continents Press).

11. Naguib Mahfouz, "The Mistake," an excerpt from *Bayna al-qasrayn* (Between two palaces), in E. W. Fernea and B. Q. Bezirgan (eds.), *Middle Eastern Muslim Women Speak* (Austin: University of Texas Press, 1977), p. 97.

12. Ibid.

13. Sharabi, *Muqaddamat*, p. 112.

14. The Mufti of the Lebanese Republic Sheikh Hassan Khalid, "Al-marʾa fiʿurf al-Islam" (The woman in Islam), *Majallat al-fikr al-Islami* 6, no. 5 (May 1975): 3–5.

15. Ahmed Shalabi, "Al-wiratha wal-wassiyya" (Inheritance and will), *Majallat al-fikr al-Islami* 6, no. 5 (May 1975): 24–25.

16. Aminah al-Saʿid, "The Arab Woman and the Challenge of Society," in Fernea and Bezirgan, *Middle Eastern Muslim Women*, pp. 373–390.

17. Albert Hourani, *Arabic Thought in the Liberal Age, 1798–1939* (Oxford University Press, 1976), p. 168.

18. Salama Moussa, *Laisat al-marʾat luʿbat al-rajul* (The woman is not a man's toy) (Cairo: Salama Moussa Lil-Mashr Wa at-Tawzi, 1953).

19. Fadela Mʾrabet, *Les Algériennes* (Paris: Maspero, 1967). See also Fernea and Bezirgan, *Middle Eastern Muslim Women*, pp. 319–358.

20. Layla Baʿalbaki, *Ana ahya* (I live) (Beirut: Dar Shiʾr, 1958).

21. Ghadah al-Samman, "The Sexual Revolution and the Total Revolution," in Fernea and Bezirgan, *Middle Eastern Muslim Women*, pp. 391–399.

22. Khalida Saʿid, "Al-marʾa al-ʿArabiyya: Kaʾin bi-ghayrihi la bi-nafsihi" (The Arab woman: An alienated being), *Mawaqif* 2, no. 12 (1970): 91–100 (a special issue on the sexual revolution).

23. Nawal al-Saʿdawi, *The Hidden Face of Eve* (Boston: Beacon Press, 1982).

24. Fatima Mernissi, *Beyond the Veil: Male-Female Dynamics in a Modern Muslim Society* (New York: Schenkman Publishing Company, 1975).

25. Markaz dirasat al-wahda al-ʿArabiyya (Center for Arab Unity Studies), *Al-marʾa wa-dowruha fi harakat al-wahda al-ʿArabiyya* (Woman and her role in the Arab Unity Movement) (Beirut: 1982).

26. Saʿid, "Al-marʾa al-ʿArabiyya," pp. 91–93.

27. Halim Barakat, "An-nizam al-ijtimaʿi wa ʿalaqatuhu bi mushkilat al-marʾa al-ʿArabiyya" (Arab social order and its relationship to the question of Arab woman), in Center for Arab Unity Studies, *Al-marʾa wa-dowruha*, pp. 53–67, or in *Al-mustaqbal al-ʿArabi* 4, no. 34 (December 1981): 51–63.

28. Barakat, *Lebanon in Strife*, p. 79.

29. E. T. Prothro and L. N. Diab, *Changing Family Patterns in the Arab East* (Beirut: American University of Beirut, 1974).

30. Ihsan Muhammed al-Hassan, *Al-ʿaʾila wal-qaraba wal-zawaj* (Family, kinship ties, and marriage) (Beirut: Dar at-Taliʿa, 1981), pp. 82, 106, 116.

31. Emile Habibi, *Sudasyyiat al-ayyam al-sitta* (The six-day war in six parts) (Beirut: Dar al-ʿAwda, 1969), p. 72.

32. Ahmed Shalabi, *Al-hayat al-ijtimaʾiyya at-tafkir al-Islami* (Social life in Islamic thought) (Cairo: Maktabat an-Nahda al-Massriyya, 1968), p. 35.

33. Jabra I. Jabra, *Hunters in a Narrow Street* (London: Heinemann, 1960).

34. Tayeb Salih, *Season of Migration to the North* (London: Heinemann, 1969).

35. Sahar Khalifa, *As-sabbar* (Jerusalem: Galilio, 1976).

36. Nura S. Alamuddin and Paul D. Starr, *Crucial Bonds: Marriage among the Lebanese Druze* (Delmar, N.Y.: Caravan Books, 1980), pp. 34–39.

37. Zuhair Hatab, pp. 45–46.

38. Fuad Khuri, "Parallel Cousin Marriage Reconsidered: A Middle Eastern Practice that Nullifies the Effects of Marriage on the Intensity of Family Relationships," *Man* 5 (1970): 597–618.

39. Muhammed Safouh al-Akhras.

40. Alamuddin and Starr, *Crucial Bonds*, pp. 63–83.

41. Ahmed Muhammed Ibrahim, "The Family System in Islam," *Majallat al-fikr al-Islami* 6, no. 5 (May 1975): 43–48.

42. Jabra, *Hunters*, p. 26.

43. Khalid Chatila, *Le Mariage chez les Musulmans en Syrie* (Paris: Libraire Orientaliste, 1934).

44. Al-Hassan, *Al-ʿaʾila*, p. 79.

45. Mohammed Barhoum, "Divorce and the Status of Women in Jordan" (unpublished manuscript, 1980).

46. Amira Abdul Munʿim al-Bassiouni, *Al-usra al-Misriyya* (The Egyptian family) (Cairo: Dar al-Katib al-Arabi, 1964), pp. 59–74.

The Charm (a short story)

ILFAT IDILBI

Translated from the Arabic by Basima Bezirgan
and Elizabeth Fernea

Her neighbor said, trying to be comforting, "What's the matter with you, Um Safi? Why make such a thing of it? You think this is the first time a man has taken a second wife?"

"How can he do this to me?" cried Um Safi, wiping her tears. "If I'd heard this from anyone but you, Khadooj, I wouldn't have believed it. I would have said no, it's gossip . . . vicious . . ." She stopped. "Oh," she cried again, "how can he do this to me, Abu Safi, after twenty-five years of marriage!"

Khadooj sniffed sarcastically. "How indeed? Sometimes I wonder about you, Um Safi. You should know by this time that trusting a man is as stupid as trying to carry water in a sieve." Then her manner changed. "But look, my dear, there's no time to waste. I'll take you to Um Zeki. She'll give you a charm to stop everything before it is too late!"

"But how?" Um Safi frowned. "You just said his wedding was set for tonight."

"Yes, yes, but Um Zeki can do wonders."

"In such a short time? In a few hours?"

"That woman can do anything, believe me. She's known for stopping weddings at the last minute, for bringing husbands and wives back together after they've fought for years. She's even managed to separate the closest and most loving of couples."

"But how?"

"Does it matter how? She just does it. But there's no point in even going to see her unless you have a gold lira. No work unless she's paid in advance. And it's a fixed price: one gold lira per job."

Um Safi hesitated. "I have a gold lira," she said.

"All right, let's go."

Um Safi rushed to dress, then she opened her own private chest and took out the gold lira. For a moment she held it tightly in her hand. Years ago she had promised herself never to part with it, this gold lira that was heavy with memories and had become a symbol of her own blessings and good fortune.

She had had many difficult times in her life, bad days, hard days, but she had never considered spending the golden lira. No, it was not a simple matter to use it.

Whenever she rearranged her chest, she would take the gold lira from its box, deep in the folds of garments. Just looking at the piece filled her with happiness, and often she would let her imagination bear her away, into the past.

Twenty-five years ago. The day she had come to this house as a bride. Many times during those years she had sat, the gold lira in her hand, looking first at the winking gold and then at the courtyard where she had worked and lived and raised her children. And she would see the courtyard as it had been on her wedding day, filled with festively dressed guests, the lemon and bitter orange trees decorated with lighted lanterns. When she crossed the threshold for the first time, she had been lucky: the traditional bit of dough on a green fig leaf, handed to her by a cousin, had stuck successfully to the wall of the courtyard. Her family had smiled and congratulated each other on this good omen, an omen that their daughter would settle peacefully in her new home and that her life would be filled with joy.

"The sacred words of Yaseen will protect you," the girls had sung. "O flower of the grove, you are the bloom of rose, of iris, that crowns the head of the sultan." The women of the bridegroom's family had welcomed her into the courtyard with joyous cries of ululation. "No, you're not too tall to be ugly," they sang, "nor short enough to be squat. You're as good as the best *halawa*, fresh and sweet, sweet." The groom's mother had taken her hand and led her to the place of honor, a platform decked with flowers, made comfortable with carpets and satin cushions. And all the time she had remembered to keep her eyes lowered modestly, so as not to be, as they said, "one of those impertinent brides who gazes into the faces of the guests."

But still she had managed to steal a glance at the courtyard, realized she would live there for the rest of her life, and had loved it then as she loved it now: a spacious courtyard with luxuriant shade trees and high arched doors with a fountain whose jet of sparkling water rose into the air and fell back, splashing, into a small silvery pool. The lilac tree had bloomed for the wedding day, its branches heavy with clusters of pale mauve flowers. When one of the girls' pretty heads touched the branches, blossoms floated gently down to decorate the courtyard floor with lavender petals. The windows and doors were festooned with jasmine, its scent stronger and sweeter than all of the perfumes worn by the wedding guests.

The twenty young girls had carried decorated candles and had circled the fountain, the flames of the candles leaping as they sang the traditional bridal song:

Blessings on the bride!
God's blessings on the bride!
O beauty,
O beauty,
O rose blossoming in the garden.

Um Safi sighed. She remembered herself then, how proud she had been of her beauty, circling with the girls, proud of her fine blonde hair that fell over her shoulders, almost reaching her knees. The *mashita* had twined glinting golden threads through her hair and a long transparent veil of white net had been fastened on her head with a wreath of lemon blossoms, the symbol of purity and virginity, of innocence.

Shouts and chants of many people outside had signaled the arrival of the groom.

An old lady had said to her, "They're singing that marriage is a harness for men, a chain, but that real men can handle it. They're singing to your husband because he's leaving the company of bachelors. But they say that if he cares well for his future wife and his home, they will shout congratulations!"

The women's joyous cries of ululation rose higher.

From under her eyelashes Um Safi had looked toward the door and seen her future husband for the first time, coming toward her, surrounded by members of his family. She cast her eyes down. A young relative of hers had whispered, "Don't forget. Don't talk to him till he gives you something for your hair."

He was before her. The *mashita* put her hands in his. She felt her chest rising and falling alarmingly, her heart pounding. Until this day, twenty-five years later, she could not explain that strange disturbance in her body. Had it been fear, awe, joy? Or all of these?

They had entered the bridal chamber. The door closed behind them. They were alone. She sat beside her husband. She felt again that strange disturbance in her chest. He was nervous, too, she thought, for he was fingering his worry beads. A moment of thick, embarrassed silence passed. Then he came close, took one of her hands and uttered, in a soft, gentle voice, the traditional first sentence of a husband to his new wife.

"You and I—against the world!" He paused. "Or is it you and the world against *me*?"

She almost looked up at him, but remembered the words of her young relative and turned her face away coquettishly.

He had smiled. "Oh yes," he said. "Now I remember." He had lifted a lock of her light hair and kissed it. "Your fair hair is like silk, my love. I shall cherish it with my life. It has no price but gold." He reached into his pocket, took out a gold lira, and put it into her hand.

At that moment she had vowed to herself that she would save the gold piece as a token of blessing, of good fortune, in memory of this wedding day. She had raised her head, meeting his eyes for the first time, and had answered him, speaking clearly and directly from the depths of her heart.

"You and I—against the world!"

She had honored that vow. For twenty-five years she had stood with him against the world, a good wife, faithful, loving, caring. She had borne him nine children, four young men now as straight and tall as palm trees, five young girls, each as beautiful as the moon, she thought. And how could he do this terrible thing to her now? Take another wife? How could he? How could he forget those years?

Maybe Khadooj was right. Men were faithless, deceitful. She had never believed that, but she realized now that her husband had changed over the years. After his uncle Bakri had died and left him the mill and the orchard, he had never been the same. He became more cross, more irritable, so short-tempered that the smallest matter seemed to annoy him. He had withdrawn more and more from family life, and was always creating excuses to be away from her. How stupid she had been! How foolish not to have noticed that something was going on! She had always had complete faith in him and had never suspected he might be thinking of someone else.

The gold lira. Yes, she would spend it. She had no doubts now. She went to Khadooj and said she was ready to see Um Zeki.

Um Zeki took the gold piece.

"After the evening prayer," she said, "go alone to the roof of your house. Circle the roof seven times, repeating this charm each time."

Um Safi nodded. But she felt oddly numb. She had done something she had sworn never to do. She had given up her gold piece, the piece heavy with memory, all for a charm to stop the marriage of her husband.

Her children said, "Mother, what's wrong? Mother, your face is so pale and sad." She did not answer. She was waiting for the call to evening prayer to end. As the *muezzin*'s cry died away, she stole away from the children, up onto the roof, as Um Zeki had instructed her.

Rain poured down. The night was full of darkness and foreboding. Fear filled her suddenly; she had not expected to be afraid. She was trembling, but she straightened up in the rain and began the first round, chanting as she had been told to chant:

"I send you Hani and Mani and the fiercest jinn of all, Khohramani the ruthless,

In his rose tarboosh and his leather slippers
To bring you back, now, now!
In any way, in any way,
From wherever you are,
Quickly, quickly, quickly!"

As she finished the verse, a bolt of thunder roared above her head. Lightning cracked the black sky, the rain fell in torrents. Um Safi froze with terror, she could not move, she felt she was nailed in place on the dark, wet roof. It seemed as though she saw before her ghosts of those evil jinns, Hani, Mani, Khohramani, in horrid glimmers of horns and tails. She thought she could hear in the distance the howling of rabid dogs and the crying of the owl.

Her heart was pounding so hard she felt it might drop down in her body or stop beating forever. "Oh, what have I done?" she moaned to herself. "These jinns are dreadful creatures." She cried out, "O Abu Safi, beloved husband, what have I done to you?" He was the father of her nine children after all, and still the most handsome man on the street, despite his age of forty-five. How could she have taken it into her head to condemn him to this horror; he would come to some terrible harm and she would lose him forever.

"No, no," she cried. "May God forgive me for the evil I have committed. Please, God, let Abu Safi live safe and sound, even if he does marry another. May God forgive me!" And she added, "And please compensate me for the loss of my gold lira."

Um Safi tried to move from the place where she stood, crying in the rain. She pushed along slowly, feeling her way with hesitant steps through the darkness along the edge of the wet roof. Then she stumbled, her foot slipped, and she catapulted down, down into the courtyard below.

But she did not die. Her fall was broken by the full branches of the old lilac tree, the tree she had watered and cared for during the twenty-five years of her marriage.

She had cried out as she fell, and her children rushed to help. Safi, the oldest son, lifted her gently down and carried her to her own bed.

"What in God's name is the matter with you, Mother?" he asked. "What were you wandering around on the roof for on a night like this?"

Um Safi turned away from him and from the other children who had gathered round her bed. She was ashamed to tell them about the charm, but she could not help saying abruptly, "It's because of your father. He's taking another wife. His wedding is tonight."

A shocked silence. Silence like the dead moment before a storm. Then the storm broke. The children all began to talk at the same time, and the babble of agitated voices grew loud, louder. Safi stood up, screaming and cursing and shouting so his words were incomprehensible. He was running out of the bedroom when his sister called, "Safi! Where are you going? How can you run off with Mother in such a state?"

"I'm going to him," he shouted, "to bring him here."

Um Safi gathered herself together. "Bring your father here? Why? What for? Where is he?"

"I don't know, Mother, but I'll find him, wherever he is, and I'll bring him back here. Wherever he is," he added, shouting wildly.

Um Safi opened her mouth and shut it again. "So that's the way it is," she said to herself. "That's the spirit, this Khohramani, the fiercest of the jinns." He had always been there, her oldest son, her strongest son. He would have helped her, but she had never asked him. She had not even thought about him. And she had wasted her gold lira and destroyed her memories.

"No, my son," she said finally. "God bless you for thinking of it, but don't confront your father now. You know how stubborn he is. I've asked for God's help. Please, don't make a scene, Safi. Don't give the neighbors something to chew on . . ."

Safi interrupted. "Don't be silly, Mother. People are already gossiping about us. So what difference does that make? Do you want me to let my father get married again so you can commit suicide and all of us can stand by and watch?"

He slammed the door behind him.

The room grew quiet. Safi had voiced everyone's worst fears, including those of his mother. Um Safi closed her eyes. A strange peace was creeping over her as she realized that her son had grown strong and independent; he was now a man perfectly capable of defending her if she needed him.

In a short time Safi returned with his father.

Um Safi closed her eyes and pretended to be unconscious. Abu Safi stood at his wife's bed. He could not meet the nine pairs of accusing eyes, and so he bowed his head in humiliation and murmured:

"There is no strength but the strength of God.
There is no power, but from God.
Fate, destiny; what is written on the forehead the eye must see.
We pray to God, we turn always to God, in his mercy."

But even the holy words spoken eloquently could not make those accusing eyes disappear. Abu Safi's sense of humiliation and shame was almost too much to bear.

"I must get the doctor for Um Safi," he said, and ran out of the house. When he came back, the children would have calmed down, he told himself. The doctor's presence would help smooth over the embarrassment of this day.

By morning, news of the events in Um Safi and Abu Safi's house had spread through the neighborhood. The women came to inquire after Um Safi. She felt poorly from the effects of her fall, but cheered up a bit when Khadooj came and whispered in her ear: "You see, Abu Safi's marriage has been stopped. The stream returns to its bed." She smiled triumphantly. "Didn't I tell you? Um Zeki is a wonder. Her charm never fails."

NOTE: *This story was translated under the auspices of PROTA, the project for translation of Arab literature into English, directed by Dr. Salma Khadra al-Jayyusi.*

New Images, Old Reflections: Working Middle-Class Women in Egypt

SAFIA K. MOHSEN

In this paper I examine the ways in which Middle Eastern women and men are reacting to the new social and political conditions created by the rapid development taking place in the Middle East today, their responses to the new challenges, and the degree to which they have been able to effect adjustments in their social relations both within and outside the domestic unit. Since Egypt is the source of most of my data, the discussion will focus on the Egyptian woman—in particular, the urban working middle-class woman. Distinction will be made, however, between the upper-middle-class and the lower-middle-class or petit bourgeois segments of the urban population. Such a distinction is made necessary because of the different ways in which current Egyptian economic policies have affected the two groups and the difference in responses to these policies, especially by women.

Sadat's "open-door" policy, which permitted easy access for foreign investment in Egypt throughout the 1970s, tended to favor upper-middle-class women, especially in the area of high-paying jobs. The readiness, even the eagerness, of that class to adopt the Western style of life made it possible for these women to translate their economic gains into changes in their family relations. Lower-middle-class women, on the other hand, found themselves facing new social conditions without adequate preparation or resources and without cultural backing for either increased public roles or for new values accompanying them. The result has been a great deal of confusion and ambivalence among both men and women that has made it difficult for women to achieve real gains either in their family lives or in their work environment. Moreover, the narrowing of the gap between the classes under the impact of rapid social change has placed the lower-middle-class woman in the position where she has not only to struggle against the psychological and cultural barriers of her own class, many of which have been created by women themselves, but also to compete with her more affluent sisters for many of the important resources, especially suitable husbands.

Economic policies since 1974 have had a profound impact on Egyptian society. Linking the Egyptian economy with the economy of the West at a time when the latter is going through a difficult phase has resulted in the importation of many of its weaknesses, especially inflation. The lifting of restrictions on imports, originally designed to encourage the importation of production goods, has resulted in the inundation of the Egyptian market with consumer goods of all kinds. Lack of governmental control over the prices of most of these goods and the eagerness of Egyptians to buy everything imported have sent prices skyrocketing. A new group of entrepreneurs has been able to amass a great deal of wealth through investing in import activities. The old and rigid class structure is giving way to a new one in which the patterns of consumption play an important role in status distinctions. Gone are the days when family background was the single most important determinant of social class, when respect and deference followed from social background rather than wealth.

For the majority of middle-class men on fixed incomes, the new economic demands have meant extra part-time jobs or temporary migration to one of the Arab countries. For women, they have meant more pressure to seek outside employment and less pressure from their families to keep them from seeking it. This has been true for both upper- and lower-middle-class women.

The Upper-Middle-Class Woman

The open-door policy has created new job opportunities for upper-middle-class women, and economic necessities permitted them to take advantage of these opportunities. Traditionally, women in that group have shown an interest in foreign education (French, English, or German) and a disdain for public (government) education. While their male relatives attended government schools and Egyptian universities as a necessary preparation for their professions, women restricted themselves to the private foreign schools. Even when an increasing number sought higher degrees, they attended such foreign institutions as American University at Cairo or went to European universities. Many upper-middle-class families consider the social environment in the government schools and universities to be inferior and did not approve of their daughters mingling with the undesirable members of the lower social strata. These families until recently have kept their daughters away from the public education system. When the policy of nationalization and expansion of the public sector under Nasser created demands for professional skills and trained personnel beyond what was available in the male population, upper-middle-class women were effectively barred from such jobs by their lack of the necessary degrees from Egyptian universities. The open-door policy, on the other hand, has encouraged private sector and foreign investment. Foreign businesses have established offices in Egypt and this has created more demand for language skills and the ability to deal with foreigners. Although most of these jobs are in the clerical field, their pay scale is several times that of the government jobs for beginning university graduates. In addition, the policy has created opportunities in the expanding field of small business. Since upper-middle-class women are more likely to have the initial capital and the necessary contacts to obtain permits and other clearances needed for establishing a business in Egypt, they have found a logical and lucrative source of income in small business. Indeed, many of these women already had acquired significant managerial skill through running their own households. Some have opened boutiques for imported goods, mainly clothes and cosmetics. Others have bought small hotels and pensions, or have capitalized on the housing shortage by renting their furnished apartments or villas to foreign visitors.

While the fields into which the upper-middle-class women entered provide attractive monetary rewards, they are also the most competitive. This is particularly true in the case of business, where women have to compete not only with other women but frequently with men, some of whom are their own relatives. Even in the clerical jobs in the private sector, where promotion and advancement are discretionary and where job termination by the employer is easy, women have to compete with others for the few openings on the higher level. This has tended to sharpen the skills of these women and provide them with feelings of self-reliance and self-esteem, which they have been able to utilize in the domain of interpersonal relations and particularly in the family.

While economic demands have encouraged women in the upper middle class to seek work outside the home, work is not viewed as an absolute necessity. It is a means of improving the family standard of living and in particular of producing extra income that can be used to buy more expensive clothes and other luxury items. Moreover, work requires very few sacrifices on the part of upper-middle-class women. Although domestics are more expensive and difficult to find than in the past, the upper-middle-class family still has enough resources to relieve the woman from major domestic duties. Unlike less affluent women, the upper-middle-class woman does not have to double her duties and responsibilities by going to work.

Of more importance is the cultural support for their public role. Upper-middle-class women adapted quickly to the westernization processes. They adapted easily to everything Western, from fads in clothes and music to smoking and drinking in public. Male/female friendships are frequent, dating is becoming acceptable, and marriage for love is gaining in popularity among this group.

Within the domestic sphere, women's public role has required some adjustment. Traditionally, husband and wife in the upper-middle-class family functioned in two separate and different spheres. The wife's sphere was that of the domestic unit and within it she had almost absolute power. The husband had very little say in such matters as the managing of household activities, the supervision of the domestic staff, or the upbringing of the children. The wife never asked her husband for advice with regard to these matters for fear that she would be viewed as incapable of running the house. Hiring and firing the domestics were her decision, and as long as his needs were met the husband did not interfere in the matter. Mothers advised their daughters when they got married to guard against the intrusion of the husband and insisted that to have a successful marriage the daughter should never allow the husband to have anything to do with running the household. The idea was that if given the chance the husband would become overbearing and unmanageable and the woman's power in the house would be undermined. A woman in her fifties told me the story of her first confrontation with her husband over the firing of the butler, who did not want to follow her suggestions:

> I was pretty young then, but I was not about to surrender to my husband's demands. When he insisted that I keep the butler because he was an old man who had been with the family for a long time, I did not say anything. The following morning my husband left for work and I told the maid to go to my sister's house for something or other. When my husband came back from work and asked why lunch was not ready, I told him if he was going to decide who is to stay and who is to be fired then he should have full responsibility for running the house and that included instructions to the servants and preparing the menus and everything. As for me I didn't mind staying in bed all day. My husband immediately got the message and apologized. I fired the butler. My husband sent him to work for his sister. That is his business but my house is my own and I decide who works there and who doesn't. This was the last time he interfered in my affairs and the house has run smoothly ever since.
>
> I did not have to discuss a budget with him. In those days there were no budgets. He gave me all the money I wanted. When I ran out of money because I bought something expensive, all I had to do was to ask for money and I got it. We did not have to count every move we made and every penny we spent the way we do now. The world has changed and all of us have changed. (Interview, August 1977)

Upper-middle-class women have traditionally enjoyed a great deal of independence from their husbands in regard to their private incomes or property. When the husband managed it for the wife it was because the wife had agreed to it. Protected by the status and power of their own families, middle-class women seemed to have a separate existence from that of their husbands.

The new economic situation has tended to narrow the distance between the domains of wife and husband. More and more husbands are participating in the managerial aspects of the domestic unit. Tight money supply has made it necessary for the husband and wife to work out the household budget together. The difficulty in finding suitable household help, the government regulations requiring the payment of social security and other benefits, the staff's general awareness of their own rights, all have contributed to a more formal relation between domestic staffs and employers, necessitating the participation of the husband in the process of their hiring and firing. Unlike the past, when domestics were considered part of the family, the new situation requires contracts and other legal documents for which the husband's experience is essential.

On the other hand, higher wages for personnel in the private sector have made it profitable for husbands to employ their own wives in clerical and sometimes managerial positions in their businesses. This is especially true in hotel administration where the work involving the management of a large cleaning and cooking staff is not so different from women's responsibilities in running their own houses. Some husbands leave the running of the business totally to their wives.

The Lower-Middle-Class Woman

The new economic demands have also pushed more lower-middle-class women into the work force. Lacking the resources needed to enter lucrative business fields, the majority of lower-middle-class women seeking work have found employment in public sector jobs, particularly in government offices.

Unlike upper-middle-class women, lower-middle-class women have taken their places in the overstaffed offices of the bureaucracy with very little to do and with promotion set according to a rigid seniority system that discourages competition. While this has resulted in less pressure, it has provided them with neither the opportunities nor the incentive to improve their skills. Many spend the major part of their office time knitting, chatting, drinking coffee, or sending the janitors to the cooperative stores to buy government-subsidized food and other household items. This long-distance household management has created a negative image of lower-middle-class women among male co-workers. Complaining about the "defection" of many of his male employees, the head of a research department in one of the ministries said:

> We hire the best people, both men and women, train them to be excellent researchers, then men get offers for other jobs in other ministries or at the university and the women are left. We start with approximately equal numbers of males and females and end up with a predominantly female staff. Women are equally good if not better, but the image is still there that women are not serious and that to them the job is low priority. Some departments in the government specifically request the Manpower Department not to send them women. They see the women worry about the house and send the janitors to buy things needed at home and say, "See, they cannot be serious about their work if all they can think about is what the best buy in the cooperative store today." Men do it, too, but we tend to view that as a sign of the man's responsibility and strength. Men are more subtle about it and do it with such authority that it somehow seems part of their jobs. (Interview, November 1977)

Women themselves seem to support that image. In a recent article Amina al-Saʿid, a leading feminist, has criticized modern middle-class women for their passivity: "The Egyptian woman is her own worst enemy. More than men, she believes in her own incompetence and has never been able to develop the self-esteem and self-reliance that the new opportunities offered her" (*Akhir Saʿa*, January 20, 1980). Al-Saʾid attributed the passivity of the current generation of women to the relative facility with which they found education and work.

> . . . they grew up in an era where education for women is taken for granted, and where jobs are readily available and family resistance to their working, thanks to the new economic pressures, is minimal. They did not have to fight for these privileges the way we of the older generation did. For us work was a symbol of freedom, of having control over our lives. The price many of us paid was high, but the crusading spirit and the novelty involved made the sacrifice worthwhile. Today middle-class women look on work as a necessity or as a chance to catch a better husband, one who can afford her comfortable living conditions without needing her income. Young women now prefer to marry a much older but well-established man than a younger but less financially able one. (Ibid.)

What Amina al-Saʿid and several other writers do not seem to realize is that these attitudes may represent a rational response to the new realities facing the working middle-class woman today. While the current social and economic conditions make it easier for women to seek education and employment, and while the public attitude seems more receptive to the employment of women, there has been very little change in the traditional views of sex roles and very little adjustment in the nature of family relations and the allocation of domestic responsibilities. Working or not, the woman remains solely responsible for the housework. Unlike the older generation referred to by Amina al-Saʿid, where domestic help was readily available and at a cost affordable by all, today's lower-middle-class woman finds it too costly to retain full-time domestic help. As a result, the expansion of her public role has been accompanied by an increase in her domestic duties.

Much of the difficulty stems from men's reluctance to accept women's new roles. Struggling to maintain dignity and control in the face of a rising cost of living and increased difficulty in supporting their families, men watched with a great deal of resentment as their wives or daughters left the home and entered the outside world with its temptations. Unable to cope with the conflict, some men are blaming women's employment for all society's problems, from juvenile delinquency to the increase in family expenditure. The writings of some of the prominent male authors reflect this antagonism toward women's expanded public role. Abdel Rahman Fahun referred to the International Year of the Woman as

> . . . the latest gimmick, and gimmicks somehow seem to be associated with women. This one is on an international scale . . . under pressure from the feminist groups, the UN agreed to designate 1975 as the year when women strive for equality, development, and peace!!! What equality is she talking about? She has already reached the level of a cabinet member, a chief editor, and has invaded new fields such as diplomacy and the police. She became equal to us in salary although we never became equal to her in paid vacations. What does she mean by peace? If she means peace at home, we the men are the first to support it. What the woman has not realized is that when she "scooped" her rights she forgot her duties, her duties to raise the children and her duties to provide the proper atmosphere in the small kingdom so that its members can produce for the good of the society. All these duties were forgotten in the woman's haste to grab other people's rights. I hereby request that 1976 be designated the year of the man so we can demonstrate to these women how much we men earn, how much we spend on ourselves, and how much we spend on them. (Al-gomhouriyya, January 30, 1975)

Many men express their feeling of insecurity by tightening their grip over the family and by exaggerating the expression of their authority over its members, especially the working wife. Lacking the social backing for their changing roles, some lower-middle-class women put up with the husband's restrictions and thus have accepted family conditions that are the same if not worse than those endured by the less educated, generally unemployed women of the past generations. A thirty-two-year-old teacher described her situation in the following statement.

All I remember from my childhood and adolescence is fear. Fear of a cruel father who never recognized the right of members of his family to express themselves, and who behaved as if he owned us, owned our thoughts, lives, and feelings. He directed his uncontrollable anger against anyone who dared disagree with him. Fear of a delicate, fragile, and idealistic mother against whom my father's anger was directed for the least provocation on the part of any of us. It was as if she was responsible for anything that went wrong in the family. I was torn between rebelling against my father's tyranny and my fear for my mother as the result of my rebellion. My mother always told us to obey my father and tried to convince us that beyond that cruel facade is a heart of gold and that he really loved us but could not express it. All she wanted was to maintain peace in the family. I used to get angry at her, blaming her for bringing us into this miserable world. I used to ask her why she had all these children, six of them, if she was not happy with my father. I kept asking her why she allowed my father to dominate her and stifle her existence as a human being. She always gave the excuse that it was her fate and destiny and that her parents did not believe in divorce especially after she had children.

It was natural that I would take my time selecting a husband so as not to repeat the tragedy of my mother. But in my eagerness to escape the conditions of my family I rushed into a bad marriage. I realized how oppressive and domineering my husband was the second week of our marriage when he used to come to the school and spy on me to see that I came home right after school and that I was not talking to my male colleagues. I complained to my mother and father but they were not supportive. My mother suggested that a child would cure his jealousy and that he was a good man and that good men are hard to come by these days.

So, it was the first child. When that did not work out, it was a second, then third and fourth child. I am now thirty-two and have four children. I can't do anything about the situation now because of the children. I find myself doing the same thing with my children that my mother did with us. I try to keep them quiet and away from my husband so he will not get angry at them and at me. I cannot support the children on my salary alone and my parents would not have anything to do with us. My husband said if I get a divorce he would give me the children and that he would not pay anything. I don't have time to go to the courts and I cannot support the children so I am staying with him until the children are independent and then I'll leave him.

This situation is well described in a lengthy interview I had with H.M., who works as a research associate at the Ministry of Health, has an M.A. in physics, and is currently completing her Ph.D. degree in public health. She is married to a physician who holds a position in the faculty of medicine. She has two children, a girl age thirteen and a boy age eleven. The interview provides an insight into the dynamics of the relationship between husband and wife, and in most respects addresses issues confronting both segments of the middle class.

H.M. describes herself as liberal in political views and social relationships but from a very conservative background.

My father was a professor of literature, my mother comes from a well-educated family. She herself was more educated than most women in her generation. She went to school overseas when her father was in the foreign service. Despite his education, my father is really conservative. It is his rural background. He never left the village psychologically. To him the village is home and until his death he visited there frequently. He kept the small house after his father died but rented the few feddans he had in the village. He always said that his roots were in the village where he spent his childhood and adolescence. My mother, on the other hand, didn't care much for the village scene and although she was always courteous to my father's relatives when they visited us in the city, she kept her distance.

I was fifteen and in high school when I was told that a suitor had asked my father for my hand and that my father had given him his word. I had never seen him before and I was not consulted. My mother was not consulted either. When she heard about it from my father after the suitor had left the house, she was really angry. But my father refused to listen to her and said it was the man who gave his word and women did not have anything to do with the whole affair. It was a crisis in the house and my father told my mother either I married that man or she would leave the house. I decided to be the victim. I married my husband. I was sixteen, he was thirty-five. One thing my mother was able to bargain for me—I insisted on continuing my education and going to the university.

My husband is not really that different from my father. He has the same attitudes and his relationship with me and the children is not that different from my father's relationship with us and my mother. The only difference is that I work and therefore have some freedom of movement and an income of my own. Other than that we do not share that much in terms of activities or even friends. Although we are in similar fields he never discusses his work with me. I know how much he makes from his work at the university, that is, his basic salary and some rough idea of how much his income is from the clinic, but any additional income he gets from public lectures or guest lectures or even overtime he never tells me about. He believes that telling everything to the wife weakens the husband and that he should have some flexibility in his income to enable him to spend some money on himself or take us out once in a while. But he mostly spends any extra money he gets on his own pleasures.

We live in a villa that we rented a long time ago and pay only fifteen pounds a month. From my salary I pay all my educational expenses, my clothes, my makeup, and my transportation. In other words all my expenses come from my salary. If anything is left, I add it to the house budget. At the beginning of each month he gives me money for the house expenses. He also pays the rent and the maid's salary (she comes three times a week), newspaper, laundry, and utilities. The rest he keeps for himself. From that he covers the car expenses. But the children's clothes and any extra expense for entertaining or for vacation have to come from the savings. The money situation is a source of conflict in the family because he does not realize that what he leaves us is not enough, not with today's inflation. As a result, I have depleted all the funds I inherited from my father and cut down on some of my personal expenses just to supplement the house budget.

When I got married I didn't think that much of the age difference. After all, I came from a traditional family and the age of the husband was not one of the things you discussed about the husband. It was taken for granted that the husband will be a lot older if you are looking for a good provider and an established man. The idea of the husband and wife growing up together is as you know a foreign idea in our society. Who wants to wait for a husband to grow up? Besides, my mother always told me that an older man looks after his wife and pampers her. Now I realize it is all nonsense. He did not marry someone young so he can pamper her, he married someone young so he can dominate her and mold her in his own idea of a wife.

He thinks a husband is a god in his own home. Everything he says has to be taken as the truth without discussion. What he thinks is right is right and what he thinks is wrong should be wrong for everyone else in the family. He believes that for the man to maintain his respect in the family he has to keep a certain distance from them. He has to be "serious" all the time, to avoid frivolousness, laughter, and jokes. The same thing applies to the wife, who should always be serious and avoid showing any sense of humor.

I live in his idea of what the world is, not my own ideas. Even all the friends we entertain are his own friends, not mine. They all are his age, from his background. He thinks they are sensible and therefore the kind of people I should associate with. Of course I have friends my own age and people I work with and like, but I do not entertain them at home. He would not see them. He thinks my friends are frivolous and lack maturity because they laugh and joke and are human. To him the ideal wife is a fat, sluggish cow with ten children who does not have any existence apart from his, a full-time wife like those of most of his friends. He still tries to forget that I work and refuses to have any social association with my friends at work. He says that they are not of his own social level because they are less professionally established and therefore his association with them would lower his status.

From an objective point of view we certainly cannot afford my not working. But the way he sees it is that if I stayed at home and quit my job I would be able to economize and save more by doing all the work myself and saving the maid's expense and also be more efficient in running the house. Every time we discuss it he says, "My mother lived on ten pounds a month, why can't you live on sixty? We don't have to live in comfort, it is all because you want to live in a given style." It is one of the sore points in our marriage. We constantly argue about it. Every time he comes back and I am not home from work we fight. Every time I ask him for more money for the house, my job is the topic of discussion. We thought about separating a number of times when I got sick and tired of his logic, but every time I retreat, I say what is the hurry? Let's postpone the decision. He is not against divorce, in fact he would welcome it. I convinced him to give the marriage another chance. He says that he married me when I was still in high school and that if he wanted a working wife he would have married one. He resents the time I spend preparing for my Ph.D. If he comes back to the house and finds me working on my research, it is the end of the world. I even had to take a leave of absence from my job without his knowledge to complete my master's.

You probbly wonder why I stay married to him. The answer is one thing: my children. I can't be away from them for a second. I view my whole married life as devoted to them and bringing them up. They are the only reason for the existence of the marriage. I feel I am building something good. They are smart and very well behaved. They are my biggest success story. I am very close to them. They consider me their friend. There is nothing that they cannot talk to me about. I cannot destroy the good thing I have built simply because I have a very uncomfortable relationship with my husband.

In the beginning of the marriage, I really loved him. I felt comfortable with him and I felt that love can develop after marriage. But soon enough he started to show his real feelings, or lack of, and to keep his distance. The arrival of the children increased the gap between us. Any time we had together when the children were not around, he spent in reading the newspaper. We even like to read different newspapers. He likes the conservative *Al-akhbar*, I like the colorless *Al-ahram*. Even when we go on vacation it is usually to a quiet seaside resort where we sit at the beach watching the sea and the children. I never go to swim, he would not allow me to wear a bathing suit. He is madly jealous that his young wife will be seen by other men. He never admits that but insists that "respectable" women do not expose themselves to the gaze of men. He is really out of the Middle Ages in his ideas. Despite that I think it is a good marriage. I have seen worse marriages among many of my friends. The husband of one of them had an affair with another woman and when the wife objected he threatened to divorce her. At least my husband does not fool around. Not to my knowledge at least. I am sure that he would not have an affair since these things usually cost money. He has to bring her presents and other things and my husband is so tight with money that he would not go along with it even if he wanted to.

People look at social change in a country like Egypt and say the whole society is changing. This is not true. It is more in appearance than reality. The reality is mine and that of thousands of women like me who have been educated and yet still live in the Dark Ages. It is the fault of the society, which treats change at the surface and not at the level of basic values. It is all right for the women to vote and get educated and so forth, but it is not all right for them to have control over their own private lives.

As the above case shows, while work has provided many women with a certain measure of economic independence, social pressures still make it difficult for a woman to seek divorce. This is especially true in the case of women with children. Some fear the possibility of losing their children under the unfair custody laws, while others face the possibility of having to support their children on their incomes alone or with minimal financial help from their ex-husbands. Collecting child support, which has been difficult in the best of circumstances, has become more so with the increased geographical mobility of the men. Many women find court battles over child support too costly or too humiliating and the returns too meager to justify the process. Economic pressures make it difficult for the woman's family to help her, and the housing shortage has made it almost impossible for the parents of the woman to provide a place for her and the children even when her income is sufficient to support them. Society still looks with suspicion upon a woman living alone without a man even if she lives with her children. Traditional attitudes toward divorced women have, therefore, tended to discourage women from seeking divorce despite the relative ease with which they can legally obtain it.

Despite the apparent changes in the aspirations of the Egyptian middle class, the most important goal for women of all classes remains very traditional. The vast majority of Egyptian women still view success in terms of a husband and a happy family life. What has changed under the impact of consumerism, however, are the means to achieve that goal. While the old virtues of good reputation and family background still play an important role, the possession of cars, expensive clothes, and stylish hairpieces also has become important in the quest for a suitable husband. These assets have become particularly significant as women have increased their activities outside the home and, therefore, lessened the need for a third party or go-between as the initiator of marriage. More men are now selecting their own marriage partners or at least making the initial suggestions. In the absence of cultural support for an open relationship between the sexes that allows the exploration of personal qualities beyond appearance, appearance has become the single most important factor in the initial attraction. For many women, particularly lower-middle-class women, neither their personal income nor that of their families is usually sufficient to provide them with the needed attractions. This has become even more difficult as the narrowing of class distance under the impact of socioeconomic changes has placed lower-middle-class women in direct competition with the more affluent ones for the same pool of husbands. Realizing their handicap, lower-middle-class women have employed a number of strategies.

A few women have resorted to illegal means to obtain the needed funds. This has been reflected in the recent increase in middle-class women's participation in crimes. In the past few years several articles appeared in Cairo newspapers and magazines calling attention to what is termed "an alarming increase" in the incidents of arrests for prostitution of female university and high school students. Most of these women were arrested in apartments rented by rich Arab visitors. Other references were made to the growing involvement of women in crimes that, until recently, were committed almost exclusively by men. Such crimes include fraud, embezzlement, and smuggling.

While the number of women involved in criminal activities remains very small, the publicity given by the Egyptian media to criminal behavior, especially prostitution, among middle-class women has tended to support the fear that women's exposure to the world of work subjects them to temptations and increases middle-class men's suspicions about the educated working woman. The image many of these men have of the working woman is of a potentially corrupt and corruptible creature, an image shared by many nonworking and some working middle-class women. It is against this background of fear, confusion, and suspicion that an increasing number of middle-class, mostly educated women are using the veil as an adaptive strategy.

Viewed as a symbol of female oppression and segregation, the veil had virtually disappeared among middle-class women in Egypt. Since the early seventies, however, a number of women, mostly university students, have started to wear very conservative attire. This ranges from a scarf, long-sleeved blouse, and floor-length skirt to a *chadur*-type garment that covers the woman from head to toe with little slits for the eyes. These women are particularly visible against the background of extravagantly dressed, heavily made-up women who constitute the majority of the female student population in Egyptian universities. Since education of women became acceptable among the middle class, the university has become the main arena for attracting a husband. Families borrow money to buy their daughters the latest in fashion, viewing it as an investment in the girls' future. It is natural that the few women who go against the trend would be viewed with suspicion. In the early seventies when the number of veiled women was still small, they were looked upon as religious fanatics (some conspiracy-minded students even thought they were communists attempting to infiltrate the powerful Muslim students' associations). As their number grew and as the trend spread outside the university to government offices and high schools, the phenomenon was taken more seriously. Some view it as part of the religious revival that produced such extremist groups as El-takfir wal-hijrah (Repentance and Holy Flight), or at least as a symbol of the rejection of westernization. Still others believe it is a product of contact with the conservative Arab countries. Egyptian women visiting these countries to work or accompanying their husbands adopt conservative dress while there and then find it difficult to change after returning home.

Whatever the explanation of the return of the veil, it has provided some lower-middle-class women with an effective means of coping with the new pressures, both in their relationship with men and in their competition with the more affluent women. By wearing the conservative attire, they are able to minimize men's suspicions about their activities outside the home. Moreover, the veil has made it possible for them to interact with their male co-workers or classmates without the sexual connotation such interactions usually carry. This has enabled these women to establish a more liberated and mature relationship with men.

> Before I wore the veil, I always worried what people might think when they saw me speak to a man in the cafeteria or outside the class. I even wondered what the man himself thought of me when I spoke with him. Since I wore the veil, I don't worry anymore. No one is going to accuse me of immorality or think that we were exchanging love vows. I feel much more comfortable now and do not hesitate, as I did before, to study with the men in my class or even walk with them to the train station. (Interview with University of Alexandria student, 1977)

Veiled women, on their part, have capitalized on the ambivalent feelings and insecurities men have toward westernized women to gain an edge in their competition for husbands. Unable to challenge affluent women when it comes to fashionable clothes and fancy cars, some women have manipulated the persistence of traditional attitudes to emphasize the old-fashioned yet still valued attributes of modesty and good reputation. The veil became an advertisement for such virtues, making possible the desired combination of education and income without the connotation of immorality westernization carries.

Referring to the veil as a strategy should not imply that given the chance these women would opt for a westernized style of life. They seem to have a genuine respect for the traditional way of life. In this regard they are not unique. They are joined by the majority of lower-middle-class women who view the old ways as offering women dignity, protection, and an easier way of life. They seem more comfortable with the old values that give primacy to the family. When they are gainfully employed, these women view their work as secondary to their domestic responsibilities. One such woman is Maisa, twenty-nine, a supervisor at the Customs Bureau in Alexandria. Although attractive, she does not wear makeup and wears a long-sleeved blouse and a loose-fitting skirt. She comes from an educated middle-class background where her father was a university professor. Her three brothers hold good government jobs. The following is an excerpt from her interview:

> I do not laugh or talk with the men around here unless it is absolutely necessary. I do not feel that anyone is restricting my freedom. Freedom is not measured by the woman's ability to make a fool of herself. I am free to choose and I am choosing to be conservative. I am sure the people around here respect me more than they respect someone like S. (another female worker in the same office) who talks and laughs with everyone and wears all these fancy clothes and comes to the office painted like a sugar doll. All those men who pretend to like her talk about her in her absence and say horrible things. Women are really foolish to think they can attract men that way. Men would have a good time with women like her but when it comes to marriage they will marry a woman they respect.
>
> I do not believe the woman has the right to choose her husband. Sure, she can express her feelings and object to someone but we women do not have the experience that the men have and my father can judge another man better than I could. I was married that way and I am happy. I have a nice home, delightful children, and a decent husband.
>
> I follow my husband's suggestions and let him decide everything about the family budget. Who wants the headache of family budget and other responsibilities? I give him my salary every month and he gives me a sum of money for my expenses and the house expenses and I live within the allowance. I believe women should work. Frankly, I would be very unhappy if I did not work, but my family comes first. If I had to choose I would not hesitate to select my family.

Such genuine support for the traditional values is not shared by all lower-middle-class women. Some follow a traditional style of life in appearance but not in spirit. While expressing their dissatisfaction with the old ways, blaming them for all social evils, these women are unwilling to risk losing the security of the old system. They are likely to justify their inability to take charge of their lives by claiming their unwillingness to hurt their families or to upset old or ailing parents. Some of these women maintain secret lives of their own while keeping the facade of traditionalism. These are the women most frequently portrayed in the fictional writings of current Egyptian authors and around whom several TV series and films have been made.

When I married I was only fifteen. My father selected my husband and I did not see him before the engagement party. The first few months were great. We went to Beirut on our honeymoon and he bought me a lot of presents. But once the honeymoon was over it was obvious that he was not the liberal man I thought he was. He never shared with me any information, never paid me any compliments, and always made me feel inferior. Every time I tried to participate in a conversation with his friends about work, he made me feel like I did not know what I was saying. Later after the friends left, he would tell me that I should not interfere in the discussion between men even if they are friends because that makes me look less feminine. I had finished my university degree when I married him but was waiting for the manpower to assign me for work. I waited for two years. When finally the assignment came in the mail, I was so happy. I thought that was my salvation. The work is terrible and the transportation is impossible but it gives me the chance to go out. I got to be very friendly with a man who works with me in the office; he is married too and lives near us. He has a car and my husband does not object to him giving me a ride. The problem is that I think we are in love now. We see each other outside the work, nothing serious, just an hour or so every day after work. Just a cup of coffee or lemonade together. He is not happy with his wife, and my husband does not think I exist. He thinks I am so conservative that he does not suspect anything between me and F. I feel guilty about it and I feel cheap, but what can I do? (Interview, September 1977)

Conclusions

The material presented in this paper shows that while Egyptian working-class women have shown a great deal of adaptability in dealing with the changing economic and social realities in Egyptian society, evidence indicates that they are somewhat disoriented by the changes occurring around them. It is one thing to maintain resiliency within the domestic sphere, and quite another to face upheavals in situations in which one has little training or sense of belonging. In Egypt, and throughout the Middle East, there is a lag between the new roles impelled by current economic demands and the persistence of traditional values regarding women's domestic responsibilities.

Women themselves are partly to blame for their inabilities to translate expanded public participation into adjustments of domestic responsibilities and relationships. It will take some time, no matter how qualified and skilled they may be at the professional level, for women to feel as comfortable and secure with their extradomestic environment as they do with the domestic one, before they can give up some of their domestic functions without feeling they have lost control over their lives.

The Ringing (a short story)

FATHIYYAH ʿAWADA
Translated from the Arabic by Tura Campanella

She put down the telephone receiver and bowed her head. She was look-ing directly into the ashtray before her and calmly counted the ciga-rettes she had smoked in the past hour. Nineteen, twenty, twenty-one, . . . she felt disgusted with herself. She began to cough and cough; the coughing would not stop. She grasped the side of the bed and pressed herself against it as though to keep her soul from fleeing her body.

The phone rang again. She lifted the receiver and shouted angrily at the unknown speaker: "Hello!"

No one answered. She repeated, "Hello!" But there was no reply.

Silence. She returned the receiver to its place and lifted up her legs, looking at her newly polished toenails. She turned to find a small note-book. She flipped through it, stopped at a page, and began to read.

The telephone rang once more. She knew who was calling. She said out loud in a high voice: "I know who you are and I know you will keep calling me without speaking."

She lifted the receiver to her ear but said nothing. The notebook lay open in her hands and she mused: "Tomorrow . . . tomorrow. Why is he calling today? Why can't he leave me and my life alone?"

The receiver was in her hand and at the other end was someone who would not speak, afraid to let her hear his voice so she could wound him with her accusing words. A single sigh was all that escaped from her.

"I wish I could speak with him!" She stared in front of her, the re-ceiver still in her hand. She saw a face whose features she told herself she was about to forget, even though she could not yet forget the feel-ings that even the memory of that face aroused in her. A rattling sound came to her across the wires.

"Coward," she said. He hung up.

Tomorrow . . . would that the date had never come, two years ago it was now. Two years.

She said to herself, How quickly life passes with scarcely a single mo-ment to grasp those we love. Love and scorn filled her. She loved him and scorned him at the same time. She desired him, but at the same time was determined to deprive herself of him. She knew that he loved her and desired her. He continually called her just to listen to her voice, not daring to speak to her for fear of her scorn.

The phone rang but she decided not to answer it this time. She would not lift the receiver so he could make the connection he wished to make.

But her thoughts became confused. Maybe the one who contacted her was just some person who annoyed people by calling them on the telephone? Or perhaps her line was crossed with another line, which caused the phone to ring constantly? She did not believe this. She found she was certain that it was he who was ringing again and again. How could her feelings deceive her since he was concerned?

The ringing stopped and she looked around her at the empty room. She suddenly was overwhelmed with fear and deadly loneliness.

She scolded herself. She could not help looking at the telephone since it was the line that connected the two of them. He heard her voice when she lifted the receiver and said hello. But she wished to hear his voice, too, and she found she could not do as he did; namely, call and then hang up after hearing his voice. If she did that, he would understand that she was the one who called him. That would make him stop calling, for he would sense the strength of her desire to return to him. And that is what she did not want.

The phone rang again for the fifth time. She lifted the receiver delicately and gently as if to greet him after a long separation, as if to embrace him, as if he were coming to her with all the love and tenderness he had in his being.

She said to him, in a voice into which she tried to pour every nuance of love, "Hello!"

He did not answer but remained silent like the sphinx, which hints at its existence without saying a word. If only he knew how much she yearned for him, she thought, he would rush to speak to her. Perhaps she was savoring the suffering caused by her self-cruelty in depriving herself of him, but that was necessary, she told herself. A month or two or even a year of deprivation would save her the suffering she would have to endure throughout her life if she yielded to him. She had thought that he would despair of her returning to him, for nearly a year had passed since they first separated. But that had not happened. The more she was on the verge of forgetting him, the more he continued to remind her of his existence and to remind her that he desired her and wanted her to marry him. He also reminded her that he was a coward when he met her face to face and so continued to call her on the phone.

She looked anxiously at the telephone while ten minutes passed, while an hour of time passed. The phone rang again. What did he want to say to her?

If he spoke, then she would know what he wanted. Perhaps he, in turn, enjoyed forsaking her and was afraid to speak with her lest she be tender and return to him after she had spoken to him harshly in the beginning, then followed these harsh words with tender, soft ones. Perhaps he wanted to live with the hope of returning to her? After she discovered he was married he still said he could not live with her, even though he was unhappy with his wife. Why not marry me, he said, but she refused. Perhaps another girl would consent to marriage with a man who already had one wife, but she would not endure having to share the man whom she loved because she wanted him completely. When she had discovered that she could not have that, she said she preferred separation, although all the warm, generous feelings of love and affection were still within her.

The telephone rang again. Tomorrow would be the anniversary of their first meeting and his persistent calling made it plain that he too still lived that meeting.

He respected her desire to separate, but he said he could not withdraw himself totally, for he said she was the one who had made him a virile man in the true meaning of the word, who had given him everything he was looking for. She wondered sometimes why they had not met before he got married, but he felt it was pointless to raise such questions after she had already refused him.

She lit another cigarette and puffed smoke from her mouth, exhaling with it the burdens that had accumulated in her. But in the clouds of smoke his image appeared to her.

The telephone was still ringing beside her. The smell of cigarettes suffocated her. The sound of the ringing seemed to her like the whizzing of airplanes. Should she return to him or not? This was the baffling dilemma that forced itself on her consciousness.

She reached her hand out to turn on the radio. The announcer reminded the listeners of the day's date, a date that bore the memory of their meeting, a memory that almost shattered her. Everything around her looked as if it were conspiring against her: the date, the radio, him, the ringing of the phone, her breath, which rose and was expelled with the cigarette smoke. She squeezed her hands tightly around her throat as if she wanted to choke everything around her by stopping her own breath.

"It is all pointless," she repeated in a high voice.

The ringing resumed. She looked at the telephone, then grasped the receiver suddenly. A sigh escaped her, a sigh bearing, she felt, all the burdens of her soul. As though she had just returned from a long and fatiguing race, she said in an exhausted voice: "Hello!"

Then she paused for a moment after uttering the word. She must make a decision here, she told herself. She must be strong, hold to her decision and every decision. The pain that would accompany that decision was inevitable.

At the other end, the man did not answer. She said "Hello!" for a second time.

The man changed his mind and replied, "Hello!"

She heard his voice.

He then said directly: "How are you? This is . . ." and he said his name to her.

It was his voice. The beloved voice that crept into her mind and emotions and stole her strength and endurance. She had known all along it was him.

Yes, this was the sound of his voice. The sound that made her heart soar to the highest places. The sound reached her now through the receiver, pulling her toward the past with all the sweetness it held pulling her toward that person who had asked about her.

What should she say to him . . . ?

Should she really tell him exactly how she was? Should she ask him about himself, too?

Should she be defeated in front of herself . . . or be victorious over her weakness and continue her struggle for strength and pride . . . ?

On the other end of the line, a man awaited her decision. He expected she would return to him in the same way she had done in the past after all the quarrels between them.

Her decision depended on his saying something else.

The silence between them grew heavy with desire for the days of the past. She was about to collapse on the threshold of her yearning and forgive him for everything as only those who love totally can forgive. She almost whispered to him: "How I have been longing to hear your voice." She almost dropped the receiver to the ground because she felt she could no longer endure this situation, which pulled her back and forth between one world and another. She knew he was waiting for a word from her after he had finally yielded and spoken.

With great difficulty, she gained control over herself. She tightened her grasp on the receiver and said in a voice into which she inserted all the strength for which he had said he loved her: "I'm sorry. There is no one by that name here."

She hung up and, as she did, she realized that her decision had been made and that he would never call her again.

Fatima: A Life History of an Egyptian Woman from Bulaq

EVELYN EARLY

The following sketch of Fatima is based on conversations held over a six-year period. Fatima is originally from an Egyptian Delta village and is presently living in Bulaq, a popular quarter of Cairo, Egypt. She has developed her own business: buying cheese and ghee (clarified butter) from markets in her home village and reselling them in Cairo. She is typical of many lower-class women seeking economic independence as a hedge both against the vicissitudes of marginality and against the possibility of divorce. In Fatima's case, neglect by her husband (and her loyalty to him through thick and thin) took a higher toll of her energy than actual divorce.

Fatima came to Cairo in 1956 when her husband sold his land and took an unskilled job in the Ministry of Culture. With time she developed her own support systems among neighbors and customers in Cairo, and they became closer than her village friends. In the late seventies, her business was booming, her health was good, and she took a major role in marrying off Muhammad, her youngest (and only son) of four children.

By the early 1980s Fatima's life was not going well. Her husband's antagonism and lack of support was not particularly remarkable, even to her. What caused her anguish was her son Muhammad's neglect. During the late 1970s he had joined the crowds of people migrating abroad to work in order to escape Egypt's dramatic inflation. He also seemed less attentive than social norms dictate, and his long absences probably exacerbated Fatima's feeling of abandonment. In Middle Eastern society the oldest son is expected to support the mother in her old age. Husbands may come and go, but children remain, not only affectively but as a source of security. It is Muhammad, not her husband and not her daughters with their own mothers-in-law to assist, upon whom Fatima had assumed she would depend in her old age. But unfortunately Fatima's relations with Muhammad's wife, Sabah, were strained much of the time. Sabah resented any attention or service that Muhammad gave his mother. At the same time Fatima was dramatically aware of the contribution from her own savings to Sabah's wedding.

The following are reconstructions of conversations with Fatima at three points: in January 1976 when I had known her over a year, in March 1976, and finally in January 1982 during our most recent meeting. The narratives are abstracted from field notes and have been rearranged and edited.

Finally, let me stress that I do not present Fatima's case as an example of hard life in Egypt. The economic straits and family disharmony could be found anywhere in the world. Fatima's creative response to her plight is in some sense an "Egyptian" response.

January 1976

This room you see me in under the staircase without windows or electricity is barely tolerable after the sunny, airy one on the top floor where I lived for twenty-four years. In that building families knew each other. There I never lacked company; we always enjoyed cooking on the landing together and in winter we would sun on the rooftop and eat tangerines. At night after our children slept, we would drink coffee together. When I went to lessons at the mosque in the morning it was easy to call Aniyat to go with me as I walked down the stairs. Now I go alone; it's not the same when you must pass several streets before you find someone to go with you.

But even without Aniyat, I still go to mosque lessons. There one can learn important facts, like the timing of voluntary prayer, which I sometimes perform in addition to the five obligatory prayers a day. These days one often encounters people who do not hold to their religion; some resort to superstitions. Remember when we visited the shrine last summer in my daughter-in-law's village and how her mother asked the shrine guardian about a fertility amulet? As for me, I place my faith in the *'awliyya'* (saints); they are the source of all good.

You ask if I see my old neighbors? And whether they've been to visit me since I moved here? No, though it is their duty to visit and congratulate me on my new home. They send their children to buy cheese but they never come themselves. I have met good people here, but we would still be living in the old house if our landlady hadn't tricked us; she asked us to leave temporarily so she could repair the building but all she wanted was to get us out and bring in tenants paying a higher rent. After all, the landlady's relatives all moved back to their rooms after the repairs were done. They are from southern Egypt and I am from the north; I was the only Delta resident in the house and they always referred to me as the *fellaha.*[1]

I have been here since my husband sold his land in the village and moved to Cairo to work as a stock clerk and later for the Ministry of Culture, but unlike my Saidi neighbors I have not been surrounded by relatives and fellow villagers (*baladiyat*). When I returned to my village this year to arrange a marriage for my son many people whom I did not know greeted me in the market place. Still, I have few ties back there;

my friends here in Cairo have become like my *baladiyat*. Friends are the people I depend on! Even family is not always to be trusted. Did my own brother have the courage to side against his wife when she demanded that *her* daughter marry *my* son? No. Do my three daughters visit me? The last time Feriayla was in town she went straight to her in-laws and did not even tell me she was here. I can't depend on my family, least of all my husband.

I must admit, Feriayla's bad manners surprised me after all the times I have traveled to be with her and after I sold my land to furnish her apartment when her father squandered her dowry. But she has suffered in her marriage. She has had several operations to cure her infertility but they always fail because her husband ignores the doctor's orders to avoid her for the first forty days. He spoiled the last operation and then he took another wife. As for my daughter Iman, she is married and has five children; she lives on the outskirts of Cairo and she does visit regularly. And then there's Nadia. She married the husband of another daughter (Nadia's sister). Nadia's sister died while still a bride. Nadia visits me often; sometimes she stays several days if she has been fighting with her mother-in-law. Nadia's sister died while still a young bride. She lived with her mother-in-law and did little but help with the cooking. One day a neighbor who envied my daughter her easy life and her youth told her how healthy she looked, and hinted her ample stomach meant pregnancy. From that moment the bride felt a pain in her abdomen; the doctors could not find a cure and within a week she was dead.

Well, at least now that my son Muhammad is engaged I can rest. I am in this hovel so he and his bride can live in the room we took across the street last year. One of my customers told me about it when the landlady was evicting. Abu Muhammad (literally "the father of Muhammad," used as a proper name for the father) hasn't contributed his share to our son's *mahr* (payment by the groom at marriage); we had to borrow from his family and now they're pressuring him to pay his share. I contributed my hundred pounds; Muhammad paid his fifty, which he saved from his work at the bindery by smoking fewer cigarettes. When Abu Muhammad retired, Muhammad took his father's position at the ministry. His father was an employee (*muwazzaf*), sitting in a chair all day, but Muhammad is a tradesman (*sana'i'i*) and works in the shop.

My husband Abu Muhammad is irresponsible; he wastes his money gambling and often he stops contributing to household expenses and eats his meals outside. I cook for Muhammad and myself but I don't feel that I have to feed *two* men! Of course I mend Abu Muhammad's clothes and make him tea; after all, we still share the same home. He says he does not want to visit his family in the village because it reminds him of his father's death and makes him sad. I know better; he does not want to repay his loan!

Several years ago Abu Muhammad and I quarreled because he gambled so much there was nothing left for household expenses. I returned to my village with my son and opened a sandwich stand there for *ful* and *ta'miyya* (sandwiches of spicy fava beans and fried chickpeas). I would never have made up with Abu Muhammad except for my son's sake. But I did come back and I used money saved from my sandwich stand to start the ghee and cheese business. As my reputation grew, I had more orders than I could carry on the train even though I went to the village every week. When I go to the village I stay with Um Ahmad, the half-blind widow whose house is across from my old sandwich stand. It is more relaxed than at my sister's or brother's, who would feel obliged to invite me for a meal. Um Ahmad fills me in on the latest news.

Who needs to depend on relatives or neighbors who are fickle and self-centered? My customers have with time become my friends; when I want to join a money-saving association, seek advice, or merely relax I turn to them. We attend each other's birth celebrations (*subu'a*, held seven days after birth), weddings, and funerals. Since I'm a merchant, I meet many people. It is not the same as being a moneylender, however. There was a woman in my village who would lend money and then request half again its sum after a week; that is interest, which is forbidden in Islam. One day boils broke out over her whole body; she soon died and her children enjoyed her ill-gotten profits while she roasted in hell. It's true I charge more if people buy cheese or ghee on installment, but this is compensation for my patience. If customers pay a lump sum they pay less because I use their money to buy more ghee right away. After all, wasn't the Prophet a merchant? It is an honorable trade.

Last week I went to see the parents of my son Muhammad's wife (literally fiancée), Sabah. His sister Nadia had suggested another candidate for her brother but it was better for him to marry from his home village; there he has a position among men. If he had married Nadia's choice he would not have known anything about her background. What would he have done at feast-time—followed her to *her* home and family? When I went last week, it was my first visit since Sabah's family insulted us during the engagement party. How? By responding to our gifts of fine dresses with a few badly cooked *fatir* (rich cakes) rather than with the expected suit for the groom. It was a disgrace but after all Muhammad's father-in-law was sick and needed an operation, so how could I complain?

Visiting in the country I can enjoy the peace, smell the fresh breeze, and watch the ducks swim in the irrigation canal. Here in the city I am cramped in this dark room. There in the village they have plenty of space and they have just installed electricity. Soon we'll be able to play the radio without batteries and they say they will bring a TV! Then we can watch movies with all those tall, blond foreigners in them.

March 1976

On the Prophet's birthday, I wanted to give Muhammad's fiancée the gifts customarily offered to the fiancée on Mawlid el-nabi. So I bought three Egyptian pounds worth of *halawa* (crushed sesame paste), three kilos of bananas, and nine kilos of oranges. My in-laws told me to take the fiancée a pound note as well. But when I found Sabah's family insisting that Muhammad come to visit them, I thought that I would give him the pound note and he could put another one with it so as to give her two pounds on his next visit. He is going next Thursday to spend a day with her. They want to see him, but he has been very sick and he must work even when sick because his position is still temporary. He cannot afford to miss any days at all, much less for a trip to the countryside. But this week when I saw Sabah in the village, she was wearing new earrings she said her father bought for her. They cost twenty-five pounds. So I figure that must be the money with which they were going to get a suit for Muhammad. Sabah's father said they would not get Muhammad a suit since he is an employee earning enough money to get his own suit. They said they've given to the best of their ability (*ʿala ʾaddi halihim*).

While in the village this week I also visited my sister's son Abdul Wahad, who is in the air force. His brother Ahmad got married last week but I did not go to the wedding because my sister and her family did not come to my son's engagement party. They didn't want to anger my brother, who was annoyed that my son Muhammad did not marry his daughter. And my sister did not pay any attention to me (*ma ʿabbarnish*)[2] while I was in the village so I could hardly pay any attention to them and I didn't even congratulate them on the wedding.

When I returned in the winter of 1982, I found Fatima ill in bed with angina. Her son was in Saudi Arabia working on a printing press like the one he worked on in the Egyptian Ministry of Culture. He was sending tape-recorded letters and money (which he carefully noted on the tape) with friends traveling to Egypt. Fatima feels her son has abandoned her in her time of need. Nevertheless, he continues to occupy a central place in her thoughts. Many times as we talked her thoughts turned to his wedding.

January 1982

Now my son Muhammad has gone to Saudi Arabia to seek his fortune. In his tapes, he tells Sabah, who is now his wife, to care for me, but does she? No. In fact, a few days ago she threw me out of her house. My sister Fikriya had come from the village to take care of me and she, her daughter, and I were staying with Sabah across the street in the room my husband and I vacated for her when she married.

Things have not been easy with my daughter-in-law. Remember last summer when she cursed me, all because she wanted her Primus stove, which I had only been storing for her at the house as a favor because she had no room? Then she dragged me by the hair into the entryway of the building. Sabah has alienated everyone in the lane and has no friends there. She has no patience with her son either; she raises him "in the street." Small wonder that he throws a tantrum every time things do not go as he would like. She does not care for him. Why, she left him for me to raise when she went off to the village in a huff two summers ago. . . .

Al-baraka fi al-ʿaʾila (the [natal] family is the steadfast support). But *should* it be my family that looks after me in my old age? It is my siblings who support me; my sister Fikriya's son came all the way from the village to ask after me. Aren't one's sons supposed to take care of one in one's old age? When my brother-in-law's son Abdul Wahad returned from Saudi Arabia, he brought me a *gellabeya*. When my son Muhammad returns he will probably bring me the same thing. Shouldn't a son bring something more than a distant relative does? You hear now on the tape recorded in Saudi Arabia how Muhammad asked his father if he needed anything, but did he ask me?

Muhammad sent his wife three hundred pounds to buy a refrigerator. He tells me in the tapes, "May God cure you" (*Rabbuna yashfiki*). But I ask you, since when did words cure someone! Did Muhammad send me money? Even people not related to me, like yourself, if they see me sick would offer me money; shouldn't one's own son do as well? Why did I spend so much to get my son married if he doesn't even ask after me now? Remember when we went to the village and the young wife in my in-laws' house arranged for us to meet her relatives whose daughter Sabah (now Fatima's daughter-in-law) was ready to marry? We went and read the Fatiha (opening chapter of the Koran) on the basis of a 250 Egyptian pound *mahr*. And we agreed that the bride's father would provide the houseware copper.

But then what happened? The day of the engagement we prepared an elaborate procession: there were eight chiffon dresses, ten bottles of sherbet, ten kilos of sugar, countless piles of macaroni, rice, and sugar.

We provided quite a display. And then the next day we waited for the bride's family to respond, expecting at least a length of cloth for a suit. What a scraggly procession they made! Nothing but *fatir* and some macaroni and rice and fruit. What poor quality the *fatir* was; it was so soggy in the middle that it all stuck together. I was so humiliated that I did not even go out to meet the procession and clap and sing like one is supposed to do at such times. The daughters-in-law of the house provided a half-hearted welcome, for to do nothing would have been unthinkable. I could not even look at that unsightly procession when it came in.[3]

I have been too sick to go to the village to market since last spring. Now I have used up all the money with which I used to buy ghee and cheese; every other week I have to go to a heart specialist. The examination costs seven pounds, but the follow-up consultation is free. The doctor is very kind and knows my case. He says, "Fatima, you are strong; look, your circulation is much better than last year. You will live." See, here are the medicines he prescribed for me today. They cost five and one-half pounds.

Some of my customer friends still pass by to see me, but my old neighbors never do. The thing that saves me now are my present neighbors (*al-baraka fi al-jiran*). The woman next door brings my water and the woman upstairs brings me food from the market. My husband is of no help whatsoever. It is better for me when I am at my daughter's for I get very sick from the anger I feel when my husband and I quarrel. You heard him just now when I said that I was not going to speak to Muhammad anymore on the tapes we send since he does not really care about me. My husband responded: "Don't talk and then he will think that you died." Do you think Muhammad would come if I died? What good would he be to me then!

NOTE: *This sketch was drawn from two and one-half years of research and subsequent visits over a period of six years in a popular quarter of central Cairo, Egypt. The research was supported by grants from the Fulbright Commission, Social Science Research Council, and the National Institute of Mental Health. During the course of my research, I was affiliated with the University of Chicago, the National Institute of Planning of Egypt, and the National Center for Sociological and Criminological Research of Egypt.*

Notes

1. *Fellah(a)*, "peasant," is commonly used to refer to Delta ruralities in northern Egypt as opposed to Saidi ones in southern Egypt.

2. The negative of the expression *yiʿabbir had*, "pay attention to someone," indicates that two people are not on speaking terms because of a mis-

understanding or slight. Egyptian traditional (*baladi*) society has degrees of "breaking off speaking" and social formulas for reinstituting relations.

3. In wedding and circumcision processions, both quantity of goods brought in the procession and quality of the chanting and singing performance of known rhymed repertoires are clear marks of a family's standing. Customarily, women sing along the way and when they reach the house they pause at the door and continue to sing. They are answered by women of the house in an extended duet.

Divorce (a short story)

LEILA ABOUZEID
Translated from the Arabic by M. Salah-dine Hammoud

The emaciated young man was suffering long moments of uneasy antic-ipation; he did not join his colleagues in their usual chat about the is-sues of the hour. He tapped his pen against his desk, looked at his watch, threw the pen down, crossed his arms and laid his head on them. Finally he rose angrily and left the office. "He's supposed to receive word about his application for promotion," explained one of the men.

A moment later, the emaciated young man returned with a dejected look in his eyes. He sat down and remained at his desk until it was time for him to go home. He walked down the halls, the rhythm of his steps in time with his breathing.

Outside in the street he got on his motorcycle and drove off reck-lessly, disregarding all traffic signs. He overtook a car from the right and swerved across the road. Moving like an expert roller skater, he at-tempted to pass a bus from the left, but as the bus came to a turn it blocked his way. He applied his brakes forcefully and was immediately thrown off the motorcycle into the middle of the road. The oncoming car that he had passed a moment earlier came to a sharp stop, its tires shrieking. The young man was bruised and scratched. A hole was torn in the right knee of his trousers as though that spot in his trousers had melted in the air. A small crowd of pedestrians collected around him and the driver of the car scolded him. Someone in the crowd helped him to stand up and handed him his motorcycle. At that moment he was overwhelmed with distress. He walked along, pushing his motorcycle on the sidewalk, and broke into sobs.

At home, his wife brought him some cotton and an iodine solution. She went back to the next room to tend to the children. They clung to-gether, motionless, as they did every time their father came home in a bad mood. He, however, went on rubbing the palm of his hand and his knee with the iodine-soaked cotton. The sting of the solution hurt and he clenched his lips and shut his eyes tightly. He did not utter a sound. He lay on a mattress on the bare floor and silence fell on what seemed to be an empty house.

He lay on his back like a corpse for some time. The evening darkness became more and more overwhelming until his brother walked in and turned on the light. He looked at the injured man's leg and heaved a sigh of relief.

"So what was rumored to be a broken leg is no more than a few scratches on your knee!" he exclaimed. "People exaggerate so much they distort the truth. Why don't you sell that motorcycle?"

There was no reply. Staring into his brother's face, he was able to see how very depressed he was. He remained silent for a while, until his injured brother finally spoke out.

"Life is depressing," he said. "I'm at a loss."

"Why? Are you going to let a small traffic accident destroy you?"

"It has nothing to do with the accident."

"Then what is it?"

"Just life in general."

"And only now you discover that things are bad?"

This question angered the emaciated young man. The veins on his forehead swelled and he shouted, "Of course not! I learned that when Father abandoned us."

"There you go again, back to the same old story! We're brothers, after all, let's be reasonable. You grew up a long time ago and Father was done with his responsibilities for you then."

"Then why did I leave school? Why did I marry a woman whom I found abandoned in the street? I am a failure on every score."

"Did anyone force you?"

"Poverty forced me! You know that well but you pretend you don't."

Silence fell back onto the house until it was interrupted by the call for the evening prayer. The emaciated young man listened attentively, and his anger dissipated. As soon as the prayer call was over, he spoke more calmly and even affectionately to his brother.

"I remember," he said, "when it used to get so cold in our room at home that I would be unable to fall asleep. But at school in the classroom I would feel the warmth spread all over my body and I would be overcome by sleep. School," he went on as a sad smile appeared on his brother's lips, "what good is school when you're hungry? Do you realize how many times Father was married? Perhaps we'll never know the exact number. Men like him, who produce delinquents, are a curse on our society. They should be banned."

"Your bitterness is too intense," put in the brother.

With a dejected, angry look on his face, the emaciated young man went on recalling. "If it had not been for holidays, we would never have seen the man at all. Remember when he insisted I go and show him who my father was? It was just before the Eid al-adha and we were playing ball as he was bringing home the sacrificial sheep.[1] I kicked the ball hard and it struck him right in the nose. It couldn't have been a better kick if I had tried to aim it at his face. He grabbed my shirt collar," he went on with a nervous laugh, his voice shaking, "he squeezed my neck so tightly that I thought he was going to strangle me. I vividly remember him looking me in the eye and saying, 'Take me to see your father, you evil omen. I am not letting go of him until I see the filthy dog who fathered him!' he yelled to the men who rushed to my rescue. 'They are doing such a fine job, littering this country's streets with outlaws.' He was humiliated, however, when he heard one of the men shout: 'He's your own son! Let go of him! You are going to kill him!'"

"You always go back to the past, every time we meet, don't you?" commented his brother. "I think your mind is deteriorating."

"The world is what's deteriorating. What on earth is happening to it?"

The two brothers remained silent for a while and only the regular rhythm of their breathing could be heard.

Then the emaciated young man further recalled, with a smile on his face, "Do you remember the story of the bicycle? I had become so obsessed by the desire to own a bike that my mother, bless her soul, was worried about me. She sold everything that was worth anything to buy me that bicycle. I was ready to die of grief if she hadn't bought it for me. Children's happiness is so essential, isn't it? And it can be destroyed by a number of things, one of which is divorce. I know that. It marks children with psychological scars that never fade."

"Well, I can't stay much longer. I have to be at work at six in the morning, as you know," said the visiting brother, looking at his watch and becoming somewhat restless. He slammed the door as he left. Silence returned to the house, which once again seemed deserted.

The next morning, the emaciated young man woke up and began to shout.

"What a mess this shirt collar is!" he cried. "Is this the shirt that I am supposed to wear to the office? I suppose I should hire someone to press it! Or should I simply go and drown in the ocean?"

His wife stood as motionless as a suspect indicted for a crime. Her children came to her for protection, and right before their eyes their father rolled the shirt in his hand and threw it in her face. Her voice climbed over his, and she shouted back.

"Don't you dare assault us anymore with your frustrations over your own failure! Don't make things any worse than they are! Don't add your behavior to everything else—depriving us of food and clothing! . . . Do you suppose I've not spoken up for so long because I worry about your own well-being? Of course not! My forbearance has been strictly for the children's sake. Otherwise, I'd be happier being somebody's maid!"

"Ah, the children!" he said. "Don't think they are going to save you."

He was flabbergasted by her boldness and taken by surprise that she was as discontented as he was. He was indignant that she was insulting his life-style and the way he treated his family. And because he was humiliated he resolved to discipline her.

But, encouraged by her own rebelliousness, she responded to his threats with another curse that made matters worse.

"You'd rather throw these children into the street, wouldn't you?" she yelled. "Exactly like your father did to you. A family tradition you want to keep, huh?"

"Go on, go on turning them against me," he said. "I know your ways."

He started toward the door in disarray, putting on his *djellaba*.²

"You'll hear from me!" he shouted as he reached the door.

He walked away and she followed, still shouting back, "Okay. Okay. Be sure you do your very best and go through with all your plans!" she cried after him.

He rushed out and went straight to the ʾ*adil*'s office where he found them just opening the office for business.³ One of the officials ushered him in and insisted that he take a seat, as though he suspected the emaciated young man might change his mind and walk out. The two ʾ*adil*s sat down at their desks.

"You are here to request a divorce, my son?" one of them inquired.

The emaciated young man nodded. The ʾ*adil* prepared to write. "I need names, and the date and place of marriage," he said, and added, "I suppose you know our fees are set."

The emaciated young man sat there reflecting upon these words when the image of a gravedigger flashed through his mind. He was suddenly amazed by the fact that some people live on the calamities of others.

"Names, please, young man. Date and place," the ʾ*adil* repeated. He wrote them down as they were given to him and read aloud what he was writing, as if he were dictating it all to himself.

When he finished the emaciated young man handed him a fifty-dirham note and departed.

Notes

1. Feast of sacrifice; one of the major religious holidays in Islam. On the condition that he is able to afford it, each head of the household is required to slaughter a sheep (traditionally) in a sacrifice ritual. The meat is meant to be shared with the poor, who are unable to afford it throughout the rest of the year.

2. A traditional Moroccan hooded outer garment.

3. Chartered judicial officials possessing enough knowledge of Islamic law to be able to witness and endorse marriage, divorce, and inheritance proceedings. Legal documents detailing such proceedings have to bear the signature of two ʾadils.

PART III
Health and Education

Improvement of the public welfare is often declared to be the ideal toward which the nation-state strives. Improved working conditions and employment opportunities, the presence or absence of conflict, and religion, education, and health are factors that affect families and thus affect women as well as men. Health and education, although only part of the total picture of any nation's general condition, are a basic measure of women's position in society. In the Middle East a woman is highly valued for her role in bearing and raising children and her fertility and sexualtiy are seen as the concern of all the members of a family. Any issue such as family planning or female circumcision that touches on female fertility and sexuality becomes a political and religious issue within society.

Family planning through contraception is not in conflict with the Koran, though abortion is considered *haram*, or religiously forbidden, "after the fetus or embryo is animated." In practice, however, limiting the size of the family may not be perceived by its adult members as being in their best interests if children are still sources of support in old age or if children are needed to work on the farms or in urban factories in times of economic distress. The late Egyptian president Gamal Abdel Nasser, in a historic 1962 television speech, supported and even encouraged the practice of family planning as the best investment for the future. One healthy child raised by a healthy mother was better than twelve sickly children raised by an ailing mother, and a small family was easier for the father to support, he said. The Grand Mufti in Jordan isued a *fatwa* or formal religious legal opinion on the subject in 1964, stating that family planning, including the use of medicine for contraception or for abortion up to 120 days of pregnancy, was permitted by Islamic law.

But many women are still torn between what they see as their own versus their nation's best interests. Given the choice, many women will stop having babies after four or five children, as Donna Lee Bowen's account of the Moroccan health system demonstrates. Most Middle Eastern governments have made determined efforts to establish free health care for their people, including family planning and gynecological clinics; as Bowen's account shows, the results are not always what the planners intended.

Female circumcision, from clitoridectomy to radical labial or Pharaonic circumcision, is not mentioned in the Koran. Forbidden in most Islamic countries, it predates Islam and is performed by women upon other women in most of the countries, both Islamic and non-Islamic, along the river Nile. The practice has long historical and ritual precedents, but in recent years both men and women in Egypt and the Sudan have banded together to work for its eradication. A 1980 conference held in Cairo by the Ministry of Health passed a unanimous resolution condemning all forms of female circumcision as detrimental to women's health and men's sexual life and hence to the well-being of the nation. In 1979 Khartoum, Sudan was the site of a conference on the changing status of Sudanese women during which an entire day was devoted to papers and testimonials on the subject. Similar condemnatory resolutions were passed. In cities along the Nile today, circumcision appears to be waning, though it is still practiced in rural areas. As Dr. Nahid Toubia, herself a Sudanese physician, points out in her paper, the effects of such a practice on women may have far-reaching consequences, and not only in the realm of physical health.

Women's health was an issue raised by Dr. Nawal al-Sa'dawi, the Egyptian physician described by many of her compatriots as the first radical feminist in the Arab world. Her books have been bestsellers in the Arab world since 1974, when *Women and Sex* was first published. Becuse of her publicly expressed views Dr. Sa'dawi was imprisoned by President Anwar Sadat in the fall of 1981; she was released after two months. Dr. Sa'dawi continues to write and lecture today and some of her work has recently been translated into English; the development of her ideas can be seen in Fedwa Malti-Douglas' translation of an excerpt from one of Dr. Sa'dawi's early novels.

Education, like health, affects the family and may also affect fertility rates, as Ann Bragdon al-Kadhi's work demonstrates. Free, compulsory public education was a basic promise of the new nationalist governments, and is often cited as the most successfully implemented of all party promises. Between 1950 and 1960, female participation at all levels of education in the Arab world increased from 1,018,000 in 1950 to 2,756,000 in 1960. Yet since 1965, when 26 percent of all students in Arab countries were female, that figure has increased to only 36 percent in 1975. Why? And what has education meant for women? Are the goals of women's education changing from teacher training to more vocational and technical education? Nagat al-Sanabary takes a look at statistics and at goals and achievements and suggests that an important beginning has been made in Arab women's education but that the pace of women's education has slowed all over the area. How can one account for this discrepancy between promise and performance, between ideal and practice? Again the interrelationship of all factors—health, education, economics, war, work, religion—must be stressed.

Mustafa Attir's account of Libyan women in a revolutionary setting introduces a new element of education: military training. Dr. Attir, however, sees military training as a crucial factor in reinforcing change in women's traditional position in Libyan society. Military training for women is not unknown; the PLO, the Israeli army, the Polisario of the Southern Sahara have recruited women, but participation in actual combat remains minimal, partly because of society's ambiguous attitude about women's place in the military.

Only by looking across geographical boundaries and from the perspectives of many forms of study can one gain a sense of the interplay between forces that, in the end, are shaping people's welfare and people's lives in the area today and determining women's status from Morocco to Iran.

Continuity and Change in Women's Education in the Arab States

NAGAT AL-SANABARY

In the Arab states, as in other developing countries, women's education has lagged behind men's. In fact, education of both women and men in these countries has been neglected for centuries due to cultural and economic decline and under the impact of Western colonialism. Even today in the Arab states millions of children of both sexes receive no formal schooling, and much of the adult population is illiterate.

Formal education for women in the modern sense was unknown in the Arab world until the early decades of the nineteenth century, when missionary girls' schools opened in Egypt, Lebanon, and Syria followed by native girls' schools toward the end of the nineteenth century.[1] By 1900 native and foreign girls' schools opened in other Arab countries, mostly under Western colonial control. For several decades only primary education was available for girls; access to secondary education came much later. Women were admitted to universities in Egypt, Lebanon, Syria, and Iraq in the late 1920s and early 1930s.

Before the achievement of national independence, educational opportunities were extremely limited for everyone.[2] Education was a vehicle for introducing a few elites into the ranks of the civil service, an area beyond the sphere of women at the time. Education was strictly class specific. Middle- and upper-class women who availed themselves of education used it for cultural refinement. Lower-class women were provided limited educational opportunities, mostly for skills in embroidery, cooking, sewing, and other crafts that had some economic value.

Only after the achievement of national independence did education become widely recognized as a vehicle for the advancement of the individual and society. Compulsory education laws affecting the two sexes were passed in most countries, and the share of the national budget allocated to education increased considerably. In many countries, education was made free of charge from the primary through the tertiary level. This was an important move that increased the access of children from peasant and working-class homes. Thus the postindependence era witnessed a major expansion of educational facilities and a major growth in both female and male enrollments. Countries such as Kuwait, Saudi Arabia, and the Yemen Arab Republic that, to use Coleman's terms, "missed both the stimulation and humiliation of modern Colonial rule"[3] as well as missionary educational activities, had a much later start in female education.

Current Status of Female Education

Over the past thirty years, all Arab governments have made considerable progress in increasing female access to education and reducing sex differentiation in education. According to UNESCO statistics, the number of female students in all levels and types of education increased from 1,018,000 in 1950 to 2,756,000 in 1960 and 8,383,000 in 1975. The corresponding percentages of female students were 30, 32, and 36 percent, respectively.

The number of female teachers increased also, from 68,000 in 1965 to 187,000 in 1975 at the primary level. During the same period the number of female secondary teachers almost quintupled, from 16,000 to 76,000.[4] The sex differential among teachers was higher at the secondary than at the primary level, but it declined due to the proportionately greater increase in the number of female teachers at the secondary level. Thus, the percentage of female teachers increased from 34 to 36 percent at the primary level and from 22 to 30 percent at the secondary level.

This expansion was due in part to a strong faith in education as a means of transforming socioeconomic conditions in these countries as well as a growing popular demand for female and male education. The commitment of the Arab governments is reflected in their increased resource allocations to education. In 1975, Arab governments spent $8,013,000 on education as compared to $1,614,000 in 1970 and $976,000 in 1965. Between 1965 and 1975, the average annual increase in educational expenditure was 23.5 percent; the share of public funds expended on education as a percentage of the gross national product (GNP) rose from 4.1 percent in 1965 to 4.6 percent in 1970 and 5.9 percent in 1975.[5] Persistent disparities between women and men in education, however, continued to exist, concomitant with lower budgetary allocations to female education.

Undoubtedly, cultural traditions play a strong role in the Arab governments' decisions on priorities and resource allocations in education. This is especially true in view of the strong sex-role stereotypes that prevail in these countries, the heavy occupational orientation of their educational systems, and the limited rate of female participation in the modern workforce.

Female Participation in Primary Education

Primary education accounts for about two-thirds of all female students in the Arab states. The number of girls enrolled in primary schools throughout the Arab world increased from 925,000 in 1959 to 2,400,000 in 1960 and 6,300,000 in 1975–76. This reflects an annual growth rate of 8.3 percent over 1960 to 1970, slowing down to 5.8 percent in 1970 to 1975.[6] However, despite compulsory education legislation and government plans to universalize primary education by 1980, about ten million girls of primary school age had no access to primary education in 1975.

Cross-country comparisons reveal that female primary education enrollment more than doubled in most Arab countries between 1965–66 and 1975–76. The rate of growth was highest in countries with initially low enrollments. In Saudi Arabia, for instance, female enrollment quintupled between 1965 and 1975.

The statistics in Table 1 show that only six Arab states—Kuwait, Lebanon, Jordan, Bahrain, Qatar, and Libya—were close to achieving equal access of girls to primary education in 1976–77. In Algeria, Tunisia, and Syria 40 percent of primary students were female. Egypt, Sudan, Morocco, and Saudi Arabia had a ratio of between 36 and 38 percent. The Yemen Arab Republic was lowest, with only one girl enrolled out of every ten students. All countries had higher female percentages in 1976–77 than in 1965–66 except Egypt, where the relative position of girls actually deteriorated.

Increased oil wealth has enabled Kuwait, Bahrain, Qatar, and Libya to achieve equal access to education for girls and Saudi Arabia to approach the level of female representation in education achieved in Egypt, Sudan, Iraq, Syria, and Tunisia, which have a much longer history of female education. This has taken place despite a more conservative traditional social structure in the oil states than in Egypt, Syria, or Tunisia, where resource scarcity has perpetuated the disparities of educational opportunities for girls. Despite its systematic plans for educational and economic development, Egypt has failed to achieve universal primary education for either boys or girls. By 1976, only 56 percent of the girls of primary school age were enrolled in school (see Table 2).

We can understand the extent of the diffusion of education among girls by examining the data on male and female enrollment ratios (that is, the percentage of those enrolled in school to the relative age group). As of 1976–77, only Lebanon and Libya had full female participation rates in primary education. Significantly, Lebanon had reached that level in the early 1960s in the absence of compulsory education legislation. Libya has been able to achieve this objective over a relatively short

Table 1. Changes in the Percentage of Girls to All Students in Sixteen Arab States by Level of Education, 1965 and 1976

Country[a]	Primary Education		Secondary Education		Higher Education	
	1965	1976	1965	1976	1965	1976[b]
Kuwait	43%	47%	37%	45%	48%	57%
Lebanon	43	46[c]	40	43[c]	18	25[f]
Jordan	42	47	28	42	32	34[e]
Bahrain	42	44	30	48	52	53
Qatar	41	47	18	46	0	57
Egypt	39	38	29	33[d]	21	30
Algeria	38	40[d]	30	34[d]	20	23
Sudan	35	37	22	32	7	16
Tunisia	34	40	28	35	18	26
Syria	32	40	22	30[d]	17	25
Morocco	30	36[d]	24	35	12	19
Iraq	30	36	24	30	27	33
Libya	28	47	14	36	8	16[e]
Saudi Arabia	22	36[d]	9	30	3	20
People's Democratic Republic of Yemen	21	30[e]	23	21[d]	27	18
Yemen Arab Republic	5	11	5	12[d]	0	10
Average	32	38	24	33	22	28

Source: UNESCO, Statistical Yearbook, 1976 and 1977, tables 4.2, 4.5, 5.2.
    [a]Rank ordered by the percentage of girls in primary education in 1965.
    [b]Most countries did not have data for 1976.
    [c]1972.
    [d]1975.
    [e]1974.
    [f]1971.

time. Kuwait also had achieved full participation rates in primary education by 1977–78. Algeria, Tunisia, and Syria are close to achieving full female participation rates in primary education. In Morocco, Sudan, Saudi Arabia, and the People's Democratic Republic of Yemen, between one-third and one-half of the girls of school age are enrolled. In the Yemen Arab Republic, only six out of each one hundred girls of school age are enrolled in school.

Clearly, the availability of resources is a major factor in the progress of female primary education. In those countries where a decision has to be made on who is to be educated, invariably the decision is made in favor of the boys, the future family providers. Here is where social and cultural traditions play a major role in determining priorities for resource allocations in education. Conversely, economic wealth tends to mitigate or counteract the influence of cultural tradition.

Countries that have not yet achieved universal equal access to primary education suffer from serious demographic problems, including a high rate of population growth (3 percent) and a relatively young population, whereby over 50 percent of the total population is under twenty

Table 2. Male and Female Enrollment Ratios[a] in Primary, Secondary, and Higher Education for Selected Arab States, 1976

Country[b]	Primary Education[c]		Secondary Education		Higher Education	
	Male	Female	Male	Female	Male	Female
Lebanon[d]	139	124	43	33	33.36	11.69
Libya	100	100	81	48	2.50	0.72
Syria	121	85	66	33	17.71	5.09
Jordan	88	79	56	42	5.33	3.00
Tunisia	117	78	26	14	6.00	2.00
Iraq	125	72	52	23	11.75	6.01
Algeria[e]	105	72	25	13	4.22	1.24
Egypt[e]	88	56	54	29	18.55	8.27
People's Democratic Republic of Yemen	107	48	30	8	1.08	0.25
Morocco[e]	77	44	20	11	5.12	1.19
Saudi Arabia[e]	58	34	34	26	5.38	1.40
Sudan	49	30	18	8	2.24	0.44
Yemen Arab Republic[e]	43	6	5	1	0.74	0.09

Source: UNESCO, *Statistical Yearbook, 1976 and 1977*, table 3.2.

[a] Expressed as a percentage of the students enrolled to the eligible age group for each level. Because of different definitions of eligible age group, enrollment ratios may exceed 100 percent.

[b] Arranged in descending order by female enrollment ratios in primary education.

[c] Does not include preprimary enrollment.

[d] 1972.

[e] 1975.

[f] 1974.

years old.[7] In the Arab states combined, ten to eleven million children of school age are added to the population every ten years.

Finally, most Arab governments have given greater attention to the expansion of secondary and higher education over the past two decades. This has resulted in a reallocation of resources and a reduction of the share of the eduction budget expended on primary education.

Female Participation in Secondary Education

Arab governments could not maintain the extremely high growth rates in education achieved in the early 1960s. Female enrollment at the secondary level grew from 87,000 in 1950 to 330,000 in 1960 and 1,893,000 in 1975. The average annual growth rate declined from 13.4 percent in 1960 to 1965 to 11.8 percent in 1965 to 1975. Despite this decline the relative position of girls in secondary education continued to improve as reflected in the changes in their percentage to all students: 23 percent in 1950, 25 percent in 1960, and 33 percent in 1975.[8]

In all Arab states, access to secondary education is still limited, as revealed by statistics in Table 2. Five countries (Egypt, Libya, Syria, Iraq, and Jordan) enrolled more than half of the males of secondary school age in 1976–77. Secondary female enrollment ratios ranged from 48 percent in Libya and 42 percent in Jordan to only 1 percent in the Yemen Arab Republic. These statistics reflect a considerable improvement in the relative position of girls in secondary education from 1965 to 1976. Progress was greatest in the oil-wealthy states: Kuwait, Bahrain, Qatar, Libya, and Saudi Arabia. Strangely, Iraq's oil wealth has not been reflected in a significant improvement in the position of girls in secondary education. This may be attributed in part to its greater emphasis on higher education, as will be shown later.

A better understanding of the level and type of female participation in secondary education may be achieved by examining data on the distribution of girls among the three types of secondary education: general, vocational, and teacher training (see Table 3).

Female Participation in General Secondary Education

In all Arab states, an imbalance between female participation in general secondary education and vocational education is found. It is as high as 100:1 in most countries, the lowest being 4:1 in Egypt and 2:1 in Tunisia, the only two countries with a relatively balanced distribution of female enrollment.

As expected, the highest growth over the period covered by Table 3 occurred in general secondary education where female enrollment ap-

Table 3. Changes in the Number of Female Students and Their Percentage to All Students in the Various Types of Secondary Education in Sixteen Arab States

Country[a] and Year	General Secondary		Teacher Training		Vocational Secondary	
	Number of Female Students	%	Number of Female Students	%	Number of Female Students	%
Egypt						
1965	244,400	29	2,552	42	27,000	21
1976	590,800	35	14,500	44	126,900	34
Algeria						
1965	29,500	31	800	33	9,700	28
1975	167,200	34	2,900	33	2,700	21
Iraq						
1965	54,300	23	2,300	41	3,800	50
1976	165,300	30	9,500	70	5,800	20
Morocco						
1965	46,700	24	200	19	3,400	23
1976	160,000	34	2,000	44	1,149	16[b]
Syria						
1965	39,700	22	2,300	33	1,100	14
1976	160,000	33	1,300	50	4,700	20
Sudan						
1965	20,900	23	500	33	0	0
1976	101,000	32	2,000	43	800	9
Jordan						
1965	28,300	29	100	100	300	9
1976	75,000	42	0	0	2,000	28
Lebanon						
1970	64,200	40	1,600	48	n.a.	n.a.
1972	72,800	43	1,800	55	n.a.	n.a.
Tunisia						
1965	17,300	27	700	15	8,100	32
1976	51,500	35	700	66	20,900	34
Saudi Arabia						
1965	1,900	8	1,200	18	0	0
1975	61,700	30	4,100	28	259	5
Libya						
1965	2,900	12	1,200	36	0	0
1976	58,600	33	13,000	60	439	9

(Table 3, cont.)

Country[a] and Year	General Secondary		Teacher Training		Vocational Secondary	
	Number of Female Students	%	Number of Female Students	%	Number of Female Students	%
Kuwait						
1965	11,500	39	400	37	0	0
1976	50,000	46	0	0	120	10
Bahrain						
1965	2,000	32	200	48	0	0
1975	8,000	50	0	0	500	24
People's Democratic Republic of Yemen						
1965	3,900	23	43	15	0	0
1974	8,000	21	169	27	123	18
Qatar						
1965	300	21	0	0	0	0
1976	4,500	47	217	35	0	0
Yemen Arab Republic						
1965	0	0	0	0	0	0
1975	22,000	10	650	49	0	0

Source: UNESCO, *Statistical Yearbook, 1976 and 1977*, table 4.5.

[a] Countries are arranged in descending order by the number of girls enrolled in 1976.

[b] 1970.

proximately doubled in Egypt and Jordan, tripled in Iraq, Morocco, and Tunisia, quadrupled in Syria, Bahrain, and Kuwait, quintupled in Algeria, and increased twenty times in Libya, and over thirty times in Saudi Arabia.

The increase in female general secondary education has been due to four main factors: first, the general expansion of primary education for girls; second, policy changes aimed at the extension of educational opportunities for women; third, the lower per-pupil cost as compared with vocational and technical education; and, most important, the availability of oil revenues and subsequent increased allocations to female education in the Gulf States.

Ironically, countries with the greatest need for education in terms of their demographic structures and the numbers of students are the ones with the fewest resources to expend on this education. Thus, in countries with high female enrollment—Egypt, Algeria, Morocco, and Sudan—the relative status of females as revealed by their percentage to all students is lower than in the smaller and richer countries such as Kuwait, Lebanon, Jordan, Bahrain, and Qatar that have lower female enrollments (see Table 3). This shows the importance of the size of the educational effort in facilitating Arab governments' endeavors to bridge the gap between educational opportunities for the two sexes.

Since only a small proportion of secondary education graduates gain access to higher education, high school becomes a dead-end for those who fail to qualify for college. Such education does not offer "professional outlets" for most of its female graduates.

In all Arab countries, teacher training and vocational/technical education receive less emphasis than general education, despite serious shortages of technicians and primary teachers.

Teacher Preparation for Primary Education

Secondary teacher training supplies primary education teachers and as such is essential for the expansion of female primary education and for the upgrading of current female teachers. Despite a major expansion, the number of those enrolled in teacher education at the secondary level is minuscule compared to female enrollment in general secondary education (see Table 3). In most countries, one female is enrolled in secondary teacher education for every one hundred in general secondary. The only exceptions are Libya, with 13,000 in teacher training as compared to 58,600 in general secondary, or a ratio of about 1:5, and Saudi Arabia, with 4,100 in teacher education as compared to 61,700 in general secondary, or a ratio of 1:15. These relatively higher participation rates in teacher training education in Libya and Saudi Arabia reflect their effort to increase indigenous female teachers and to replace foreign Arab women teachers.

One factor behind the low emphasis on female teacher education at the secondary level is the continued class stratification within Arab education, despite all efforts at democratization. Arab governments have been more responsive to pressure, mostly from middle and upper classes, for an academic education geared toward university. This is in contrast to teacher education, which draws its students from the peasant and working-class people. In fact, recent observations in small towns and villages in Egypt and other Arab countries indicate that primary school teaching has become a means of social mobility for lower-class girls. Teaching also provides added income, a marriage asset under stringent economic circumstances.

Furthermore, the low value attached to secondary teacher education contradicts the traditional Arab view that teaching is the most suitable profession for women. Whereas primary school teaching, to which this education leads, is a "feminine" profession worldwise, only four of twelve countries for whom data are shown in Table 4 have increased the level of female participation to 50 percent or more of the total teacher training enrollment. Most Arab governments continue to concentrate their efforts in training male rather than female teachers.

Female Participation in Vocational and Technical Education

A recent and significant development is the increased access of girls to vocational and technical secondary education. In 1960, seven Arab states (Sudan, Jordan, Bahrain, Qatar, Saudi Arabia, the Yemen Arab Republic, and the People's Democratic Republic of Yemen) had no provisions for vocational education for girls. Additionally, two other countries (Libya and Lebanon) had no public vocational institutions for girls, but did have several private fee-charging coeducational vocational schools to which girls were admitted.[9] But by 1976–77, only the Yemen Arab Republic and Qatar did not provide female access to vocational education.

The number of girls enrolled increased considerably, expecially in countries with a relatively long history of female access to vocational education, notably Egypt, Tunisia, Iraq, and Syria. By 1976–77 female enrollments in these countries were as follows: 126,900 in Egypt, 20,900 in Tunisia, 5,800 in Iraq, 4,700 in Syria, 2,700 in Algeria, and 2,000 in Jordan. This was partly due to pressures from UNESCO, which held a special conference on vocational education for girls in 1969 in Kuwait. However, all the remaining countries still have very small female vocational education enrollment. In Egypt, Syria, Tunisia, and Jordan, the position of girls in this education improved over the 1965 to 1976 period. In Morocco, Iraq, and Algeria, however, the position of women in this education has actually deteriorated, despite growth in enrollment.

Vocational education at present does not necessarily prepare women for active participation in the economy. This is particularly true of the so-called Feminine Education, or Technical Education for Women, which is mostly an education in home economics, child care, sewing, and handicrafts. A report by UNESCO voiced serious reservations about it. Several countries took steps to reform "feminine education." For instance, Egypt has extended its scope to encompass commercial and industrial training. Egypt and Tunisia seem to have made the most progress in relating vocational female educational enrollment to human resource requirements.

The number of countries allowing women access to technical fields is small. Egypt, Tunisia, Syria, Morocco, Lebanon, and Jordan allow for female access to industrial secondary education in great numbers. Certain traditionally female fields such as textile and garment making, however, have a predominantly female enrollment and thus are merely an extension of the maternal and domestic role.[10] However, girls also enroll in more technical fields such as electronics in Egypt, laboratory technician education in Lebanon, Morocco, and Tunisia, and engineering assistants in several countries.[11]

Commercial secondary education is attracting increasingly large numbers of girls in some Arab states. A study by UNESCO found that the subjects commonly chosen by girls were typing, stenography, accounting, bookkeeping, and other secretarial office skills. Employment opportunities in these traditionally female fields have been good, especially in the private sector.

Although rural women and girls have worked in agriculture for centuries, their access to agricultural education is limited. One explanation is given by Chabaud: no one admits that agricultural work "should take the form of a real skilled occupation."[12] This condition limits the options for rural women and maintains their status as low-paid or unpaid unskilled agricultural workers.

Female Participation in Higher Education

Over the past two decades, all Arab governments have made a concerted effort to increase female participation in higher education. Thus female enrollment in this education increased at a much higher level than in the preceding two levels: from 6,000 in 1950 to 28,000 in 1960 and 237,000 in 1975, growing at an average annual rate of 15.7 percent in 1960 to 1965 and 15.1 percent in 1965 to 1975. The percentage of females increased from 12 percent in 1950 to 17 percent in 1960 and 28 percent in 1975.[13]

The growth in female enrollment was greatest in the oil-wealthy states in their newly established universities. Meleis, al-Sanabary, and Beason have demonstrated the remarkable progress achieved in female education in Kuwait since 1966.[14] Saudi Arabia and Libya also have made remarkable progress in a very short time. In countries with a long tradition of higher education for women, notably Egypt, a good deal of uncontrolled growth has been facilitated by the establishment of regional universities. Popular demand for more education has made it politically difficult to curb the growth of higher education in Egypt.

In most Arab countries, women have benefited from the growing acceptance of coeducation in universities and admission policies based solely on academic scores. Theoretically, no girl can be denied access to the college of her choice if she has the qualifying grades and if female access to that particular college is available in her country. However, higher education is still highly selective in all countries, and the proportion of women students to the relative age group is low (see Table 1). The most talented, and probably the most financially able, are usually admitted into higher education, and in some universities scholarships are given to high achievers regardless of need. The access of rural and working-class women to higher education is restricted by obstacles such as inferior quality secondary education, lack of family support and low family aspirations, inability to incur the direct and indirect costs of education, geographical distance, and early marriage. Thus, despite various democratization efforts, one would concur with Chabaud that ". . . with a few exceptions, women students come from a more affluent environment than men students . . . there are still more boys from a working-class background going to university than there are girls."[15]

In the Arab states access to the various fields of study is also class specific. Middle- and upper-class women are more likely to get into scientific and professional education where lower- and lower-middle-class women are more likely to choose humanities and social sciences, education, agriculture, and nursing.

Comparison of the distribution of female enrollment in the various fields of education reveals several interesting facets of higher education for women in these countries (see Table 4). In a group of twelve Arab countries for whom data are given in Table 4, female distribution among the various fields of study in higher education was highest in social sciences (51,875) and humanities (48,163), followed by education (33,350), medical sciences (23,432), natural sciences (16,545), law (12,977), agriculture (11,752), and engineering (10,000).

As in Western countries, female higher education enrollment is still concentrated in the humanities and social sciences. In 1975–76, the percentage of women to all students in the humanities ranged from a high of 71 percent in Kuwait to a low of 20 percent in Libya. Several Arab universities, notably in Algeria, Egypt, Iraq, Syria, and Lebanon, continue to produce thousands of women with humanities, law, and social science majors whose career prospects are usually very poor. Graduates in the professional and scientific fields have much better prospects of finding a good job immediately after graduation. Women have not begun to take advantage of this reality and are choosing the sciences and professions.

Teacher education claims the third largest female enrollment in all Arab states combined: 33,350 in the twelve countries for whom data are given in Table 4. Qatar's female higher education enrollment is all in education, and the majority are in this field in Bahrain. In all countries, with a sizable enrollment of women in education, their percentage to all students ranges from 67 percent in Syria to 13 percent in Sudan. Quantitatively, Egypt and Iraq enroll the largest number of women in education. This is not only to supply their own ever-growing demand for teachers, but also to satisfy the need of other Arab countries. Saudi Arabia and Kuwait have vastly expanded their own facilities for training women teachers in order to reduce their reliance on expatriates. Additionally, most countries supplement trained teachers with college graduates from other disciplines.

Medical sciences constitute the fourth field that claims relatively high female enrollments in most countries. The proportion of females to all students in this field ranges from 53 percent in Jordan to 18 percent in Sudan. It must be noted, however, that the medical sciences include nursing education, where enrollment is all female. Arab countries vary greatly both in the level of development in the field of medicine and in the relative position of women in it. Egypt, Iraq, Tunisia, and Syria have the highest female enrollment in the medical sciences. High female enrollment in the medical sciences can be attributed to government efforts to improve the level of health care, to the rising aspirations of women for a good profession that may be combined with women's traditional role as a homemaker,[16] and to the Muslim aversion to having female patients treated by male doctors.

Attitudes toward women's educational and occupational options vary according to the degree of traditionalism or modernity. Modernizing countries like Iraq, Egypt, Syria, and more recently Tunisia and Algeria have a more balanced distribution of higher education students among the various fields of study. In the more traditional states with relatively short histories of higher education for women, there is a greater emphasis on traditionally female fields such as humanities, education, and social sciences and to a lesser extent on medicine. For instance, in a study of the attitudes of educated women in the Gulf States, Kotb found a striking preference among college women for teaching, medicine, and social work as the most suitable professions for women.[17] Similarly, in an earlier study conducted in Egypt, Lebanon, Syria, and Sudan, Badran found that in spite of the increasing female participation in paid employment, there is still a general feeling in these countries that women should not work outside the home and that opposition to women's employment in-

Table 4. Number of Female Students and Their Percentage to All Students by Field of Study in Higher Education in Selected Arab States, 1975

Country[a]	Human-ities	Education	Fine Arts	Law
Egypt[c]	20,000	15,000	2,300	6,500
	43%	32%	32%	19%
Iraq	4,550	8,000	310	820
	40%	52%	35%	17%
Syria	6,100	3,170	520	1,080
	34%	67%	25%	14%
Algeria	2,700	54	123	2,043
	40%	40%	11%	20%
Lebanon[d]	4,500	1,100	180	480
	27%	60%	21%	13%
Morocco	2,200	1,150	0	1,180
	27%	21%		14%
Tunisia	1,660	360	150	400
	37%	26%	28%	24%
Saudi Arabia	2,950	1,500	0	0
	23%	41%		
Kuwait	1,056	1,090	0	148
	71%	66%		35%
Sudan	1,160	85	81	265
	23%	13%	15%	16%
Jordan[e]	554	1,435	0	0
	32%	35%		
Libya	733	404	0	61
	20%	28%		3%
Total for twelve countries	48,163	33,350	3,664	12,977

Source: UNESCO, *Statistical Yearbook, 1976 and 1977,* table 5.1.

[a] Arranged in descending order by the total number of female enrollment.

[b] Includes an additional 552 female students listed in the original source as unspecified.

[c] 1974.

[d] 1969.

[e] 1974.

Social Sciences	Natural Sciences	Engi- neering	Medical Sciences	Agri- culture	Total Female Enrollment[b]
34,800	5,500	5,600	12,700	8,974	111,470
35%	38%	13%	27%	22%	29%
5,860	2,870	2,670	1,940	1,260	38,270
36%	34%	18%	33%	16%	33%
1,900	2,050	1,100	1,700	970	18,640
23%	26%	11%	24%	12%	25%
1,271	2,944	330	2,607	131	12,170
19%	22%	6%	34%	15%	23%
1,330	430	7	409	27	8,910
13%	20%	0.9%	33%	10%	23%
1,750	412	38	1,700	31	8,440
16%	17%	4%	26%	2%	19%
1,070	820	107	1,410	82	6,070
23%	27%	6%	35%	8%	26%
730	54	0	80	0	5,310
15%	4%		20%		20%
1,400	770	19	129	0	4,610
53%	47%	15%	100%		57%
1,100	250	36	233	188	3,410
15%	16%	3%	18%	12%	16%
460	256	0	400	12	3,120
35%	23%		53%	13%	34%
204	189	100	124	77	1,890
12%	26%	7%	20%	11%	16%
51,875	16,545	10,000	23,432	11,752	212,310

creases where jobs are limited.[18] Nonetheless, thousands of Arab women have disregarded society's expectations and have ventured into educational and occupational fields previously dominated by men. Thus, probably the most remarkable achievement over the past twenty-five years has been women's increased access to engineering and the natural, physical, and medical sciences, which, in several Arab countries, are superior to those in many advanced Western nations.

It is remarkable that eleven of the thirteen Arab countries with engineering schools admit women, and in several countries the number and the percentage of women to all students is high for a nontraditional field. In 1975–76 the highest female engineering enrollment was in Egypt (5,600, or 13 percent of its total engineering enrollment). In Iraq 2,670 (or 18 percent) and in Syria 1,100 (or 11 percent) of the total enrollment was female. In these countries, female engineering enrollment ranges over all specialties from civil to nuclear engineering. Engineering has become an attractive educational and occupational field for a growing number of Arab women because of its high status and employment prospects in an increasingly industrializing Arab world.

Female participation in agricultural education is limited in all countries except Egypt and Iraq. In these countries, women do not willingly choose agriculture, but are usually assigned to it according to their scores in the General High Secondary Education Certificate and the availability of space in agricultural colleges.

Conclusion

Although much remains to be done, Arab governments have made remarkable progress in improving the access of girls and women to all levels and types of education. In assessing the status of women's education in the Arab countries, it is important to recognize the great differences in history, resources, demographic structure, general level of educational development, and the level of commitment to female education that exist among the various Arab states. While traditional thinking strongly influences government policy on educational options and opportunities for women, the translation of tradition into policy is more subtle and complex than Westerners generally perceive.

Despite a common Islamic cultural background among Arab states, differences in income levels at the national and individual family levels have assumed major significance in determining the level and type of female participation in education. Thus wealthy countries are increasingly moving ahead of the more modernized countries with a long tradition of female education. This is especially true of primary education, whose progress has been curtailed in the latter by lack of resources and a vastly growing population. Similarly, girls and women from the middle and upper-middle classes, especially in urban areas, have benefited most from the vast expansion in female education. This is not to deny the important role of education in promoting social mobility for a growing number of talented working-class women.

Major discrepancies still exist between female education and the socioeconomic needs of the various Arab states, despite their utilization of educational planning. Much progress has been made in advancing female access to vocational, scientific, medical, and professional education. Nonetheless, the education of most women is only remotely related to their needs and the needs of socioeconomic development. Dead-end secondary education and female concentration in the humanities and social sciences limit the options of most graduates from these fields. Thus, most women are still channeled into traditionally prescribed adult female roles due to the persistence of sex-role stereotypes.

Furthermore, social stratification in all Arab countries is reflected in inequities in educational systems. Thus, in several countries the gap continues to widen between the illiterate female masses and the growing elite of educated women produced in increasing numbers from free public higher education. In between are women with middle-level education and lower-status occupations.

Scarcity of resources in most Arab countries makes it necessary to continue selective educational systems with closed entry. In these systems merit rather than sex should be the criterion for access to education. Many Arab governments are now in a special position to promote educational changes favorable to all citizens. Educational reforms are under way in all countries to reduce sex differentials in education. But whether or not women's education equity will be achieved or is realistically seen as a goal, only future developments will tell.

Notes

1. For a detailed discussion of the impact of Christian missionaries on girls' education, see Nagat al-Sanabary, "A Comparative Study of the Disparities of Educational Opportunities for Girls in the Arab States" (Ph.D. dissertation, University of California at Berkeley, 1973), pp. 268–293.

2. Ibid., pp. 318–358.

3. James S. Coleman (ed.), *Education and Political Development* (Princeton, N.J.: Princeton University Press, 1965), p. 35.

4. UNESCO, *Statistical Yearbook, 1976 and 1977* (Paris: UNESCO, 1977 and 1978), table 2.1.

5. Ibid., table 2.11, p. 103.

6. Ibid., p. 83.

7. UNESCO, *Survey of Educational Progress in the Arab States since the*

Meeting of the Ministers and Directors of Education in Beirut, February 1960 (Paris: UNESCO, 1966), mimeographed in Arabic, p. 7; Mohammed A. el-Ghannam, "Education in the Arab Region Viewed from the 1970 Marakesh Conference" (Paris: UNESCO, 1971), p. 8.

8. UNESCO, *Statistical Yearbook, 1976 and 1977*, table 2.1.

9. UNESCO, "Access of Girls to Technical and Vocational Education in the Arab States" (Paris: UNESCO, 1969), mimeographed, pp. 9–10.

10. Jacqueline Chabaud, *The Education and Advancement of Women* (Paris: UNESCO, 1970), p. 63.

11. UNESCO, "Access of Girls," p. 14.

12. Chabaud, *Education and Advancement*, p. 59.

13. UNESCO, *Statistical Yearbook, 1976 and 1977*, table 5.2.

14. Afaf Meleis, Nagat al-Sanabary, and Diane Beason, "Women, Modernization, and Education in Kuwait," *Comparative Education Review* 23, no. 1 (February 1979): 115–124.

15. Chabaud, *Education and Advancement*, p. 102.

16. Kathleen Howard-Merriam, "Women, Education and the Professions in Egypt," *Comparative Education Review* 23, no. 2 (1979): 262.

17. I. Y. Kotb, "Attitudes of University Women in the Arabian Gulf States towards Some Social Issues" (Kuwait, 1975) mimeographed in Arabic, pp. 38–39.

18. Hoda Badran, "The Arab Woman and National Development: A Study of Three Arab Countries, Egypt, Lebanon, and Sudan" (paper prepared for the seminar on Arab Women in National Development, Cairo, September 24–30, 1972).

Growing Up Female in Egypt
(from *Mudhakkirat tabiba*)

NAWAL AL-SAʿDAWI
Translated from the Arabic by Fedwa Malti-Douglas

Dr. Nawal al-Saʿdawi, a physician and leading Egyptian feminist, has received visibility in the West mainly for her outspoken views on such issues as women's sexuality and the practice of clitoridectomy. She was born in 1931, received her medical degree in 1955, and has practiced in the areas of gynecology, family medicine, thoracic surgery, and psychiatry. She is the author of important feminist studies as well as numerous short stories and novels. The following selection is the first chapter of Mudhakkirat tabiba *(Memoirs of a female physician), a novel first published in 1965 that chronicles the development of a female physician. It includes her childhood, medical education, and adult years to the age of thirty. Although the life described in this book is not that of the author, the crossing of the genre of fiction with that of autobiography gives the text much of its immediacy.*

The struggle between me and my femininity began very early . . . before my femininity sprouted and before I knew anything about myself, my sex, or my origin . . . indeed, before I knew what hollow had enclosed me before I was tossed out into this wide world.

All that I knew at that time was that I was a girl, as I heard from my mother. A girl!

And there was only one meaning for the word "girl" in my mind . . . that I was not a boy . . . I was not like my brother . . .

My brother cuts his hair and leaves it free, he does not comb it, but as for me, my hair grows longer and longer. My mother combs it twice a day, chains it in braids, and imprisons its ends in ribbons . . .

My brother wakes up and leaves his bed as it is, but I, I have to make my bed and his as well.

My brother goes out in the street to play, without permission from my mother or my father, and returns at any time . . . but I, I do not go out without permission.

My brother takes a bigger piece of meat than mine, eats quickly, and drinks the soup with an audible sound, yet my mother does not say anything to him . . .

As for me . . . ! I am a girl! I must watch my every movement . . . I must hide my desire for food and so I eat slowly and drink soup without a sound . . .

My brother plays . . . jumps . . . turns somersaults . . . but I, whenever I sit and the dress rides up a centimeter on my thighs, my mother throws a sharp, wounding glance at me, and I hide my shame and impurity . . .[1]

Shame and impurity!

Everything in me is shame and impurity, though I am a child of nine years!

I felt sorry for myself.

I closed the door of my room on myself and sat crying alone . . .

The first tears of my life were not shed because I failed in school or because I broke something expensive . . . but because I was a girl!

I cried over my femininity before I knew it . . .

I opened my eyes on the world with enmity between myself and my nature.

I bounded down the steps three at a time to get to the street before I finished counting to ten . . .

My brother and his friends, sons and daughters of the neighbors, are waiting for me to play cops and robbers . . . I have received permission from my mother to go out . . . I love to play! I love to run as fast as I can . . . I feel an overflowing happiness whenever I move my head, my arms, or my legs in the air . . . and I run in great bounds, hindered only by the weight of my body, which the earth draws to itself . . .

Why did God not make me a bird so I could fly like a dove, but instead made me a girl? It seemed to me that God preferred birds to girls . . .

But my brother does not fly . . .

This fact comforted me a bit . . . I felt that boys, despite their wide freedom, were incapable, like me, of flying . . . and I began to always search for the areas of weakness in men to console me for the weakness that my femininity imposed on me.

I do not know what happened to me while I was jumping . . . I felt a violent shiver running through my body and a dizziness in my head ... Then I saw something red!

"What is this?"

I was extremely alarmed, I stopped playing, mounted the stairs to my house, and locked myself in the bathroom to search secretly for the explanation of this grave event . . .

But I did not understand anything . . . And I thought that this might be a sudden illness that had stricken me . . . So I went in terror to ask my mother . . .

I saw my mother laughing happily . . . I was amazed that my mother could confront this hideous sickness with such a broad smile . . .

My mother saw my surprise and confusion and took me by the hand to my room, where she told me women's bloody story . . .

I stayed in my room for four days in a row, not having the courage to face my brother, or my father, or even the servant boy.

They have all certainly become aware of my shame and impurity . . . My mother has undoubtedly betrayed my new secret . . . I closed the door on myself to explain this strange phenomenon to myself . . . Was there no other way for girls to mature, other than this unclean way? Is it possible for a person to live for days under the control of his tyrannical, involuntary muscles? God undoubtedly hates girls, so he tarnished them all with this shame . . .

I felt that God had sided with boys in everything . . .

I got up from my bed, dragging my oppressive existence, and looked in the mirror . . . What is this?

Two small protrusions had grown on my chest!

Oh! If only I could die!

What is this strange body that surprises me every day with a new shame that increases my weakness and my withdrawal into myself?!

I wonder what else will grow on my body tomorrow? Or, I wonder through what other new symptom my tyrannical femininity will erupt!

I hated my femininity . . .

I felt that it was chains . . . chains of my own blood that bind me to the bed so that I am unable to run and jump . . . chains from within my own body . . . that shackle me in fetters of shame and disgrace so that I withdraw within myself, hiding my dejected existence . . .

I no longer ran . . . And I no longer played. . .

These two protrusions on my chest are getting bigger and they quiver whenever I walk . . .

I stood sadly with my tall, slender frame, hiding my chest with my arms, and watched, with sorrow, my brother and his companions playing . . .

I grew . . . I outgrew my brother, though he was older than I . . . I outgrew the other children, so I withdrew from them and sat by myself thinking . . .

My childhood came to an end . . . a short, breathlessly fast childhood . . . No sooner did I experience it than it slipped away and left me a mature woman's body carrying within it a ten-year-old child . . .

I saw the eyes and teeth of the doorkeeper shining in the middle of his coal-black face . . . He approached me while I was sitting by myself on his wooden bench, following my brother and his friends with my eyes, while they ran and jumped . . .

I felt the rough edge of his *galabeyya* touching my leg and I smelled the strange odor of his garments, so I moved away with disgust; but he drew near me again and I tried to hide my fear from him by watching my brother and his companions playing, but I felt his rough, coarse fingers groping around my thighs and ascending under my clothing! . . .

I got up in terror and quickly ran away from him . . .

This repulsive black man is also staring at my femininity?!

And I ran until I entered the house . . . My mother asked me the reason for my alarm . . . But I could not say anything to her . . . Perhaps I was afraid or ashamed, or both . . . Or perhaps I thought that she would reprimand me and that there would not be between us that affection that would make me tell her my secrets . . .

I no longer went out in the street . . . And I no longer sat on the wooden bench . . .

I fled from those strange, rough-voiced and mustached beings that they call men . . . and I created a special world for myself designed by my imagination . . . and I made myself the god of this world, and I made men into weak, ignorant creatures charged with serving me . . .

I sat in my world on my high throne arranging the dolls on the chairs and placing the boys on the ground, and I would tell stories to myself . . .

No one disturbed my life alone with my imagination and my dolls except my mother . . . with her many orders that never ended . . . the house and kitchen chores . . . the ugly, limited world of women, from which emanated the odor of garlic and onion.

No sooner would I escape to my small world than my mother would drag me to the kitchen, saying, "Your future lies in marriage . . . You have to learn to cook . . . Your future lies in marriage . . . Marriage! Marriage!"

That loathsome word that my mother repeated every day until I hated it . . . And I never heard it without imagining in front of me a man with a big belly inside of which was a table of food . . .

In my mind, I conncted the smell of the kitchen with the smell of a husband . . .

And I hated the word "husband" and I hated the smell of food.

My old grandmother remained silent amidst the chatter and looked at my chest . . . I saw her worn eyes contemplating the two new protruding buds and weighing them . . . Then I saw her whispering something to my mother . . .

I heard my mother say to me: "Wear the light-blue dress so that you can come in and greet the guest who is with your father in the salon . . ."

I smelled the odor of conspiracy in the air . . .

I used to greet most of my father's friends and serve them coffee . . . And sometimes I would sit with them and listen to my father while he told them about my success in school, and I would feel happy and sense that my father, by recognizing my intelligence, was freeing me from the gloomy world of women, from which emanated the odor of onion and marriage . . .

But why the light-blue dress? That new dress that I hate . . . On the front of it was a strange pleat that rested on my breasts and increased their prominence . . .

My mother looked at me searchingly . . . She said, "Where is the light-blue dress?"

I answered angrily: "I will never wear it!". . . She saw the stirrings of rebellion in my eyes, looked at me sadly, and said, "Then smooth over your eyebrows . . ."

But I did not look at her . . . And before opening the salon door to enter, I ran my fingers through my eyebrows, mussing them up . . .

I greeted my father's friend and sat down . . . I saw a strange, frightful face with a relentless, scrutinizing gaze that resembled that of my grandmother . . .

My father said, "She is first in her class this year in junior high school . . ."

I did not see any expression of admiration in the man's eyes at these words . . . But I saw his scrutinizing glances hover around my body and settle finally on my chest. So I stood up in terror and left the room, running as though a demon were chasing me . . .

My mother and my grandmother met me at the door with a passionate anxiety and said in one breath, "My God! . . . What have you done?"

I uttered a single shriek in their faces, ran to my room, and locked myself in . . . Then I went to the mirror to look at my chest . . .

I hated them! Those two protrusions! Those two small pieces of flesh that circumscribed my future! I wished that I could tear them from my chest with a sharp knife!

But I could not . . . I could only hide them . . . compress them with a thick corset to flatten them . . .

This long, heavy hair . . . that I carry on top of my head everywhere

. . . It hampers me every morning, burdens me in the bath, and burns my neck in the summer . . .

Why is it not short, free, like my brother's hair? He does not carry it on top of his head, nor does it hamper him or burden him.

But my mother rules over my life, my future, and my body, even down to the locks of my hair . . .

Why . . . ?

Because she gave birth to me? But what is her merit in having given birth to me? She pursued her normal life like any other woman, and then I came along without any act of will on her part in one of her moments of happiness . . . I came without her knowing me . . . without her choosing me . . . and without my choosing her . . .

I was imposed on her as a daughter and she was imposed on me as a mother . . .

Is it possible for someone to love a being who has been imposed on her? And, if my mother loved me despite herself, instinctively, then what virtue is there in this love? And is she thus superior to the cat who, at times, loves her kittens, but, at other times, devours them?

Is not my mother's harsh treatment more painful to me than if she were to devour me?!

And if my mother loved me with a true love whose aim was my happiness and not hers, then why are all her orders and desires in contradiction with my comfort and happiness?!

Can she love me while putting chains every day on my feet, on my hands, and around my neck?

For the first time in my life, I went out of the house without asking permission from my mother . . .

I walked in the street, and the challenge had given me a kind of power, but my heart was beating from fear . . .

I saw a sign that said "Ladies' Hairdresser". . .

I hesitated for an instant and then went in . . .

I watched the locks of my hair twisting between the blades of the sharp scissors and then falling to the ground . . .

Are these the locks that my mother spoke of as woman's crown and throne? Does woman's crown fall to the ground like this, in a single moment of decisiveness? I felt great contempt for women . . . I saw with my own eyes that they believed in worthless things of no value . . . And this contempt for them gave me a new strength that permitted me to go home with a firm step, and I was able to stand up before my mother with my short hair.

My mother uttered one loud scream and gave me a sharp slap on the face . . . Then more and more slaps followed . . . while I remained standing . . .

As though I had become frozen . . . as though the challenge had made of me a force that nothing could shake . . . as though my victory over my mother had made of me a hard substance that did not feel the slaps . . .

My mother's hand would crash against my face and then fall back from it, as though it had crashed into granite . . .

How is it that I did not cry? I was the one who would be made to cry by a single shout or a light slap.

But my tears did not fall . . . My eyes were wide open, looking into my mother's eyes boldly and strongly . . .

My mother continued to slap me . . . then she collapsed on the couch, sitting, repeating in a daze: "She has gone crazy!"

I pitied her when I saw her face sink in defeat and weakness. I felt a strong desire to hug her, kiss her, and cry between her arms . . . to say to her: "Reason does not lie in my always obeying you . . ."

But I pulled my eyes away from hers so that she would not be aware that I had witnessed her defeat, and I ran to my room . . .

I looked in the mirror and smiled over my short hair and the flash of victory in my eyes . . .

I knew for the first time in my life what victory was like . . . Fear leads only to defeat . . . and victory can only be won through courage.

The fear that I used to feel toward my mother left me . . . That great halo that made me dread her fell from her . . . I felt that she was an ordinary woman . . . And her slaps, which were the strongest things she possessed, I no longer feared . . . because they no longer hurt me . . .

I hated the house except for my study . . . I loved school except for the home economics class . . . I loved the days of the week except for Friday . . .

I participated in all the school activities . . . I joined the acting club, the speech club, the athletics club, the music club, and the drawing club . . . But this was not enough for me; instead, I got together with some of my girlfriends and I created a club called the Friendship Club . . . Why did I choose the word "friendship"? I did not know . . . but I felt that deep within me was a great longing for friendship . . . for a great big friendship that nothing could satisfy . . . for vast groups of people who would keep me company, speak to me, listen to me, and go off with me to heaven . . .

I did not believe that any achievement would suffice me . . . it would not extinguish the fire burning in my soul . . . I hated the repeated,

monotonous lessons . . . I used to read the material once . . . once only
. . . I felt that repetition would suffocate me . . . kill me . . . I wanted
something new . . . new . . . always . . .

I was not aware of him when he entered my room and when he stood
beside me while I sat reading my book until he said, "Wouldn't you like
to relax a little?"

I had been reading for a long time and felt tired. So I smiled and said,
"I would like to take a walk outside."

"Put on your coat and let's go."

I put on my coat quickly and ran to him . . . I was on the point of putting my hand in his so we could run together, as we used to do when we
were children, but my eyes fastened on his and I suddenly remembered
the long years I had not played and during which my feet had forgotten
how to run and had grown accustomed to walking slowly like adults . . .
So I put my hands in my coat and set out slowly beside him . . .

I hear him say, "You have grown."

"And you also."

"Do you remember the days when we used to play together?"

"You always used to beat me at running."

"And you always used to win at marbles."

We laughed a long time . . . A lot of air entered my chest and it in-
vigorated me, making me feel that I was recovering some of my lost
childhood . . .

He said, "I want to run a race with you."

I said confidently, "I will beat you."

He said, "Let's see . . . !"

We drew line of the ground . . . and stood next to each other . . . He
yelled out: "One . . . two . . . three . . ." And we took off running the
course . . .

I was about to reach the finish line before him, but he grabbed me by
my clothing from behind so I stumbled and fell to the ground, and he
fell next to me . . . I lifted my eyes to him, breathless, and I saw him
gazing at me with a strange look that made the blood rise to my
face . . . Then I saw his arm reach for my waist . . . and he whispered in
my ear with a rough voice, "I will kiss you."

My whole being shook with a violent, strange shudder and I wished
for an instant—it flashed through my senses like lightning—that his
arm would reach further and embrace me strongly . . . strongly . . . But
my strange secret desire, emerging from my hidden depths, changed
into an intense anger . . .

But my anger increased his persistence, and he grabbed me with an
iron hand . . . I do not know where the strength came from that made

me push his arm far away from me, and lift up my hand and then let it fall on his face in one violent slap . . .

I tossed around my bed confused . . . Strange feelings flood my being . . . and many phantoms pass before me . . . But one vision lingers before my eyes . . .

My cousin lying on the ground next to me with his arm almost wrapped around my waist and his strange glances piercing my head . . .

I closed my eyes to float with my specter, who began to move his arm until it wound strongly around my waist . . . and he moved his lips until they touched mine and pressed upon them with force . . .

I hid my head under the covers . . .

Am I sincere?! This hand of mine that rose and slapped him is the very same hand that trembles in his imaginary hand?!

I wrapped the covers tightly around my head to shut out this strange illusion, but it slipped under the covers to me . . . So I put the pillow on my head and I pressed it with all my strength to smother that stubborn specter . . . and I kept pressing on my head until sleep smothered me . . .

I opened my eyes in the morning, when the sunlight had dispersed the darkness with all the ghosts that lurked in it . . .

I opened the window . . . The invigorating air entered my chest and it destroyed the remnants clinging to my vision from the delusions of the night . . .

I smiled scornfully at my inner self, this cowardly self that shakes out of fear of me when I am awake and then sneaks into my bed in the dark and fills the bed, surrounding me with specters and illusions!

I finished my secondary studies and I was first in my class . . . Then I sat thinking: What course do I follow?

What course can I follow since I hate my femininity, detest my nature, and disown my body?!

None but denial . . . challenge . . . resistance!

I will deny my femininity . . . I will challenge my nature . . . I will resist all the desires of my body . . .

I will prove to my mother and grandmother that I am not a woman like them . . . I will never spend my life in the kitchen peeling onions and garlic . . . I will never devote my life to a husband who eats and eats . . .

I will prove to my mother that I am smarter than my brother, than man, than all men . . . and that I am capable of doing all that my father does, and still more . . .

NOTE: *I would like to thank Dr. Nawal al-Saʿdawi and Dr. Sherif Hetata for reading and commenting on the translation. Responsibility for the text and the title of the selection, however, is my own.*

Note

1. In the original the word is ʿ*awra,* meaning that which is impure, defective, illicit, and, as a result, must be covered. It also means genitals.

Ideology, Value Changes, and Women's Social Position in Libyan Society

MUSTAFA O. ATTIR

During the past two decades, Libya has been undergoing major social change, and the position of women is one social domain experiencing dramatic change. This paper describes traditional values related to women and the attempts to change these values, along with the results of these attempts, during the periods from independence in 1952 through 1969 ("change within tradition"), the decade of the 1970s ("equal but different"), and the 1980s ("destruction and rebuilding").

Traditional Views of Women

The traditional view of women in Libyan society is a manifestation of a cluster of cultural values, some deeply rooted in the Arabic-Islamic tradition, others modified from African and Mediterranean civilizations. Major traditions and attitudes might be described as follows.

1. *Women are physically and mentally weak in comparison to men.* Within a household, the wife traditionally plays a supportive role. She prepares food and feeds and cares for children. Meals are prepared according to the husband's desires; he eats alone and is served first. A wife always has to be ready to provide any services her husband may need, including sex. Only rarely is a wife the primary income producer; when she assists in earning the family income, her role is a minor one.

In rural areas, women participated widely in activities outside the house, but only men performed important and difficult tasks such as drilling a well, building a farm house, or harvesting crops. On these collective occasions, women prepared food, brought water, and sang songs of encouragement.

In the past when a girl approached the age of marriage, her parents decided whom she should marry. Marriage was not an equal partnership in Libya. A male could have more than one wife at one time, and he could divorce his wife whenever he wished. Divorce procedures were very simple: a husband simply announced before two adult males that he was divorcing his wife. Theoretically, a wife might ask for a divorce, but in almost all cases it was the husband's decision.

2. *Women are beautiful, soft, and temperamental.* According to this value set, a woman aspires to possess beautiful clothes and jewelry. The quantity and quality of both are related to her family status. At the time of marriage, traditionally it is the husband's responsibility to present his bride with jewelry and expensive clothes, the exact amount of which is specified by the bride's parents or guardians. Women must wear their jewelry and expensive clothes on numerous occasions, and on some of these a woman from a well-to-do family may wear as much as two or three pounds of gold.

Women are not socialized to be leaders because they are considered temperamental and overly sensitive. Therefore all leadership roles traditionally have been reserved for men at all levels of Libyan society.

3. *Women are sex symbols and a source of shame.* Traditionally, women were to be carefully protected. Over the years, numerous means and procedures of protection developed. As children girls played only with other females and attended all-female schools. As they reached the age of eleven or twelve, they began to wear garments that covered their entire body, including their face; these were worn whenever they left their houses.[1] Young women did not go to the market, and their clothes were purchased by males. They traveled only with a male member of their family. This protection or veiling process was extended to names also. Female names were not to be revealed to males who were not members of the family.

Females married in their early teens, with the marriage ceremony taking place in a gathering of males only. Invitations went out to family members and friends. Whenever a written invitation was used, it stated the name of the bridegroom and referred to the bride as the daughter of Mr. So-and-so. Once married, a female rarely heard her name spoken by males, including her husband.

To leave Libya, a female citizen had to apply for an exit visa and include a letter from her father or her husband stating his approval of the trip. This letter was necessary even if the female was traveling with her father or husband. If her father was not present (that is, deceased), an unmarried female was expected to have an adult male (normally a relative) as guardian. In rare instances when an adult relative was not available the court appointed one, either a family friend or a respected citizen in the community.

Change within Tradition

Although social change has taken place throughout Libya's history, the year 1952 marks a very significant milestone. During that year Libya became an independent state. During the forty years preceding independence, Libya was either an Italian colony or under British or French administration. Leaders of the newly created state immediately began emphasizing that Libya had been, for the last fourteen centuries, part of the Arabic-Islamic world. Many Arabic-Islamic traditions were restored or re-emphasized.

Since 1952 all political leaders have emphasized their commitment to Arabic and Islamic values. However, the society's dominant rules, regulations, and laws reflect the results of a long history of interaction between Arabic-Islamic values and those that belong to other cultures and civilizations, primarily African and Mediterranean.

During the 1950s and 1960s Libyan political leaders encouraged modernization, but always within the context of preserving major traditional values. In practical terms this meant that the speed of social change was slow. Education was considered the most important means of modernization.[2] In spite of a scarcity of economic resources during the early days of independence, schools and teaching facilities received the largest proportion of government budgets. Citizens responded with great enthusiasm by sending their children to school. A law was introduced that made elementary education compulsory for all children. Even so, parents preferred to send their daughters to girls' schools, where only female teachers were employed, and to marry them at an early age.[3] As a result, female education lagged behind male education during the 1950s and 1960s (see Table 1).

Simultaneously, females in small numbers began to seek employment outside of the household. Government regulations did not discriminate against women in salaries, and men and women received commensurate income for the same job. As Libya became more modern, the proportion of jobs requiring education and technical skills grew significantly. The educational process lagged behind in this development, however, with the result that women were only eligible for those jobs requiring little or no training and that could be performed in segregated quarters. Thus, women tended to occupy positions such as housemaids or office janitors. Even today the proportion of women in the labor force, excluding farming, remains very small: 7 percent in 1980, an increase of less than 2 percent since 1964.

During the early 1950s, a set of regulations was introduced to organize family life. As a consequence, women were given the right to choose their marriage partner, and the legal marriageable age for women was established at sixteen years. Both husband and wife were permitted to seek a divorce. Furthermore, the regulations specified that a divorce proceeding had to be conducted through a court and follow certain legal

Table 1. Development of Education in Libya, 1950 to 1979

	Levels of Education					
	Elementary Schools		Preparatory Schools		Secondary Schools	
Years	Total Students	% Female	Total Students	% Female	Total Students	% Female
1950–51	32,089	11	0	0	628	2
1955–56	65,163	17	2,585	1	1,170	2
1960–61	120,433	19	9,465	5	1,946	6
1965–66	195,274	28	20,270	11	4,586	12
1970–71	350,225	37	37,047	18	8,441	15
1975–76	556,176	46	122,359	32	18,069	22
1978–79	600,747	47	191,574	40	27,122	23

Source: Several issues of Libyan Arab Republic, Ministry of Planning, *National Accounts.*

procedures. Specific references were made as to who gets what in terms of property and children. In reality, however, tradition continued to dominate.

Libyans adopted many aspects of Western life-style, including clothing. However, women as well as men did not entirely abandon the traditional style of dress after adopting European fashions. Women began to aspire to own both traditional and European clothing and jewelry items. As the economic conditions began to improve, newly added items of clothing and jewelry grew in quantity and value.

During the early 1960s, women received the right to vote and participate in political life. They also received the right to sell and buy property that they could own independently of husbands, and they obtained the right to form their own associations. In reality, however, these rights existed only on paper for all but a very small group of women. Unveiling began among a few urban women. Soon this group grew larger. But this did not mean women could participate in daily activities on an equal basis with men. The unveiling phenomenon was limited to walking to school or to work. Even so, most of these women did not go shopping or participate with men in social or political activities. Women's associations began to form in the major urban centers. The activities of these associations consisted largely of social gatherings and organizational meetings.

| Levels of Education | | | | | | |
| Vocational Schools | | University | | Total | | Student Ratio to |
Total Students	% Female	Total Students	% Female	Total Students	% Female	Total Population
115	23	0	0	32,832	11	2.0
1,125	18	31	0	70,075	16	6.1
3,122	12	678	3	135,644	18	10.0
5,475	31	1,787	8	227,392	26	14.0
8,465	23	4,442	9	408,620	34	21.2
24,033	51	11,243	14	731,880	43	32.3
40,173	56	12,295	20	871,911	45	34.0

Equal but Different

By the 1970s, educated women numbered in the tens of thousands and could be found at all levels in the educational system (see Table 1). Also, oil revenues became relatively large and the wealth from exporting oil began to spread across the population. At the beginning of the decade, the newly installed revolutionary regime announced new policies and promised to carry out major social change, including equal rights, obligations, and participation for women. At the same time, the ideology emphasized that the sexes are physically different and, therefore, they have different duties to perform in society. Family life was regarded as sacred, and priority was given to preserving and maintaining its continuity. The role of a woman as mother was to be highly respected. Therefore, she was assumed to take full responsibility in rearing the children. Islamic values were to be emphasized, but the oil wealth was to be invested in modernizing the country within the shortest period of time. The general goal was to enhance the quality of life of every citizen.

Practical steps were taken to bridge the gap between males and females in education. The level of compulsory education was raised to the ninth grade, coeducation was encouraged at the elementary level, schools were built in every town or village, and punitive measures were introduced against parents who failed to send all of their school-age children to school. As can be seen in Table 1, these actions led to a tremendous increase in female education during the 1970s.

Women were encouraged to actively participate in political life but within the framework of the official ideology. They were encouraged to seek formal means to settle family problems and to obtain their full rights. Women were given the right to approve of their husband's taking a second wife, and a divorced woman was permitted to keep the house while her ex-husband found another dwelling.⁴ However, most of the new rights did not significantly change the position of women. Traditional norms remained very strong.

The only change of any real importance to women during the 1970s was in the area of education. Illustrative results emanating from increased education included widespread unveiling, especially in urban centers, greater female participation in shopping and driving, as well as intracity travel without a male companion.

The opportunity of women in the labor force remained small. On the one hand this was due to the emphasis on the traditional role of female as mother and homemaker. On the other hand the highly emphasized goal of modernization within the shortest period led to a dependency on foreign labor, which comprised 41 percent of the national labor force in 1980. Thus, actions were not taken to facilitate Libyan women entering the job market. Even in what are considered "female dominant" jobs such as nurses, secretaries, and flight attendants, foreign women rather than Libyan women were employed.

As per capita income grew larger every year, Libyans became more and more dependent on modern, imported goods. The society became increasingly consumer-oriented. Differences in the number of imported goods between the 1960s and the 1970s were quite significant. Presently, the list of imported household goods includes thousands of items, ranging from needles to furniture.

Many individuals have suggested that increased education will lead to major changes in the Libyan woman's traditional social position and roles. This, though, has not occurred, and the primary reason is cultural. Because men control all leading roles in Libyan society, they emphasize values that reflect this fact. As a consequence, the decade of the 1970s can perhaps be best characterized as "equal but different," reflecting official government policies. However, upon examining the values emphasized in the educational materials, it is apparent that these values do not adequately reflect the widely publicized official policies. For example, Table 2 profiles the portrayal of the sexes in elementary school books used during the decade of the 1970s. Among the illustrations that depicted teachers in a classroom setting, only 18 percent of the teachers

Table 2. Representation of Males and Females in Reading Books of the Elementary Level [a]

| | Percentage | | | |
Representation	Male	Female	Both	Total
Instructor in the classroom	82	18	0	100 (17)
Instructor in the house	91	9	0	100 (23)
School activities	100	0	0	100 (18)
Poet	100	0	0	100 (32)
Writer	75	25	0	100 (4)
Historical figure	83	17	0	100 (12)
Names	90	10	0	100 (130)
Photographs	80	4	16	100 (109)

[a] Table constructed from reading books at grade levels three to six; survey done by Mrs. Amna Krekshi, my research assistant.

were female in spite of the fact that 44 percent of the elementary school teachers during the latter part of the 1970s were female.

Although official policy emphasized that the mother has major responsibility for rearing children, only 9 percent of the pictures showing a learning process taking place in the home portrayed a female doing the instructing. Despite the fact that the society is equally divided between the sexes, only 10 percent of the names mentioned in the analyzed books were female ones.

Destruction and Rebuilding

When the 1980s began, 35 percent of the population was enrolled in academic institutions; of these, 47 percent were females. More than 50 percent of the students who were enrolled in vocational schools during this period were females, while the percentage of females at the university level reached 24 percent. At the elementary level, over half of the 800,600 students were attending coeducational schools. All institutions at the university level were coeducational.[5]

The male-female ratios for faculty were quite different, however. Only 9.5 percent of the university instructors during this period were females. Interestingly, though, most of the superintendents in elementary schools for girls were females, and women comprised at least half of the superintendents of coeducational, preparatory, and secondary schools.[6] Simultaneously, however, there were few female doctors, engineers, laboratory technicians, heads of university departments, lawyers, or computer programmers.

In adddition to traditional areas of work, Libyan women in 1980 could be found in banks, department stores, and government offices. However, only 7 percent of the national labor force consisted of females. Unveiled women became commonplace in the streets of urban areas, although their participation in the decision-making processes outside the home remained negligible. Almost all leading roles in the society were assumed by men. Traditional rules remained: a female could not marry or leave her house or her country without the permission of a male guardian.

Although the proportion of men marrying more than one woman at a time is minimal, occurring in not more than 3 percent of all marriages, the fact that this phenomenon still exists illustrates the unequal status of marriage partners. And women's traditional interest in jewelry and expensive clothes has become even stronger, and the male guardian continues to have the final word in virtually all major issues within the family.

As the decade of the 1970s approached its end, new policies regarding the status of women were introduced. These simply stated that there are no differences between the sexes and emphasized the need to treat men and women equally. Before the close of the decade, a number of steps had been taken to implement these policies. At the same time, though, individuals who opposed the new policies developed procedures to slow their implementation.

With the emergence of the 1980s three steps toward reaching the goal set by the new policies were taken. These can be summarized as follows.

1. *All students who are in secondary schools and above are required to have military training.* Both male and female students at the secondary school level are required to wear a standard military uniform to classes, attend daily military exercises, and participate in occasional military activities away from school. Military training is supervised by regular (male) military officers. These rules are altered somewhat for university-level students. These students are not required to wear uniforms when attending classes, but they do have to attend training camps.

2. *Girls are encouraged to enroll in women's military academies.* The first female military academy opened its doors in 1979. Graduates of this academy have been promoted to the rank of lieutenant. Preparations are now under way to open other specialized military academies for women such as air force and marine institutes.

State-owned television and radio stations carry daily programs encouraging parents to send their daughters to these military academies.

Application forms must be accompanied by a number of documents, in-cluding a high school diploma, birth certificate, approval of a male guardian, etc. However, female students are requested to make partial application first, submitting the numerous documents at a later date.

3. *Females are encouraged to form revolutionary committees.* Revo-lutionary committees may be formed in schools, places of work, and in the communities at large. The major task of such committees is to de-velop a core group of believers in President Qaddafi's third world theory. The president will implement it both inside and outside of Libya and develop procedures to guard the revolution and minimize corruption.

In a recent paper, Barakat developed a theoretical model to represent the relationship between the lower social status of Arab women, the culture as a whole, and the social and structural systems. According to this theory, to uplift the low status of Arab women a revolutionary change has to take place within the social structure and the social sys-tem of the society.[7] This reflects what the Libyan political leaders have in mind and what they are planning to implement during the 1980s. The only steps taken so far in Libyan society, however, are the three steps described earlier that center around military training and revolu-tionary committees. These steps essentially represent the ideas of one political leader.

But is it feasible to try to raise the status of Libyan women to a level equal to that of men? If feasible, how long will this process take? What kinds of social problems may develop? Changes can occur on a number of levels (family, community, society, etc.), although the present discus-sion will be limited to potential impact on the family.

The three steps that have been taken so far are expected to produce a major transformation of women's social position and social role. The present government assumes that military training of women will lead eventually to the development of a "new woman." This "new woman" will have a strong self-identity and confidence in her ability to perform many tasks traditionally reserved for men. She will also abandon some of the traditional activities of women. For example, she is expected to pay less attention to fashion and jewelry and to actively participate in decisions regarding family life, community, and society.

If given a choice, most men and women would oppose female military training. Such opposition, however, is not tolerated by the government. Revolutionary committees, which are not constrained by government laws or regulations, are expected to play a major role in eliminating op-position to new policies.

Women's military training programs can be implemented in several ways: (1) people attending school will receive military training only while they are in school, (2) school-age females will receive military training throughout their school years and afterwards, or (3) all women irrespective of age will receive military training.

Approach one limits military training to students; thus, the training will cease as the individual leaves school. Those who oppose military training for women will keep their daughters out of school or send them to evening schools. This is the approach currently being used. Only students at the high school level and above receive military training. Any female not complying with such a requirement is forced to drop out of school. Such a female wishing to continue her education must enroll in an evening school. Parents are required to submit a legitimate excuse when enrolling a daughter in such an educational program. If this approach continues, military training will have a negligible impact on changing the social position of women. However, such an approach will not satisfy the goals of the present government.

If the second approach is adopted, the emphasis will then be on the next generation. The assumption underlying this approach is that the young are less committed to tradition, welcome new ideas, and, therefore, will adjust easily to change. Parents would have to send all their children to day school; dropping out of school would not be tolerated. A new set of regulations and laws eliminating official differences between the sexes would need to be introduced. Organizations and institutions currently in existence to help the family in the socialization process would be strengthened, with more authority and responsibility assigned to them. New, formal organizations would be developed to take over some of the responsibilities that the traditional extended family presently assumes. This, in turn, would lead to more chances of female-male interaction, which would pave the way for the development of new kinds of female-male relationships. Such relationships would impact on the family of the future in the following ways.

1. Marriage will not be arranged by the parents but rather will be based on the free choice of the individuals involved.

2. Families will be nuclear, independent, and small.

3. Increased male participation in household activities and a new division of labor within the family will develop.

4. Most traditional customs related to the formation of a new family will be abandoned, especially the material aspects and the lavish expenditures. Marriage will become a personal matter rather than an extended family activity.

5. Less interference will be allowed in the life of a nuclear family from members of the extended family and relatives.

6. Services such as child care will be provided by formal organizations rather than by members of the extended family and relatives.

7. Women will actively participate in economic, social, and political activities outside of the home.

8. The family will no longer play the most important role in the socialization process. Other formal organizations will share such a role with the family. Some of the organizations may even have a stronger impact on the individual than will the family.

The third approach, if it is adopted, would require that all women, irrespective of age, would have to start military training and continue it indefinitely. Few men or women would willingly accept such a practice (although the government, as previously mentioned, would not tolerate opposition). There are, though, several major obstacles to the implementation of such a policy. The current average family size is large, and present dietary habits require home-prepared meals involving considerable time and energy. Males have been socialized to take no part in traditional housewife activities. Therefore, if this third approach is implemented, it will lead to a great deal of confusion, role conflict, and tension. Men who are not happy with this policy but cannot forbid their wives and daughters from participating in military training will look for some means to release their anger and tension. Moreover, such an alternative may lead to female defiance of traditional male dominance, with some behavior perhaps taking a violent or deviant form. Accordingly, this third approach, at least during a transition period, might be characterized as resulting in (1) a vague division of authority and responsibility in the family, (2) more male-female disagreements and quarrels, (3) the development of new types of male-female relationships, (4) a high incidence of psychologically broken homes, and (5) a high rate of juvenile delinquency.

Conclusion

The social status of women in Libya has always been defined in terms of values that reflect the dominant ideology, that of the male who happened to be the political leader at the time. Recently, however, as in many parts of the contemporary Arab world, women's role and status have been the center of a great deal of discussion, writing, regulations, rules, and laws. The process of attempting to change the roles and status of women consists of three distinct stages. The first stage began in 1952 when Libya became an independent state and ended in 1969 with the First of September Revolution. The official ideology as well as the ideology of those individuals who participated in the activities related to women during this stage seemed to acknowledge most of the traditionally held beliefs about women—that women, biologically and psychologically, were only fit to play supportive roles. As such, women were to be respected provided they maintained their position in the home and engaged in activities that did not require direct male-female interaction.

The second stage took place from 1969 to 1979, the first ten years of the current revolutionary regime. During this stage, the official ideology was centered around the principle that the sexes are equal but different. Thus, the sexes were to have equal rights as long as major traditions were preserved. Given obvious biological differences, men and women were each assumed to have a unique social role. Members of each sex were admonished to assume the roles that had been culturally prescribed to their sex. However, some of the traditional barriers between the sexes were eliminated. The impact of this policy was eventually seen in the spread of female education, unveiling, and female participation in family-related activities outside of the home.

The third stage began with the decade of the 1980s. Although this stage has just started, the widely publicized official ideology appears too revolutionary for the contemporary Arab world. Males and females are viewed as completely equal; ideas of biological and psychological differences have been abandoned. Males and females are encouraged to perform the same tasks and play the same roles. The first step in implementing this ideology is reflected in mandatory military training for all males and females. Although other parts of the Arab world have prescribed military training for women, such a practice until now has been voluntary.

This last ideology, the ideology of the third stage, will involve major value changes if it is implemented. It can either be carried out over a long period of time (gradually and naturally) so that comparable changes take place in other parts of the social structure, or by forceful means in a relatively short period of time. If the latter occurs, changes will be accompanied by other phenomena that, according to present Libyan cultural values, will be considered social problems.

The drive toward equal rights for Libyan men and women alike has accomplished many goals, even though women in modern Libya are not treated equally in all respects. Recently, this drive has gained new momentum. This may lead to the establishment of a society where the sexes are completely equal, or to the development of a society torn by social problems and conflicts. The 1980s may prove to be the most important period in the history of contemporary Libya with respect to determining the fate of its society.

Notes

1. Females in rural areas do not normally wear a veil. Since relatives reside in the same area, a rural woman rarely encounters strange men. When

she does, she either covers her face or averts it while talking with an unrelated male.

2. M. O. Attir, *Modernization and Development: Results of an Empirical Study in Libya* (Tripoli: The Arab Development Institute and the University of Garyunis, 1980), pp. 50–53.

3. Males taught in girls' schools in some eastern coastal towns as early as the mid 1940s. A few elementary schools in the south have been coeducational since the early 1950s.

4. In the past, a divorced woman had to return to the house of her original family. She could only take jewelry and clothing with her.

5. Local university education, first established in the mid 1950s, has always been coeducational.

6. School superintendents are called heads of popular committees, but they perform more or less the same tasks of a schoolmaster or superintendent.

7. H. Barakat, "The Social System and Its Relation to the Problems of the Arab Woman," *Al-moustaqbal al-Arabi* 34 (December 1981): 51–63.

Women and Public Health in Morocco: One Family's Experience

DONNA LEE BOWEN

In Morocco, as in many other new nations, the public health service was designed to provide free or inexpensive health care. Organized under the Ministry of Health in 1956 (after independence from the French), the service encompasses all areas of health from psychiatry to obstetrics and provides needed services from disease prevention in oasis villages to sophisticated surgical operations in urban hospitals.

The health network in Morocco is organized in an upward-moving pyramid with the local clinic at the bottom. Anyone needing medical care reports to the local clinic (*dispensaire*) to be seen by nurses. There is generally no doctor at this level. If the case is serious enough or proper treatment is not available one is referred to the next level, the health center (*centre de santé*). Cases can be referred from there to the district hospital and in complex cases to the large hospitals at the provincial, regional, or national levels where more specialized facilities are available.

Since public health care is free, the demand exceeds the limited supply, so patients have devised three methods that strengthen their chances of seeing medical personnel. The first is queuing; that is, service goes to the one prepared to wait the longest. Persistence is also important for patients to survive the long system of referrals from clinic to health center to hospital. The ones who last the course are those who genuinely need care, but the toll in suffering is high. The second method is personal influence. Whenever possible, no matter how tenuous the relationship, "pull" is used to advance people to the head of the line. A third method, often commented upon but officially ignored, is the bribe. Patients accuse paramedical personnel of being constantly on the take and state that bribes are necessary for even the simplest tasks to be performed, including referral to the doctor.

Medical supplies for the public health service are often limited. In addition to the normal supply and demand, the expansion of health facilities and the attempt to distribute drugs to newly created provinces have resulted in severe shortages.

Dissatisfaction with the public health service brings new customers to private pharmacies. In North Africa a wide variety of drugs available in the West only through a doctor's prescription are freely sold over the counter. Perhaps because people are paying for value received, popular faith in pharmacy medicine runs higher than in that dispensed by public health. Pharmacists are also often very helpful in listening to symptoms, diagnosing, and prescribing.

Even though free care is theoretically available, patients prefer to use private physicians. In the cities an office visit costs $5.00 to $7.00 and if patients can save the money they will willingly spend it. They charge that public health doctors are ineffectual. A survey of users of a rural health clinic yielded further interesting results. Users initially maintained that the health care was good in their area but later stated they would not want to return to the public health clinic. Complaints listed included unfriendliness and superciliousness of paramedical personnel, the necessity of bribes, the attention paid to important or wealthy men, and the failure of the treatment. Only a third of the sample surveyed had ever used the medical facilities, even though 60 percent lived within two kilometers of the clinic and hospital.

Doctors themselves, however, are accorded a high level of respect. In the past Morocco relied on foreign doctors from France and Eastern Europe, but thanks to new medical schools, cadres of Moroccan doctors have entered the health system. Almost half the doctors practicing in Morocco work in the private sector and over half of these practice in the five largest cities, thus leaving the rural areas inadequately serviced. Public health doctors are allowed to operate private practices as well, and doctors often assume part- or full-time administrative posts. This removes them from contact with patients, so the bulk of the practice thereby falls on the nurses and the paramedical personnel.

Paramedical personnel, mostly trained in Morocco, numbered around eight thousand in 1971. The majority are men since Morocco, like most Muslim countries, discourages nursing as a career for women. The most highly trained are the graduate health assistants (*adjoints de santé diplômes d'état*), some of whom are also certified specialists in areas such as radiology or sanitation. Their training is equivalent to the baccalaureate. The licensed health assistants (*adjoints de santé brevetés*) finish four years of secondary education, the last two of which are special training for their program. The health aides (*aides sanitaires*) are products of a special crash course, now discontinued, that provided minimal training to meet the urgent need for personnel immediately following independence. However, today health aides still account for about one-third of the entire paramedical corps.

Women in the Public Health System

For a Moroccan woman, correlating the factors that maintain her good health and that of her children can be a full-time job. The web of doctors, dispensaries, nurses, medicines, and hospitals that make up the public health service constitutes a new and forbidding world that takes time and initiative to manage. The complexity of the public health system demands guidance if she is to unravel the possible services and clarify what possibilities for help are available. Thus many women have doubts about entering the public health sector with its unknown and seemingly arbitrary system, its remote and omniscient doctors, haughty nurses, guarded hospitals, and battery of foreign medical terms. Retreat into the traditional sector therefore remains a real possibility, the sector where illness is attributed to supernatural causes and help is sought from a sympathetic and accessible religious man or a practitioner of traditional medicine. Another avenue is the relatively efficient private sector health system, but this is expensive.

The need for relief from sickness and help with ill children will draw a woman into the complex system of health care and force her to take action. For lower-class women, lack of money must be compensated for by expenditure of time, initiative, and imagination.

Health care is not just a question of having a doctor diagnose one's ills. Rather it involves available money, choice of services, family logistics of time and transportation to visit medical facilities, and days of waiting. When pregnancy or avoidance of pregnancy is involved other health concerns enter the picture or are intensified.

Given the amount of effort required, the woman must be both very ill and very determined before she will seek help in the public health system. She must be ill enough to be forced to seek professional help and determined enough to go through all the necessary steps to assure success in her venture.

Family Planning

The question of whether or not to have another child is of paramount concern for young mothers. Society, family, and traditional values pressure women to bear many children, but issues of health and finances necessitate a couple's reconsideration of its family size.

On the one hand a woman's status is determined by her children. A girl becomes a woman when she marries, but she is truly accepted by society and her new family when she bears a son. High infant mortality rates force women to have as many children as possible. The children, when grown, will supply their parents with security for their old age since no social security or pension plans exist for the general populace.

The national demographic profile is at odds with this scenario, however. Economic and demographic experts predict disaster if Morocco's high (3 percent) growth rate does not decline. Projections estimate that the population of Morocco, already estimated at over twenty-two million, will reach 37.5 million in the year 2000 and 56.6 million in 2020 (population estimate, World Population Data Sheet, 20th edition). Yet young parents desiring large families see no connection between a fifth child and the massive problems of hunger and crowding predicted by demographers. The pressure to lower the birth rate therefore falls upon the government and necessitates implementation of a national family planning program. Ironically, better medical standards and improved sanitation have lowered mortality rates and are thus partially responsible for the higher growth rate. Another component in the equation is a rise in education and general income levels, both of which show a strong correspondence with lower birth rates. All of these expensive programs, however, put further strain on already tight national budgets.

The young mother is the focus of the tension between the different government plans. Oblivious of the Moroccan demographic profile, aware of her future dependence on her children, she recognizes immediate arguments in support of having another child but also fears the ramifications of another birth. In the final analysis, the woman's health is often the decisive factor that mitigates against continual pregnancies.

Use of contraception is not, however, a simple matter. The family planning program in Morocco lends little support to the mother. Family planning clinics are available throughout the public health system, but they are under separate control and not generally housed with the regular health clinic facilities. The clinics dispense birth control pills and IUDs. Therapeutic abortions have been legalized if the mother's health is in danger, but are unavailable in the public sector and relatively expensive ($250 to $300) in the private sector.

The intrauterine device (IUD), the first contraceptive method introduced, was popular with planning officials because of its high usage continuation rate (it is difficult to remove once inserted). But it was unpopular with many women. Aversion to its use stemmed from fear, a fear that increased with inadequate medical explanations and follow-up service. Once inserted, IUDs were rumored to penetrate directly to the heart and kill the user. Sterility was also attributed to its use.

Interest in the IUD declined sharply after birth control pills were introduced in Morocco in 1969. Then the most widely used means of contraception, the pill was adopted by 93.5 percent of all new acceptors. In 1974 the percentage of pill users was 81.9 percent. Its effectiveness, however, is negated by the ease with which it may be discontinued or misused and by the side effects of nausea, bleeding, or headaches.

The System: Theory versus Practice

While in theory the Ministry of Health tried to account for most contingencies, in practice another variable had to be reckoned with—the human factor. Perhaps the most effective way to demonstrate how the Moroccan public health system works for women is to describe one family's 1972 experience.

Khadija, the young wife of the family, was then twenty-five and about six months pregnant. She loved to talk. Children were her main subject, and I was eager to listen as I was working on maternal and child health issues. Khadija had two girls and two boys then aged eight, seven, five, and three. Ahmed, her husband, was employed regularly by the army.

Following the birth of her youngest boy, Khadija began taking birth control pills. After taking the pills for almost two years, a pain started in her stomach and "shot up like a needle into her chest." Expensive food containing lots of protein would alleviate the pain, but the family was unable to afford a good diet of meat and eggs. Khadija ate more and more bread and couscous, seeking relief with bland food. When she was unable to fast during the month of Ramadan, she finally went to see a public health doctor who told her to stop the pills. The pain subsided and within three months she was pregnant again.

Large families are expected and praised in Morocco. As Khadija said, "Having four or five or six children is considered nothing here." But her four were enough. "Everything is so expensive now; people just can't tell us to have more children . . . And my husband—he has a good heart, but he's a donkey. He doesn't understand things." She confessed she was not reconciled to bearing this fifth child.

I asked shyly if she had even thought of an abortion. She said that she had definitely considered the possibility and had talked about going to the hospital to abort the baby (a procedure then illegal in Morocco); however, relatives and friends had convinced her it was forbidden by God. Her husband said no also. Khadija did not seem convinced by the illegality of abortion, but was impressed by the social and religious pressures. Still, the general economic malaise could not be denied.

"This year vegetables are more expensive than ever before, and they grow by seeds and the help of God! I spend 100 riyals ($1.25) every day for bread alone plus five riyals for the use of the oven. Heavens, I myself eat three loaves of bread a day and my husband and older son eat more. And unemployment. There's no work. The king and the government officials and the rich merchants all have enough to eat and drink and a place to sleep. From their Mercedes or their offices, they don't even see people with our problems, much less have similar problems . . .

"They try to teach us about religion. They put the old men on television where they talk about how we should behave, the kinds of clothes we women should wear to cover up our bodies. But no one over twenty listens to those men. How can working women wear veils and long clothes?" I shrugged, having that morning watched a woman clad in caftan, hood, veil, and sunglasses zoom past me on her Mobylette. "If we stay at home we can dress that way. But at least we're not as bad as those Muslims in Egypt and the East. They're not at all like us."

I asked whether good Moroccan Muslims are allowed to use family planning measures. She hesitated, then answered that they weren't forbidden if the woman's stomach (an all-purpose description, here meaning womb) was empty. "Every day at noon and at eight in the evening family planning information is shown on television. They say that taking pills is better for your health and makes it easier to educate your children. Of course, it's bad for prostitutes to use the pills and never have children. But if you have children already and don't want more—it's all right."

I told her I had a friend, Dr. Zuhra, who was a gynecologist. After her baby was born I could arrange for her to see Zuhra and find a better way of birth control, perhaps an IUD. She agreed and her eyes lit up at this new idea.

In November, Khadija gave birth to a healthy boy. Her mother, Fatima, reported that she was fine, but "her head wasn't all right." "No doubt, it will pass if God wills it," she said.

Khadija was vague, said her mother, but also irritable. She fussed at the children; she was often in tears and not able to cope with the day-to-day routine. I said, "Khadija must see a doctor." "OK," Fatima said, "I'll see that she does." I promised to inquire about public health system facilities for psychological care.

I learned that a hospital in Salé, across the river from Rabat, handled such cases. Fatima had also been told about the hospital in Salé and had taken Khadija to see the local doctor through whom all referrals were made. Khadija had an appointment for the following week. I was impressed with the efficiency of the system as I had been led to believe that it was riddled with corruption and malpractice at the best of times.

Next week I asked for news. "Oh, Khadija didn't see the doctor," Fatima replied. "She waited, someone asked her what was wrong, took a few notes and made another appointment."

"She didn't see any doctor?"

"Oh, no, she has to go back next week and see the doctor then. It's a terrible nuisance—she's so far away." Khadija, coming from Youssoufia, had to take two separate buses and allow an hour and a half for a trip that takes ten minutes by car.

Two months later, in January, Fatima came to see me. "It's Khadija," she said. "You told her that after her baby you'd take her to see your friend, the doctor. She needs to see her now," she continued. "She has terrible pains here," pressing her lower parts, "whenever she urinates."

By now, having learned a little of Moroccan public health routine, I knew that Khadija's doctor in Youssoufia would have to refer her to the *maternité*, the next step up the health ladder. "But he has," she assured me. "Khadija has the paper." "Then she should just go," I said. "No, no, no," she interjected forcibly. My Western grasp of Moroccan realities was obviously deficient. "You know Zuhra. You must make the appointment. Then it will all be all right. You'll see."

Miraculously I found Zuhra on the first try; I made an appointment for Khadija and one for myself for the next afternoon. "No time to get nervous," I told Fatima. "Khadija must be here by 2:00 P.M. so we can be there by 2:30. She mustn't forget the paper from her Youssoufia doctor."

We arrived at the clinic gates promptly at 2:30. As I ushered Khadija through, a small man came running up and asked us where we were going. I took a firm grip on Khadija's arm and in my best French said, "To see Dr. Ben M'hammad." Khadija pulled out the precious referral slip. The man looked briefly at the totally illegible scrawl and waved us on. We chose the most official-looking entrance and stepped inside, Khadija somewhat insecurely, owing to her borrowed high heels and the mounting panic I sensed in her. My own bravado, I realized, came from years of trusting my family doctor.

The maternity hospital, formerly Rabat's major hospital during the French occupation, was old, with high ceilings, wide hallways, and walls painted a dull blue-gray. No signs were apparent in either Arabic or French. I looked around hopelessly, but not even the customary guardian was evident. I intercepted a nurse rounding a corner and asked for Dr. Zuhra's clinic station. We went to the end of the corridor and up a small staircase, where a French nun pointed ahead. A moment later Zuhra herself appeared through the door, giving directions to an orderly in a blood-stained apron. She smiled briefly at us, promised to call us in a few minutes, and dashed back through the swinging doors.

Two metal folding chairs stood against the wall; a woman sat in one and I seated Khadija in the other. Not even the brilliant Moroccan winter sun could penetrate the grayness of the decor. The halls were narrow, the ceilings low, but the result was not cozy. The walls were gray, the windows grimy and unwashed, and gray metal water pipes, festooned with cobwebs, climbed the corners and ran along the conjunctions of wall and ceiling in every direction.

Finally the doors swung open, and a stretcher-cart bearing a middle-aged woman in a worn brown caftan passed in front of us down the hall. Then Khadija's neighbor was motioned through the doors by a male nurse and two other women appeared at the head of the stairs, one leaning heavily on the other. Khadija indicated the two empty chairs, but the women ignored her and settled on the floor in the position of eternal patience. One, in a rose-colored caftan, pushed her black veil down and murmured a solicitous question to her obviously ill friend. The friend shook her head slightly and pulled her veil under her chin. Her cheeks were gaunt, her eyes dark and shadowed. She stared straight ahead, paying no attention to the movement around her.

Watching the stark face of the woman squatting on the floor, staring out the grimy windows, I began to feel real fear. I was only waiting for a routine examination, I told myself; I had really come only to give Khadija courage. But what if something was really wrong with me? Would I trust the doctors in their smeared jackets or the nurses with their minimal education? Could I possibly be cured in such poor sanitary conditions? Khadija and the women next to me had no choice and in effect knew no other alternative.

Zuhra's voice, giving orders to a patient, preceded her through the swinging doors. She pressed a scribbled note into the hand of the patient. "Don't lose this," she told the woman sternly. "You must show it at the door when you return next week." She ushered Khadija and me into a huge high-ceilinged room with an obstetrical examination table precisely in the middle, a chair, and a set of scales against the wall. A single faded chart illustrating proper nutrition had been tacked to one of the bare gray walls.

Zuhra directed Khadija to remove her undergarments and lie down on the table. Then she vanished. Khadija seemed used to this, for she handed me her small change purse containing the doctor's authorization, then modestly followed Zuhra's directions. She seemed, however, to remove nothing, and climbed onto the table, still clad in caftan and hood. "Don't forget about the IUD," she said. "Ask when I can get one."

Zuhra reentered, produced her forceps, and sent me out of the room. After the initial examination, she invited me in, directed a stream of impressively pertinent questions to Khadija, and nodded quietly at the answers. She told me in English that all would be fine. Now it was my turn. Khadija dressed and waited outside. After my examination, Zuhra pulled the chair away from the wall and sat down opposite me.

Khadija, she said, had a cyst near the entrance to her vagina. This was evidently what was causing her pain. Removal would be a simple operation and could be performed here in the maternity clinic—the next Friday if Khadija could arrange it.

Khadija was delighted by the quickness of the examination and the simplicity of the proposed treatment. But things did not quite work out as planned. Once Khadija was under anesthesia in the clinic, Zuhra decided not to perform the operation; Khadija would have to go to the hospital. What was wrong? Khadija was obviously very ill as it took her almost a whole day to come out from under the anesthesia and she was dizzy and nauseated for a second day. Zuhra had told her to return Wednesday to see her. Could I accompany Khadija again? Now she was very frightened and didn't want to go alone.

Zuhra assured me on the phone that Khadija's illness was due to her reaction to anesthetic. However, when ready to operate Zuhra realized that the cyst was also attached to the wall of the urinary tract, making removal more sensitive. Since she was a gynecologist, she preferred to turn the procedure over to a urologist; she would recommend a good one and phone him personally after she saw Khadija Wednesday.

Wednesday afternoon Khadija and I again braved the gates of the *clinique maternité*, passed the gatekeeper, and took places on the bench near Zuhra's office. When Khadija's turn came, we entered the small office and sat on metal chairs. Zuhra explained the situation and pressed an appointment card into Khadija's hand. "Take this to the fourth floor of Avicenne Hospital. The urologists' offices are there," she said. "The doctor was a colleague of mine in medical school and he is very good. You'll be better off with him performing the operation."

The second operation required a stay in the new hospital of Avicenne, a fair distance out in a suburb of Rabat. Located at a major crossroads, the hospital was edged on one side by a forest, on the other by fields leading to the main Casablanca road. A pretty setting but difficult to reach. Though the hospital was served by a bus line, several changes were necessary. Khadija and I took a taxi.

The hospital complex was white and formidable, five stories high, containing four major wings and a host of other associated buildings. The taxi dropped us in front of the main gate. Again we had to present an appointment slip in order to be allowed to the main door of the hospital. We climbed stairs and determined that Zuhra's friend was stationed here and would be in soon. Again we sat down to rest on a bench across the hall.

Avicenne is a fairly new hospital. The corridors were clean and the patient areas seemed bright. Hospital staff in blue jackets pushed carts back and forth, carts bearing meal trays or sparkling clean medical equipment. The nurses were quiet and unobtrusive. Khadija and I sat, backs against the blue wall, and discussed the question foremost in her mind: how she could spend days in the hospital and continue to nurse her baby. We'd gone over, around, and under the subject but had reached no decision.

After half an hour a young woman, a patient in robe and slippers, came out of a nearby room. Anxious for company, she began to tell us her life story. She had been part of the Moroccan National Health System for two years, having first consulted a public health doctor in Tafilalt, a river oasis area in the far southeast of Morocco. From there she had been referred from local dispensary to provincial hospital to regional hospital to area capital and finally here to Avicenne in Rabat. The medical establishment was still unsure about her case, but she had undergone every possible test and consulted more doctors than anyone else in the hospital. In the process she had remained cheerful, seen all of Morocco, and learned Arabic. As a teenager growing up in a Berber-speaking village she had had no exposure to Arabic until she began her journey into the medical labyrinth. She had not only mastered the system but also the language. The young woman was very blasé about the whole process. She was also very pleased to be in Rabat, to have arrived, so to speak, at the pinnacle of her current profession as patient.

Fifteen minutes later the doctor appeared, handsome, quite young, grave and distant. He and Khadija disappeared into an examination room and she emerged a few minutes later clutching a paper. The doctor told me that the operation was simple, but that they would prefer that Khadija stay in the hospital a few days. I explained that Khadija was a nursing mother and she preferred to spend a short enough time in the hospital so that she could continue to nurse the baby. The doctor agreed.

On the following Thursday, Khadija admitted herself to the hospital. Her husband, Ahmed, acccompanied her through the necessary paperwork. As Ahmed was in the army many dozens of extra forms pertaining to Khadija's case had to be filled out. The doctor said she would only be there three days. She had left a partial day's supply of milk at home for the baby and brought a breast pump with her. Ahmed came by every evening on his motorcycle to pick up some milk while Khadija's mother tended the children and fed the baby.

On the weekend I went to Avicenne to visit Khadija. I had to push upstairs against a crowd of relatives and friends. I found Khadija sitting up against pillows and talking to her husband. She looked extremely healthy and quite bored. As it turned out, nothing had happened. Khadija had been scheduled for the operation on Friday afternoon but the doctor had been called away and the operation was delayed for two or three days. Khadija was not to leave the hospital.

Khadija's concern was for her baby, and she faithfully pressed the milk from her breasts so Ahmed could take it home each evening on his motorcycle. Other than working and bootlegging mother's milk out of Avicenne, Ahmed tried to stay home as much as possible and help his mother-in-law care for the home.

On Monday the operation was again postponed and finally the date was set for a week later. Neither Fatima nor Khadija seemed unduly concerned. I, on the other hand, was beside myself. "How," I asked Fatima, "can the hospital afford to keep people occupying beds? What about the stories we hear of sick people being turned away from doctors, fobbed off with two aspirin and sent home? Furthermore, what about the expense? How could they afford to keep people there for extra weeks? And what about poor Khadija who wants to be at home with her baby?" Fatima shrugged and I began to understand how the Berber girl from Tafilalt had spent two years wandering through the Moroccan health service.

The week passed. Khadija was bothered by the nursing problem, but it gave her a great advantage in the ward where a nursing mother was a rarity. The staff recognized her status and accordingly brought her food promptly and often included extras.

Khadija had few complaints, perhaps taking her enforced idleness as her due after her struggles following the last baby. Finally the operation took place. Fatima reported that Khadija had reacted far better to the anesthesia this time and within a few hours was awake and coherent. She had asked for me and so I went once more to the hospital at Avicenne.

I walked into Khadija's ward, dumped my presents on her bed, and examined her face anxiously. She looked triumphant; her color was excellent. She said she felt fine; her breasts were still more bother than the operation but she was well accustomed to that by now. She was delighted with the presents.

"The operation," she said nonchalantly, "was nothing." The doctor was not concerned, the problem was not grave. The whole operation had taken less than half an hour and the anesthesia wore off rapidly.

I asked if the doctor checked on her. "No, only the nurses on their normal rounds."

"You're sure everything's all right?"

"Of course, no bleeding and little pain."

Khadija recovered rapidly from her operation and resumed regular life with her family immediately after her release from the hospital. Two months later she visited Zuhra for an IUD.

I went to see her before leaving for the United States, but she was at her sister's house. I sat outside in the afternoon sunlight with her mother. Khadija was fine, said her mother, but she herself was a bit ill.

"Now," she told me, "it's time for Khadija to watch over me. The children are my great joy, and Khadija is as helpful and kind as any mother could wish."

Women's Education and Its Relation to Fertility: Report from Baghdad

ANN BRAGDON AL-KADHI

Education level has been recognized as an important discriminator of sociological variables in most societies. In Iraq, public schools for girls are a relatively new phenomenon. This report indicates that schools have been and continue to be mediators in role transformation of women from traditional family-defined identities typified by high fertility.

Public school education for girls began in Ottoman-administered Baghdad in 1899 on an extremely limited scale and grew through 1913, when there were twelve schools with a total of 756 pupils and thirty-two teachers. These schools were attended primarily by daughters of urban bureaucrats. World War I brought disruption to the system, but under the British mandate primary schools were reopened and a secondary school for girls was established in 1929. The absolute number of schools and females enrolled in schools continued to increase, although the percentage of age-eligible females enrolled remained low until the late 1970s. United Nations figures indicate that in 1978 90 percent of seven- to twelve-year-old girls were enrolled in first-level studies. (Second-level thirteen- to eighteen-year-olds and third-level nineteen- to twenty-four-year-olds showed smaller enrollment rates—31 percent and 5.9 percent, respectively.)

In a field study of a girls' middle school (grades seven, eight, and nine) done in 1975–76 in al-Adhamia, an older and established middle-class neighborhood of Baghdad, the impact of education upon female roles was observed and analyzed. Schools have been an important mediator in transforming female roles in a variety of ways and at different levels. Education corresponds to a number of life-style variables, including dress, employment, participation in social and political activity, and family roles. The impact of education on family roles and reproductive behavior is intensified by the fact that there is near universal employment of women with diplomas. Traditional child care and family life have been influenced by the employment of women, most notably evidenced by a trend toward smaller family size.

Information regarding levels of education and number of children born to mothers of students enrolled at the research school and the teachers was collected by questionnaire and analyzed. The sample was divided into five groups according to educational level. The results are summarized and illustrated dramatically in figure 1. The women with no education have the largest number of children and increased levels of education correspond directly with a decrease in family size. This quantitative evidence supports the contention that education is a powerful

Figure 1. Fertility in Relation to Education Level of Women

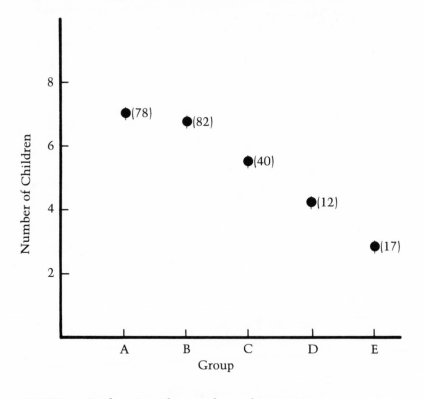

GROUP A: Students' mothers with no education.
GROUP B: Students' mothers with some or all of primary education.
GROUP C: Students' mothers with middle school education.
GROUP D: Students' mothers with secondary education.
GROUP E: Teachers with college education.
Numbers in parentheses are sample size; vertical lines represent standard deviation.

discriminator of populations and their behaviors as indicated in the significant area of family life and size.

References

Al-Kadhi, Ann Bragdon. "Schools as Mediators in Female Role Formation: An Ethnography of a Girls' School in Baghdad." Ph.D. dissertation, State University of New York at Buffalo, 1978.

UNESCO. *Statistical Yearbook, 1972* and *1980*. Paris: UNESCO, 1973, 1981.

The Social and Political Implications of Female Circumcision: The Case of the Sudan

NAHID F. TOUBIA

Amputation of the clitoris and sometimes even of the external genital organs goes hand in hand with brainwashing of girls, with a calculated merciless campaign to paralyze their capacity to think and to judge and to understand. For down the ages a system has been built up which aims at destroying the ability of women to see the exploitation to which they are subjected, and to understand its causes. A system which portrays the situation of women as a destiny prescribed by the Creator who made them as they are, females, and therefore a lesser species of the human race.   —Nawal al-Saʿdawi

Female circumcision is a form of social injustice that has been given new attention in the last few years. Despite the considerable number of publications available on this topic most of the literature is on the medical aspects and physical complications of the operation (Hathout, 1963; Shandalla, 1967; Huber, 1969; Verzin, 1975; Cook, 1979; among many others). In recent years, however, a psychological dimension was added to the problem (Karim and Ammar, 1965; Baashar, 1979; Shaalan, 1979). Documented psychological complications and the possible effect of the practice on the process of socialization and psychosexual development of women have posed questions that have been previously suppressed (Mustafa, 1966).[1] In more recent years, a series of broader studies has been conducted with a more socioeconomic theme in an attempt to identify some of the factors that play a role in the continuity of the practice (al-Dareer, 1979; Assaad, 1979).

Despite the diversity of the literature and the different approaches of the authors and researchers, all share either a descriptive or speculative attitude and any attempt at analysis seems to concentrate on a single aspect of the problem; that is, linguistic, religious, economic. Although one cannot deny the wealth of information gathered from these writings (from Miss Woolfe's letters[2] to the recent collection of works presented at the WHO seminar on the topic in Khartoum in February 1979), one cannot help feeling that something has remained unsaid.

I was born and brought up in Sudan and was taught in its schools. I myself have experienced the process of socialization of women in a country that derives its cultural history and social structure from two major sources: ethnically heterogeneous tribal Africa and the great philosophic Ideal of Islam. Being a doctor I also experienced the medical system of two countries: Egypt, where I received my medical education, and Sudan, where I practiced.

Although the medical complications of female circumcision are great, I believe these are only the side effects and are by no means at the root of the problem. For the last fifty years (and to a great extent even now) it was believed that physical health was the only reason for condemning the act. Consequently the solution was seen to lie in the hands of the medical, nursing, and midwifery personnel within the context of their professional roles, ignoring or neutralizing their position within the dynamics of power in the society (Taba, 1979; Baashar, 1979; Minority Rights Group (MRG) Report no. 47; Modawi, 1977).[3] As a result, a 1979 national survey in Sudan gives the incidence of infibulation as still at 82 percent.

I believe that to understand the purpose of a particular act, why it came to be, who benefits from it and who loses, which are the strongest links in the protective fence that surrounds it and which are the weakest, one needs to unravel the social politics of everyday life. Identifying society through defining the class, sex, and ethnic and cultural component of its interacting groups may explain the relations of power that dominate and therefore why a particular rule or practice persists.

I also believe that we cannot isolate one form of "injustice" against women without due consideration of all other factors, historical and economic, that contribute to the subordinate position of women. This does not apply to the "local" scene only but must be extended to the international community as new modes of sex discrimination are being imported from the capitalist countries to replace the traditional systems in the recipient underdeveloped country. Another important issue is the separation and marginalization of women's issues outside the mainstream of academia and research, especially in regard to development theory in the Third World.

Reading the literature with the basic understanding of the sociological process in mind, one cannot help but notice that there are certain agreements and preferred assumptions underlying most of these writings whose sociopolitical nature is not seriously questioned or submitted to a more detailed analysis. I will here attempt to explore some of these assumptions and question their validity.

The Mystification of Ritual

The practice of female circumcision has often been described as having the strength of a religious belief (Modawi, 1977; Mustafa, 1966; Taba, 1979; Baashar, 1979; MRG Report no. 47). It has been given the names "custom," "ritual," "tradition," "social taboo," among others. The implicit and explicit message is that it is something inherited from an untraceable past that has no rational meaning and lies within the realm of the untouchable sensitivity of traditional people.

Sudan, as I previously mentioned, has at least two definite major sources of cultural heritage. There is evidence that the African tribal system had in the past and still sporadically preserves a matrilineal and/or matrifocal family system (Hassan, 1967; Goode, 1970; James, 1978). Islam as a great ideal invaded and conquered these African cultures, absorbing them. If we examine the definition of women's sexuality in these merging social systems, we may begin to understand why members of the new system cultivated extreme measures to surpress women's sexuality.

Without unduly glorifying a past matrilineal age in Africa, one can still pose the possibility of a family system in which women had a different and a more positive role to play. The modes of production that prevailed in the past required women to occupy a larger space in public life. This undoubtedly gave them more freedom of movement, acquisition of knowledge, and experience and therefore more social power. But over time, through the process of capital concentration and surplus accumulation, women's spheres gradually diminished to their present boundaries within a strongly developed form of patriarchy. Within sub-Saharan Africa where this process is still under way, women's sexuality is defined in connection with the natural, the wild, and the uncontrollable.

In Sudan, remnants of this image of women prevail despite centuries of farming and domestication and are scarcely different from the image of women and female sexuality among the Bakwair of the Cameroon, described by Edwin Ardener (1975). If we compare this definition of women's sexuality to that of Islam as described by Mernissi (1975) and Antoun (1968), based on their interpretation of Imam al-Ghazali, we will find they do not contradict but complement each other. Unlike Western Christian culture and its later product, Freudian psychology, Islam recognizes woman's sexuality as even stronger than man's (Goode, 1970). It also warns that it is a power that if used properly will give pleasure to the Muslim man, but if unleashed would bring destruction not only to the individual or the family but to the whole Muslim nation. The two methods that Islam recommends for managing this feminine sexual desire are, first, to satisfy it and, second, to confine women within very strict, well-defined limits.

If we combine these two very strong definitions of female sexuality, the wild and the powerfully destructive, then the measures to contain it will have to parallel it in strength in order to avert danger and allow the emerging system to survive. So, although Islam does not openly favor female circumcision and the operation is not performed in most non-African Muslim countries, Islam may have provided the ideal that reinforced an ongoing process of increasing subjugation of women. It was clearly not difficult for the benefactors of the order to adopt the new ideology and use it in their favor without facing a major contradiction.

A Woman's Domain

Another common statement is that circumcision is a sacred women's ritual (Modawi, 1977; Taba, 1979) performed by women on women, whose persistence reflects the inherent conservative nature of women.

We may ask the question: do women in Sudan really control their lives enough to have their own domain and to dominate it? Is the woman's quarter a place where she exercises the full realization of her being or is it a place of confinement ruled by powers beyond her control? In a patrilineal, patrifocal, patriarchal, polygenic extended family system, women are the tools for gaining social honor. Yet they experience honor only indirectly, through the honors of their men, families, or tribes. There is no room for them to exercise social rites outside of those set by the system. Where women's sexuality and sensuality and their counterparts, virginity and purity, are a source of moral and social prestige for men, where they are an indirect economic investment or a directly exchangeable commodity for financial gain, the risk of losing control over them is not truly in the hands of the women.

May I suggest that through the propagation of the process of "desexualizing" the young girl, both physically and psychologically, women are protecting themselves from the consequences of possible deviance. Thereby social deviance is not punished after the act but before it, to minimize the risk of its occurrence. In another sense we can say that the existence of women's sexuality in itself is considered a form of deviance, as defined by Becker (1973): ". . . deviance is not a simple quality present in some kinds of behavior and absent in others. Rather, it is the product of a process which involves responses of other people to the behavior." He adds: "Whether a given act is deviant or not depends in part on the nature of the act (that is, whether or not it violates some rule) and in part on what other people do about it."

In short, women may want to avoid being victimized for the existence of their sexuality, and since they do not possess the economic, political, and social power to defend this sexuality, they suppress it. We may go even further and postulate that women, by some unconscious (or maybe conscious) process, prefer to destroy the parts of their body that threaten their physical existence and suffer all the complications that may follow rather than face their fate if they were even suspected of misusing their sexuality.[4]

However, this interpretation of the fear of punishment may be too direct and a more subtle process may be in action, as described by Shirley Ardener (1978) in *Defining Female*. She states: "Among all the different mechanisms which keep women in their place, perhaps the most effective is the notion that the place is designed for their own good and that of their families." She then explains how women as the subordinate group may take part in tightening the "locks" around their own "imprisonments." "Members of muted groups instead of ignoring the dominant group or merely tolerating its demands, may even go further and accept the burden of maintaining or 'policing' a system which to the onlooker appears to disadvantage them."

The women who actually perform the operation on other women may be mothers, aunts, grandmothers, the traditional village circumciser, or the trained midwife or nurse. Each of these groups may have their reasons or roles to play in enforcing the rules of the dominant group. The older woman in the family gains special privileges of power and freedom in society, and she has to be seen to use them properly if she is to keep these status privileges. She does this by ensuring that the rules of the dominant group are being followed and that the system is not disrupted.

Midwives and trained nurses in Sudan occupy a very low socioeconomic status and are labeled with a moral stigma. Their official or government salaries are very low in relation to the general cost of living. Circumcision is an important source of extra income (Graunbaum, 1980). On the other hand, they use their skills and expertise to enjoy a certain amount of social power. This would explain the failure of the health education programs to alter the practices of these midwives and nurses. Appeals to their "sisterly solidarity" with members of their own sex will be ineffective unless they are combined with real change in their social and economic status.

The "inherent" conservatism of women is not so inherent as it is a direct result of their confinement to the private domain. If women were to be exposed more to the faster-changing public sphere through more educational facilities, more employment and equal chances in the different fields of work, and reduced responsibility of care for the family, they might prove to be even less hostile to change than men. For they will soon discover that they are the ones who will gain most from it. Women might have the consciousness of their situation, yet the circumstances of their existence might not allow them to express that consciousness.

The "Absolute" Value of Education and Medicine to the Third World

Nobody would disagree with the importance of increased education and health facilities to an underdeveloped country. It is rather ironic, however, that the same educationalists or policy makers who may discuss the benefits and shortcomings of different educational systems and what purposes they serve in socializing children toward a particular class, ethnic, psychological, or sexual orientation in a literate society would speak of *one* education when it comes to introducing more educational facilities to countries with high illiteracy rates. The same attitude applies to health facilities when nobody questions the moral value of modern medicine, which is taken to be an absolute value in itself.

This is the position taken by international organizations and local groups in favor of abolishing female circumcision. They continue to believe that the advance of education and modern medical facilities will overcome obsolete practices like circumcision. This was the conclusion and guideline for policies made by almost all those involved with the campaign against the practice from as early as 1924 under the British colonial administration to the present day under the banners of the United Nations. Since 1924 women have been educated at all levels. Yet in my experience only a tiny minority of those who received a higher education (i.e., secondary school or university) have escaped the operation of circumcision.

There is more than one issue involved in the question of women's education. First there is the discrimination women suffer in the distribution of the already meager educational facilities, both in terms of number of schools available for girls and the quality of education they are offered. Another important issue in education is its content. The process of reinforcing traditional women's roles and the division of labor according to sex have worked hand in hand with male intellectual elitism in the Sudanese educational system. In the sixteen years I spent in private and government schools in Sudan and in the experience of my family and friends, no information was given about female circumcision. More important, we have not received any education or instruction to help us understand our bodies or to explore our position as women in society. The curricula are totally male oriented (but that is not to say they are neutral) and the only exclusively feminine education we received was cookery, home economics, and needlework.

In the medical schools of the Sudan and Egypt the topic of female circumcision is again ignored, together with any information on women's sexuality. And although the "primary" sexual organs and reproductive parts of the female genital system are studied in detail, very little if anything is mentioned about the external genital organs of the female and least of all their function. The clitoris as a functioning organ is never mentioned in teaching and since it has no place in the British and American gynecology and anatomy books due to the influence of Freudian psychology it is not considered worthy of mention. The case with the male genital system is very different and along with an explanation of the reproductive and hormonal function the anatomy and physiology of the organs are explained within the context of their sexual functions.

As a house officer in Sudan I witnessed hundreds of women suffering from vasicovaginal fistulas.[5] It is a humiliating condition whereby women are constantly leaking and smelling of urine and are rendered untouchable by their community. It was never explained in medical school that the high incidence of this condition was directly connected to infibulation, although its incidence is repeatedly recorded in medical papers and specialized journals.

As we worked in gynecology clinics filled with hundreds of women desperately seeking a solution to their chronic pelvic infection or sublevel fertility, we realized exactly what this meant to them in a place where a woman's fertility defined the reason for her existence. With time, we also learned to define these women as neurotic, depressed, or as malingerers. We were never taught that these women lived an extremely frustrated sexual life, that many were trying to avoid their marital duty (as they see it) of giving sexual pleasure to their husbands for fear of the pain from the scar of pregnancy and its complications. Others were desperate to fulfull their womanhood and prove themselves worthy by bearing children. All felt guilty, inadequate, and in a constant state of depression. All these living examples of an important social problem were ignored and the pathological processes were only partially explained, and in bare medical terms. The connection between these complications and infibulation was rarely if ever mentioned. Exploring "sex as a variable in analysing the professional construction of illness," according to Judith Lorber (1975), might "provide important data on how seemingly scientific knowledge is shaped by the social biases of the producers and users of that knowledge."

The solution of the problem through modern medicine, if not handled properly, could mean a handover of the material and status benefits of the operator (midwives, other women) to the more powerful social group (doctors). This would promote the larger process of the changing modes of female subjugation, with a change from control by the traditional system to control by modern capitalistic means. It may be worth mentioning here that the official policy of the medical profession until February 1979 was not the total abolition of female circumcision, but the promotion of clitoridectomy under more hygienic circumstances as a substitute for infibulation. This process of "modernization" of the operation has acted (and continues to act) as a reinforcement and endorsement of the practice, especially as these "modern" facilities are not available expect to the higher strata of the society, members of which always act as models for the aspirations of the less privileged groups.

Conclusion

Female circumcision, unlike male circumcision, is an act of ablating the sensory organs of a woman's genitals as a means of removing her sexuality while retaining her reproductive functions. The common wisdom of traditional people recognized the clitoris and external genitals as the target organs of female sexual gratification,[6] and by removing them they have succeeded in greatly hindering women's ability to achieve that gratification but not in reducing her sexual desire (Karim and Ammar, 1965; Baashar, 1979). This aggression against female sexuality is only a part of the total process of subordination of women to facilitate the use of their reproductive and productive powers by the patriarchal society. The effects of the operation must be seen beyond their direct physical complications. The process of psychosexual development of the girl is affected directly by the operation itself and indirectly through its social meaning and implications. The act, if seen within the context of creating the overall code of "modesty" described by Antoun (1968), may explain many modes of feminine behavior and the relationship between the sexes prevalent in the society. The self-image of the teenager and later the grown-up woman is shaped to a great extent by this process of socialization. It may create the extremes of severe sexual frustration, fear of sexual desire, and a humiliating sense of shame and guilt for its existence. It may also partially explain exaggerated traits of self-denial, lack of assertiveness, and a fatalistic attitude many women have toward themselves. It may underlie the lack of confidence and drive in taking up risk and challenge that has been interpreted as the conservatism previously mentioned. This does not apply only to a woman's private life, but extends into her modes of participation in public life. The question then arises, can we isolate one physical act against women's sexuality and attempt to abolish it without changing the whole social fabric of the society? Can women be freed from their sexual oppression[7] under patriarchy without changing the conditions of their economic exploitation under feudalism and capitalism? On the other hand, can changing the material, social, and economic conditions under which women live lead to their total emancipation from their sexual oppression? These and many other questions need to be asked and tested in practice as well as in theory. It might be useful, however, to look at two instances where the practice of female circumcision was markedly reduced by two different processes.

In Egypt until the 1950s the practice was very popular in the rural areas and still had a strong hold among the urban population. In the following two decades of Nasser's regime, the practice showed a marked recession toward the periphery and its remnants were found in areas least affected by the social revolution and among groups who benefited least from the revolution's economic reforms. This could be paralleled to the overall changed conditions for women in real terms: equal opportunities in education, skill training, and employment and full political rights, backed by a constitution that stressed the importance of the equality of women for the success of the revolution. The legislation in 1953 banning all forms of circumcision was the least popularized and no special campaign was singled out for it. As Egyptian women gained ground at all levels, an obsolete practice such as female circumcision could not persist against the new tide of a rising feminist consciousness.

The second example is Ethiopia. When the Eritrean People's Liberation Front occupied large areas between January 1977 and December 1978, as part of their social reforms they campaigned against and successfully banned genital mutilation and forced marriage. Later, after the Front's retreat from these areas, the practice did not return and many women from other areas joined the liberation army to avoid forced marriage or the knife (MRG Report no. 47).

The first example demonstrates how the actual change of the material, social, and political position of women leads to changes in their consciousness of their sexual oppression and in their powers to change it. In the second the change took place not in material and social conditions but in political awareness and participation in an armed struggle; women began to fight for their social, sexual, and economic rights. I believe we cannot separate these two mechanisms as they feed into each other through a synergistic process.

To Marx's statement "It is not the consciousness of men [and women] that determines their existence but on the contrary their social existence determines their consciousness," we have to add the experience of the feminist movement, which has demonstrated that the changing of women's consciousness is a way for them to begin to fight to change their own social existence.

NOTE: *This paper was delivered at a conference entitled "New Research in Sudan" at the University of Durham, Durham, England, summer 1981.*

Notes

1. Mustafa states, "Tiganni, who was the only psychiatrist in the Sudan for several years, does not recollect meeting any psychological problems caused by circumcision. On the contrary, he thinks it is a custom that is as strong as a religious conviction and provides a 'happy social occasion' for Sudanese women who normally enjoy little in the way of entertainment" (Tiganni al-Mahi, private letters, 1965). Tiganni al-Mahi was one of the four vanguard Sudanese doctors who signed the 1945 report that condemned Pharaonic circumcision together with the British medical services in Sudan at the time.

2. Miss Woolfe was a British midwife who, together with her sister, wrote the earliest reports on their practical experience with female circumcision in the 1920s. (Sudan Archives).

3. Dr. S. Modawi (a senior gynecologist in Sudan) in his 1977 study of the records of 2,526 women in Khartoum and Medain found that 2,507 were infibulated by the original or modified method, twelve had had clitoridectomies, and seven were uncircumcised. He noted that "although the habit is still practised in some parts of the Sudan it is gratifying to note that it is gradually dying out." He still holds that "the most effective line of attack was a medical one."

4. See Nawal al-Saʿdawi (1980) on the social punishment of female sexuality in Arab countries.

5. A false passage between the bladder and the vagina created during difficult labor by the death of the tissue separating the two organs. This narrow passage in an infibulated woman will be obstructed if she is not defibulated.

6. In the West the situation is very different. The Christian culture denied women's sexuality until Freud recognized the libido. However, at the same time Freud did not recognize the clitoris as an organ of sexual gratification for the "mature" woman, hence the psychological clitoridectomy of the European and American woman. It was not until Masters and Johnson (1966) rediscovered the clitoris and Virginia Sherfie (1966) started questioning Freud's definition that the attitude toward female sexuality in the West changed.

7. As defined by Eisenstein (1979).

References

Al-Dareer, A. "A Study on the Prevalence and Epidemiology of Female Circumcision in Sudan." *WHO/EMRO Technical Publications* 2 (1979). (Report of a seminar held in Khartoum, February 10–15, 1979).
Al-Saʿdawi, N. *The Ḥidden Face of Eve: Women in the Arab World.* London: Zed Press, 1980.

Antoun, R. "On the Modesty of Women in Arab Moslem Villages: A Study in the Accommodation of Traditions." *American Anthropologist* 70 (1968): 671.

Ardener, E. "Belief and the Problem of Women." In S. Ardener (ed.), *Perceiving Women*. London: Malaby Press, 1975.

Ardener, S. "The Nature of Women in Society." In S. Ardener (ed.), *Defining Female*. London: Croom Helm, 1978.

Assaad, M. "Female Circumcision in Egypt." *WHO/EMRO Technical Publications* 2 (1979).

Baashar, T. "Psychological Aspects of Female Circumcision." *WHO/EMRO Technical Publications* 2 (1979).

Becker, H. "Outsiders." In *Studies in the Sociology of Deviance*. London: Macmillan, 1973.

Cook, R. "Damage to Physical Health from Pharaonic Circumcision of Females: A Review of the Medical Literature." *WHO/EMRO Technical Publications* 2 (1979).

Eisenstein, Z. "Developing a Theory of Capitalist Patriarchy and Socialist Feminism." In Z. Eisenstein (ed.), *Capitalist Patriarchy and the Case for Socialist Feminism*. New York: Monthly Review Press, 1979.

Goode, W. *World Revolutions and Family Patterns*. New York: Free Press, 1970.

Graunbaum, E. "The Movement against Clitoridectomy and Infibulation in Sudan: Public Health Policy and the Women's Movement." Paper presented at the annual meeting of the American Anthropological Association, Washington, D.C., December 6, 1980.

Hassan, Y. F. *The Arabs and the Sudan*. Edinburgh: Edinburgh University Press, 1967.

Hastrup, K. "The Semantics of Biology: Virginity." In S. Ardener (ed.), *Defining Female*. London: Croom Helm, 1978.

Hathout, H. M. "Some Aspects of Female Circumcision." *Journal of Obstetrics and Gynecology* 70 (1963): 505–507.

Hosken, F. *The Hosken Report—Genital and Sexual Mutilation of Females*. 2nd ed. Lexington, Mass.: Women's International Network, 1979.

Huber, A. "Die weibliche Beschneidung." *Zeitschrift für Topenmedizin und Parasitologie* 20 (1969): 1–9.

James, W. "Matrifocus on African Women." In S. Ardener (ed.), *Defining Female*. London: Croom Helm, 1978.

Karim, M. and R. Ammar. *Female Circumcision and Sexual Desire*. Cairo: Ain Shams University Press, 1965.

Lorber, J. "Women and Medical Sociology: Invisible Professionals and Ubiquitous Patients." In Millman and Kanter (eds.), *Another Voice*. New York: Anchor Press/Doubleday, 1975.

Lowenstein, L. "Attitude and Attitude Differences to Female Genital Mutilation in the Sudan: Is There a Change on the Horizon?" *Social Science and Medicine* 12 (1978): 417–421.

Marx, K. *Capital*. Vol. 1, *Process of Capitalist Production*. Moscow: Foreign Languages Publishing House, 1954.

Mernissi, F. *Beyond the Veil: Male-Female Dynamics in a Modern Muslim Society.* Cambridge, Mass.: Schenkman, 1975.

Minority Rights Group Report no. 47. "Female Circumcision, Excision and Infibulation: The Facts and Proposals for Change." 36 Craven Street, London WC2N 5NG.

Modawi, S. "The Impact of Social and Economic Changes on Female Circumcision." *Proceedings of the Third Congress of Obstetrics and Gynaecology.* Khartoum, April 1973, Sudan Medical Association Congress Series no. 2, 1977.

Mustafa, A. Z. "Female Circumcision and Infibulation in the Sudan." *Journal of Obstetrics and Gynaecology of the British Commonwealth* 33 (April 1966): 302–306.

PMC guide du Sudan 1980. Planning and Management Consultancy, P.O. Box 1672, Khartoum, Sudan.

Shaalan. "Clitoris Envy: A Psychodynamic Construct Instrumental in Female Circumcision." *WHO/EMRO Technical Publications* 2 (1979).

Shandalla, A. A. "Circumcision and Infibulation of Females." *Sudan Medical Journal* 5 (1967): 178–212.

Sudan Archives. Miss Woolfe's letters. Cir. Sec. 44/2/12.

————. "Report on Female Circumcision in the Anglo-Egyptian Sudan." Sudan Medical Service, Khartoum, 1.3.1945. I Reports 4/1/1.

Taba, A. "Female Circumcision." *WHO/EMRO Technical Publications* 2 (1979).

Verzin, J. A. "Sequelae of Female Circumcision." *Tropical Doctor* 5 (1975): 163–169.

PART IV
War, Politics, and Revolution

Conflict—local, national, or international—has characterized the Middle East for the past fifty years. During that time, of course, conflict has been in evidence throughout the world, but because of the attention of the Western media, the Middle East seems to be a major focus of strife. This attention is due to the area's position within spheres of interest of the great powers. Further, the nationalist strivings of different countries in the Middle East have affected and been affected by Western politics and economics.

Turkey declared its independence in the 1920s, but most other countries in the Middle East and North Africa did not gain freedom from colonial rule until the 1950s. Since that decade, every nation in the area has experienced changes in political leadership, some of them violent. The one exception is Saudi Arabia, which was never occupied by Western colonial powers. While the rest of the area was in the process of political transformation, Saudi Arabia continued to be ruled by the House of Saud, which came to power in 1932.

Most recently, the Iranian revolution of 1978 sent shock waves throughout the Islamic world. As of 1983, the war in Afghanistan had not ended, nor had the Iraq-Iran war. The struggle in the southern Sahara was still in progress and the Arab-Israeli conflict far from settled. The possible long-term effects of these events in the region are yet to be analyzed in the West and the events themselves only superficially known. We hear about the battles, but not the battles' aftermath. We know little of the painful day-to-day rebuilding of homes, markets, trade routes, schools, and hospitals or of the settlement of refugees. Lebanon, however, is something of an exception. Following the 1982 Israeli invasion, much information has come out of Lebanon, a country whose people have faced civil strife since 1975 and that has also been a battleground in the Arab-Israeli conflict.

Wars affect the lives of young and old. Where warfare has not consumed their relatives and their friends, destroyed their homes and their sources of livelihood, it has blunted aspirations and ideals, shifted personal goals, and disrupted traditional family patterns. Some observers have argued that prolonged violent conflict encourages men and women to cast off old roles and to develop new and more egalitarian male-female relationships. However, current evidence indicates that after the immediate situation of common danger has ended, women and men revert to older patterns. This was true in Algeria after the ten-year struggle against French rule, and the materials presented here not only corroborate the Algerian experience but suggest that we in the West who have not experienced such conflict first-hand tend to romanticize the battle or revolutionary situation when we see it as an arena for equalizing men's and women's roles.

Not all women can play heroic roles or even become directly involved in the conflict. In a Palestinian refugee camp in south Lebanon in 1981, a mother of five, when asked what the role of women should be in revolution, replied, "A woman must do what is required of her. She may have to learn to use a gun. But a woman with small children, what can she do?" Her husband, a commando fighter, said, "Women are precious in revolutionary situations. Through bombs and shells, they keep life going."

The materials that follow are expressions of individual people's views presented in different forms. Fadwa Tuqan, a widely published and respected Arab poet, writes about the effect of war on her family and her friends, who are Palestinians, refugees, and exiles. But many other ethnic groups are exiles and refugees in the area today. The excerpt from Emily Nasrallah's novel describes friendship between women, a friendship affected by separation during the civil war. She hints, however, at other problems, at other kinds of distances between women in Lebanon based on class or on economic or educational differences.

Rosemary Sayigh's paper, "Encounters with Palestinian Women under Occupation," deals directly with the problem of the relationship between the ideology of the "national problem" and the ideology of the "woman question." She places the issue in its specific social context and, through interviews with women of many different interests and involvement in politics and resistance, provides us with a clearer picture of what the Palestinian woman herself sees as her problems. The role of the Palestinian woman is quite different from the role of a Western woman, she points out, adding that "for liberal Western feminists the family rather than the state is the source of women's oppression, and they have traditionally attacked 'patriarchy' at the family level without looking at larger political/economic frameworks that organize family relations." Women speak here for themselves and ask for a just policy that includes them in both the nationalist and feminist spheres. But, Sayigh cautions, "theorization is of no use if it does not make contact with people's real lives," and states that we still only poorly understand the conditions of Palestinian women's lives, their reactions to those conditions, and their very considerable achievements.

The Beirut teenagers whose world was shattered by the civil war of 1976 are now young adults trying to deal with a new disaster and rebuild their country after the 1982 Israeli invasion. Some of their underlying feelings and beliefs and recollections of the 1975–76 war are summarized

in the sociological study undertaken by the newspaper *L'Orient de jour* in cooperation with a
Beirut research center. In the course of the study
nearly nine hundred Lebanese men and women
between the ages of sixteen and twenty-two were
interviewed.

Of course, Lebanon is hardly representative of
the entire Middle East. Different ideological conflicts and varying economic and political situations have produced the refugees, the divided
families found throughout the area in many countries today. Yet human suffering is the same, the
effects as catastrophic no matter what the context
or underlying ideology. We have fewer reports
from other areas, but the effect of conflict on a
single individual is eloquently stated in "The
Aunt of Rafiq," Daisy al-Amir's short story about
an unnamed young woman who works for an unnamed cause in an unnamed country. What is
happening to me? Who is responsible? What are
we doing with our lives? The situations may
differ, but the questions are the same. The young
women as well as the young men in the Muslim
Middle East are asking such questions daily. The
answers are not yet forthcoming.

Poems

FADWA TUQAN
Translated from the Arabic by Tim Mitchell

BETWEEN EBB AND FLOW

When words
on falsehood's tongue
turn jellied
I shrink and withdraw,
blend back, diminished,
within myelf, contract.
Wherever the way is jellied
I step aside, avoid the sticking
of humankind and shun
the pathway's quick-silvered untruth,
hold myself together, lest I slip,
test each foot on the soapy ground,
my clenched palm untendered.
I loathe the touch of things, loathe
the ugliness of smiles and curse
the sly animality of man.

But when I am embraced by a child
who touches to my weary face
the nap of his cheek,
his tender palms,
and fingers of a lily
on which no talon ever grew
and his two eyes look down on mine
like a heaven the angels of light
have rinsed in a cool dawn

my heart stretches and grows large
its enclosing walls break loose
the polar river gushes through
trees spring up within
and from exile
to my spacious heart returns
the face of man.

A PAINFUL LONGING

We are still under anesthetic
still asleep on the couch
year passes after year
after year after year
the very earth shakes us and the roof
collapses sod upon sod
and the falsehood is drawn over us
from the top of our head
to our feet

Brothers! Inevitable you say?
Ahh, oh Vietnam
if a million warriors
from your heroes
an east wind dropped
over the Arabian desert
pillows would be furnished
and a million fecund daughters of Arabia!
.   .   .   .

Sir, my apologies, madam.
So painful is this longing
yet we have nothing left
from you, save a clattering
of voices, the basic things we've lost.
We've grown weary, my friends,
of sprinkling sugar on the dead.

ETAN IN THE STEEL NETTING

"One morning, one of the kindergarten children at the kibbutz of Ma'uz
Hayim asked: How long must we go on guarding our country?"

Beneath the Tree
branching larger
in wild enlarging rhythms
beneath the Star
building the dream's
bloodied walls, stitching
in steel threads the net
that pulls him down and plunders
him his movement
Etan opens his eyes, the human child,
and asks within this veil of darkness
the meaning of the walls and the wire
and the passing legs of amputated time
clad in khaki, in death's austerity
in smoke, in sorrows

If the Star would fortell the truth, if . . .
but the Star . . .
         So sorry

Etan my child you are drowning in lies
and the landing stage as well
in a sea of lies, submerged
pulled down by the swollen
reptile-headed
thousand-limbed
dream
Ahh
stay human my child!
I dread and fear for you
growing bigger within this net
in this time on amputated legs
clad in khaki, in death's austerity
in fires, in sorrows

I fear my child, lest the human in you
be killed,
be dragged down by the fall
tumbling
    down
        down
            down
                into the abyss

A SMALL SONG TO DESPAIR

*Dedicated to Aisha Ahmed Auda in return for the inspiring letter she
sent me from the Central Prison, Nablus*

. . . when he stretches, pulls, tears, pounds,
shakes me
plants date-palms in me
ploughs the garden of my soul
and brings it clouds
then the rain pours down upon it
the trees turn to leaf
and I know
that life remains a friend
and that the moon
though it stray from me
shall know toward me its path

The Kalashnikov Generation

MAROUN BAGHDADI and NAYLA DE FREIGE
Translated from the French by J. M. McDougal

The material that follows is adapted from a series of articles that appeared in Beirut's French-language daily newspaper, L'Orient de jour, *during the spring of 1979. At that time the worst of the battles of the 1975–76 civil war had ended. The articles resulted from a research project designed to explore the effects of the war on the youth of Lebanon. The material is based on the responses of a random sample of nearly nine hundred Lebanese youth between the ages of sixteen and twenty-two to a set of fifty-four questions prepared by the authors in cooperation with a Beirut research institute. The sample was drawn from a cross section of the society—nearly all political parties, religious groups, and socioeconomic levels were represented. (Note: A Kalashnikov is a Russian-manufactured gun used extensively in recent wars worldwide.)*

At the age when one dreams of America or of streetcorner adventures, at the age of carefree living, of first loves, first sorrows, and first failures, youth in Lebanon have had to confront the sordid, implacable, and deadly reality of war—the folly and excess of adults. A fine introduction to the world these thousands of young people were given—this nightmare of an unending war of attrition! Thus was the Kalashnikov generation born: fruit of fanaticism, racism, intolerance, violence, and corruption. And, as we shall see, this generation began to achieve its liberation only at the end of a long and painful birth.

Seventy-three percent of the school-age Lebanese youth (sixteen to twenty-two years of age) who answered our questionnaire are seriously interested in politics: 91 percent read one or two political newspapers every day, 56 percent have aligned themselves with political parties, and of these 61 percent were members of these parties during the war. Finally, 32 percent carried arms during the war (43 percent of the men and 13 percent of the women).

These statistics are eloquent. The idea that the Lebanese seek only the "good life" must be abandoned. In the shadow of its most anarchic and pluralist democracy, Lebanon henceforth can take pride in having the most profoundly political youth in the Arab world. Whereas neighboring states rarely are able to mobilize their youth (rarely do they want to) around invigorating themes of exemplary national achievements, Lebanon has developed one of the most explosive concoctions in the region: young people who are not willing to dissociate politics from their everyday lives and personal happiness. Thus, Lebanese youth are expiating for their parents the numerous sins of carelessness and individualism accumulated since independence. Our young continue to ski, to dance, to drink, to go to the cinema, to read—to live. But they also make war, are active in combative political parties, and daily devour the current political scene. They no longer consume politics; they practice politics with their very bodies.

What is it exactly to be seriously involved in politics? For Michel it is "taking one's future in hand and forgetting family conventions"; for Fouad it is "to be involved more and more in reality." For Joseph it is perhaps more pressing. Joseph doesn't want to think of the future, but rather the present: "It is this moment I seek to control, for we must once and for all be rid of those who traffic in our destiny." These young people have had it. They are fed up with their elders deciding for them. They want to take a more active part in forming the society in which they want to live. All were rudely awakened to a nation on fire. Each in his own way realized that a little of their future was disappearing in flames. And they saw above all that war could not be made without them.

"They needed us. We had to fight. And I can assure you from the bottom of my heart that I got involved for me . . . only for me. I didn't have to think about my elders. They had only to leave.

"You know, I had so often heard my father over the years telling stories, silly things, that I had only one thought: to go see if all that was true. And for once he wasn't off." Kamal was seventeen years old in 1975. He had never seriously read a newspaper. "The sports page maybe. . . . Do you realize, they teach you all year at school to knock a ball around, and then one day, you find yourself on a barricade knocking around with a rifle against a guy on the other side who used to knock around the same ball. I thought about that a lot . . . sometimes at night, after drinking a little. Got a lot of crazy looks. I imagined everything was like a basketball game. Really. Since then, I've learned that one distraction is like another. To read the newspapers to look for the names of the dead. It was a game. Sometimes there were names I recognized."

Antoine's politicization is less cynical. He saw it coming. His father had always been involved in politics and often received apparently important people who would regularly announce the imminence of unavoidable catastrophes. Antoine was bored during these luncheons and was reproached for being too interested in motorcycles and girls. That was true until the day he refused to leave Lebanon and accompany his father and all the family to France. "I learned everything all of a sudden. Before, we didn't understand anything about it. There were too many combinations. The war clarified everything."

Here then, we have the summary point of view of thousands of young people who suddenly awoke to politics when it began more and more to resemble a game of "cops and robbers" or a basketball game, only with real dead and wounded. Politics became "purified." There was no more talk, no more pretentious lectures, no more demagogic speeches . . . there was a call to war and that was all. Fight or keep quiet. Keep quiet or die. Suddenly there were people dying for their ideas. This solidification of politics on the field of battle certainly created a new political result, one that was physical and immediate. Death became the immediate penalty for a logistical or strategic error. It was no longer a formal game, but rather a Machiavellian Russian roulette. Short-sighted politics were relegated to the rear. In front were left only those ready to play the game to the end, the end being unavoidable—death. The intrusion of risk must have been a factor determining the massive adherence of youth to a system of politics that had for two years become a deadly poker game.

Sami is twenty. His mother always repeated that there were only two idols to venerate: "Notre Dame de Harissa, for she watches over Jounieh, and Camille Chamoun, for he watches over Lebanon."

Sami still believes in them. "The president is our conscience, our honor, our pride . . . for me he symbolizes the resistance to every form of foreign oppression and the irreversible attachment to our identity, to our roots. My father was a peasant. He sacrificed everything to give us life and as much learning as possible. I must never forget that. Someone like Camille Chamoun constantly reminds me of that sacrifice."

But there is also Karim, who is finishing his science exams and who will go to the United States if everything goes right. "I lost two years of my life believing that something could change. But each side is as bad as the other. All sharks. No one will come out of this war clean. It got all of us dirty."

This disgust is revealing. It is a sort of index of a generation that wants to reject the abuses, the compromises, and the failures of the preceding one, all the rottenness upon which we have built our quasi-state.

Throughout the youths' narrative runs an unbearable anguish about the war. But if we emphasize the positive results of the war, as Mounir Chamoun likes to do, we have to mention the new autonomy that has been achieved by the young over the last three years. They found themselves in a situation of having to decide on their present and, to a certain extent, on their future.

Jihad, who was at all the fronts, was fascinated by the warriors' bearing behind their "Doushkas" in the jeeps.[1] "I did everything to get behind one of those guns and I got there. It was like airborne water-skiing! It was behind my 'Doushka' that I found my independence. It's true. One day I went home after a week's absence. And my vision of my parents had completely changed. I looked at them differently, and they couldn't understand anything. I found my father pitiful, really pitiful. And me, I was so powerful, yes, powerful. Do you understand this sensation of force, of sudden power, to have in your hand your own life, your own death?"

Charles: "I don't regret anything. I keep feeling an immense pride at the idea of having fought for my country. And my country is my home, it's this piece of land my ancestors inhabited. It is in their image, in the image of their struggle over the centuries to protect themselves from invaders. Now my pride has no match except for my contempt for all those who left during the fighting. Those who want to taste the fruits, but who fled the harvest. Well, we made the harvest, and now eternally they owe us their survival. Listen, it's worse than that: I have much more respect for the fighter on the other side than I did for my neighbor who fled."

Tony: "We were fighting with our backs to the sea. In a way, we had this grandiose feeling of fighting for our own civilization. In the end, we don't care about the West. Our civilization is our way of life, this mélange of cultures, this sweet life, the Mediterranean, the blue sky. I'm not being poetic. Maybe a little, but we needed a lot of poetry, a lot of romanticism to carry out this absurd war."

Samir, twenty-one, was at the siege of Tell Zaatar.[2] "Zaatar was agony for me. I began to doubt myself, really. At the time, I didn't dare talk too much. I wasn't sure . . . The impression of having gone too far. You know, like when you fire a rocket and you hear the cries of children afterward. I'm sure it was in my head. An illusion. Yes, an illusion. It's just to say that at the end I was completely out of touch with everything. I couldn't get by without the strength of pills . . . 'speed' and such. Today, when I think about it, it's like a nightmare."

A nightmare of mud and blood. It had rained that day at Damour.[3] It had also rained the day after Quarantaine.[4] And the memories of Jihad and Pierre will always be stained with mud and with blood. Jihad: "You know, the photograph of the little girl with her doll dragging in a sea of blood? That was my first vision of Damour. And then the cries, the cries of women and children. I surprised myself when I realized I was firing in the air so as not to hear the cries. Even in my sleep I heard the cries and again I saw the little girl and her doll. One day I had drunk and smoked a lot; I don't remember any more; I talked about Damour to my friends. They didn't give a damn about it. They didn't understand anything. They told me we had to avenge the Quarantaine."

Quarantaine. Pierre was there. "I didn't toss off the champagne. Nor did I vomit. Yet you can be sure that I went through the most extraordinary battle of my life. When I think about it, I see myself vomiting gobs. There was this body of this old woman next to a tree. Hideous. And afterward I felt this incomprehensible need to go to confession. But I couldn't tell the priest anything, nothing. I didn't kill in cold blood. Never. But the awful sensation of having dirtied my hands. It's ridiculous, isn't it. . . ." The kind of disgust that lives on in the memory of hundreds of young people. But this feeling is rarely admitted because the standards are of pride, of power, of duty fulfilled. So the disgust and horror linger, but as uncertainty and doubt.

Marwan sketched the war for us, and his watercolors carry the traces of a memory definitively slaughtered and scorched. A dominating color, maroon, was "the ever-present bloody mud."

The kinship with death is an antagonistic one, mixed with revolt and defeat. A suicidal relationship. What could be more contradictory than the powerful instinct for life that one feels at the threshold of adulthood and this awful death administered by the most tragic of wars? What a sad entry into life, through the doorway of military regimentation. Macabre, bloody . . . but egalitarian, isn't it, Joumana, so proud of having carried arms, so proud of having won your equality in risk, in danger, in death?

Joumana: "It was a chance . . . and I had to seize it in flight. I went through two training camps and no one wanted to believe that I'd finish. Finally, I went into the streets, carrying weapons, and I fought. I'm not ashamed to admit that my femininity blossomed during the war. I've never thought of femininity as standing in front of a mirror daubing make-up on my face. I was only concerned with having the same rights as any man, for it was *our* destiny, all of us, that mattered." Neither a woman with her cosmetics nor a tomboy, Joumana, twenty, says: "It's enough to refuse the pre-established roles: women in the house, men in combat."

All the women did not stay at home.

Many involved themselves in the reality around them. Lina, who was in the secretariat of a political party: "The political mobilization was just as important as the battles. We had to create a psychological mobilization to keep people in a perpetual state of alert. We had to support the fighters."

Marcelle benefited from her training at the Red Cross by doing voluntary work in a party dispensary: "I can assure you that they needed us. I'm not joking."

There is also the eternal nurse as portrayed in films and novels; the sweet, tender woman who alleviates pain. It is Siham, and Carol. It is all those who felt the need to make themselves useful in caring for the wounded who came back day and night from the front. "In every woman there is a nurse sleeping," says Carol, who nevertheless admits she was exposed to growing ennui in her volunteer work.

And finally there are the *pasionarias*, the inevitable female mobilizers in all tragic and interminable wars. Mouna, Nadine, Colette, and others who drafted the leaflets, distributed provisions, organized collections, and held hundreds of meetings, debates, and discussions. They made war as the war allowed and as the society would tolerate. For there was a certain resistance to be overcome in the face of this intrusion of women (too rapid for some) into politics. Politics was still a man's responsibility, wasn't it?

Joumana, who fought, called their relation to war "physical." She speaks of it as though it were an obvious substitute for the familial cocoon. "My boyfriend left me two months after the beginning of the fighting. He couldn't put up with the idea of me being at the front while he stayed home. I forgot all about it quickly. In fact, I didn't think anymore about it the very next day. I didn't feel like seeing him anymore." The weapon for the woman was a tool that sowed death, but also "an instrument one comes to understand, that gives you security and confidence in yourself: no man can take you when you have one."

Joumana speaks of her Kalashnikov as "a new power," a re-found sexuality: "My charm, my only attraction was in my Kalashnikov. The rest was secondary." A morbid response, but it was one that Joumana was quick to rationalize: "It is, if you want, my way of vengeance, my way of saying 'the hell with it!' to my family and to all those who never understood anything about my desire for independence. You know, before the war I was talking about leaving. I was fed up with everything and I was going from one disappointment to the other with the same disillusionment. Finally, I was almost embittered. I was anxious and bored. My friends were bored . . . they smoked a lot, they got drunk all the time and were slowly degenerating. I was just like them in this agony since we were living through the same experience. Today, I feel that I've gotten away from that . . . a little in my own way, maybe. That's to say, in the most extreme way."

Joumana the extremist, so extremist that today she has only one desire: "making war again as soon as possible." If not? "If not, I'll leave . . ." Joumana, twenty-two, who still happily dreams of the outbreak of hostilities; she will either leave or make war. In fact, it is this intolerable situation of "no war, no peace" that people like Joumana can't live with.

Young men and young women have both lived through the same tragedy—some on the front, and some behind the lines. This has, perhaps, permitted women to increase the territory of their independence, for they were needed in the war. But, as always, as in times of peace, a division of labor was the rule: to the women went the subsidiary jobs—clerical, medical, organizing supplies. But we must also realize that the war contributed to the rapprochement of the sexes. Women and men, side by side, took part in the same combat.

Nayla: "We were united and equal in death, and we knew that day after day." Unity and equality in death were there for whomever looked for them on the macabre battlefield.

Pierre: "Death? I didn't really think about death. Death is always in front of you, or beside you, or behind you. It's never you who are going to die. Death is fear. If you catch that virus, you're screwed. When you're on the battlefield and the bullets are whistling in your ears, you must not doubt. One wrong move and you're off on the long trip."

Jihad: "Death is the others, those who die next to me. I never imagined my own death, but I did see the death of others."

Marwan: "I felt dead ten times during the war. But I don't regret any of those ten. I'm not crazy, but I assure you that for every fear there is a corresponding death."

Joumana: "I'm not dead and I certainly don't want to think about it now. Because I want to fight again. When you're there on the front, death is in the air. You breathe it. It's not an abstract thing like it is in the philosophy books."

Samir: "I told my friends that if I were gravely wounded I wanted them to finish me off. Above all, not to take me home. It was the only obsession I had. . . ."

Fady: "I was afraid to die alone, abandoned by my friends. I only fought along with my friends. I was sure that if I fell, they would carry me away."

Sami: "We didn't talk about death. You die and that's it. Death is an instant. I haven't lived it yet. That's why I can talk to you now."

And yet death, risked and played with, was always present. It was, traditionally speaking, a phony war: fighting in the streets, the Battle of the Motels, the mountain battle, the sieges of Quarantaine and Tell Zaatar. It was a strange war, as Joe said so well: "It was a little like a festival. With a bizarre joy. It was a war that fit us. We were suddenly the masters of a city that had frequently scorned us."

Samir: "We were everywhere. We were the kings. I suddenly felt that everything could belong to me. We went into marvelous houses, palaces like you see in the cinema. Beirut was at our feet."

But today all that has changed, at least for some of these young people. It is no longer a war of men, but a real war. The Kalashnikov war is over, now it is a full-scale war, the war of exchanging artillery fire. We can better understand the disillusionment if we realize that today these young people must run to shelters to protect themselves from bombs.

Joe: "The war we're leading today is really shitty. It's a war of wearing out the other, a war of endurance. This war that throws us into the shelters is unbearable."

This war is unbearable for the many who were there for adventure, the fresh air, and for friends. This new war is too regular. Too serious. Before, they died unconsciously, in fresh air, in movement. They fought. Today they die in one place, buried under debris and dust.

But many are still ready to die like others before them.

Why do they die? Why do they look for death? God and country. Country and family. Family and land. Land and honor. Honor alone. The family alone. The country alone.

Farid: "The country, our country. Independent. Purged of these bad elements. Cleaned up. Purified. We want to live with respect."

Jihad: "For the disinherited. All of them. It is our war. The war of the poor."

Sami: "For the country and my family, and for Lebanese sovereignty."

Marcel: "For the country, against feudalism, corruption, and foreigners."

Marwan: "For democracy, for the unity of Lebanon."

Nagi: "For secularization, unity, and democracy."

Jamal: "For the Arabism of Lebanon and its unity."

Nayla: "For socialism and women."

Fadia: "For honor."

Khalil: "For me."

Outside there is war. Yet everywhere the instinct to live still flourishes—the need to survive no matter what the cost. This entails the repudiation of anything that might reduce or limit the chances of survival. Such urgency has swept away restrictive and repressive norms of conduct. Now there are fewer rules and the new code of physical and moral movement is anarchic and flexible. Family constraints are reduced and the social constraints shifted elsewhere. The family hasn't actually exploded . . . it has suffered the same inevitable distortion that the society at large has had more or less to accept.

This relaxation of social constraints has contributed to creating a favorable climate for new human relations. The degree of autonomy recently acquired by young people confirms their new independence, their relative tolerance, and their extreme politicization. Even the image of the couple and the family has changed. Their physical relations are very different from those of their parents. One must remember that the survey dealt with young people who were attending university; still, the figures are surprising. Fifty percent of the youth admit to having had sexual relations (76 percent of the men and 21 percent of the women, of whom the Christian/Muslim ratio was about even). More than 56 percent of these 50 percent (28 percent of the total interviewed) had these relations in the period of second adolescence (from sixteen to nineteen years of age). Fifteen percent (a large proportion) had their first sexual relations before sixteen and 7 percent after nineteen. This represents a real affirmation of sexual autonomy among young people. There has also been an increase in sexual activity among the younger age groups, mainly attributable to the dissolution of family constraints.

Youth are "liberating" themselves. In a sometimes disorderly way, they are breaking the taboos and are abandoning their guilt at the threshold of their incomplete adolescence. Certainly they have become fiercely independent: they have invented a freewheeling amorous language whose vocabulary is primarily instrumental, and many of them are losing their sacred idols—even John Travolta doesn't hold their attention longer than a season. But in this sudden emancipation, today's youth also are losing a large part of their romanticism. In fact, romanticism is already the property of another generation.

Today the youth no longer walk secretly in dim, dark streets. They no longer send passionate messages nor keep intimate diaries. They do not often dream. They only get involved in practical matters; they reject melancholy reveries. The war has diminished their ardor a little and maybe rusted their imagination. The girls don't faint anymore at the first kiss and the boys no longer say "I love you" as feverishly as before. Today it's more like "I feel good with you," or "I feel good," or, for the most jaded, "It's OK." You can also keep your mouth shut and just put on your shoes. That's called "floating off." High-flying lyrics—"that's weird." Lover's desperation—"that's all over with." Werther died a long time ago.

The cycle is irreversible, the movement has already begun: 48 percent of the youth (67 percent of the boys and 33 percent of the girls) think that premarital relations are necessary and 30 percent think they are acceptable. Only 14 percent reject them. Sexual tolerance is evident among the majority.

For many young people (mainly in families of the higher income levels) their first sexual experiences occurred during a long voyage to Europe where the mores facilitated, if not accelerated, sexual autonomy in the past. But there are also 49 percent who have had no sexual experience. Thus the weight of the old society is still present and the few wartime years of moral relaxation are not enough to jar completely the ideology of a country that is still deeply subjected to religious pressures. Sexuality remains a traumatizing force at least for the majority of young people because the culture surrounding them still contributes to making it so. Joseph has not yet had a real sexual experience "because of the lack of opportunity." Fady hasn't because he's "looking for his great love." Aida: "I'm keeping myself for the father of my children." Hanan hasn't because "my father would kill me." Samir: "Girls are all bitches." Mounir: "I'm too young and I don't go out much." Siham: "I want to keep one chance to get married." Wadad: "It's a sin." And Najila: "My mother told me about her own catastrophic experience with my father." Najila, for whom sexuality is stained by sin, the original sin. Najila, who doesn't want to "sully" herself and who will probably go to a convent. At least that's what she says. She will thus preserve her chastity. And everything will be in order in a spiritual paradise.

But what to do? Wait for Prince Charming, curly and blond or dark and handsome? Who will deliver the maiden from her immaculate phantom? Women still fear "this inherent brutality in men," as Jocelyn says. Still, maybe with a little sweetness, a lot of tenderness, our young men may be able to succeed in appeasing the fears of Jocelyn, Rima, in allaying all those misgivings of women that make up their fear of leaving childhood behind.

Despite some of these uncertainties and ambiguities among the young people, we find a clear increase in tolerance and an understanding of change. Their expressed tolerance is based on better knowledge of life and on a better attitude toward the other person. They grant the other the liberty to change, to be different. As they are open to the world and become more sensitive to the sounds of a society in mutation, sexuality tends more and more to take on a healthy pace, accompanying a psychic opening up to the world. They say they no longer walk into marriage as into a pagan ceremony where the sacrificial beast must bleed to be agreeable to the gods. Marriage has become a place of encounter.

For Simone: "The premarital experience is necessary, absolutely necessary. It is vital for the psychological health of the couple."

Dany: "How can you pretend to know someone if you are ignorant of his body? Physical attraction is primordial. It's instinct. It's essential."

Amin: "I don't want to marry an unknown, and I wouldn't want to be an unknown to my wife. It is through the body that feelings travel."

Faced with life and a threatening future, the youth, male and female, henceforth want to assume the same responsibilities. Thus, in regard to the socioprofessional integration of women, 55 percent say they are enthusiastic and 21 percent express an evident tolerance to let women do what they want. Five percent say they would forbid their wives to work. The young people are tending toward a sort of egalitarian relationship based on mutual respect and reciprocal consideration.

For Michel: "It's a guarantee of evenness in a couple to share the responsibilities." For Kamal: "It is vital that each has his own life, his own interests." For Nayla: "No one should be the blind follower of another." For Colette: "I would never accept the pre-established role of wife in the home, caring for children and cooking." For Isaam: "We must not repeat the errors of our parents. Those who hold repressive machismo ideas represent only the last resistance to an irreversible evolution. This evolution is based on a new rather positive rapport between boys and girls."

The war, by reducing social pressures and familial constraints, has facilitated, if not favored, contacts between young people. It has reduced the distance. The menaced social group became a community in spite of itself. Seventy-three percent of the youth affirm that the war made their relations more free. Eighteen percent think that no real change occurred. This liberty in relations testifies to a sexual relaxing of tension within the new generation. Forty-three percent of the youth (many more Christians than Muslims) feel attraction and 32 percent well-being in the presence of the opposite sex. Twenty percent (more Muslims than Christians) say they feel indifferent. Ten percent feel timidity. The war imposed a new sociability through a network of relations forged over and over again and under dramatic circumstances.

The image of the couple has improved, male-female relations have become more healthy, and the young have acquired a great degree of autonomy. But this autonomy is often to the detriment of the family. The young people now keep their distance from their elders. The war, having relaxed the rigid kin ties, has thus stretched family relations to their limits. The family as an institution does not appear so much dislocated as decaying.

The society still seems far away from the time when young people leave the family home to live alone, to live their lives by themselves according to their own rules. The structure of Lebanese society does not yet allow such an evolution. But the parents are no longer the supreme reference and authority. To the question, "From whom would you ask advice on choosing your spouse?" 61 percent of young people responded, "No one." That is to say they wouldn't consult anyone and they're proud of their independent decision. Only 20 percent would consult their friends and 23 percent their parents. Thus, parents are placed at the same level of importance as friends.

Michele: "Why should I ask advice from someone? I hope I can be sure enough of my choice not to do such a silly thing. I would never imply that my parents, who without a doubt hope the best for me, are incompetent. But we don't have the same criteria. I wouldn't be marrying his parents and he wouldn't be marrying mine."

Samir: "My parents? I'll tell them of my decision, but their blessing is not necessary. It's a matter of my life, not theirs. I owe them respect and love. That's enough, isn't it?"

Fadija: "Ask for advice? That means I would be hesitating. I won't hesitate on the choice of my husband."

Despite their experiences, 75 percent of the Lebanese youth see their future in Lebanon. Further, 91 percent believe that their generation will have an influence on that future. They believe their influence will affect social (74 percent) and cultural (71 percent) areas; their vision of the future is still tinged with hope. Fifty-seven percent think that soon Lebanon will be united under a new national organization. But that is the point of view mostly of the Muslims and atheists in the group. The Christians lean more to the opinion that Lebanon will be federated or divided into provinces.

Hicham: "If this war does not result in a new country, it will truly be a catastrophe. All the deaths will have been in vain. All during the war, we felt we were doing this to improve and change our country. Real change."

Andre: "The only perceptible change is in our determination to be independent. We are not changing, why should we change? We are evolving, perhaps."

Selim: "It is almost impossible to unite the country in the name of some newly discovered national entente. It's foolish to believe in unity here where all our efforts have been based on division. The important thing is to recognize our differences and respect them."

The war has developed the young's autonomy at two levels: the level of judgment and the level of behavior.

During truce times and cease-fires the family tried to recover its authority and mend itself. The ultimate recourse is in repression: 31 percent of the young think the war has made their parents more severe and 34 percent believe the war hasn't changed a thing in the attitudes of their mothers and fathers. But, faced with these wrenching developments, where the young have broken the chains of parental authority to liberate themselves and to live better, the family appears more and more like an institution gutted by the crisis.

The youth of Lebanon, this "Kalashnikov Generation," has been radically affected by the 1975–76 war and the failed attempts to resolve the issues that brought it about. Some of the changes have been for the better, we can honestly say, and some for the worse. The final result is yet to come.

What They Read

91 percent read one newspaper, many read two.
Most popular independent nonpartisan presses:
> *Al-nahar* (Arabic), *L'Orient de jour* (French), read by all persuasions and all social levels.

Others:
> *Al-safir* (Arabic), 30 percent, Muslims.
> *Amal* (Arabic), 19 percent, Christian petit bourgeoisie.
> *Watan* (journal of the National Movement), 10 percent, Muslims, atheists from low-income groups.
> *Nida* (organ of the Lebanese Communist party), 5 percent.
> *Ahrar* (organ of the Lebanese National party), 5 percent.

Their Most Admired Figures

None, 23 percent, Muslims, Christians.
Myself, 11 percent, Muslims, Christians.
Kamal Joumblatt, 11 percent, Muslims, Christians, atheists.
Camille Chamoun, 7 percent, 5 percent Christians, 2 percent Muslims.
Pierre Gemayel, 3 percent, Christians.
Gamal Abdel Nasser, 3 percent, Muslims.
Others cited: Gandhi, de Gaulle, Hitler, Khomeini, Arafat, Antoun Sa'ada, Karl Marx, Ché Guevara, Castro, the Prophet Muhammad, Jesus Christ, Michel Berty, Saad Haddad.

Qualities Most Admired

Patriotism, 28 percent.
Intelligence, 22 percent.
Courage and power, 21 percent.
Honesty, 15 percent.

What They Do for Fun

Go for walks (promenade), 50 percent.
Visit friends, 43 percent.
Go to the cinema, 32 percent.
Go to nightclubs, 15 percent.
Go to restaurants, 12 percent.

Notes

1. A nickname for the Kalashnikov.

2. A Palestinian refugee camp in the predominantly Christian suburb of East Beirut. It was besieged by Phalangist Christian forces in August 1976 and fell after a fifty-three-day siege, during which three thousand Palestinians were killed and three thousand wounded. (Figures quoted in the notes are from Walid Khalidi, *Conflict and Violence in Lebanon: Confrontation in the Middle East* [Cambridge: Harvard University Press, 1983].)

3. A Christian Maronite town in South Lebanon. On January 20, 1976, one day after the fall of Quarantaine, Damour was overrun by Palestinian and Lebanese nationalist forces in retaliation for the attack on the Maronite Christian Palestinian refugee camp of Dbaiyeh. The death toll reached five hundred and the town was burned.

4. A slum area of East Beirut inhabited by Muslim Lebanese and some Palestinians. It was attacked by the Phalange on January 19, 1976. The death toll approached one thousand, mostly civilians, and nearly twenty thousand people were left homeless.

Those Memories (from the novel)

EMILY NASRALLAH
Translated from the Arabic by Mohammad Khazali

Chapter 2

Two years ago Hanan left her elegant home in the al-Ramla al-Baida area of Beirut.

I still recall how she came to me on that cold morning, overcome by anxiety, sunk in a mysterious ocean of bewilderment.

"Farid has decided to leave for London," she said. "He believes that there is not much future for his work in Lebanon. So he has signed a contract to work for a British company."

"What about the children?"

The question popped out spontaneously. I did not intend to pry, as that would only have increased her bewilderment. If Farid had decided to work in London, then the children would be with him and he would send them to a school that suited his aristocratic taste. Thus would he satisfy his constant yearning for expatriation.

Farid never let an occasion pass without criticizing Lebanese society: the life-style, the manner of raising children, and the moral degeneracy. And he always yearned for the day when he would escape from the "human hell," as he used to call it, and take his children out of it and into a "civilized world." I would always confront him and try to dissuade him for the sake of Hanan—Hanan, who is deeply rooted in the soil of Beirut, who loves her country in all its beauty and all its ugliness; the tolerant and modest Hanan, who knows how to understand and forgive the mistakes of others and who does not set herself up as a judge over others or wave a sword over the heads of the defenseless and the weak.

I would tell Farid, "Escape does not solve the problem. The responsibility of saving Lebanon lies with you and your peers among educated youth."

He would always turn a deaf ear and close the subject, saying, "I am no social reformer. I am neither a politician nor an artist. I am a man who likes to live in peace. Therefore I will not let the monsters swallow me and my children. I will run with them to the far ends of the earth for the sake of their future."

I would always argue with him. "But Hanan does not share your opinion. You are forcing her to leave."

He would respond decisively, "She is free. Let her stay here beside her mother. But for my part, nothing will stand between me and my decision."

Hanan would lower her head calmly. Farid is stubborn and not to be argued with. Maybe she had tried a lot and wearied of the game. Here she was now, totally resigned, withdrawn into herself and hiding her true feelings. Only when we are alone together, and only then, would she reveal her thoughts. "To you I'm an open book," she would say. "So easy to read." "With you I relax and shed my worries. The flow of our conversation washes away my pain. Do you realize that, Maha?"

Indeed, I realized that fully. My heart grieved for my friend's pain and I felt helpless to change her situation. There are limits to a friend's interference. Farid is sure that he is right, seeking happiness and stability, even through escape.

Hanan is content with her lot. The woman submits to her man. He is her master. This is what the schoolbooks had taught her.

Two years went by. During that period I received news of Hanan from traveling friends. I learned that Farid had bought an elegant house in the suburbs of London, that his work was steadily progressing, and that he was on his way to considerable wealth.

A woman follows her husband while he looks for work, the ladder of his ambition and his glory. Farid's work had led him to one of the plateaus of wealth while his homeland was sinking into the abyss of misery. He would boast to his friends that he had prophesied the eruption in Lebanon and that his prophecy had come true. He had been able to rescue himself and his family at the right time.

This news reached me and increased my anxiety over Hanan. I know her well enough to understand that her silence does not mean content.

I would wonder, How is she able to survive in that land of frost and fog, she who always sought the cozy, warm corners. She who passionately loves the sea of Beirut and its golden beaches!

I would think, and wonder about her fate and the fate of many friends who had left the country while the sky of Beirut rained down missiles and shells and the horror isolated us in shelters and underground vaults where we spent our nights waiting for death, until morning came and then we would start to check on each other and to feel our limbs to see if they were still there.

In those hard moments I would ask myself, Do I wish to be away from my country at its dying moment? Do I envy Hanan and the others like her who ran away? My conscience evoked her reprimanding image, and I regretted my doubts.

Hanan had not chosen her exile, just as she had not chosen the path her life had taken.

Her mother had managed her affairs for her, and her mother had shared Farid's opinion and had tried to convince her only daughter to leave.

"Go, my daughter, go. The future of your children is the most important thing in your life."

And Hanan would respond, "But leaving will take me away from you."

Then the mother would answer, with a reassuring smile, "I will visit you now and then. Go and God be with you."

But her mother's visits, even if they were lengthy, did not give Hanan the complete support to which she had been accustomed.

My doubts continued until one day I received a letter from Hanan written in English.

Dearest friend,

How I yearn for you, and think about you and miss you. I miss you a lot. How are you? What is occupying your thoughts, and who shares them with you during those hard times?

I need not say that I respect you and value you and appreciate your good spirit, and often I wish that you were living near us in this small town in the suburbs of London.

Here we have many treasures of knowledge, for London is an important center of culture and it has much that nourishes the soul and mind.

I just finished reading *The Book of Mirdad* in English. I believe that Mikhail Naimy is a great writer and this book of his is one of the greatest books written in our age. Naimy's work offers a great deal of mental nourishment, but in *Mirdad* one finds nourishment for one's soul. Here our Lebanese writer has reached the level of the prophets. How much I regret that I did not have the pleasure of talking to this great man when I lived in the same city with him for years. Do you think I will have the chance again?

You know how much I yearn for inner growth. I am always looking for a way to realize that goal, to gain more wisdom and patience, so I may be able to survive in this frozen human environment. I miss our quiet visits and long for conversations about what really matters in life.

I tell you, the more we learn and the less we care for material things, the better we are to understand life in some depth. Then we stand happily and freely, watching life pass by without allowing it to crush us.

I feel sorry that the "storm" that swept across Lebanon has taught people so little of what they ought to know. Some let emotions sweep and destroy them. So now as the war quiets down, they find themselves crushed, melancholic, empty, and broken-hearted.

My dear Maha, read the spiritual books. They are the spring of inner tranquility and they give consolation and peace.

I want you to stay as I knew you, steadfast in the face of storms, pre-

serving that inner calm. I want you to remain a pillar in your environment as you always have. And I wish you all the peace in this new year.

> Your friend,
> HANAN

I folded the letter and put it away. And I thought that Hanan was introducing new ideas into the pattern of our dialogue.

So this is how she spends her time! She tries to benefit from contemporary civilization. She reads Naimy's English book in order to understand him better. Can that be a sign of Farid's total domination?

There are many things to occupy me, yet the words of Hanan kept
echoing in my mind. My friend was no longer an individual person. The
companion of my college days had become a symbol. She represented
the thousands of Lebanese citizens who have been led to the roads of
diaspora by the war.

Hanan, in her letter to me, had been trying to defend a situation that
she did not choose or control, a situation that she had been led into,
with no regard for her own will, in total submission to the will of her
husband on one side and the orders of her mother on the other.

When she chose to write me this letter, she was reassuring me that
the expatriation had not severed relations between us and had not
erased the memories of past days.

She had come to me in the same way that a believer goes to the con-
fessional. She had told me about all the confusion, desolation, and alienation that was oppressing her. But she in her few words had not specified her feelings.

I thought, How many times before had Hanan been lost on the roads
of life? Her new expatriation had increased her sense of loss, but it had
added more strength and depth to our relationship.

Chapter 10

Her voice collided with the particles of air in my room, creating a commotion around me, and I felt that electrified waves were shaking my
being.

Here she was, pulling me out of my own space and time and stealing
moments of rest from me as she steals the drowsiness from my eyes.

"Hanan, can I get a cup of tea for you? You're shivering from the cold.
Here, take this coat. Put it around your shoulders."

I tried to bring her back to me by talking. By any means available I
would try to bring her back to reality to shorten what she intended to
reveal.

But she would always escape between my fingers just as drops of mercury slip in their own way to settle in the container they have chosen.

Hanan persists in her stubborn ways. She gained this stubbornness while she was away from me, during her years of aversion. . . . No, "aversion" is not the right word. I would say her "compulsory absence."

Before her last absence she had taken several trips outside Lebanon. She had not told me in advance and not once had she come to say good-bye to me. I lost all trace of her for years.

But whenever she returned from a trip, she would get in touch with me and her presence would shake the world around me and the mercury would slip through my hands once again.

"Hanan, what did you say?"

"A cup of tea is what I need. . . . It's four in the morning, isn't it?"

Only her lips are with me. Her eyes are wandering to some place far away. I tried to move from my place to get her what she had asked for, but she pulled me by the hem of my dress.

"Stay here," she begged.

I smiled while I kept going.

"The tea needs someone to bring it, Hanan. I'll be with you in a minute."

"Then I'll come with you."

She followed me to the kitchen, wrapping herself in the coat and dragging her feet.

"I'm scared to stay by myself. Dawn has not come yet . . ."

She threw herself in the kitchen chair and waited silently. When I handed her the cup of tea she started to sip it greedily.

"This is the best tea I've ever had. Do you remember the tea at the Michelene? You used to describe it as tasting like water that had trickled through the roof!"

I spoke to fill the emptiness.

"But at the Michelene café we enjoyed a kind of serenity."

"Indeed! You remember that? . . . Yes, serenity and peace. . . . Those are days that will never come back, Maha, no matter how much we would like them to. They will remain memories . . . those days, I mean."

"Of course they will never come back. You are living in London and we are digging ourselves out from under the debris of the war."

"In London the future is for children. For children to grow up. Myself, I am afraid of that future. I refuse to think about it. Life in London is paradise for children and pleasure for youth and students . . . for young and mobile types. But the city is hell for the elderly. This is a problem for me and I don't know what to do about it."

I said, sarcastically, "It's not time yet to think about old age. You're in the prime of life."

Hanan paused for a few moments before she continued.

"Maha, some turning points force you to leap years. And the change that we are living in forced us to face many problems we had postponed. When you are a stranger in another country, you can't help facing this problem. I lived it through my mother and her experience in London. Before her illness, she used to go out to the park every day and among the hundreds of people she never found anyone who would say hello to her. She would come back to our house very sad and depressed. And her feeling of estrangement, of being uprooted, increases all the time. The problem of belonging somewhere is a problem human beings must face through all the years they live no matter where they travel."

She continued. "But it is different for my children. They are growing up in the London atmosphere and when they are grown up, we will be strangers, a burden to them, an obstacle in their way."

I interrupted her, saying, "This is true of parents and children everywhere."

But Hanan shook her head in disagreement.

"No. Here we are ready to sacrifice. We do not cut our tie to the past. But there, children look out only for their pleasures. They look always forward. The disabled go to special institutions. They die alone. Take my mother, for example. If it weren't for the way we were brought up we would have put her in one of the nursing homes, because she needs constant care these days."

I objected. "But she is not disabled to that extent!"

"A stroke is not a joke, and it has left her half paralyzed. She will be like this forever. But the deepest wound she has suffered is estrangement. If she were here in Beirut friends would be visiting her daily to pass the time with her. Their company would lighten her burden . . . Life there in London is total loneliness, as if man had gone back to the womb and all the exits had closed behind him. . . . Do you understand what I'm saying?"

I nodded reassuringly. "Yes, Hanan, I understand. And I can't tell you now 'come back to your precious city . . . come back to Beirut.' Because coming back to the old Beirut is impossible."

"But I yearn to return now, today. My city, my beloved, needs me. If I could only embrace it with my arms, soothe its pain, heal its wounds! O Maha, I cannot describe the emotions that are exploding inside me."

"Why don't you put all this in writing?"

Hanan responded sadly. "Writing in exile is an impossibility."

At an earlier time Hanan had chosen exile. She had left her father's mansion and taken refuge in an isolated monastery, entrusting her daughter Randa to a governess who would bring her up under the supervision of Hanan's mother.

I had said to her at that time, "You are looking for problems instead of solving them." And she had responded hastily, "Life at home is unbearable. The atmosphere suffocates me and I'm not able to keep up with my studies. My father was satisfied with this arrangement and my mother accepted reluctantly."

I said jokingly, "And from the monastery you will graduate with a charming story under your arm."

"No, no. I will keep up my studies in peace and quiet, far from society's fury and triviality."

"Actually, Hanan, you are already far from the society in which you were raised," I had said, "and the proof is this round hole in the sole of your shoe!"

We laughed, and Hanan's eyes had watered as she said, "You notice everything . . . I was not paying attention to my shoes . . ."

"I'm careful about noticing such things," I had said, "just as I am careful to mend my own shoes and clothes. . . . I have to protect my back in this city of Beirut that judges so by appearances. . . . And when you have only one pair of shoes, like me, then you look after them with a passion."

We had laughed together at that. The difference in our social class, we were implying, would not stand in the way of our friendship. There was a human bond between the two of us rejectionists: Hanan, who rejected absolute adherence to her luxurious environment that enslaved her with its material trappings and its rigid traditions, and I, who refused to be a slave to an environment that shackled me with its poverty and its limited horizon.

On this plateau we had met and become friends. There developed between us that complete understanding and harmony that the years of separation and estrangement were unable to disturb or change.

Here Hanan sat holding her tea cup in an elegant way. She sipped the tea. Then her eyes wandered a little, and the heavy silence hung between us. And for a moment, Hanan makes me forget time and space and takes me to our cozy corner in the café Michelene, as if we were back in the old days . . . and as if there were no years of separation between us, and marriage and children.

Her lips murmured, "This is better even than the five o'clock tea in London."

I said jokingly, "It is the tea of four o'clock in the morning, Beirut time."

Suddenly she turned to me and asked, "Do you believe that it will be built in the near future, Beirut? . . . What do you think? What do people feel?"

My answer came in question form. "What are your feelings?"

"I cannot define them."

A strange contradiction of emotions was moving restlessly inside me and I tried to tell Hanan.

"When I first contemplated the extent of the damage and walked through that vast cemetery from Debbas Plaza to the Holiday Inn, I thought that tens of years would pass before this dark page would be turned and the face of Beirut shine again. But when I reached the al-Rawshah area and stood in front of the little shops and makeshift stands, watching the energetic movements of the merchants who were starting over, a different feeling overwhelmed me. I understood that an awesome, strong man, a man whom calamities cannot defeat, exists here on this land. He is planted in the heart of the soil like the oak tree or like the cedar on the mountain.

"The war did not uproot this man and there is no power that can erase his name from the book of existence.

"I stood contemplating him, that awesome man, who seemed to be standing in front of the savage ocean, facing the tempest, challenging it even, his eyes filled with a determination to survive.

"From my visit to al-Rawshah I returned with a sense of hope and promise . . . And I tell you, Hanan, it won't be long before the rubble of destruction disappears, and the elegant stores return again to embellish the capital's bosom. . . . and my beloved Beirut will once more be the jewel of the East.

"And you will return to it then."

Hanan interrupted me.

"Be quiet, Maha, or you will make me feel worse than I do already. I no longer deserve to live here, because I did not suffer one moment for the sake of this city. I did not walk one step on the road of Golgotha. Therefore I cannot aspire to walk in the Resurrection procession."

Encounters with Palestinian Women under Occupation

ROSEMARY SAYIGH

The dilemma for anyone setting out to examine the situation of Palestinian women is both practical and ideological: the need to decide whether or not there is a problem of women independent of the collective national problem, and what is the correct relation between the two. Any attempt to escape this dilemma leads either to a feminism that ignores the effects of Ottoman/British/Israeli oppression on Palestinian social/family structures or to a nationalism short on social content. For liberal Western feminists the family rather than the state is the source of women's oppression, and they have traditionally attacked "patriarchy" at the family level without looking at larger political/economic frameworks that organize family relations. Further, by viewing families in non-Western societies through the prism of the domestic/public dichotomy, they have exaggerated women's exclusion from the "public" sphere as, by assigning families to the relatively unchanging realm of culture, they have underestimated the political functions that families assume in precapitalist societies, and most strongly where colonialism has crushed indigenous political structures. This means that women's resistance to colonialism from within the family has been minimized as well as the emotional and cultural forms it takes simply because of their relative absence from formal political organizations. Finally, while Western feminists see clearly the limits to freedom placed on women by families (especially in the Arab/Muslim world), they do not perceive as clearly the range of activities women carry on within the limits of family life nor the resources offered them by their family networks.

The feminist/nationalist debate in Palestinian circles has proved rather sterile so far, unable to move beyond statements of principle, reactionary or progressive. The weakness of the feminist statements is that they have all, except for that of the Popular Front for the Liberation of Palestine (PFLP), been the product of individual women[1] without organizational roots, easily discounted by the mainstream as Western-oriented and bourgeois. On the other side, the topic is of such low priority that the only considered statement is that of Munir Shafiq,[2] who expresses in quasi-Marxist terms the Fatah preference for avoiding the "woman question."[3] PFLP leader George Habash gives women's liberation the same priority as national and class liberation, but his arguments remain abstract and alien,[4] not geared to the conditions and culture of the Palestinian masses nor worked into a program of social change. However, more than other groups, the PFLP and DFLP (Democratic Front for the Liberation of Palestine) have put real effort into changing the practice of gender relations within the party. Being doubly a minority, their women show greater solidarity with each other than do Fatah women. Further, their work among the mass of women is more systematic, more directed toward change, more supported by their leadership. It is mainly they who have kept up pressure on the Fatah-dominated executive committee of the GUPW (General Union of Palestinian Women) to keep the "woman issue" on the agenda. Real progress was being achieved in Lebanon before the recent war in terms of discussions, seminars, and positions taken by leading Fatah women,[5] progress that would certainly have been translated into pressure on the resistance leadership to expand women's participation and pay more attention to their concerns (for example, change in family law).

Outside the range of position papers and programs, there has been an extraordinary development since 1965 in what women undertake, particularly in areas like Lebanon and Occupied Palestine where crisis has been continuous. This is not to say that women's activism is in itself a sufficient guarantee of irreversible change in gender relations; definitely this cannot happen without a policy of radical social change at the leadership level. But, if it is properly used by the women's movement and the progressive forces, it does provide a campaign basis for change "at the top."

Part of the interest of the women's situation in Occupied Palestine, apart from their increased involvement in resistance, is the emergence of new groups with a more radical stand on class and gender relations than those of the national movement outside. These will be described briefly in the following paper along with a selection from meetings with women in Occupied Palestine made during a brief visit in 1980.

Escalating Resistance

Since Camp David the tempo of resistance has accelerated, involving all strata of the population of the West Bank. Students, schoolchildren, and women have been particularly visible, almost as if a new division of labor has emerged with men's obligations as family providers moving them out of political roles. Every day brings fresh evidence of women's activism. A typical incident is the arrest of eight women in Nablus (including Mayor Shak'a's wife) on charges of illegal demonstration and throwing stones at the vehicles sent to break them up. Women I was advised to meet were hard to disengage from a maelstrom of sit-ins, demonstrations, press conferences, and other national/social work. Of those I managed to meet, most had been interrogated and/or imprisoned.

Between 1967 and 1979, according to a recent researcher,[6] 1,229 named women have been arrested or detained, but this is definitely an undercount since it omits over 150 names for which no other details were obtainable, mass detentions such as those in Gaza in the early 1970s, and cases not reported in the press. Cases of administrative detention are generally not reported though detention may last for periods longer than a year. This is an impressive record that totally explodes the "silent," "passive" Arab woman image as well as the idea—sometimes encountered— that Palestinian women are less involved in the national struggle than were their Algerian sisters. The difference is that they have had less media exposure.

A lawyer who defends many Palestinians on political charges says that women resist interrogation better than most men, attributing this to women's lesser daily-life contact with Israelis. Another explanation is that men's involvement in politics is "natural," part of their male role, so that many who get drawn in are not particularly heroic. Women, on the other hand, usually have to defy the "government" of the family before they defy the occupation; hence, those who cross the line between sentimental and active resistance are a courageous minority with a minority's capacity for stubbornness and secrecy.

The inevitability of interrogation is taken for granted by all the women I meet; indeed it has become an initiation rite marking their graduation to an (adult) national role, the abandonment of the (child/women) domestic one. R.F. tells me unemotionally of her two weeks in the Moscobiya, when they tried to force her to sign a "confession" that she belonged to the PLO. Apart from interrupted sleep and continuous discomfort, interrogation was accompanied by forced stripping, name calling ("prostitute"), and threats of rape.

Schoolchildren have increasingly been subjected to violence. It is no longer rare for schoolgirls to be arrested or harassed in class by occupying forces who break in, using tear-gas bombs and a rich assortment of riot-control equipment. The effect is repercussive: teachers in Jerusalem comment on the ever-earlier politicization of girls.

A meeting in Jalazun with the family of one fifteen-year-old prisoner, Intisar al-Sheikh Kasim, makes very clear what all the testimonies of political prisoners show: the occupation deliberately uses family relationships for control and collective punishment. The life of the al-Sheikh Kasim family was completely disrupted for the three weeks of

Intisar's interrogation (first in Ramallah, then in Moscobiya). Each day her mother or father accompanied her for the day-long sessions; it was her mother who was there the day she was beaten; she sat in a corridor, unable to do anything while her daughter screamed. Her father (a building laborer whose father owned olive-growing land near Lydd) lost two weeks' pay and faced a lawyer's fee of twenty thousand lira. The family has also suffered from Intisar's press exposure; her father told me he would not forbid his daughter taking part in demonstrations but did not like her photo in the newspapers. Knowing that the authorities could easily disrupt his daughter's education (as they have done in many other cases, especially in Jalazun), he had signed a statement denying allegations of his daughter's beating.

Everyone engaged in resistance, from the most active to the mildest form, knows that their families will suffer if they are caught. Parents are often jailed along with children accused of resistance or for refusing to tell of their whereabouts. The homes of militants are blown up or sealed off, sometimes even houses where they have lodged in the past (as in the case of one of the teachers currently on trial). When children stone or petrol-bomb Israeli vehicles, the occupation invariably responds with curfews and punishment of the whole community.

Girls and women are vulnerable because they are females, not just because they are Palestinian. Many men who had otherwise resisted interrogation have broken down when threats were made against their sisters. Rasmiyeh Odeh's father was forcibly involved in his daughter's sexual violation in a complex attempt to shame both of them.[7] All possible combinations of family-bound male/female feelings—love, fear, shame, protectiveness—are employed to shock and break down resistance. Up to now, this form of pressure has not been successful: the politicization of women appears to be increasing rather than lessening. but the fear is that the occupation will not draw the lesson that its family punishment policy is a failure, but will rather conclude that it has not been pushed far enough.

Local Women Leaders *(Shakhsiyat)*

Palestinian women under occupation are highly visible in social work that takes on a national significance under present conditions. With the growth of their access to education, they are also becoming an important element in intellectual and productive work. The term *shakhsiya* is used here, as it is used colloquially in the West Bank/Jerusalem area, to indicate prominent women involved in social/national work. It implies a forceful personality and a leading social/family status.

Historically, the *shakhsiyat* (like their male counterparts) emerged in

a situation of intermittent mobilization against a powerful foreign occupation in a society composed of deeply rooted local lineages, where
social structure remains relatively stable and repression prevents nationwide organization. The local leader role is evidently class bound,
yet within its class limits there remains a significant difference between
the Jerusalem leader-families, those of the more important provincial
towns (like Gaza, Jaffa, and Acre), and those of small townships and
large villages. One finds a growing radicalism as one moves outward (in
space) and downward (in wealth). The same transformation of the role is
also evident over time, with the *shakhsiyat* of today much more overtly
political than those of the Mandate period.

The *shakhsiya* has never been by any means purely an ascribed role,
even though incumbents come from "known" families. It involves hard
work, commitment, and efficiency. Perhaps some of the great ladies
elected to the executive committee of the first Arab Women's Union in
1929 were brought in because of their family connections, but the esca-
lation of violence through the course of the Mandate would certainly
have weeded out all but the most committed. After 1948, with the national movement apparently annihilated, there was even less scope for
tokenism: those who continued to be active were only the most dedicated. This is the period when many of the best-known *shakhsiyat*
showed their mettle: ʿAndalib al-ʿAmad set up an orphanage and hospital in Nablus; Zulaykha Shihabi, secretary-general of the first Arab
Women's Congress, started projects for the refugees near Jerusalem;
Widad Khartabil kept the Union going in Lebanon and set up women's
projects and an orphanage; and the Halabi sisters rescued Palestinian
peasants' designs in their Jerusalem workshop. Similar projects, and
similar women, were to be activated by the June 1967 war.

As a group, the local women leaders have certain things in common
besides the fact of coming from "known" (property-owning) families.
Their activities, though intense, fall within the boundaries of the socially acceptable (for example, social work), they are broadly nationalist
but do not join political parties or groups, and they are strong culture
loyalists, careful not to disturb existing structures of class and gender
relations.

Each town, each village has its own local women leaders. In Gaza, the
woman everyone counsels me to meet is Sitt Yusra Berberi (whereas in
Lebanon and Israel women leaders are called *ukht*, "sister," in the occupied territories a touch of feudalism is retained in the widely used
sitt, "lady"). Member of a well-known nationalist family, Sitt Yusra refused to continue her work as inspector of girls' schools under the Israelis
and now devotes herself full-time, but on a volunteer basis, to the
Women's Union.[8] It contains a large orderly day-care center (one of four)

where working mothers can leave children from four months to five years old.

The person behind the order, Sitt Yusra, is a straight-backed lady with iron-grey hair, flat shoes, a simple black suit. It is more for her defiant stand toward the occupation, however, than for her efficiency that other Palestinians admire her. As headmistress from 1950 to 1958 of Gaza's only girls' high school, she brought up a nationalist generation, among them Um Jihad, said to be Fatah's first woman member.

She emphasizes the national importance of the kind of social work the Women's Union does. "We help prisoners and needy families, educate children and bring them up with a nationalist consciousness. We help working women, and the wives and daughters of martyrs and prisoners." Gaza has a population upward of 441,300 (1977), most of whom are refugees, and there is little employment, whether for unskilled workers or university graduates. An unusual number of women are without male support (owing to the ruthless repression of the early 1970s), and several thousand are bussed daily to work in Israeli factories. The means the Women's Union has to confront the problems of the mass of women are minute.

Closer to Jordan and to funds, the West Bank situation is less stagnant. Most of the occupied territories' 150 charitable associations are located here, and women's role in them is crucial: every township and large village has its association and its active women leaders. Dr. Amin al-Khatib, president of the Federation of Charitable Associations, admits their preponderance in work that has taken on a national importance under occupation: "Women are more active than men—it's a fact and I can't deny it." But he notes another significant fact: before 1967 women *headed* the voluntary societies as well as forming the bulk of active membership; now, they still do most of the work but men have tended to take over the leadership. Men leave social work to women unless they are blocked from normal political activity; when social work becomes national work, men move into leadership.

In Ramallah, Sitt Um Khalil's (Samiha Salameh) Inʿash al-ʿUsra (Society for the Preservation of the Family) is greatly admired for its growth and success. The Inʿash started out in 1965 with one hundred Jordanian dinars—just enough to rent two rooms, hire a sewing teacher, and recruit ten girl students. Now there is a three-story building with thirty-two rooms, sixty-seven employees, and a monthly payroll of 2,500 dinars. There is also a day-care center for the children of working women, thirteen literacy centers in nearby villages (run in conjunction with Bir Zeit University), help for 130 needy families, and a sponsorship scheme for war victims and the children of martyrs and prisoners. The Inʿash also markets the products of about two thousand women who work at home. Local doctors and dentists have been enlisted to give treatment to ten cases each a month. There is also a food-processing factory.

Successful in its mixture of social work and profit making, the In'ash has moved into the cultural field. It has a folklore museum and a magazine, *Culture and Society*, that is widely read by Palestinians outside for its contribution to the post-1967 renaissance of Palestinian culture and identity. A study of a West Bank village (Turmus'ayya), a collection of proverbs, and research into women's traditional handicrafts are further enterprises in this line.

Um Khalil is very much the center of this spreading network of projects. She is a woman of energy and drive who now lives alone with her husband. (All of her children are abroad and only one can return to visit her. Two sons were deported, one was imprisoned.) Like Yusra Berberi, Um Khalil is loved because she symbolizes defiance to the occupation. Her social work has spilled over into demonstrations and sit-ins; she has been imprisoned six times. The occupation has tried to interfere with the In'ash's activities by closing down most of its village centers, but the maintenance of Jordanian law in the West Bank has given the charitable societies their small basis for action.

I asked Um Khalil if she thinks women's earning power is improving their position in the family. "Yes, it is. In the past men wouldn't let women go to meetings; now they *ask* them to go. Village people used not to let their daughters have education; now many are in university." But she is no feminist: "When a girl begins to earn money she may begin to impose conditions on her family. We don't encourage such a spirit in our girls. To open the door too wide would cause a bad reaction." For her, social concern and nationalism are inseparable. "This is the way to liberate our land."

Before 1967, the charity-running middle and upper classes used to draw a hard line between social work and politics, viewing the first as respectable and the second as suspect, but the occupation has had the effect of obliterating the line and legitimating the expansion of women's social role into a national/political one. The difficulty will be to sustain this expansion once the national problem is solved, but if there is any good to be found in the long-drawn-out nature of the Palestinian struggle it is that mass and women's participation may have irreversibly changed sex and class relations.

Where an earlier generation of local women leaders turned belatedly to mass work without real knowledge of mass conditions or culture, those who have assumed this role after 1948, though not from the masses, have been much closer to them than the great ladies who founded the AWU in 1929.[9] They are not separated from the women of villages and camps by high status, great wealth, foreign education, or different life-style; they talk the same language, cook the same food, perform the same domestic duties. Reflections of this role can be found in any camp or village, and from its pervasiveness one can guess that it meets the subjective needs of women for a public sphere of action, the cultural/social restraints of the local community, and the overall oppression that maintains fragmentation by blocking nationwide organization.

Um Khalil well illustrates the way the *shakhsiya* role has changed in response to growing national mobilization: she comes from a small land-owning family in a small township (al-Bireh), she is not highly educated,[10] and her own involvement is nearly total, leaving the bare minimum for domestic/social obligations. But in other ways she carries on its traditions: her organizational style is personal and charismatic, and the directing nucleus that she has mobilized to work with her remains essentially uni-class, a group of friends who trust each other.

Israeli Variations

In Israel, political and economic oppression have blocked the emergence of a Palestinian leadership, male or female, and women's domestic role has been deepened by land confiscation, the spread of capitalist relations of production, and the cultural conservatism that has been one reaction to alien domination. Surveillance and lack of public funds have prevented the emergence of local development projects on the scale of the West Bank, and women's absence from the few that exist is as marked as their presence on the other side of the Green Line. Palestinian women who work outside the home (14.2 percent of all women aged fourteen and over in 1978) tend to be absorbed into the dominant Israeli institutions and have little time for extra community work. Women's public role is thus more limited here than elsewhere, yet the shadow of the *shakhsiya* is still visible. I hear of several active women in the villages of Galilee, and there is a Women's League in Acre running a kindergarten and teacher-training workshop. In Nazareth there are several groups, including the Democratic Women's Movement (affiliated with the Communist party),[11] whose president is Samira Khoury.

Ukht Samira bears a strong resemblance to the *shakhsiyat*: the same energy, the same simple life-style (very different from that of most bourgeois women), the same mingling of domestic and public roles. Like them, she began to work in response to national crisis. When in 1948 her training to be a teacher was interrupted, she joined with a few friends to help the refugees who poured into Nazareth from the surrounding villages. In that period, the Jewish forces would surround refugee quarters, round up the men, and threaten to deport them in an attempt to get families to leave. Samira's group distributed food and clothing (there was no international relief organization inside Israel) and led demonstrations against deportation threats. "We felt the pressure to organize, saw people helpless, without consciousness, ignorant, felt we must teach them, lead them." From this early social/national work grew the first women's group, the Union of Democratic Women, later to become the Democratic Women's Movement (DWM). Samira joined Rakah (the Communist party in Israel), thereby losing her teaching job, and the same year married a fellow teacher and fellow party member, Fuad Khoury.

Contacts with Palestinian women's groups were only made after 1967, and have remained restrained by the presence of Jewish members in the DWM. All but seven of the DWM branches are in Arab areas. Peak activities are the three big annual celebrations: Woman's Day, Children's Day, and Worker's Day. Recently instituted summer work-camps bring up to two thousand volunteers to Nazareth each year.

Rakah has a strong following in the villages, but women's liberation is not part of its aim there. There continues to exist a de facto gender separation both in villages and towns, with women members meeting separately and engaging mainly in social activities on the old, pre-1948 pattern. The problem with "starting from reality" is that, without a clear policy of change, one tends to get stuck there.

To some members of the younger generation, increasingly drawn to the Abnaꜥ al-Balad (Sons of the Country) movement, Rakah seems insufficiently radical on the "woman question," and their criticisms are parallel to those that can be heard in the West Bank or Lebanon. Younger women find the *shakhsiya* generation anachronistic. In Jerusalem a young professional woman told me: "The problem with that generation is they need to be constantly worshipped. But we have to work from a sense of obligation, not for praise. Besides, their methods are outdated." What divides the local women leaders from the category I am calling the "women intellectuals" is primarily a generation gap, sharpened by crisis-accelerated change.

The Women Intellectuals

The category of women intellectuals came to maturity after 1948. Their movement into universities and professions must not be viewed as a response simply to economic pressures or to "modernization"; it was also a reaction to national crisis, part of the collective quest for revival. As a group, they are educated to a more advanced level than the *shakhsiyat* (for whom universities were not available in Palestine) and are more specialized. They are also more likely to be employed, and the organiza-

tiòns they join are more likely to be professional or political, not charitable. Their nationalism has a more ideological, more book-learned
flavor. While older women in their youth competed with each other
from family and local power bases, younger women are divided along
party and ideological lines. Another important difference is the much
broader class spectrum from which the women intellectuals come;
though still overloaded at the upper end (because of the maldistribution
of education), they include women from the petit bourgeoisie, villages,
and camps.

In using the term "woman intellectual" I am keeping in mind the distinction that Nakhleh makes between an intellectual and someone who
is university educated.[12] While entrance to university remains restricted
by class, oppression and crisis are creating, along with growing literacy
and mass communication, the conditions for a new "mass intellec-
tualism" that does not overlap with the official education system,
particularly not with its upper levels. Because of continuing pressures
toward early and universal marriage and because of their relative exclusion from tertiary education and the professions, Palestinian women are
a large part of this phenomenon. For this reason I include within the
category not just the prominent women whom every journalist hears of,
but also the thousands of anonymous primary school teachers, laboratory assistants, nurses, students, and literate housewives.

L. is a social worker from a small village near Jerusalem. Her family
belongs to the class of medium landowners that provided fighters and
local leaders to the 1936 revolution. Her father, with whom L. was jailed
a few years back, has been imprisoned twenty-three times under the
British, the Jordanians, and now the Israelis. As *mukhtar* he still refuses
to use an Israeli stamp. One of her brothers is in prison, another has
been deported.

Some women intellectuals such as Raymonda Tawil and Sahar
Khalifa attack the family subordination of women from a straight feminist standpoint. Others like Hanan Ashrawi have a theory linking
women's oppression to collective weaknesses that impede liberation.
But most people continue to see the "woman issue" solely in terms of
freedom or rights rather than in terms of a whole society changing its
structures. I suspect the majority would agree with L., who says, "I
would feel guilty if I asked for more rights as a woman at a time like
this."

R., a teacher of sciences, represents the largest occupational sector
within the female labor force. Her profession is one that attracts the majority of qualified women: it's approved by society and easy to combine
with marriage. Often teachers come from families of small shopkeepers,
civil servants, or small farmers. R.'s father was a teacher in the public

system. She is from Jerusalem, where education for girls has the oldest roots. Her home was full of books, visitors, political talk. Her father wanted all seven of his children to go to university, but the year R. finished high school the Jordanian government retired him without a pension. Somehow she got to Ain Shams University in Egypt, where she studied physics and chemistry and graduated the year after the annexation of Jerusalem. Unmarried, R. still lives with her family in Jerusalem and commutes some twenty kilometers to work daily.

She tells me of the Graduates Club and the Civil Servants Club, focuses of national/cultural activities in which she takes part. In July 1979 she directed an exhibition for the first Palestinian Social Conference that brought together all the charitable associations. The occupation had tolerated their activities as local groups, but meeting together gave them a dangerously national character. There were arrests, and R. was one of those taken in for interrogation.

"It took place in the Moscobiya and lasted more than a month. They try to give you the idea that they know everything about you. They kept accusing me of belonging to the DFLP. I stuck to my position that I have no links with any organization, that I have a political stand, but my activities are social."

I had first met R. on a one-day bus trip to Gaza with members of the Women's Action Committee, a new group launched from the Ramallah area. Unlike the charitable associations, whose structure reproduces class boundaries (the middle class directs *for* a needy clientele), WAC members include professional, clerical, and factory workers. Other signs of difference: it is moving fast to outgrow its local origins; it is trying to avoid the paraphernalia of institutionalism (offices, elections, etc.); it is an all-women group, combining in its manifesto the goals of women's, class, and national liberation. R. says: "We formed the committee because the older societies did not encourage working women. They only give money and services, don't have development projects, don't try to change consciousness. We go to women, try to involve them in social and political activities. At first the older societies resented us as newcomers. This has been a big problem. But now some of them help us." Classical income-generating projects for women are geared to women working at home and are practical but limited, without any effect on the social and cultural conditions in which low-income women live. WAC is focusing on literacy classes and social centers in camps and villages. To find out more about the problems of working women and housewives they recently conducted a field study[13] in the Ramallah area, where there is a concentration of industrial projects employing women. As far as I know, this is the first study to be done by any Palestinian women's group.

Women in Science. The proportion of Arab women now entering the "hard" fields of science, medicine, and engineering is probably higher than in the United States.

M. teaches biology at Bir Zeit University and is deeply concerned about the deteriorating public health situation in the West Bank. The military authorities closed two hospitals and froze health facilities when they occupied the West Bank, and there is ever-increasing population pressure on inadequate resources. Medical personnel are too few and are demoralized by poor equipment, lack of funds, and a heavy workload. M. began collecting public health data two years ago and is now trying to involve her students.

There are indications that infant mortality rates are rising (a reversal of the overall Palestinian trend), but the only studies so far have been based on samples too small for conclusive evidence. Still unanalyzed data from the Zbaydat village study undertaken by Bir Zeit for the Mennonites indicate a level of more than one hundred deaths per thousand.

Women Intellectuals in Israel. Some of the special difficulties faced by women intellectuals in Israel emerged in an evening's discussion with girl students at the Hebrew University. Out of a total Arab population of 570,000, only two thousand (about 0.35 percent) are in Israeli universities, and of these only a handful are female.[14] The difficult *bagrut* (high school equivalency) exam in Hebrew and special college entrance tests form the first barrier (apart from inadequate access to secondary schools). Then there is the difficulty of gaining access to the field of their choice. All I met had to switch; it is almost impossible to enter pharmacology, medicine, or engineering. University fees are high and there are no public scholarships for Arab students. This and the difficulty of finding jobs after graduation make many families draw back from investing in university for their daughters.

The narrowness of chances for Palestinian girls to get higher education in Israel does not mean that the "woman intellectual" does not exist but that the category of woman intellectual must be seen differently in the Palestinian context. The reality of being a minority has produced a mood of acute rebellion among young people against class and family structures that are seen to transmit Israeli oppression. Both in Nazareth and in a village near Haifa I encountered small women's study circles (none of the members were university educated) eagerly reading Nawal al-Sa'dawi, the Egyptian radical feminist. Z., a young newly married woman from Q., tells me that she only found confidence to speak on politics in the presence of men after reading al-Sa'dawi.[15]

In Z.'s generation (or a minority of it), rebellion against Israeli oppression and the patriarchal family are fused. For them, the idea of Palestine has become the symbol of this larger belonging. Z. expresses something of this: "When I was small we didn't even know the word 'Palestine,' we used to think Jenin was in Jordan. On Independence Day we used to carry the Israeli flag. But now children know; they sing 'Biladi'[16] even though it's forbidden. This year some of them refused to take part in Independence Day." To this new Palestinianism (which is the driving force of Abna⊃ al-Balad) is linked Z.'s drive for autonomy as a woman and a part in the struggle. She supports birth control, seeing clearly the way large families pin women down in the home, and not only women but men, too, drawing them out of politics through heavy economic obligations. She intends to have only two children, whether or not they are boys, and to bring up daughters in the same way as sons. She thinks all women should be able to provide for their families in case their husbands are inprisoned.

Later, in an Abna⊃ al-Balad meeting of both men and women, I met other girls like Z., most unmarried, though there was also an older woman with two small children who had been a candidate for the local council. The rapporteur was a competent girl in a Muslim headscarf (a reminder that it is possible to be both pious and progressive). Because of the difficulty of desegregating the sexes after so long, the women also met separately to discuss problems such as family restrictions on attending meetings. The group discussion leader, a young man who steadily encouraged the women to participate, made a statement on the movement's stand toward women's liberation: "The main stand of Abna⊃ al-Balad toward the issue of women is that we must destroy all traditional values and all obstacles to the participation of women in struggle. Our main goal now is to form women cadres who will reach the stage of taking part in all levels of organization so that they will be able to work side by side with men for the liberation of women. This is one of our fundamental principles, not a minor point." He and other speakers stressed the links between capitalism, Zionism, and the domestication of women.

The Third Category

The third category I have suggested is not valid, for there are no "ordinary" women. Labels like "uneducated," "illiterate," "housewife," and "traditional woman" are all unsatisfactory and loaded with elitism, but they do point to the way schooling has increasingly become a discriminating factor between women, shattering the older unity of a similar domestic/social role and a shared protection by (read subordination to) the family.

Regions, classes, and a whole generation still exist who have hardly been touched by education. Outside the cities and the middle class, few women over thirty-five are schooled, and though not numerically pre-ponderant in this young population (50 percent under eighteen), they undoubtedly account for most of what remains of female illiteracy (re-cently estimated at 40 percent for the West Bank).[17] In some peripheral areas like the Negev there are still no girls' schools at all. Bedouins still have highly inadequate public schooling, though richer bedouin fami-lies are sending daughters to private schools. Girls in the poorest areas—refugee camps, villages, city slums—may have elementary schools but not the secondary levels that open the door to skilled employment.

Wherever girls are excluded from secondary education they remain subject to pressures toward early marriage (a form of economic se-curity), large families, and exclusion from acceptable employment. Cur-rent conditions of internal colonialism, brought about mainly by land confiscation, are increasingly forcing unqualified women into the labor market to work in Israeli factories or on plantations at discriminatory wage rates. This trend is, of course, much more advanced in Israel, but it can be seen too in the occupied territories in spite of their greater scope for national industry and public services.

In Qariya (not its real name) we visited one of the new village facto-ries that employs girls. It is financed by Jewish capital from Haifa but has a local "partner" who supervises production. About twenty-five un-married girls and two slightly older married women "foremen" work from 7:30 A.M. to 3:30 P.M. with two quarter-hour breaks, machine-sew-ing women's dresses. For this they are paid three and a half dollars a day. This wage is lower than they could get in larger factories outside the village, but their families prefer that they remain in the village because of their fear of Muslim Brotherhood violence: two buses that carried women to work were burnt last year. In Nazareth, the same pay differ-ence is found between the large, Histadrut-organized factories and the small, backstreet workshops.[18]

In spite of low pay and strict control (they must not talk between breaks), the girls seem happy to be away from home. Their political con-sciousness is awakened: they have already carried out two strikes, one to get paid regardless of electricity cuts, the other for a 10 percent pay increase. This year they refused to work on Yawm al-Ard (Land Day).

It is true that in certain areas, particularly Gaza, even secondary edu-cation does not necessarily lead to skilled employment. The ratio of girls in secondary school in Gaza is higher than most other parts of the country where Palestinians are dispersed,[19] but there is heavy un-employment. Whatever the importance of schooling in determining women's status, it has no clear relationship to participation in national struggle. Everyone who has been in prison confirms the wide age and class range of women prisoners.

Another important form of "ordinary" women's resistance—not remarked because taken for granted—is the capacity for staying put. If the Palestinian emigration rate out of the occupied area is much lower than Israelis would wish, this is not a little due to women who make no special pleas for an easier life.

If "ordinary" women cannot be distinguished from the other two categories in their Palestinianism, I think they can in the degree to which they suffer from the occupation. Indeed, one of the reasons why it is so necessary to bring them into view, even while knowing so little about their conditions and feelings, is that if one considers *only* the *shakhsiyat* and the intellectuals, one leaves room for a false link between their "advancement" and Zionist intervention. That Israel has nothing to do with women's increased education or wider public participation is clear from a comparison of Israel and the West Bank,[20] or Occupied Palestine and Lebanon. But it becomes even more obvious if we consider the broad effects of the occupation on the third category in particular; that is, on women who have no chance to "compensate" through interesting work or a leadership role.

The psychological strain on "ordinary" women of threats to their families is hard to measure, but one can get some idea by reading accounts of the curfew in Hebron after the deportation of Mayor Qawasmeh. The mayor's wife suffered a breakdown when, soon after her husband was deported, troops threatened to shoot one of her children playing in the garden. There is no Palestinian wife/mother in the occupied territories who has not gone through similar traumas.

A different set of problems arises from Israeli "de-development" policies, which starve Palestinian communities on both sides of the Green Line of funds needed for social infrastructure. As unpaid family/social labor, women's workload automatically expands to fill in deficiencies in public facilities. Inadequate public hygiene means more time spent cleaning. Poor transport and health facilities mean more time spent carrying sick children to clinics, more time spent waiting for care. Inadequate water and fuel supplies mean more time spent on housework.

Samira Khoury, president of the DWN, in an interview given in Nazareth implicitly recognized the double burden. She began by speaking of

. . . the neglect of Arab towns and villages and discrimination between Arab and Jewish localities. For example, Affuleh with a population of 14,000 gets a budget of 250 million lira, while Nazareth with 45,000 has just had a budget of 180 million lira refused.

In the so-called mixed cities (Acre, Haifa, Jaffa, and Lydd) the situation is even worse because the Arabs live in separate quarters that are starved of municipal funds. They can't develop, can't build schools and kindergartens or sports centers. It's the same in the villages. Children are learning under the trees without equipment, without even lavatories.

It's the same story with the Ministry of Health: medical facilities for Arab areas lag far behind. The Histadrut gives health insurance to all its members, but their clinics only exist in Jewish centers, and Arabs, especially from the villages, can't always reach them. In a recent measles epidemic, many children died because their mothers couldn't reach the clinics.

Of course, such conditions affect women psychologically. They are always under the strain of problems and anxiety. The bad economic situation affects them, inflation, unemployment. Their men often have far to go to work, there are many checkpoints, and if they are a few minutes late they are sent back, and lose a whole day's pay.

In the conditions of internal colonialism that characterize the situation of Palestinians under occupation, women can only be seen as "advancing" if we focus exclusively on political consciousness and eliminate from view the deterioration in women's situation caused by forced proletarianization and the transformation of the indigenous household from a center of multiple activities—social, cultural, economic—into a dormitory for workers and schoolchildren. Beyond this there is the problem of woman's centrality as a symbol of social order. With Palestinians increasingly polarized between progressive and reactionary currents, women are likely to pay a heavy price for over-visibility. Here again, Israeli hegemony, seen as modern and Western, has strengthened ideological countercurrents that place false emphasis on "our" women remaining traditional. Men's fear of loss of control over the female sector, of a sexual revolution, of emancipation on the Israeli model (with miniskirts and premarital sexuality falsely equated with emancipation) have added new dimensions to the "woman problem." I hear of an increase (more in Israel and Gaza than the West Bank) of honor crimes and daughter and wife beating, and though such things are not publicized, they point to the need for a national policy not based on an idealization of the Arab past or the Arab family, but on understanding of the new, complex realities that are emerging.

Up to now much of the debate around Arab women (and Palestinian women in particular) has been infertile because it has employed polarized and abstracted concepts—the ideal Muslim woman, the sexually emancipated Western woman—that cut the debate off from all exchange with reality. Theorization is of no use if it does not make contact with people's real lives; neither the conditions in which Palestinian women live, nor their reactions to those conditions, nor their very considerable achievements are studied or understood. Probably few Palestinians believe deeply in the simplistic slogan that women's liberation will come through participation in the national struggle, but no sustained intellectual effort has been put into getting beyond that slogan. Not a priority for the revolution? But this is a revolution that, blocked in the short run from achieving its full national targets, is compelled to think more deeply than others about social change.

Notes

1. For feminist statements, see May Sayegh, *The Arab Palestinian Woman: Reality and Impediments* (Beirut: GUPW, 1980, in Arabic and English); Raymonda Hawa-Tawil, *Mon pays, ma prison* (Paris: Seuil, 1979); and Nuha Abu Daleb, "Palestinian Women and Their Role in the Revolution," *Peuples méditerranéens* 5 (October–December 1978): 35–46. May Sayegh is a Fatah member but without strong following on this issue.

2. Munir Shafiq, "Mawduʿat hawla nidal al-marʾa" (Themes on the struggle of women), *Shuʾun Filastiniya* 62 (January 1977): 200–227.

3. Fatah is the majority group within the Palestinian Liberation Organization led by Yasir Arafat.

4. George Habash, *Hawla taharrur al-marʾa* (On the liberation of women) (Beirut: Information Centre of the Rejection Front, n.d.). The PFLP also published a pamphlet in 1970 by K. Abu Ali entitled *Muqaddimat hawla waqiʿ al-marʾa wa tajribatiha fi al-thawra al-Filastiniya* (The revolution and the liberation of women issue) (Beirut: GUPW, 1975). For an individual PFLP statement, see Rasmiyeh Odeh in S. Antonius, "Prisoners for Palestine: A List of Women Political Prisoners," *Journal of Palestine Studies* 9, no. 35 (Spring 1980): 29–80.

5. To commemorate International Women's Day, March 8, 1982, the *PFLP Bulletin* took the unusual step of interviewing Jihan Helou, a leading member of the Fatah cadre and a member of the GUPW executive committee. *PFLP Bulletin* 61 (April 1982).

6. Antonius, "Prisoners for Palestine."

7. Ibid.

8. Several branches of the pre-1948 Arab Women's Union survive in Occupied Palestine where the GUPW (founded in 1965) is prohibited.

9. See M. Mogannam, *The Arab Woman and the Palestine Problem* (London: Herbert Joseph, 1937), pp. 70–73 for details. Among executive committee members were Mrs. Jamal Husseini, Mrs. Mousa Alami, and Mrs. Ouni Abdul Hadi.

10. *Shakhsiyat* of Yusra Berberi's generation were the first, almost, to be university educated (Matiel Mogannam had a law degree); Palestine lacked a university. Today, the enrollment of Palestinian girls in tertiary level education is probably one of the Arab world's highest.

11. Concerning the attitude of Arab Communist parties to the "woman issue," K. Abu Ali remarks that before 1948 Rakah had a "European ap-

proach" because of its Jewish members, but that this was later modified to take into consideration prevalent social customs and values.

12. K. Nakhleh. *Palestinian Dilemma: Nationalist Consciousness and University Education in Israel* (Shrewsbury, Mass.: AAUG, 1979).

13. *Hawla awda' al-mar'a al-Filastiniya fi al-manatiq al-muhtalla: Dirasa maydaniya* (The situation of Palestinian women in the occupied territories: A field study) (Ramallah, 1980).

14. In Bir Zeit about 40 percent of students are female. In the other West Bank universities the figure is slightly lower.

15. One of Dr. al-Sa'dawi's books is now available in English: *The Hidden Face of Eve* (London: Zed Press, 1980).

16. "My Country," best known of Resistance songs and unrecognized national anthem.

17. Based on data from the literacy survey undertaken recently by Bir Zeit University.

18. The Histadrut is the Israeli labor union.

19. See *Statistical Yearbook 1977–78* (Vienna: UNRWA-UNESCO Department of Education, 1979), p. 19.

20. See F. S. Nasru, *Education in the West Bank: Government Schools 1968–1976/77* (Bir Zeit: Bir Zeit University Documentation and Research Office, 1977), for evidence that girls' enrollment in school has suffered in the West Bank as a consequence of parents' fear of Israeli army violence.

The Aunt of Rafiq (a short story)

DAISY AL-AMIR
Translated from the Arabic by Tura Campanella

She looked out of the window at a green forest. The last rays of sunshine would not let the trees become dark yet, and a total silence seemed to cover all of the universe as though with a smooth, unwrinkled robe.

She sat down in the rocking chair. The chair rocked as usual but today she was not moved. The chair did not even squeak like it usually did. Where to find a sound in this silence?

She turned on the radio. A loud voice was speaking in a strange language. What was the announcer saying? What was his commentary on the strange music? Could other voices answer him? Was there no Arab voice in this profound exile of hers?

Tonight was the last night she would spend in this strange country. The mineral baths and the massage had ended in the morning and the attendant had smoothed the last heavy application of black mud onto the ailing parts of her body.

The doctor said in the strange, broken langauge of this country that she needed physical, mental, and emotional rest.

"Physical rest! Mental rest! Emotional rest!!" he repeated.

She told the doctor she would be unable to obtain any of these rests that he prescribed.

"Why not?" he had asked.

She could not respond. How could she make him understand who she really was? How could she explain the responsibilities that rested on her shoulders, on her head, on her arms?

She had tried to conceal her real identity in this strange country, tried to disguise herself so no one would know she was here, resting her body, her mind, and her emotions.

It was the doctor in her own country who had decided that she was near collapse and needed a retreat where there would be no work or responsiblity, only relaxation, sleep, and a pleasant atmosphere. Her brother had nodded, but said after deep thought and careful consideration, "And who will help me while she is gone?"

The strange doctor had continued to question her. What do you do that causes such total exhaustion, such great tension?

She had been puzzled about how to answer. Should she have explained the nature of her work? Should she have said that she is the sister of her brother? In the end, she had said nothing.

When she had left to go to the strange country, her brother had told her not to speak of her work to anyone. "If the Arab tourists recognize you," her brother had said, "they will say, aha, the militants behave in a bourgeois manner even though they say they are the militants, the leaders, and the fighters. They will say you are the sister of the militant, the sister of the leader, and the sister of the fighter. Thus you must not behave like a bourgeois."

And he continued to tell her, "Remember, the feeling of fatigue is a bourgeois trait. The collapse of the body in the face of responsibilities is a bourgeois trait. And the frailty of nerves in the face of exhaustion and wakefulness is a bourgeois trait."

Her brother had, after all, devoted himself totally to the cause. He had been infused with enthusiasm from the first moment he became aware of the concerns of the homeland. He was the only son in the family, she was the younger sister. She was influenced by what he said and believed in what he did. She was moved by his strong personality and began to voice his opinions and repeat what he said. Then he began explaining the cause to her. She soon found herself engaged in a major military operation. Her brother made her a comrade in the struggle. This increased her commitment to the cause and she spent all her time working.

But her brother—. Despite his enthusiasm and his work for the struggle, her brother managed to find another comrade, a comrade of a different kind. Her brother's new comrade entered his life through an easy door and became a pampered wife. She, his sister, remained his comrade in struggle.

Other people knew this perfectly well. They knew that she, his sister, was truly his confidant, that every major secret was told to her alone. They knew that behind her brother's unique, captivating personality stood his sister—a solemn pledge to the cause, consulted before all his speeches were made, before all his policies were announced.

But women are assumed to be more talkative than men and people tried to follow her, to ask her questions, direct and indirect. She had passed the test, however, and remained steadfast, not answering any of the tantalizing questions, until her brother's supporters and followers called her the sister of men. They had honored her. They had given her a rank, the rank of those who are known through their brothers!

Soon she recognized that the cause was more important than all human desires and to give it total attention she dissociated herself from the world of women. No visits to the hairdresser or the dressmaker, no trips to the market or morning social calls. For such visits wasted time. She needed the time for the cause.

When her brother's wife bore a son, Rafiq, her brother became known as the father of Rafiq. She found this preposterous. She also found it strange that her brother began to spend part of his time evaluating his son's toys, while her own responsibilities to the cause increased. And she came to be called the aunt of Rafiq. They had elevated her to a new rank, that of the aunt of Rafiq. She was no longer called the sister of men. Had men suddenly become little children?

What if she had been called the mother of Rafiq? The idea had not occurred to her before. She remembered an offer of marriage, long ago. She had been engaged very young to a man whom she did not see except through the gifts that his mother and sister gave her. . . . Then her father had decided that her fiancé was not suitable and she had returned the gifts.

She had asked, "Why wasn't he appropriate? Why had he been appropriate at one time and not now?"

Her father never answered this question, neither when she asked him herself nor when she sought an explanation from her mother. "Your father thinks this is best for you," was all her mother would say.

She wondered what had happened to those gifts and who was wearing them now.

Whenever her brother returned from a trip, he brought gifts for his wife, his son, Rafiq, and for his friends. For her, he always brought a bundle of new political books.

Once she saw her brother's wife with guests, one of whom was revealing the future to her in a cup of coffee. Then she gave the guest her own cup to tell her future.

In the evening her brother asked in disbelief, "Is this your intellectual level? Have you stooped to the point of wanting to know the future from a cup of coffee? *We* make the future, *we* are the ones who build it. Do we need to look in a cup to tell us what we have to do, or what will happen?'

She asked once what would happen if she stood before the mirror admiring herself as her brother's wife did.

Her grandfather said, "She is a wife, and must make herself pretty to please her husband. But as for you, are you making yourself pretty to please your brother's friends? And what would people say if one of them got interested in you?"

Her brother added, "What if, God forbid, one of them loves you? People would say that I allowed you to participate in a national cause in order to find you a husband. Your proper behavior makes you immune to criticism and your pride in being the sister of men is enough for you." Her brother had laughed merrily. "Isn't that so, aunt of Rafiq?"

She went back to looking out the window. The green forest surrounding the hotel was darker now. The sun had set some time ago. The moment of the sunset had passed and the long dark night had arrived. She had been careful to avoid being watched and recognized while she was here. But this was her last night in this strange country, and she had never explored the life of the night here. She had gotten to know the streets leading to the sanitorium, the massage room, and the room for mud applications. What had she seen in this strange country other than the mineral baths? Even in her room, what had she looked at other than the walls, the ceiling, and a window overlooking the forest, green during the day, darkening at evening, and black at night, that dreary time of her own sleeplessness.

The bell rang, announcing the hour for dinner. Usually she did not go down to the hall but ate dinner alone in her room. Tonight, however, her final night in this strange country, she decided to go down to the restaurant and sit at a corner table away from the gaze of the curious.

For the first time she approached the restaurant, a brightly illuminated room crowded with people. The room next to the restaurant had a sign above its door in red light; "Bar," it said in many different languages.

During the day the room was empty and locked. Night was another world, a new world with which she had not been familiar during the three weeks of her exile. Had the long quiet nights studying political books in her room rested her and made her happy? Was the restaurant forbidden, so she had dinner in her room? Why had the world of the night frightened her? Wasn't she the fighter, sister of men, aunt of Rafiq? Was she more courageous during the day? Why had she eaten her lunch every day in the infirmary restaurant, which was filled with the old, disabled, and sick? And why had she limited her breakfast to the mineral water from the drinking fountain in her room?

She knew why she had kept to herself. But she could not believe that she actually had passed three long weeks in a medical program that claimed to have given her rest physically, mentally, and emotionally! It was time to return home. To the cause. To the work. In her own country, night would connect with day once more and women and men would be considered equally.

Men and women, men and women. She seemed to hear her brother say, "Have you forgotten that you are the sister of men, the aunt of Rafiq?"

After all of this struggle and self-denial and sacrifice, why had she still not reached the point of being called by her name?

Was it not an honor to be a woman? A woman *only*? Why is a woman always the sister of men, the aunt of a child. . . . Why was she not at least the *wife* of a man?

She had finished eating her dinner and had not noticed that the sweet had been placed on a plate in front of her.

She looked about the restaurant . . . At some tables sat men, at others women, and at a third both sexes sat together. And she . . . she alone of all the people in this room could not say, if asked, at which table she belonged.

She kept staring at the tables. Did all the people eat the same food? She noticed that in addition to the food, some people had glasses of wine. Here was a world where wine was allowed for both sexes. Her eyes searched for a waiter. She would ask him for a glass of wine. She sat glued to her chair while her eyes looked for him. She saw the waiter serving food, chatting with the people sitting next to her, exchanging conversation with them. Occasionally laughter arose and, sometimes, a loud burst of laughter!

The waiter passed by. He did not seem aware of her presence. But she had not wanted to be recognized all during these three weeks! She had hid herself more years than she wished to remember so that she would not be noticed by others. Of course, this waiter did not give her a glance. He did not even turn his head.

A voice rang out. She realized after a moment that it was her voice calling. The waiter came to her. She asked him for a glass of wine. He stared at her in astonishment and disapproval. She repeated her request.

He said, "You want wine now, when dinner is over? We are in a restaurant attached to a hospital; the time has passed for ordering wine with dinner."

He paused and pointed outside.

"The bar is on your right as you exit from the main door. They can serve you wine until the sun rises tomorrow."

He left before hearing her reply. Had the waiter provoked her deliberately? Did he know who she was? Even though she had disguised herself these weeks, that did not mean that she was nobody. There, in her own country, a thousand and one individuals desired to talk to her, the sister of men, to learn something about her or her affairs or the affairs of . . . of . . . of her brother.

For the first time she asked herself to what had she dedicated her life? To the cause, or to her brother?

The waiter presented her with a check. She signed it and stood up proudly, confident of her reputation in her own country. Tomorrow she would be at home, where people honored her and expected her to speak eloquently.

She walked out of the main door of the restaurant. There was the word written in numerous languages in red light.

Music drifted out of the bar. She entered. The room was crowded and filled to the ceiling with smoke.

She walked among the occupied tables to a small table in the farthest corner. She sat down. The table remained empty, and she was pleased that no one had recognized her.

She wondered if she should ask for a glass of wine? Did she want red or white? Which was known to give a person more courage?

She looked around but no one was watching her. She could ask for whatever she wanted and nobody would even give her a glance. Was that a comfort?

The light in the bar was faint and the clouds of smoke surrounded her. No one could see her in the semi-dark. Was that what she wanted? That no one would see her?

Someone stopped by her table. He gestured toward the empty chair. She motioned with her head that he could help himself to the chair and he did. His features resembled those of the natives of her country and so she turned her face away from him.

The fingers of your hands are lean like the fingers of a man, her brother had said. She withdrew her hands and put them in her lap. The man sitting at her table was not looking at her, but turning his head this way and that. She followed his eyes to a statuesque blond girl with a beautiful face. The blond girl was carrying a tray with glasses and bottles on it.

The sister of men looked attentively at the face of her table companion. In it was grief and longing. The waitress was near the neighboring table but she turned and laughed toward them.

The waitress came over and whispered to her table companion. A word the sister of men, the aunt of Rafiq, did not understand, a word in the language of the people in this strange country. But the table companion was a stranger, too; that was better. But . . . why was that better?

On the next round, the waitress stopped for some moments and again on another round. Some minutes passed.

The table companion turned and looked at her . . . She told herself he could not have recognized her. He was a stranger, and he did not know that she was the sister of men, the aunt of Rafiq. He was looking at her directly, at her, herself.

Then he looked down at the empty table before her, and then up at her again.

His eyes asked, "Have you finished?"

And she nodded, "Yes."

PART V
Religion and Law

Religion in the Middle East is not part of the social structure, it *is* the structure, according to John Williams. This is a strikingly different perception of religion than is generally found in the West, where the separation of church and state is a basic cornerstone of thought and action. If, however, the basic social paradigm is religious, what is now happening in the Middle Eastern Muslim world—legal reform, renewed interest in Islamic practice, a turn to modest dress and veiling among women—is not simply a revival of religion or a return to a religious state, but an attempt to reorganize and restructure what already exists, a combining of older ideas with new attitudes arising from the clash of Western and non-Western thought.

For millions of men and women, Islam is the only shared condition that predates the colonial period. Islam is also the basis for most of the laws on the books in a majority of Middle Eastern countries. While legal reform is in progress, it may seem contradictory that at the same time the need to assert Muslim identity seems to be growing throughout the area. Again, neither are new phenomena. Reform and reinterpretation of laws (particularly family law, which affects women's lives directly) have been ongoing processes since the death of the Prophet Muhammad. Confirmation of Islamic values and the assertion of Islamic identity in the face of outside secularist or religious challenges are recurring themes throughout Muslim history. Even during the past two cen-

turies of Western presence (since 1798 when
Napoleon invaded Egypt), many social/political
Muslim movements are documented. The Mah-
dist revolt in the Sudan at the end of the nineteenth century and the rise of the Muslim Brotherhood as a political force in Egypt in the 1920s
and 1930s are the most dramatic, well-known examples, but Islamic associations have flourished
throughout the modern history of the Middle
East, movements involving all levels of activity
from prayer and study to revolution.

For Westerners, discussions of Islamic movements often raise questions about the position of
women within them. Zaynab al-Ghazali, the
Muslim activist whose autobiographical excerpts
appear in the following pages, does not specifically mention women as a group. Thus Westerners
may be led to assume that women are excluded
from the movement Hagga Zaynab describes.
This assumption is the result of our own ethno-
centrism, for it is quite clear from the tone of
Hagga Zaynab's remarks and writings that when
she speaks of Muslims she is speaking of all Muslims, men and women. The division between
male Muslims and female Muslims does not exist—in thought and in principle. In practice,
of course, separate organizations for women exist and have existed in the past. The number of
those organizations seems to be increasing today,
and they take such forms as women's study
groups (Egypt), women's *sofreh*s and *rozeh*s (Iran),
women's *kraya*s or prayer groups (Iraq), and sis-
terhoods in the lodges dedicated to holy figures
(North Africa). Muslim women's groups therefore
have to be seen in context as modern versions of
older institutions, adapting to the changing needs
of women. For example, the Muslim Women's
Cooperative Association in Egypt is currently
housed in Cairo in a modern multistory building
near al-Azhar mosque and university. The association provides supervised dormitory space for
women students who do not have family homes
in the city and child care for married women stu-

dents, filling needs that did not exist fifty years ago when few women studied at any university and those who did lived under the protection of their natal families. Another women's cooperative association provides volunteer teachers for children's religious classes, much like our own Western volunteer Sunday school teachers. Still another recruits women medical students and practicing doctors and lawyers to donate their services to the poor. Many men's organizations offer similar opportunities. Clearly, it is Islamic groups that have stepped in to fill some of the gaps as the society changes and the extended family is pulled apart by time, space, and migrant labor. (This was the case in America in the nineteenth century when the first groups offering assistance to divided families, working girls, and students came from the churches.)

Even the development of the women's movement, particularly in Egypt, reflects the continuing importance of Islam. Huda al-Sha'rawi is the pioneer Egyptian feminist who, with Seza Nabarawi, was the first woman to publicly cast off the veil. In the West, these two women are seen as leaders of the major women's movement that split off from the nationalist parties and operated independently after 1923. But as we read Hagga Zaynab's autobiography, it becomes clear that the women's movement took two directions. Hagga Zaynab was part of Huda al-Sha'rawi's early Feminist Union, but she resigned in the thirties to form the Muslim Women's Association, which looked not to the West for inspiration but to Islamic teaching.

Legal reform in Islam is an issue facing both men and women. Family law, the last legal area to remain untouched by Western-influenced civil codes in many countries, is a political issue of great importance for all Muslims. The Shi'ite 'ulama in Iran are attempting to restate and reinterpret women's position in the 1980s on the basis of precedents established in past legal decisions, as the paper by Shireen Mahdavi indicates.

The strengths and weaknesses of Egypt's new family law, passed in 1979 after years of negotiation, is analyzed by Aziza Hussein. For just as legal reforms have developed and changed over the centuries in Western Europe, so that lawyers in America today still debate the difference between analyzing the law and introducing policy, so Muslim laws are still being rescrutinized and reinterpreted. The results are promulgated by fiat in some countries and by often painful compromise in other countries, where both conservative and liberal forces seek to establish positions. Current family laws in many Middle Eastern countries vary widely. Eric Mueller, an American Muslim scholar, offers a useful analysis of their origins and development.

The issue of veiling or modest dress, especially among women, is an expression of the changing and shifting reorganization of Islamic society, as yet incomplete, in which many people with many different points of view are trying to look back at a common identity and forward to new and pressing needs.

Western commentators have tended to assume that modest dress is a step backward since they view the veil as a symbol of repression. This view of the veil is one that appears again and again in the West, partly because the veil is indeed a dramatic visual symbol. The veil attracts us to a face that may not be seen and at the same time signifies a boundary that may not be crossed.

Such a barrier or boundary between men and women exists in some form in all societies. But the veil as a visible barrier calls up in the viewer a complex reaction. We tend to believe that those who look out (through the veil) suffer from the same exclusion as those of us who look at the veil and its hidden contents. However, we have no right to make such an assumption. Much depends on who makes the decision to veil—whether it is imposed or self-selected.

New patterns of veiling and conservative dress are evolving throughout the Middle East. Are they the result of a woman's own choice or a public imposition on a woman's freedom to choose? Data from Iran are still incomplete, but in Egypt social and economic changes have given a new significance to forms of conservative dress.

Until recently, veiling and conservative dress had been declining steadily in all parts of the Islamic world. Walking on the streets of Turkey, Lebanon, Iraq, Tunisia, Morocco, Algeria, Jordan, and Egypt, a visitor would find a veiled woman the exception rather than the rule. Yet it has continued to be the rule in Saudi Arabia, the Yemen Arab Republic, and some areas of Afghanistan and Pakistan. And now patterns are shifting again.

Western and Middle Eastern attitudes toward the veil have often been seen as an indication of attitude toward values associated with the veil. These values include that of chastity, a prescribed role for women in the family, and, above all, unequal female access to divorce, inheritance, and child custody. If these injustices are reformed, many Middle Eastern women say, the use or nonuse of the veil will become unimportant.

But the veil has been used over the centuries for political, religious, and social purposes, and thus is a symbol within the society itself that can find new uses—"an outward sign of a complex reality." The donning of modest dress or, as some women call it, "Islamic dress" is a personal statement in response to new and changing social conditions. It does not necessarily include the veil.

In Egypt this is a new phenomenon. Women are not "returning to the veil," for the garments they are designing for themselves and wearing in the streets of Cairo are not like the older garments worn before the turn of the century—the *milaya*, the head scarf, the long full black dress. They constitute a new style, developed only in the past ten years. The head scarf, the turban, the fitted long dress, or the loose full dress are adaptations on an old theme, with new expressions and new implications.

The second point is that Islamic dress today is a middle-class and upper-middle-class phenomenon, found mostly among educated working women. The majority of those taking up modest dress are young, in their early twenties, and many are in the universities and professional schools throughout Egypt. As a medical student at Tanta put it, "I think of Islamic dress as a kind of uniform. It means I am serious about myself and my religion but also about my studies. I can sit in class with men and there is no question of attraction and so on—we are all involved in the same business of learning, and these garments make that clear."

The young women who are wearing Islamic dress are often the daughters and granddaughters of women who wear Western dress. Some sociologists within Egypt suggest that this is evidence of a form of rebellion, a rebuff to a parental generation whose efforts have not, as expected, improved conditions in Egypt. Economic conditions in Egypt are indeed better for a small percentage of the population, but for the majority of Egypt's people the bright future promised in the fifties has not materialized. In this sense the new garb carries a political message: it is a dramatic, nonviolent protest against the establishment and its policies as well as against the influence of the West.

But a political statement in Islamic countries is also a religious statement. A small minority of Christians (Copts, Armenians, Nestorians, Eastern Orthodox Catholics, Roman Catholics) live in Egypt, but nearly 90 percent of the population is Muslim. Since the Muslim religion is part of everyday life, religious affiliation is part of one's social identity whether or not one practices a religion or even believes in it. Therefore, far from a simple statement of religious affiliation, the wearing of Islamic dress is related to the very basis of social life in Muslim countries. The growing use of Islamic dress has been observed in Egypt, Jordan, Lebanon, Libya, Morocco, and Algeria.

The wearing of Islamic dress also relates to the individual's sense of belonging to a group and sense of her own identity. Although in Egypt some men also wear a form of Islamic dress (a long, loose, homespun shirt, a white skullcap, and beard), this is less common than among women. Such male apparel may be politically risky these days as it suggests sympathy with what their critics term "Muslim extremists."

A third important point to be made, and one women stress repeatedly, is that the choice to wear Islamic dress is a personal choice and must come "from inner religious conviction." Although stories are told by Westerners of organized Muslim groups paying women to wear Islamic dress, these seem generally to be unfounded. While many women make their own choice, however, they are likely to be influenced by their peers, and the decision is one hotly debated within families and with different groups of friends.

In addition to the genuine religious motives avowed by many young women, the wearing of Islamic dress has many practical advantages. As one young woman put it, "My family trusts me implicitly, and now that I wear this dress, they are not worried if I stay out later than usual or mingle with friends they do not always approve of. In this dress, my reputation remains intact, for everyone knows that it is a respectable garment. People thus respect you if you wear it."

Complete veiling is found in Egypt among a small number of women who cover themselves completely, including their hands. They take the Koranic injunction, "and tell the believing women to draw their garments close around them," to its logical extreme or beyond and say they are emulating the wives of the Prophet, who remained hidden from public view. They describe themselves as devoted to God and unwilling to enter the public workplace.

But the majority of women wearing Islamic dress do not seem to feel this way, nor are they

able to isolate themselves, given the economic realities of Egyptian life. They see themselves as
making a statement or taking action at a time
when individual action is difficult, action that
strengthens their own position within the society.
They attend colleges and universities, work outside the home, mingle with men in classes and on
the streets.

In crowded conditions, such as the streets of
Cairo and the packed public buses, Islamic dress
does offer some protection against importuning
and aggressive sexual advances by men. But of
greater significance is that the new phenomenon
of women working outside the home places many
men and women in new situations, close to each
other for long periods of the day. This places a
strain on the traditional boundaries between men
and women and may also jeopardize the reputation of the young women. For while it is true that
many of the outward signs of the older Egyptian
society—seclusion of women and segregation of
women from public workplaces, educational institutions, etc.—have disappeared, traditional attitudes are slower to change. The wearing of Islamic dress is a practical, simple way of stating
publicly, "I am a respectable Muslim woman.
Leave me alone."

The veil or modest dress, then, is a complex
symbol that can have multiple implications and
different impacts. Manipulated in one way, it can
become a symbol for conservatism or for reaction
against modernization; utilized in another way, it
can become a symbol for a new Islamic approach
to the solutions of old and new problems. However it is used, it means different things to different people within the society, and it means different things to Westerners than it does to Muslim
Middle Easterners.

Women in the Muslim Middle East, like men,
find themselves in a society radically different
from that of their grandparents. Not all are of the
same opinion about how to deal with the situation. Despite differing viewpoints, however, the

majority seem to agree on one point: whatever the future, it should reflect Islamic tradition. Women and men may argue about the means to achieve that goal, but their overall commitment to it is clear.

Revitalizing Old Ideas: Developments in Middle Eastern Family Law

ERIC MUELLER

The Islamic world is heir to one of the most sophisticated legal systems. Over the centuries the Shariʿa, or Islamic law, developed from verses of the Koran and from the decisions of the Prophet Muhammad and his early companions into a versatile and complex system of legal opinions, precedents, and judgments. In a sense, "systems" would be a more appropriate characterization, since Islamic law embraced many different schools and tolerated a large variety of opinion on almost every topic. These different views were the natural result of the complicated process of development that produced the phenomenon of "Islamic law," a legal system that deals with every facet of Muslim life. But the Shariʿa was not brought down from a mountain in finished form, carved into stone tablets. Muhammad's "way" was a flexible, dynamic adaptation of general principles to specific situations as they arose.

Muhammad the Prophet began his religious career preaching in Mecca. Although he attracted many followers, he remained simply a religious teacher. Nevertheless he was viewed as something of a threat by the tribal oligarchy that controlled long-distance trade through Mecca and relied on tribal allegiance to exercise its control. Muhammad's message, on the other hand, not only decried social inequality but also addressed itself to all men regardless of tribal affiliation. Thus the Islamic message tended to undermine the tribal bonds that ensured the Meccan oligarchy its pride of place.

Muhammad was invited to Medina in 622 C.E. to be the arbiter of disputes that at that time frequently flared up between the tribal groupings resident in the city. Since he was of a different tribal background and thus neutral, Muhammad could pass judgment without becoming the catalyst for further tribal feuding.

Muhammad, then, regarded as arbiter of community affairs, was naturally asked to give rulings, orders, or injunctions on any topic that might arise and cause discord. Therefore, not only did he make pronouncements on how the Muslims should pray and fast (actions that Islam takes to be more social than individual), he also had the obligation to establish proper methods of taxation, marriage and divorce, commerce, treaties of war and peace, and rules for personal and public sanitation. Any issue that concerned the members of the growing community in Medina was brought to the Prophet for his judgment.

The Law was developing even at that early period as Muhammad took the specifics of each case into account. Thus one finds different statements on a given topic depending on the time the judgment was made. In addition, some issues never arose, or arose only once in the Prophet's lifetime, and as a result there is little information as to what Muhammad's views on such questions might have been.

After the death of the Prophet Muhammad in A.D. 632, his first four successors, the so-called pious caliphs, carried on the tradition of flexibility. Not infrequently one finds statements by these leaders that have no precedent in Muhammad's career or that refine his practice markedly. For example, the second successor, ʿUmar ibn al-Khattab, refused to cut off the hands of thieves who had stolen out of hunger.

The early successors, although they preserved the Prophet's rulings on many issues, clearly felt that the specific injunctions were themselves mere forms and that it was the intent of the Prophet's legislation that was essential. Thus, although Muhammad alone was the lawgiver and the successors were obliged to carry out the "Laws of God," the early successors believed that laws had to be understood and reinterpreted to remain true to their original intent. Though Muhammad had laid down the laws, the successors felt fully able to interpret, adapt, and even supersede them in an effort to make sure that the original intent was followed.

This does not mean that the successors considered themselves prophets—they did not. However, during their time the Shariʿa retained its original ad hoc nature, whereby the merits of each case were adjudged in the light of general principles. The law continually developed, and the successors in their secular authority were fully empowered to preside over and guide that process.

When the authority in the Muslim state passed to the dynasty of Bani Umayyah (the caliph Muʿawiyah and his heirs), this situation changed. Muʿawiyah, the son of one of Muhammad's arch enemies and heir to the Meccan oligarchy, had no aura of religiosity about him. Many of his successors were known for their dissolute lives. With the Umayyad dynasty one can truly speak of an Islamic state (as distinct from the more vague "Islamic community"), a state with a king and a regular army. The first four successors had ruled more or less on the basis of their personal popularity. Muʿawiyah and his successors ruled primarily on the basis of strength.

This signified a major change for Muslims. The early, semitribal, more egalitarian social order was reflected in a legal system that was developing in tandem with social change. But under the Umayyad state, the law grew more rigid as it was employed by rulers as a theoretical justification for state control. On the one hand the leader began to be seen as more subject to the law and less qualified to modify or change it; on the other hand the leader could enforce the law with the help of his troops.

Although traditional Islamic theory maintains that Islamic law attained its final form with the passing of the age of the first four caliphs, such was not actually the case. Mu'awiyah and his successors were no longer sources of Shari'a legislation, but it was under their rule that religious scholars collected and organized the various rulings of the Prophet and his first successors and created a legal system. During this period of formation, from about A.D. 700 to 900, all four Sunni schools of law emerged and the main collections of prophetic statements (Hadith) were compiled.

Parallel with the crystalization of state-sponsored "orthodoxy," numerous movements appeared in opposition to the state. These adopted alternative religious views that are (naturally) called "unorthodox." The Shi'a was the first "sect" to be constituted. The Khariji movement followed, rejecting the Shi'a as well as the majority of the community. Throughout the Umayyad and 'Abbasid times the orthodox religious scholars spent no little time combatting "pernicious" heresies of various Shi'a groups, the radical Qaramita, the hostile if passive Sufis. Thus the term "traditional Islamic law" stands in fact for a whole variety of groups and opinions. Some have been accepted as orthodox, others have the aura of rebellion about them. All of them claim to draw upon the same sources, the Koran and the practice of the Prophet.

Since the eighteenth century, the gradual integration of the Islamic lands into the world market and the impact of Western colonialism have brought about massive and relatively rapid social changes in Islamic societies. Legal practices have had to come to grips with these changes in one way or another. The Ottoman empire for centuries supplemented its version of orthodox Shari'a with *qanun* laws, the secular decrees of the sultan. Other governments in the Muslim world have followed this pattern by passing a variety of *qanun* laws to deal with rapidly changing times and conditions.

The Shari'a, supposedly being divinely ordained, was viewed theoretically as perfect and unchanging. But social, economic, and political change tended to produce gaps between the obvious intent of Shari'a legislation on the one hand and the effect of its literal application on the other. Furthermore, even traditional Shari'a exegesis recognized that specific injunctions could be dispensed with or modified if the society's well-being was at stake. In addition, Shariʿa embraced a very wide range of different attitudes and interpretations.

By the twentieth century, then, the stage was set for the tide of reformist legislation that has modified or replaced traditional law. Personal status, marriage, and family laws are some of the most notable examples of attempts at legal reform, and today new laws continue to be enacted. These laws are of great interest because of the way in which the legacy of Shariʿa is combined with the imperatives of modern legislation.

Recent family laws from three Arab countries (Iraq, Egypt, and the People's Democratic Republic of Yemen) provide good examples of the new reformist trend. To some extent these laws are incompatible. Different countries—even different Arab countries—face distinct social problems requiring specific legal solutions. Generally, though, the legacy of the regions is similar, and the laws differ primarily as a result of the differing views of the authors of particular pieces of legislation. These different views in turn are not simply personal, but reflect different class and social perspectives and political ideologies.

The most far-reaching set of laws under consideration is the Family Law of the People's Democratic Republic of Yemen (PDRY). The PDRY is the first Arab state to embrace Marxism-Leninism as its official ideology and, as one might expect, its laws reflect a radical social outlook. Yet even here a large part of the Family Law is merely a restatement of long-held Shariʿa interpretations. "We researched the old books of *hadith* to show that we had not created anything; everything is in Islam. We only gave vitamins to old ideas to have them triumph," a former member of the committee that drafted the Family Law commented.[1] The Yemeni law, for instance, accepts the Islamic "prohibited degrees"[2] of marriage, including prohibition by fosterage as well as by blood relationships. Before remarrying, a Yemeni woman who is widowed must wait for four months and ten days, while a Yemeni woman who is divorced and not pregnant must wait only ninety days, just as the Shariʿa specifies.[3] Thus, Yemen's Marxist leaders are not willing to import Western-style legislation wholesale without regard for local values and customs.

All three countries prohibit marriage without the consent of both bride and groom. All require the involvement of the official court system. But the PDRY is the only one of the three to prohibit polygamy, except in very specific cases such as barrenness or critical disease, and then only with the court's special consent.[4] Further, the first wife may divorce the husband if he avails himself of such permission.[5] Taking a second wife is grounds for divorce in Egypt as well, but only if the first wife initially withheld consent for the husband's second marriage.

The Yemeni law alone of the three places the legal burden of support of the family equally on both the wife and the husband, assuming both are financially capable.[6] The assumption is made in Egypt and Iraq that the wife should be supported by the husband, this being the traditional Shariʿa position. In the PDRY the compensation for divorce is discussed in a more egalitarian framework, though admittedly one that remains close to fundamental, traditional Shariʿa principles: the woman, should she initiate the divorce, pays no more than the value of the *mahr*, or dowry, and the man, if he initiates the divorce, pays no more than one month's support.[7] Traditionally, in Islamic marriage the groom presents his bride with a *mahr*, part of which he pays in cash and the rest of which remains on paper until death or divorce effects its transfer to the woman's estate. Traditionally, if a woman divorced, she was expected to return the part of the dowry she had actually received. Thus the Yemeni law in effect preserves the traditional divorce processes while at the same time setting them on a legal foundation of sexual equality.

The laws of all three countries have similar acceptable grounds for divorce. All three mention arbitration efforts to forestall divorce, although the Iraqi and Egyptian laws are much more specific than the Yemeni law. The practice of arbitration rather than immediate divorce is of course Koranic in origin.

In sum, all the family laws reviewed here incorporate major elements of the Shariʿa as well as modern reform legislation. Or, to be more precise, the Shariʿa itself has been reinterpreted in reformist or even radical ways. None of the family laws seeks the mechanical imposition of Western legislation on Islamic society. Yet there remain great differences among these Islamic countries' modern legislation. The Iraqi and Egyptian codes are reformist in nature while the Yemeni law seeks to establish totally new relations between men and women—a sweeping revolutionary objective. In all, however, the flexible legacy of the Shariʿa is clear and powerful. This is an indication of the enduring vitality of Islamic law, which in different interpretations can continue to fulfill many and various social functions depending on the perspective of the interpreter.

Notes

1. "Freedom Takes Time," *The Middle East* 100 (February 1983).
2. The People's Democratic Republic of Yemen, *Family Law: Law No. (1) of 1974 in Connection with the Family* (Aden: 1974), part 1, chap. 3, p. 10.
3. Ibid., part 3, p. 16.
4. Ibid., part 1, chap. 2, pp. 9–10.
5. Ibid., part 2, p. 15.
6. Ibid., part 1, p. 12.
7. Ibid., part 2, pp. 15–16.

Recent Amendments to Egypt's Personal Status Law

AZIZA HUSSEIN

In June 1979 Egypt's National Assembly approved amendments to the Personal Status Law. The amendments, presented by presidential decree in the form of a package deal, were the first revisions to be made in fifty years. The procedure followed in guiding them through the Assembly was in accordance with the new Egyptian Constitution and was designed to avoid polemics and filibuster during the debate over this very sensitive issue. The amendments left unchanged the right of the Egyptian husband to divorce and to marry more than one wife. However, they balanced these privileges with responsibilities, within the religious framework, that had never before been given legal expression.

The amendments were carefully formulated to forestall any unnecessary confrontation with conservative religious elements. The extreme fundamentalists could not be won over anyway, being totally opposed to the very principle of codification. In their view the Shariᶜa (Islamic jurisprudence), which is based on the Holy Koran, the Sunna, and the interpretations of the old theological schools, is in itself sufficient as reference and guide for the judges as well as for the individual conscience. Their point of view is completely at variance with present-day thinking of social reformers who are concerned about the social and psychological effects of the old laws on the conditions of women and the well-being of the family.

Fundamentalist views apart, all previous efforts to amend the Personal Status Law had foundered over the attempt to curtail, by legal means, the right of the husband to divorce his wife at will and to marry more than one woman. That right was considered to be God-given and as such should not be restricted or tampered with. There have always been divergent views on this issue among the religious authorities, but somehow the conservative elements had been able to exercise enough influence to keep the laws unchanged.

The pragmatic approach is demonstrated in the amendments by a decree from President Sadat that gained the support of various women's groups, among them our Cairo Family Planning Association (CFPA).

Two years earlier our organization had launched the first systematic effort in support of amending the Personal Status Law. We organized meetings and seminars, made judicious use of the mass media, and drafted a comprehensive model for a family code.

It was the first time that this question had been tackled by a nongovernmental organization on a long-term basis and with appropriate funding (from IPPF [International Planned Parenthood Federation]), staffing, and expertise. Equally important, it was the first time that a link had been forged between the security of the woman within the family and family planning as such.

When the long-awaited amendments were made public, they were by no means a carbon copy of the code drafted by CFPA. There were many omissions that, at first glance, caused some disappointment. Soon, however, this group, which had played a constructive role in campaigning for change, realized that the amendments represented good interim legislation that addressed itself to some very basic problems without creating undue friction and confrontation on the social, religious, or political levels. In fact, President Sadat had even succeeded in winning over the religious leadership, which spoke up in favor of the amendments in such a manner as to surprise even those who had themselves campaigned for change. The three most influential leaders—the head of al-Azhar Mosque, the Grand Mufti, and the Minister of Wakfs—were jointly interviewed on television in an hour-long appearance during which they gave full endorsement to the new legislation and offered religious justification for the changes.

There were rumblings, of course, from the fundamentalists and from other traditionalists in the rural areas. Defenders of male superiority from the lower middle class complained that men were becoming the victims of discrimination. These same groups had been equally displeased with the new legislation that gave women a quota of thirty seats in the National Assembly, another innovation by President Sadat in his efforts to improve the status of Egyptian women.

What, then, were the amendments and what were the particular issues to which they addressed themselves?

The main grievances against the Personal Status Law centered on the arbitrary and unilateral rights of the husband to divorce his wife and his absolute and unquestioned right to marry more than one wife, as well as the laws relating to parental rights and obligations. The laws regarding legal capacity, property rights, and the right of the wife to retain her maiden name remained unchanged. These laws have always been a source of pride to Muslims, since under Islam women had been given these rights centuries before they were acquired by women in non-Muslim countries.

Divorce and Custody

The husband continues to retain the right to divorce his wife without recourse to the courts, the reason given being that a court action would lead to the disclosure of private family affairs and might even result in a scandal that would be harmful to everyone concerned. Of course, religious considerations are also a factor. However, the procedures that must be followed under the new amendments place certain restrictions on men.

1. The husband must register his divorce before witnesses at a Registrar's Office and his wife must be officially and immediately informed. Failure on his part to inform her makes him liable to a penalty. No such restrictions existed before.

2. The divorced wife is entitled to an alimony equivalent to one year's maintenance plus a compensation equivalent to two years' maintenance, and this amount could be increased by the court in cases of extra damage or the termination of a long marriage. The first installments of this sum are to be paid automatically to the wife via the Nasser Bank, which is empowered to collect them by various means from the husband. Under the previous law, the wife was entitled to an alimony equivalent to one year's maintenance.

3. The husband who divorces his wife must guarantee her a home if she has custody of his children. He must either find them a home or move out himself.

4. As for custody, the divorced wife automatically gains custody of her children under the age of ten for boys and twelve for girls, subject to extensions by a court decision to fifteen for boys and until marriage for girls. The previous law gave the mother custody of her children only until age seven and nine for boys and girls, respectively, subject to extensions to nine and eleven.

5. Under the old law a wife could obtain a divorce only by a court decision on the basis of specific grounds. The new amendments fix a deadline of nine months for "court mediation." If attempts by the court to reconcile the couple fail, the divorce is granted without further delay. This has resolved one of the most burning issues and has narrowed the gap between men's and women's rights in divorce.

Polygamy

Polygamy has long been a cause of outrage and a symbol of degradation for women, especially among the educated class, even though, admittedly, it is rarely practiced. The very existence of the man's right to marry another wife has had a damaging psychological effect on women, especially in the lower socioeconomic strata. Moreover, the husband could remarry without having to make his action known to his wife.

The amendments do not restrict a man's right to marry more than one wife, but they do place practical constraints on him. The husband now has to notify his wife of his intention to marry another woman. He must also inform his wife-to-be of his present marital status. In fact, secrecy was the major factor in making polygamy relatively easy to practice in certain circumstances. Furthermore, the first wife is entitled to a court divorce within a year of her knowledge of her husband's marriage to another woman. In such a court decision, the second marriage is regarded as damaging to the first wife and entitles her to compensation.

Right to Work

Another important and new aspect of the amendments is the confirmation of women's right to work. This right is not contingent any more on the husband's approval.

In the past, a woman who worked against her husband's wishes was legally placed in the category of *nashez*, meaning "disobedient." As such she lost her right to maintenance by her husband, who had the right to neglect her. The wife's right to a court divorce was very much jeopardized by the disobedient status. The new amendments have rectified this irregularity in the old law.

NOTE: *This essay is excerpted from a chapter in* Religion and Politics· *(Westview Press, 1981).*

An Islamic Activist: Zaynab al-Ghazali

VALERIE J. HOFFMAN
Translated from the Arabic by Valerie J. Hoffman

Zaynab al-Ghazali al-Jabili calls herself the "mother" of the Muslim Brotherhood, a reference to her seniority in age and her leading role as teacher and propagator of the Brotherhood's cause in Egypt. The Muslim Brotherhood was founded in 1928–29 by Hasan al-Banna in Ismailia and called for a total integration of Islam into all aspects of Egyptian public life. Zaynab al-Ghazali became active in the Brotherhood in 1949, but at that time she already had thirteen years of active involvement in the Islamic da'wa (call or mission) through her own organization, the Muslim Women's Association. After a Brother made an attempt on Nasser's life in 1954 the Brotherhood was outlawed, though its vast influence and activities continued. In 1965, when there was a new round of arrests of Brotherhood members, Zaynab al-Ghazali was among those imprisoned and tortured. She was released six years later.

The story of her imprisonment is told in her book, Ayyam min hayati (Days of my life, Cairo and Beirut: Dar al-Shuruq, n.d.). What follows is a translation of portions from an interview I conducted with Hagga Zaynab at her home in the Cairo suburb of Heliopolis on June 17, 1981, and from the second chapter of her book. Both the interview and the book are very revealing of her ideas, her background, her relationships with those who were close to her, and the inner workings of the Brotherhood during a period of regrouping after dissolution.

The book aims mainly to expose the Nasser regime's persecution of the Muslim Brothers, and Zaynab al-Ghazali consciously depicts the Brotherhood as a peaceful and peace-loving association of pious Muslims, with no reference to its numerous internal conflicts or to the Brotherhood's violent tendencies. Zaynab al-Ghazali was editor of the section of Al-da'wa magazine entitled "Toward a Muslim Home." This section includes a mini-magazine for children with a feature entitled "Know the Enemies of Your Religion" that encourages children to hate and fear Zionists, imperialists, and evangelicals, who are accused of working to undermine Islamic religion and society. Al-da'wa was banned in September 1981 along with a number of other religious publications.

Although to the best of my knowledge the Muslim Women's Association has not functioned as a legally incorporated society since its dissolution in 1965, Zaynab al-Ghazali remains an active lecturer, teacher, and propagator of Islam. Furthermore, the recent Islamic resurgence has made a particular appeal to women. Numerous religious associations have women's sections, and most mosques now have Koranic lessons for women once a week. Far from ignoring women or considering their role as secondary, Islamic religious organizations have come to emphasize the essential contribution Muslim women make toward creating the Islamic family. In the words of one author, women are "the foundation of the virtuous Islamic society." These are words that are echoed in many Islamic writings.

Following are excerpts from the 1981 interview with Hagga Zaynab.

QUESTION: How did your contact with the Muslim Brotherhood begin?

ANSWER: The Muslim Brotherhood is the association of all Muslims in the world, so it is natural and imperative for every Muslim to be in contact with it. If I did not have contact with the Muslim Brotherhood, that would be strange and incomprehensible according to sound Islamic understanding, but the fact that I have had contact with it is natural. My contact with it began at the beginning of 1939. It was a direct contact with the martyred *imam* and renewer of the faith,[1] Hasan al-Banna.

Q: How did you come to know him?

A: I came to know him because he is an *imam* and a renewer of the faith, calling people to God. At that time I was actively propagating Islam, calling people to God. . . . I was working in the general headquarters of the Muslim Women's Association, which I founded in A.H. 1356/A.D. 1936.

Q: How did you come to assume this role?

A: At the time I was eighteen years old. I was working with Mrs. Huda al-Sharawi in the women's movement, which calls for the liberation of women.[2] But I, with my Islamic upbringing, found that this was not the right way for Muslim women. Women had to be called to Islam, so I founded the Muslim Women's Association after I resigned from the Feminist Union.

Q: At first you were with Mrs. Huda al-Sharawi, and then you discovered—

A: That this was a mistake.

Q: Why? How did you discover that this was wrong?

A: Islam has provided everything for both men and women. It gave women everything—freedom, economic rights, political rights, social rights, public and private rights. Islam gave women rights in the family granted by no other society. Women may talk of liberation in Christian society, Jewish society, or pagan society, but in Islamic society it is a grave error to speak of the liberation of women. The Muslim woman must study Islam so she will know that it is Islam that has given her all her rights. . . .

Q: But why were you convinced at first of the validity of Huda al-Sha'rawi's movement, but later changed your mind? What brought about this change of mind?

A: Studying, reading, and attending lectures and Islamic meetings.

Q: So you established the Muslim Women's Association when you were eighteen, by yourself.

A: Yes. I called women together for Islam.

Q: Was it successful?

A: Very.

Q: What were its activities?

A: Our goal was to acquaint the Muslim woman with her religion so she would be convinced by means of study that the women's liberation movement is a deviant innovation that occurred due to the Muslims' backwardness. We consider the Muslims to be backward; they must remove this backwardness from their shoulders and rise up as their religion commands, as it should be in Islamic lands.

Q: So there were lessons for women?

A: There were lessons for the women. The association also maintained an orphanage, offered assistance to poor families, and helped reconcile families. It attempted to give useful work to young Muslim men and women who were unemployed; that is, they helped in religious activities. The association also has a political opinion, that Egypt must be ruled by the Koran, not positivistic constitutions.

Q: You say that your contact with the Muslim Brotherhood was natural. Do you think that the Muslim who is not in the Brotherhood is not a true Muslim?

A: He is a deficient Muslim, and the remedy for this deficiency is for him to join the Muslim Brotherhood.

Q: What is the goal of the Brotherhood?

A: The return of the Islamic state, which rules by the Koran and Sunna.[3]

Q: Would there be states other than the Islamic state?

A: The Islamic nation possesses one-third of the world. Geographically, we are richer than the rest of the world, in oil we are richer than the rest of the world. So why are we backward? Because we are not following our religion, we are not living in accordance with our constitution and laws. If we return to our Koran and to the Sunna of our Prophet, we will live Islam in reality, and we will control the whole world.

Q: Do you think it is wrong for there to be something called Egypt, Saudi Arabia, or Pakistan?

A: They remain. But there would be a federation, like the United States.

Q: What methods does the Brotherhood use to attain its goal?

A: Very simple methods. We teach the child his religion, and that he should be governed by nothing but the Koran and should govern by nothing but the Koran. That is all. The day is coming when we will see the whole nation upholding the Koran. When all the people say, "Our religion is Islam," no ruler will be able to say, "I don't want Islam."

Q: Have you seen changes in the Brotherhood in the many years you have been with it?

A: Of course. Whenever one goes deeper, one becomes more refined, stronger. Of course, the Muslim Brotherhood passed through martyrdoms, imprisonments. Brothers were taken to prison, exiled from their country. All these trials gave them power, experience, wisdom, and an ability to patiently endure, so they will not be content unless they are following this path.

Q: Do you think the Brotherhood is stronger now than it was before?

A: Much stronger. Because it learned from the experience of persecution from such people as Gamal Abdel Nasser. It has become wiser, more knowledgeable, in better contact with God, knowing more about human nature.

Q: What is the role of women in the Muslim Brotherhood? Are there many women like you?

A: The Brotherhood considers women a fundamental part of the Islamic call. They are the ones who are most active because men have to work. They are the ones who build the kind of men that we need to fill the ranks of the Islamic call. So women must be well educated, cultured, knowing the precepts of the Koran and Sunna, knowing world politics, why we are backward, why we don't have technology. The Muslim woman must study all these things, and then raise her son in the conviction that he must possess the scientific tools of the age, and at the same time he must understand Islam, politics, geography, and current events. He must rebuild the Islamic nation. We Muslims only carry arms in order to spread peace. We want to purify the world of unbelief, atheism, oppression, and persecution. . . . Islam does not forbid women to actively participate in public life. It does not prevent her from working, entering into politics, and expressing her opinion, or from being anything, as long as that does not interfere with her first duty as a mother, the one who first trains her children in the Islamic call. So her first, holy, and most important mission is to be a mother and wife. She cannot ignore this priority. If she then finds she has free time, she may participate in public activities. Islam does not forbid her.

Q: Must all women marry in Islamic society? Is there no place for the single woman?

A: Marriage is a sure Sunna in Islam. There is no monasticism in Islam. Men must marry unless they have an excuse, that is, an illness. Women are also excused if they have an illness. But marriage was instituted to reproduce children and to establish the family, which is the fundamental unit in building the Islamic state. Marriage is a mission and a trust in Islam. Sexual life in Islam is a necessity for both men and women, but it is not the first and last goal of marriage. It is to preserve the human race, establish the family, build the man and the woman, to build the ruler, to bring about righteous government. . . . Any sexual relations outside marriage are totally prohibited. When a man has relations with his wife, it is Sunna that they both wash themselves. And it is Sunna that before he approaches her he says, "In the name of God, the Compassionate, the Merciful. God, protect us from Satan." He begins in this way, because it is a human duty, a duty imposed by God, a divine duty.

Q: You were married?

A: I married twice. I found that [my first] marriage took up all my time and kept me from my mission, and my husband did not agree with my work. I had made a condition that if we had any major disagreements we would separate, and the Islamic cause was the essential. My second husband knew that I left my first husband because of the cause. He gave me written agreements that he would not come between me and my mission, but that he would help me and be my assistant. And in fact we had an enjoyable married life in which there was cooperation, love, faithfulness to God, and purity of soul and conscience. We separated only when I was sent to prison, and he died twenty-one days after I was sentenced. After that, since I had done my duty in marriage, I was free to give all my time to the cause.

Q: You said it was your father who had the greatest influence on you in your Islamic upbringing. Who was he, and how did he influence you?

A: He was Sheikh al-Ghazali al-Jabili, a scholar who completed his education in al-Azhar.[4] He refused to accept a government job, but he was a big cotton merchant. When it was not the cotton season, he devoted himself to preaching Islam. He went around the country, exhorting the people, preaching in the mosques on Fridays, teaching the Islamic call and religion. He always used to say to me that, God willing, I would be an Islamic leader. That's what he used to say to me. He would say, "Huda al-Sha'rawi does this, and Malak Hifni Nasif does that, but among the Companions of the Prophet Muhammad, may God bless him and grant him peace, there was a woman named Nusayba, the daughter of Ka'b al-Mazini.[5] He would tell me of how she struggled in the path of Islam, and then he would ask me, "Whom do you choose? Do you choose Huda al-Sha'rawi, or will you become Nusayba, daughter of Ka'b al-Mazini?" And I would say to him, "I will be Nusayba, daughter of Ka'b al-Mazini." So I decided to be a Muslim woman.

From *Days of My Life*, chapter 2, pages 26–41.

My connections with the Muslim Brotherhood were not new, as the foolish would have people believe, for its history goes back to the year A.H. 1357/A.D. 1937.

On that blessed day, long ago, in about A.H. 1358, approximately six months after the founding of the Muslim Women's Association, I first met the martyred *imam*, Hasan al-Banna. This was after a lecture I gave to the Muslim sisters in the Brotherhood headquarters, which at that time was in 'Ataba Square.

The guiding *imam* was preparing to create a division for the Muslim Sisters. After first stressing that the ranks of all Muslims must be unified and there must be no differences of opinion, he asked me to head the Muslim Sisters' division. That would mean incorporating the newborn of which I was so proud, the Muslim Women's Association, and considering it a part of the Muslim Brotherhood movement. I no more than discussed the matter with the general assembly of the Muslim Women's Association, which rejected the proposal, though it approved of a first cooperation between the two organizations.

We continued to meet together, though each of us held to his own opinion. The Muslim Sisters' division was founded without changing our Islamic relationship at all. I tried, in our last meeting in the headquarters of the Muslim Women's Association, to appease his anger by promising to take it upon myself that the Muslim Women's Association be one of the supports of the Muslim Brotherhood on condition that it retain its name and independence, which would be more beneficial to the cause. But this too did not please him as a substitute for incorporation. Then events happened quickly, and the incidents of 1948 occurred.[6] A resolution was issued dissolving the Brotherhood and confiscating its possessions, locking up its people and throwing thousands into prison camps. The Muslim Sisters did things for which they received much gratitude. One of them was Mrs. Tahiya al-Jabili, my brother's wife and my cousin; from her I learned many of the details, and for the first time I found myself longing to reconsider all of al-Banna's opinions and his insistence on complete incorporation. On the morning following the dissolution of the Muslim Brotherhood I was in my office in the headquarters of the Muslim Women's Association, in the same room in which I had had my last meeting with the guiding *imam*. I found myself sitting at my desk with my head in my hands, weeping bitterly. I felt that Hasan al-Banna was right, and that he was the leader to whom allegiance is due from all Muslims, to strive in the path of God to restore the Muslims to their responsibilities and their true and rightful existence, the apex of the world, which they will lead as God wills, and which they will judge by what God has revealed. I felt that Hasan al-Banna was stronger than I, and more sincere in unambiguously spreading and proclaiming the truth.

Such courage and boldness are the clothing that should be worn by every Muslim. Al-Banna had worn it and called us to it.

Then I found myself calling my secretary and telling her to get me in touch with Brother ʿAbd al-Hafiz al-Sayfi, whom I commissioned to carry a verbal message to Imam al-Banna, reminding him of my promise in our last meeting. When he returned to me with his greeting and appeal, I summoned my brother, Muhammad al-Ghazali al-Jabili, and asked him to deliver a slip of paper either by himself or via his wife to the guiding *imam*. On the paper was written:

"My lord, Imam Hasan al-Banna:

"Zaynab al-Ghazali al-Jabili approaches you today as a slave who has nothing but her worship of God and her total devotion to the service of God's call. You are the only one today who can sell this slave at the price he wishes for the cause of God the Exalted.

"Waiting for your orders and instructions, my lord the *imam*. . . ."

My brother returned to arrange a hasty meeting in the headquarters of the YMMA.[7] It was to happen as if it were a coincidence. I had no lack of justification for being there, for I was on my way to the YMMA hall to give a lecture. I met Mr. al-Banna and said to him as we went up the stairs, "By God I pledge allegiance to you, to work to establish the state of Islam. The least I can offer you to achieve it is my blood, and the Muslim Women's Association with its name." He said, "I accept your pledge of allegiance. The Muslim Women's Association may remain as it is." We separated on the agreement that we would be in touch by means of my brother's family. The first charge I received from the martyred *imam* was a commission to mediate between al-Nahhas and the Brotherhood. At that time Mustafa Pasha al-Nahhas was outside the government; the late al-Nahhas appointed Amin Khalil to try to bring an end to the misunderstanding, and the martyred *imam* was pleased with this choice; I was the contact.[8] One night in February 1949 Amin Khalil came to me and told me, "Immediate steps must be taken for al-Banna to leave Cairo. The criminals are conspiring to kill him." I found no way to contact him directly, because my brother had been imprisoned. I tried to contact the martyred *imam* in person. While I was on my way to get in touch with him, I got word of the assassination attempt and that he was taken to the hospital. Then the news of his bad condition quickly got worse. He departed as a martyr to his Lord, with the prophets, the truthful, the martyrs, and the upright, and they are the best companions.

My grief was intense and my desire for revenge against the criminals was bitter; I made no attempt to hide it. The government of the coalition of parties came into power and issued an order dissolving the Muslim Women's Association. I opposed the order in court, which ordered us to resume our activities during the government of Husayn Sirri Pasha in 1950. The lawyer was Mr. ʿAbd al-Fattah Hasan "Pasha." Then came the Wafd government, and the Brotherhood resumed its activities. At that time its allegiance was to the guiding *imam*, Hasan al-Hudaybi. On the first day of the opening of the general headquarters of the Muslim Brotherhood, I wanted to announce my faithfulness to the cause in an indirect way, and may God ordain whatever He wills in the matter. So I contributed the most expensive and precious piece of furniture in my house, an arabesque parlor set inlaid with mother of pearl, to furnish the office of the General Guide.

All was calm and peaceful. The martyr ʿAbd al-Qadir ʿAwda[9] visited me and thanked me for the donation, and said, "I am happy that Zaynab al-Ghazali al-Jabili has become a member of the Muslim Brotherhood." I said, "May it be so, with God's permission." He said, "It is so, praise be to God."

Events passed in a calm and friendly atmosphere between me and many members of the Brotherhood. Then the revolutionary military government came under the leadership of Major General Muhammad Neguib, who had visited me only a few days before the revolution accompanied by Prince ʿAbdallah al-Faisal, Yas Sirag al-Din, Sheikh al-Baquri,[10] and my brother ʿAli al-Ghazali on the occasion of Prince ʿAbdallah al-Faisal's visit to Egypt. The Brotherhood was sympathetic to the revolution, and so was the Muslim Women's Association, for a while. Then I began to feel that things were not going as we had hoped, and this was not the revolution we had anticipated, a crowning of previous efforts at the hands of those who were working to save this country. I began to express my opinion to other members of the Brotherhood. When ministerial positions were offered to some Brotherhood members, I expressed my opinion in the magazine of the Muslim Women's Association that none of the Brotherhood should pledge loyalty to a government that does not rule by what God has revealed, and whoever does so must separate from the Brotherhood, and that the Brotherhood must define its position, now that the government's intentions had become clear.

The martyr ʿAbd al-Qadir ʿAwda visited me, asking me to postpone writing on this subject. So I withdrew two issues of the magazine. Then I resumed writing until the martyr ʿAbd al-Qadir ʿAwda visited me for the second time, this time bearing a command from the General Guide ordering me not to write on this subject. I recalled my pledge to al-Banna, may God have mercy on him, and I believed that loyalty was transferred to al-Hudaybi, so I obeyed the order.

From that time on my pledge of allegiance governed my behavior, even in such matters as the peace conference in Vienna. I did not travel until I had obtained permission from the guiding *imam*, al-Hudaybi.

Time passed, and then came the events of 1954 with its infamies and calamities, which revealed Gamal Abdel Nasser for what he really is: an enemy of Islam, fighting it in the persons of its propagators and the leadership of its movement.[11] Heinous death sentences were passed on the top Islamic leaders: the martyr and councillor ʿAbd al-Qadir ʿAwda, a man of virtue, a scholar of al-Azhar, a pious man, for whom the British leadership in the canal zone in 1951 offered a reward of 10,000 pounds to whomever brought him in dead or alive; Sheikh Muhammad Farghali, who was given to the imperialists dead without any loss to the British treasury; and the other noble martyrs.

Even the great struggler for God, Imam Hasan al-Hudaybi, was sentenced to death, though the sentence was not carried out because he was suddenly struck with a severe angina in the heart and was taken to the hospital. The doctors said he had only a few hours to live, so at that point Abdel Nasser issued a pardon for him, expecting to read his obituary in the papers the next morning. But God's power foiled his stratagem. The *imam* lived. Every life term is fixed by God. Yes, he lived, to again render services—and what services!—to the Muslims and to lead the Islamic call in its darkest hour. He demonstrated an ability to steadfastly cling to the truth while he was ill with a number of diseases. This baffled his torturers and caused them to take him to the war prison once more and torture him in the most hideous manner. But he continued to cling to the truth, taking the road of those who follow the call until he came to see the end of Abdel Nasser and his clique, while he survived, raising the banner of truth and the unity of God in which he believed, involved with every kernel of his being. He was steadfast, and allowed himself no weakness or languishing in the religion of God. He refused to be lenient with himself and remain in his home, disapproving only in his heart, as some religious scholars allow and practice.[12]

Indeed, I remember how brave and noble he was when some of those who felt things had gone on too long and who suffered from some weakness wanted him to be lenient and write to the tyrant expressing support for him and asking his pardon. They asked Imam Hasan al-Hudaybi for permission to do that. At this he uttered his famous words: "I will not force anyone to be determined and stand with us, but I tell you, the Islamic call never stood a single day with those who were soft."

He said that when he was an old man of eighty years. He remained in the Mazraʿat Tarra prison until the last group of prisoners was released after the death of Abdel Nasser.

We return again to the details of the events of 1965.

In 1955 I found myself drafted into the service of the Islamic call without an invitation from anyone. It was the cries of the orphans who lost their fathers to torture, and the tears of the women who were widowed and whose husbands were behind prison bars, and the old fathers and mothers who lost their heart's delight. These cries and tears penetrated my innermost being. I found myself feeling as if I were one of those responsible for the loss of the starving and the wounds of the tortured. I began to offer a little help.

But the numbers of the starving increased day by day, as well as the number of those who were naked, and the news of the martyrs who died under the whips of the debauched apostates, the cruel infidels. Schools and universities needed money, supplies, and clothes, and landlords were demanding rent. The problem grew more difficult, the burden grew heavier, and the hole in the garment grew larger, especially after a year and a half. It was precisely the middle of the year in 1956 when some of those who had been in prison but not sentenced were released. Some were in direst need of someone to provide them with money, food, clothes, and shelter. All of this was happening while the Muslims were in the good country, in Egypt, which veered with those who led the revolution; no one was aware of his duty. On the contrary, we found many religious scholars and sheikhs who washed their hands of those who struggled in the cause of Islam.

All those who were released, even those who wept at the tragedy and were in pain, hid their pain and their tears out of fear, lest the tyrant accuse them of being Muslims. When my grief at what had happened became overwhelming and I found no way out of it, I went to visit my honorable teacher, Sheikh Muhammad al-Awdan. He was one of the very few men of al-Azhar who were sincerely pious, and I used to ask his advice on everything pertaining to the Islamic cause and the religious sciences. He believed, as I did, that the fact that the Muslim Women's Association had not merged with the Brotherhood could prove useful to the Brotherhood at a later time. He knew of my pledge of allegiance to al-Banna, and he blesssed it and supported it. Likewise he knew of my loyalty to the cause after al-Banna's martyrdom, and he accepted it.

I sat with him and told him of the tragedy of the families, and he listened to me in profound grief. I finished what I had to say by explaining what I thought of doing within the limits of my capabilities. I saw that it was not enough for us to grieve while people in the circles of those involved in the Islamic cause, those who were obedient, those who struggled in the path of God, cruelly suffered from hunger, whip lashes, and nakedness and women and children were homeless; our grief was not enough to make the word of God paramount. I saw that as president of the Muslim Women's Association, God willing, I could help the families of the Brotherhood as God enabled me.

The sheikh kissed my head and wept, saying to me, "Don't hesitate to offer any assistance. God is the one who blesses our plans." I again explained to him my position in the association and my complete confidence in the women who were its members. The sheikh said to me, "It has become your irrevocable duty to not hold back any effort in this path and the work you are doing. Place it between you and God the Blessed and Exalted." Then he added, "The only salvation for Islam by God's commandment is these tortured Muslim Brothers. We hope only in God and in their devotion and efforts in the path of the call. Do all you can, Zaynab." So I did in fact all I could. I spent my efforts to offer something, though no one knew that I was doing anything. I gave one or two individuals what I could, saying these things were sent to me and I was only charged with seeing that they were delivered to them.

Then I learned that the virtuous mother, the great struggler in the path of God, the wife of Mr. al-Hudaybi, also took great pains, along with some other noble and virtuous women in the Muslim Sisters, including Amal al-ʿAshmawi, wife of the councillor Munir al-Dilla (she was head of the Muslim Sisters),[13] Khalida Hasan al-Hudaybi, Amina Qutb, Hamida Qutb, Fathiyya Bakr, Amina al-Jawhari, ʿAliya al-Hudaybi, and Tahiya Sulayman al-Jabili.

My contacts gradually widened. I contacted Khalida al-Hudaybi in extreme secret, then Hamida Qutb and Amina Qutb. All of this was for the sake of the tortured, the children, and the orphans.

My first meeting with ʿAbd al-Fattah Ismaʿil[14] was in 1957 in the season of the pilgrimage. I was in the port of Suez at the head of a delegation from the Muslim Women's Association going on the pilgrimage. Among those bidding us farewell was my brother, Muhammad al-Ghazali al-Jabili. I saw him coming toward me, accompanied by a man whose face was clothed with light and reverence, averting his eyes. My brother introduced him to me, sayng, "Brother ʿAbd al-Fattah Ismaʿil, one of the young men who was best loved by the martyred *imam*, Hasan al-Banna. The honored Guide loved him and had absolute confidence in him. He asked me to introduce him to you in this way, so you would know him." The Brother greeted me and said, "God willing, I will be with you on the ship." I welcomed him, and he left.

We climbed up into the steamship and it moved far from the shore. I busied myself with the needs of the delegation of the Muslim Women's Association. When I went to my room to rest after lunch, I heard a knock on the door. I told the person to come in, but the knock came a second time, and the person who knocked had moved away from the door. When he heard my voice permitting him to enter for the third time, he came in. It was the Brother whom my brother had introduced to me at the pier. He said humbly with his head bowed, after greeting me, "I know, with praise to God, that there was a vow of allegiance between you and the martyred *imam*, Hasan al-Banna, after a long dispute." When I asked him how he knew this, he answered, "From the martyred *imam* himself, may God rest him in peace." I asked him what he wanted, and he answered, "That we meet in Mecca for the sake of God, to speak of what al-Banna wanted of you, God willing."

These words were simply expressed and well intentioned, soft in their simplicity, strong and truthful, with heavy responsibilities, carrying the implication of a command that leaves no room for thought.

I said, "God willing, in the house of the Muslim Women's Association delegation in Mecca or in Jidda." When he asked for the addresses, I told him of two Brothers in Jidda whom he said he knew, Sheikh al-ʿAshmawi and Mustafa al-ʿAlim, either of whom could guide him to where I was staying in Mecca and Jidda.

The Brother bid farewell and left.

One night in the month of the pilgrimage I had an appointment after the evening prayer with the late sheikh, Imam Muhammad ibn Ibrahim, Grand Mufti of the Kingdom of Saudi Arabia at that time. We were studying a memorandum I had given to His Highness the King in which I explained the necessity of educating the girls in the kingdom. I asked him to hasten the implementation of this plan, explaining that this was in the kingdom's best interests. The memorandum was transferred to the mufti, who asked to see me.

I spent two hours studying the plan with him. When I left him, I went my way to the Gate of Peace, intending to go around the Kaʿba, when I was stopped by a voice calling my name and greeting me in the Islamic fashion. I turned, and there was ʿAbd al-Fattah Ismaʿil. He asked me where I was going. When he heard I was going to go around the Kaʿba and then to the house where the delegation was staying, he accompanied me to the mosque, and we went around it together. After performing the prayer that accompanies the circumambulation, we sat facing the proper direction and he began to talk about what was on his mind.

He asked me my opinion of the resolution to dissolve the Brotherhood. I answered that it was a legally invalid resolution. He said, "That is the matter I wished to study with you." When I asked him to visit me in the house where the delegation was staying, he thought it an inappropriate place to discuss such matters for fear of Nasser's spy networks. We agreed to meet in the construction office of the sacred places of Mecca, the office of a righteous man, Sheikh Salih al-Qazzaz. We met there, but he whispered to me that it would be better for us to meet in the sacred place. So he left on agreement that we meet behind Abraham's abode.

After two prostrations of the circumambulation, we sat behind the Zamzam building near the place where Abraham stood, and he began to talk about the invalidity of the resolution to dissolve the Muslim Brotherhood and the necessity of organizing the ranks of the Brotherhood and resuming its activities. We agreed to get in touch after returning from the holy land with Imam Hasan al-Hudaybi, the General Guide, to ask his permission to work.

When we turned to go, he said, "We must be linked here by a vow with God to struggle in His path, and not to waver until we gather the ranks of the Brotherhood and separate out those wo do not want to work, whatever their circumstances and status." We made a vow to God to struggle even to the point of death in the path of His call.

And I returned to Egypt.

In the first months of 1958, my meetings with ʿAbd al-Fattah Ismaʿil became more frequent, both in my home and in the headquarters of the Muslim Women's Association.

We studied the affairs of the Muslims, attempting with all our might to do something for Islam, to restore to this nation its glory and its creed, beginning with the life of the Prophet, blessing and peace be upon him, and the pious ancestors, and those who came after them, deriving our program from the Book of God and the Sunna of His Messenger, may God bless him and grant him peace.

Our plan of action aimed at bringing together everyone who wanted to work for Islam to join with us. All this was only studies and setting up rough outlines, so we would know the way to go. When we wanted to start working, we had to ask permission from Mr. Hudaybi, as General Guide of the Brotherhood, because our legal studies on the resolution to dissolve the society ended in the conclusion that it was null and void, because Abdel Nasser has no claim to allegiance, and cannot command obedience from the Muslims, since he is fighting against Islam and does not rule by the Book of God.

I met with Mr. Hudaybi to ask his permission in my name and in the name of ʿAbd al-Fattah Ismaʿil, and he granted us permission to work after several meetings, in which I explained to him the purpose and details of the studies ʿAbd al-Fattah and I had done.

We decided to begin the work by having Brother ʿAbd al-Fattah ʿAbduh Ismaʿil conduct a survey throughout the length of Egypt at the level of the province, the administrative center, and the village with the aim of finding out which Muslims wanted to work and were suitable to work with us. We would begin with the Muslim Brothers, to make them the first nucleus of this coming together.

Brother ʿAbd al-Fattah Ismaʿil began his tour, starting with those Brothers who were released from the prisons and who had not been sentenced, to test their mettle: did the persecution affect their determination, and did imprisonment make them withdraw from what might expose them to imprisonment once again? Or were they still loyal to the cause, ready to sacrifice everything, great and small, in the path of God and the support of His religion?

The survey was necessary so we might begin to work on firm ground, so we might know who was really suitable. Together we studied the reports ʿAbd al-Fattah Ismaʿil brought from each region, and I would visit the General Guide and inform him of what we had agreed upon and the conclusions to which we had come. If we presented him with descriptions of the difficulties we would encounter, he would say, "Keep going, and do not look back. Do not be misled by the titles or reputations of men. You are building a new structure from its foundation."

Sometimes he would support what we presented to him, and sometimes he would give some instructions. One of his instructions was that we add to our sources of study the *Muhalla* of Ibn Hazm.[15]

In 1959 our studies ended, and we drew up a program of Islamic education. I call God as my witness that our program consisted of nothing but the education of the Muslim individual so he would know his duty toward his Lord, and the creation of the Muslim society, which will of necessity be separate from pagan society.[16]

Since the activities of the Society of the Muslim Brotherhood were halted due to the pagan resolution of dissolution of 1954, it was necessary for these activities to be secret.

My work in these activities did not prevent me from fulfilling the duties of my mission in the general headquarters of the Muslim Women's Association or cause me to neglect my family duties, though my noble husband, the late Muhammad Salim Salim, noticed the frequent visits of Brother ʿAbd al-Fattah and some of the pure Muslim youth to our house. My husband asked me, "Are the Muslim Brothers having activities?" I said, "Yes." He asked me about the extent and type of these activities. I said, "They are to restore the organization of the Society of the Brotherhood." When he began to ask me probing questions, I said to him, "Do you remember, dear husband, what I said to you when we agreed to marry?"

He said, "Yes. You stipulated certain conditions. But now I'm afraid for you, that you will expose yourself to the tyrants."

Then he was silent, his head bowed. I said to him, "I remember well what I said to you. I told you that day, 'There is one thing about my life that you must know, because you will become my husband; if you still agree to marry me, then I must tell you, on condition that you not ask me about it later. I will not go back on my conditions with regard to this matter. I am the president of the general headquarters of the Muslim Women's Association. This is true, but most people think I adhere to the political principles of the Wafd party. That is not true. What I believe in is the mission of the Muslim Brotherhood. I am linked with Mustafa al-Nahhas by personal friendship; but I have given my oath of loyalty to Hasan al-Banna to die in the path of God, though I am not planning a single step toward entering the circle of that divine honor. But I believe I will take this step some day—in fact, I dream of it and hope for it. On that day, if your personal welfare and economic work conflict with my Islamic work, and I find that my married life interferes with the way of the call and the establishment of the Islamic state, then we will separate.'

"On that day you lowered your eyes to the ground. Then you lifted your head, and your eyes were filled with tears. You said, 'I asked you what material goods you wanted, and you asked for no dowry or wedding gifts. You stipulated that I not keep you from the path of God. I didn't know that you had any ties with Mr. al-Banna. What I knew was that you had a disagreement with him over his request that the Muslim Women's Association be incorporated into the Muslim Brotherhood.'

"I said, 'Praise be to God; we came to an agreement during the persecution of the Brothers in 1948, before al-Banna's martyrdom. I had decided to banish marriage from my life, and to devote myself entirely to the call. I cannot ask you today that you join me in this struggle, but it is my right to stipulate that you not interfere with my struggle in the path of God, and that the day that responsibility places me in the ranks of the strugglers, that you not ask me what I am doing. Let the trust between us be complete, between [me and] a man who wants to marry a woman who gave herself to the struggle in the path of God to establish the Islamic state when she was eighteen years old. If there is a conflict of interests between marriage and the call to God, then the marriage will come to an end and the call will remain in my whole being.'"

Then I stopped speaking for a moment. I looked at him and said, "Do you remember?"

He said, "Yes."

I said, "Today I ask you to keep your promise. Don't ask with whom I am meeting. I ask God to give you a portion of the reward of my struggle as a grace from Him if He accepts my work. I know that you have the right to give me orders, and it is my duty to obey you. But God is greater in our souls than ourselves, and His call is dearer to us than our own selves. We are in an important phase in the life of the cause."

He said, "Forgive me. Do your work, with God's blessing. May I live to see the day that the Brothers achieve their goal and the Islamic state is established."

The work and activities increased, and the young men crowded into my house night and day. My believing husband would hear the knocks on the door in the middle of the night and get up to open the door. He would escort the visitors to the office, then he would go to the maid's room and wake her, asking her to prepare some food and tea for the visitors. Then he would come to me and wake me gently, saying, "Some of your sons are in the office. They look like they have been traveling or working hard." I would dress and go to them, while he went back to sleep, saying to me, "Wake me if you pray the morning prayer together so I can pray with you, if that's no bother." I would say, "God willing."

And if we prayed the morning prayer together, I would wake him so he could pray with us. Then he would leave, greeting those who were present in a fatherly way, full of warmth, love, and compassion.

In 1962 I met with the two sisters of the martyred *imam*, the legist and great struggler in the path of God, Sayyid Qutb, with the agreement of Brother ʿAbd al-Fattah ʿAbduh Ismaʿil and permission from Mr. Hasan al-Hudaybi, the General Guide of the Muslim Brotherhood. The purpose of this meeting was to contact Imam Sayyid Qutb in prison to solicit his opinion on some of our studies and to ask for his guidance.

I asked Hamida Qutb[17] to convey our greetings to Brother Sayyid Qutb and to inform him of the assembled society's desire to study an Islamic course under the guidance of his views. I gave her a list of references that we were studying. This included the *Tafsir* of Ibn Kathir, the *Muhalla* of Ibn Hazm, *al-Umm* by al-Shafiʿi, books on the unitarian religion by Ibn ʿAbd al-Wahhab, and *In the Shadow of the Qurʾan* by Sayyid Qutb.[18] After a short time Hamida returned to me with instructions to study the introduction to *Surat al-anʿam*, second edition. She gave me a section of a book, saying, "Sayyid is preparing it for publication. It is called *Ma'alim fi al-tariq* (Signposts on the way)."[19] Sayyid Qutb had written it in prison. His sister said to me, "When you finish reading these pages I will bring you more."

I learned that the General Guide had read portions of this book and had given the martyr Sayyid Qutb permission to publish it. When I asked him about it, he said to me, "With God's blessing. This book has fulfilled my hopes in Sayyid, may God preserve him. I read it and re-read it. Sayyid Qutb is the great hope for the call now, God willing." The General Guide gave me portions of the book and I read them. He had them so he could give permission for them to be published. I confined myself to a room in the home of the General Guide until I had finished reading *Ma'alim fi al-tariq*.

We recommended our studies in the form of short pamphlets distributed to the young men for them to study. Then they would be extensively studied in group discussions. Our ideas and goals were in agreement, so the plan of study incorporated the instructions and pages brought to us from the martyred *imam*, Sayyid Qutb, may God have mercy on him, while he was in prison. Those were good nights and unforgettable days, holy moments with God. Five or ten young men would gather and read ten Koranic verses, reviewing their precepts and ordinances and all their implications for the life of the Muslim servant. After we had fully understood them, we would decide to go on to ten other verses, following the example of the Companions of the Prophet, peace and blessing be upon him.

Those days were sweet and good. A blessing from God surrounded us as we studied and studied, training ourselves and preparing men for the cause, with youth who were convinced of the necessity of preparing to establish the call of truth and justice. We believed in the absolute necessity of preparing future generations in the persons of these young men, whom we hope will be the teachers who will guide and prepare the coming generations.

Among the decisions we made, with the instructions of Imam Sayyid Qutb and the permission of Hudaybi, was that the period of training, formation, preparation, and planting belief in the unity of God in hearts would continue. This was accompanied by the conviction that there is no Islam without the implementation of Islamic law and government by the Book of God and the Sunna of His Prophet, so that the precepts of the Koran would be supreme in the life of the Muslims. We decided that our training program would last thirteen years, the duration of the call in Mecca, with the understanding that the foundation of the Islamic nation now is the Brothers who adhere to the law and precepts of God.

We insisted on performing all the commands and prohibitions revealed in the Book and Sunna within our Islamic circle, and that obedience to our *imam*, to whom we had given our oath of loyalty, was necessary, since the establishment of the punishments of Islamic law was not imminent—although we believed in them and defended them—until the Islamic state was established. We were also convinced that the world today does not have a foundation that would supply the necessary attributes of the Islamic nation in a complete way, as had been the case in the days of the prophethood and the rightly guided caliphs.[20] Therefore it is incumbent on all Muslims who want to see God's rule and the consolidation of His religion on earth to join in the struggle until all Muslims return to Islam and the true religion is established—not slogans, but an actual, practical reality.

We also studied the condition of the entire Islamic world, searching for examples of what had existed before in the caliphate of the rightly guided caliphs and of what we wanted in God's society now. We decided, after a broad study of the existing painful reality, that there is no single state corresponding to that ideal. We excepted the Kindom of Saudi Arabia, with some reservations and observations that the kingdom must rectify and correct. All the studies confirmed that the nation of Islam does not exist, although some states have raised slogans claiming they established God's law.

After this broad study, we decided that after thirteen years of Islamic training for young men, old men, women, and girls, we would conduct a comprehensive survey of the country. If we found that the harvest of those who followed the Islamic call, believing that Islam is both religion and state and convinced of the necessity of establishing Islamic rule, reached 75 percent of all the individuals of the nation, men and women, then we would call for the establishment of the Islamic state and demand that the state establish Islamic law. If we found that the harvest was 25 percent, we would renew the teaching and study for thirteen more years, and more if necessary, until we found that the nation was ripe to accept Islamic government.

It does not matter if generations come and go; what matters is that the preparation be continuous, that we keep working until our term of life ends. Then we will give the banner of "There is no god but God, and Muhammad is the Messenger of God" to the noble sons who come after us.

We were in contact with Mr. Muhammad Qutb with the permission of the General Guide, Mr. Hudaybi. He used to visit us in my house in Heliopolis to explain to the young men what they could not understand. The young men would ask him many questions, and he would answer them.

Notes

1. The *imam*, from the beginning of the Islamic community, is the one who leads the prayer in the mosque. Originally it was the Prophet himself, and after him his successors, the four caliphs, who filled this office; thus, *imam* came to be a title for the ruler of the Muslim community and in theory claims to the title should not be multiple. In the passage from her book translated here, the title *imam* is applied to Hasan al-Banna, Hasan al-Hudaybi, Banna's successor, and Sayyid Qutb, who became the intellectual leader of the Muslim Brotherhood. "Martyr" (*shahid*) is also used as an honorific title, appropriate for a Society that claims that "death in the service of God is the loftiest of our wishes," for by martyrdom the Muslim attains the highest rank of piety. Hagga Zaynab refers to Hasan al-Banna as *al-imam al-shahid*, "the martyred *imam*." ʿAbd al-Qadir ʿAwda and Sayyid Qutb are also rarely referred to without the title of martyr. "Renewer of the faith" (*al-mujaddid*) is a title of even rarer honor. It refers to a tradition that God would send a renewer of the faith to the Islamic community in every century; Hagga Zaynab seems to believe Banna was the *mujaddid* for his century.

2. Huda al-Shaʿrawi was the famous leader of the women's liberation movement in Egypt in the 1920s. After attending the International Women's Union conference in Rome in 1922, she shed her face veil and founded the Egyptian Feminist Union in 1923.

3. The Sunna is the exemplary behavior of Muhammad, the Prophet of Islam, as depicted in the Hadith literature. Although the Hadith is not a revelation from God, it is considered, along with the Koran, as one of the foundations of Islamic law. Later Hagga Zaynab refers to marriage as a "sure Sunna"; that is, marriage is the approved practice and the Hadith does not contradict or cast doubt on this.

4. Al-Azhar University, founded in A.D. 972, emerged after the thirteenth century as a major center of learning. Much of its prestige has faded with the establishment of a modern, secular educational system in Egypt, but it continues to be the center of Islamic religious learning for Egyptian and many foreign students. In Egypt it draws most of its students from the countryside and is known for its conservatism.

5. Malak Hifni Nasif (b. 1886), also known by her nickname, "Bahithat al-Badiya" (seeker of the desert), was a prominent writer and lecturer on feminist and social issues. She was one of the first Egyptian women to graduate with a teaching diploma in 1903 and she publicly campaigned for women's education. Although there was a companion of the Prophet named Kaʿb ibn ʿIyad al-Mazini (listed in al-Dhahabi's *Tajrid asmaʾ al-sahaba* [Biographical dictionary of the companions of the Prophet], ed. Saliha ʿAbd al-Hakim Sharaf al-Din [Bombay: Sharaf al-Din and Sons, 1970], vol. 2, p. 33, no. 352), there is no listing of a Nusayba bint Kaʿb al-Maziniyya. It is probable that Hagga Zaynab was referring to Nusayba bint Kaʿb ibn ʿAmr al-Ansariyya, who was also of Mazin and was known as Umm ʿAmmara (ibid., p. 308, no. 3714). This Nusayba was famous for her distinction as a warrior

in the battle of Uhud. She is mentioned in the works of Ibn Sa'd, Ibn Hisham, al-Baladhuri, al-Muqaddisi, and Ibn Hajr, among others. A summary of their accounts may be found in 'Umar Rida Kahhalah, A'lam al-nisa' fi 'alamay al-'Arab wa-al-Islam (Women in the Arab-Islamic world) (Beirut: Mu'assassat al-Risala, 1977), pp. 171–175.

6. In 1948 the government believed the Muslim Brotherhood was planning imminent revolution: a cache of arms was found in the Muqattam hills in January and another in Isma'iliyya in October, the Brothers were believed to be involved in the coup d'etat in Yemen, a respected judge was assassinated by a Brother, the confiscation of Society papers brought to light the existence of the Brotherhood's Secret Apparatus, and the Brothers were accused of inciting riots at the university in which the Cairo police chief was killed. The Society was dissolved by government order on December 6. For details, see Richard P. Mitchell, The Society of the Muslim Brothers (London: Oxford University Press, 1969), pp. 58–67.

7. The Association of Muslim Youth (Jam'iyyat shubban al-Muslimin), commonly called the YMMA and thought of as the Muslim answer to the YMCA, was founded in 1927. It was actually more militant in its orientation than its constitution professed, according to Heyworth-Dunne, and both interacted and competed with the Muslim Brotherhood but never achieved anything like the latter's organization and strength. See J. Heyworth-Dunne, Religious and Political Trends in Modern Egypt (Washington, 1950), pp. 11–14.

8. Mustafa al-Nahhas was leader of the Wafd party, which rivaled the Muslim Brotherhood as champion of the anti-British nationalist movement prior to the revolution of 1952. The Wafd came into power a number of times prior to 1952, with Nahhas as prime minister. Relations between the Wafd and the Brotherhood were usually antagonistic, with periods of cooperation and mutual support when their interests coincided. As Hagga Zaynab explains later, she had a personal friendship with Nahhas, but did not agree with the Wafd platform.

9. 'Awda was a lawyer and al-Hudaybi's deputy, but he quickly became part of the leadership clique antagonistic to al-Hudaybi (Mitchell, Society of the Muslim Brothers, footnote p. 108). 'Awda favored cooperation with the Revolutionary Command Council government until the February 27, 1954 demonstrations in support of General Neguib against the RCC. 'Awda played a prominent part in the demonstration and distributed pamphlets hostile to the regime; Mitchell calls his behavior a miscalculation of the situation that "proved to be a fatal error" (ibid., pp. 129–130). In the aftermath of a Brother's attempt on the life of Nasser, 'Awda was among the six Brothers who were publicly executed (ibid., pp. 160–161).

10. Sheikh Hasan al-Baquri was a member of the Muslim Brotherhood's Guidance Council. Later he became minister of Awqaf under the revolutionary government, for which he was expelled from the Brotherhood.

11. See ibid., pp. 125–162, for the details of the growing enmity between Nasser and the Brotherhood that culminated in the dissolution of the Broth-

erhood, an attempt on Nasser's life, and the imprisonment and torture of Brothers.

12. Hagga Zaynab's unambiguous praise for Hudaybi's resolve and leadership was not unanimously felt, as Mitchell's account of the history of the Brotherhood makes clear (ibid., pp. 111–126, 139, 142–150), and opposition even took the form of one attempted "coup," though Hudaybi apparently had the support of the rank and file. Hudaybi's distaste for violence, emotionalism, and the separate leadership of the Secret Apparatus brought him into conflict with the leaders of the latter group.

13. Munir al-Dilla was a member of the Guidance Council and advisor of Hudaybi. "It was in his home and at his inspiration that the name of Hasan Ismaᶜil al-Hudaybi . . . was first mentioned as a candidate for the post of general guide" (ibid., p. 85). He was sentenced to life imprisonment with hard labor after the attempt on Nasser's life.

14. ᶜAbdal-Fattah Ismaᶜil, Hagga Zaynab's chief collaborator, was also arrested in 1965 and was executed along with Sayyid Qutb in 1966.

15. Abu Muhammad ᶜAli ibn Hazm (A.D. 994–1064) was a famous theologian and legist of Muslim Spain. He belonged to a school known for its rigorously literal interpretation of the Koran and Hadith and is therefore called *al-Zahiriyya*, "those who adhere to the apparent meaning" (*al-zahir*). His *Kitab al-muhalla bil-athar fi sharh al-mujalla bil-iqtisar*, a commentary on the Hadith, belongs to an earlier period when he was an ardent follower of the Shafiᶜi school (*Shorter Encyclopaedia of Islam*, ed. H. A. R. Gibb and J. H. Kramers [Ithaca, N.Y.: Cornell University Press, 1953], p. 148).

16. *Jahili*, a reference to pre-Islamic times. She compares modern Egypt to the "times of ignorance" (*al-jahiliyya*) that existed in pre-Islamic Arabia. In the interview, when she speaks of women's liberation in a "pagan society," she uses the word *kafir*, "unbelieving" or "infidel." In that context it could just as well read "atheistic society."

17. Hamida Qutb and Zaynab al-Ghazali were the only women brought to trial in 1966 along with the Brothers, including Sayyid Qutb. They spent five years together as cellmates. At the end of her book, Hagga Zaynab describes her grief at being released while her "daughter" remained in jail.

18. Ismaᶜil ibn ᶜUmar ᶜImad al-Din ibn Kathir (A.D. 1301–1373), an Arab historian of Damascus and pupil of Ibn Taymiyya, wrote a classic Koran commentary (*tafsir*). Abu ᶜAbd Allah Muhammad ibn Idris al-Shafiᶜi (A.D. 767–820), founder of one of the four schools of law, grew up in Mecca but lived the latter part of his life in Egypt, where his tomb in Cairo is a major shrine. *Kitab al-umm* (The mother book) is a seven-volume collection of his writings and lectures. Muhammad ibn ᶜAbd al-Wahhab (A.D. 1703–1787) was founder of the Wahhabiyya community, the spiritual force behind the Saudi dynasty in Arabia. The Wahhabiyya call themselves *muwahhidun*, "unitarians." They derived their doctrine from the school of Ibn Hanbal as interpreted by Ibn Taymiyya, who attacked the cult of the saints in many of his writings. Portions of Ibn Taymiyya's works are pub-

lished in pamphlet form in Cairo bookstalls today; he continues to inspire Islamic "fundamentalists."

19. Jane I. Smith notes that this book, critical of the regime, made Qutb so dangerous in the eyes of the government that he was executed, along with six other Brothers, in 1966 (*An Historical and Semantic Study of the Term "Islam" as Seen in a Sequence of Qur²an Commentaries* [Missoula, Mont.: Scholars Press, 1975], p. 205.

20. The "rightly guided caliphs" are the first four successors to leadership of the Islamic community after Muhammad's death: Abu Bakr, ʿUmar ibn al-Khattab, ʿUthman ibn ʿAffan, and ʿAli ibn Abi Talib. Hagga Zaynab's comments reflect a common perception of the pristine condition of early Islamic society, which has suffered a steady disintegration in morality and religious integrity ever since. This view ignores the fact that ʿUmar and ʿUthman were both murdered, the latter for corruption, and ʿAli was never universally recognized as caliph. He was even suspected of approving of ʿUthman's murder.

The Position of Women in Shiʿa Iran: Views of the ʿUlama

SHIREEN MAHDAVI

The position of women in Iran has passed through many stages since the Islamic conquest in A.D. 651. During the Mongol period, women held high political and social positions. But after Shiʿism was declared the official religion by the Safavids in 1501 the status of women declined.

This situation, circumscribed by Koranic injunctions and elaborated by the interpretations of classical commentators, became permanently fixed during the Safavid period (1501–1722) at the hands of religious scholars (mujtahids) who constituted the religious establishment in the new, "officially" Shiʿa nation-state.[1] The great mullabashi, Muhammad Baqir Majlisi (1627–1699), may be said to have written the final word on the subject.[2] The possibility of interpretation (ijtihad) by later scholars was inherited by the religious leadership of the Qajar period that assumed effective power in 1795 under Agha Muhammad Khan.[3]

Major political and social changes in world history began to exert their influence on Persian history during the early nineteenth century. These changes, which ultimately brought about a constitutional-parliamentary system of government in Iran in 1905–06, did not much affect the position of women. The beginnings during the Qajar period of what may be termed the emancipation of Iranian women underwent more momentous changes in the twentieth century under the two rulers of the Pahlavi dynasty (1925–1979). These developments, however, appear to have suffered a setback under the regime of the present Islamic Republic of Iran.

The position of women in Iran today is directly linked to Shiʿism, and thus a brief historical glance at its origins is useful.[4]

Muhammad was the nabi (prophet) to whom Islam was revealed, but ʿAli ibn Abi Talib was the wali (guardian) who, the Shiʿites believe, preserved the faith forever. Muhammad was rasul Allah, "the messenger of God"; ʿAli was wali Allah, "the friend of God." The two expressions are enshrined in the adhan, or call to prayer, in the Shiʿa world. The position of Muhammad is easy to understand; that of ʿAli, as it was developed by Shiʿa scholars throughout the ages, is much more complex.

To understand it one has to examine the two aspects of Shi'ism, the political-historical and the religious-theological, that are the foundations of the Shi'a sect of Islam.

When Muhammad began to preach the new faith in Mecca in A.D. 610, 'Ali was a young man, one of the early believers. In addition, he was Muhammad's first cousin. As an orphan, Muhammad grew up in the household of 'Ali's father, who gave the Prophet crucial support. 'Ali was a heroic figure in the early days of Islam, and even during the Prophet's lifetime a group of friends congregated around 'Ali and became known as his *shi'ah* (party or faction). 'Ali's position became even greater when he married Fatima, Muhammad's favorite daughter. It was thus expected that 'Ali would play a leading role in early Muslim history. This he did, but his position was fraught with difficulties. These problems and the manly (*mardanah*) way in which 'Ali tried to overcome them made him a tragic hero, a role that he passed on to his immediate descendants.

'Ali was expected to succeed Muhammad in the leadership of the Muslim community (*ummah*) following the Prophet's death in 632, but three older men preceded 'Ali in the line of succession (the caliphate). When 'Ali's turn finally came, Islam's center had already shifted away from Mecca and Medina. The governor in Damascus (who was the scion of the leading family in Mecca before Islam, the Bani Umayyah) made a successful bid for the leadership of the Muslim community in opposition to 'Ali and his supporters. 'Ali was later assassinated, and his younger son Husayn, who made a valiant attempt to seize control of the leadership, met with a tragic death at Karbala in A.D. 680. 'Ali's claim to the leadership based on "legitimate right of succession" persisted for centuries but was not successful, and the challenges were often repressed by bloody persecutions at the hands of the rulers in power. His followers became known as the Shi'a faction of Islam.

In the meantime, Shi'ism split into many sects, the largest of which is the Ithna'ashari (or Twelver) branch, the one observed in Iran today. It was this branch that achieved success in 1501 when the Safavid dynasty adopted it as the "official" religion of the country. It continued to be so during the Qajar period (nineteenth century) and was finally written into the Persian constitution of 1905–06. It received its ultimate sanction under the present Islamic Republic of Iran.

Such are the political-historical developments of the Shi'a movement in Islam. The religious-theological developments, on the other hand, provided the ideology that kept the movement alive and nurtured it in a scribal tradition that ensured its uninterrupted continuity. This aspect of Shi'ism was the product of the *'ulama*, better known in Iran as the *mujtahid*s.

The majority of Muslims accepted the dictum (which seems to have found consensus quite early in Islamic history) that, with the death of the founder, answers to religious problems would be found in God's book, the Koran. For this reason, the word of God (revealed to the Prophet) was collected very early to be used as the source book for all subsequent Islamic learning and law. The leadership of the community (the caliphate) remained primarily a secular office, and with time a class of learned scholars (*ulama*) developed to interpret the Koran. The Koran itself, then, combined with the Hadith, or traditions and sayings of the Prophet, became a kind of religious authority or institution at the same level of authority with the ruler (caliph, king, shah, sultan) and the government administration. Since the *ulama* in their various gradations and functions ministered to the needs of the community (religious, legal, educational, etc.), their ties with the people were always close, and as such they may be described as the living conscience of the common people or perhaps even as the "loyal opposition" to the autocratic rule of the despotic head of state and his representative.

Among the Shiʿas this class of *ulama* (or *mujtahids*) appears to have grown among the circle of scholars who surrounded the Sixth leader (the *imam*) of the Shiʿa community circa A.D. 750. His name was Jaʿfar, and the Shiʿa School of Law of the Ithnaʿashari branch is called Jaʿfari after him. (The Sunnis, at about the same time, developed four such schools: Shafiʿi, Hanafi, Maliki, and Hanbali.)

The *mujtahids* base their right of interpretation of Islamic principles on a time-honored concept called *ijtihad*. This is essentially a personal "exertion" (a kind of soul-searching struggle, which is the root meaning of the term *ijtihad*) aimed at arriving at a proper understanding of the meaning of religious dogma as found in the Holy Book. The *mujtahid* achieves the elevated degree of *ijtihad* through total immersion in religious studies, which are normally passed on from one religious scholar to another. The personal approach in the Islamic tradition has always tended to guard against the development of a hierarchical system.

Interpretation of Islamic law also involves the interpretation of the position of women. Today in Iran, a country that officially follows the Shiʿa interpretations of Koranic injunctions, the most prominent contemporary interpreters of the Shiʿa position on women have been three *ulama*, or *mujtahids*: ʿAllamah Tabatabaʾi,[5] ʿAllamah Nuri,[6] and Ayatullah Mutahhiri.[7] All are the product of classical Muslim learning, which stresses law and theology as well as a deep knowledge of Arabic. An analysis of their arguments may cast light on the current view of women's position in Iran.

All three men begin with history, arguing that women in the ancient and the pre-Islamic world had no rights and were not even considered human beings, and that Islam elevated the position of women by giving them legal rights. They also state that Islam did not invent the veil (hijab) but that it existed in other cultures and civilizations prior to Islam. They see the Iranian woman's demand for liberation as a corrupting imitation of the West.

The argument for the improved position of women in Islam as opposed to the immediate pre-Islamic past is a forceful one. Islam, when it overwhelmed the Middle East in the seventh century, was not just a new religious system but a powerful social revolution that completely altered the way of life of whole societies, including family life and the role of women. Theoretically, Islam did give women rights. But there are certain assumptions in the Islamic approach to women that in practice serve to limit their role.

The primary assumption is that men and women are not equal because they are biologically different. The biological differences affect both sexual needs and mental ability. Women menstruate and reach menopause; men remain virile at all times. Men are rational; women are emotional. In practice, these differences lead to divisions in work, needs, and social life. Women are seen as a disturbing element to men in their conduct of everyday life. This causes difficulty, because the male's sexual desire is seen as uncontrollable.

Such assumptions affect interpretations. The Koran says a great deal about the position of women but much of it has been interpreted in such a way as to become socially restraining and to justify men's rights and superior position. These interpretations have become incorporated into the Shariʿa, the totality of Islamic law and "way of life." The most important among these are the family laws, which govern women's lives and, in their present form, confirm the authority of the male in matters of divorce, child custody, marriage, and inheritance. These laws provide that women should inherit half a man's share and be protected in case of divorce, but they also form the basis for such current practices as veiling, polygamy, and temporary marriage (mutʿah, which is forbidden in Sunni Islam). These are the practices that, from a modern point of view, are seen as disadvantageous for women. Therefore, the opinions and the interpretations of the mujtahids concerning these practices and the case for the superiority of men will be examined below in some detail.

The case for the superiority of men over women in Islamic society is based upon Koran IV: 34, which states:

> Men are the maintainers of women [qawwamun ʿala an-nisaʾ], with what Allah has made some of them to excel others, and with what they spend out of their wealth. So the good women are obedient [qanitat], guarding the unseen as Allah has guarded. And as to those on whose part you fear desertion [nushuz], admonish them, and leave them alone

in the beds, and chastise them [*udrubuhunna*]. So if they obey you, seek not a way against them. Surely, Allah is ever Exalted, Great.[8]

Different translations and interpretations of this verse portray man as manager, superior, or simply preferred by God.[9] But all are used to justify male divorce or male guardianship of children after divorce.

The celebrated thirteenth-century Sunni commentator Baydawi explains in detail the different ways in which men are superior to women. He says that God has preferred men over women in the following matters:

> . . . that of mental ability and good counsel, and in their power for the performance of duties and for the carrying out of divine commands. Hence, to men have been confined prophecy, religious leadership, saintship, pilgrimage rites, the giving of evidence in the law courts, the duties of the holy war, [and] worship in the mosque of the day of assembly [Friday] . . . They also have the privilege of electing chiefs, have a larger share of inheritance, and discretion in the matter of divorce.[10]

The classical-medieval interpretations of this and other Koranic verses pertaining to women have more or less endured in the writings and views of later scholars. The ideas have been slightly modernized, but have essentially remained unchanged. 'Allamah Tabataba'i, for example, in reference to this specific verse, states that the only limitations imposed by Islam on women as emotional and affectionate beings are those realms in which intellect and reason are required and that must be separated from emotion. These include three main categories; namely, the holding of positions in government, the assumption of the profession of judges, and the need to participate in holy war.[11]

'Allamah Nuri, on the other hand, starts his argument for the superiority of men over women by quoting a series of facts and figures concerning physiological differences between men and women such as the size of the heart, the weight of the brain, and the size of the skull.[12] The psychological differences, according to him, are that women are affectionate and emotional and have weaker nerves. Men, however, are wise and intellectual and have strong nerves, which make them more qualified to strive, struggle, and campaign against the odds of everyday life.[13] Nuri considers these differences sufficient grounds for not giving women the right to divorce. According to 'Allamah Nuri,

> Its great impediment is women's special mentality which like spring weather and infantile temperament is in a state of constant flux. She falls in love at the slightest sign of affection and, at the slightest sign of bad temper, starts a bloody feud. Its great impediment is women's limited mentality. She screams at the slightest misfortune, pours buckets of tears, and seeks protection. Its greatest impediment is the

pride, conceit, and selfishness of women which knows no bounds. She is ostentatious, full of affection and pretension, and is constantly inclined to show off. She is never able to use a power like the right to divorce at the necessary time, and the slightest pretext is enough for her to display her pretensions to power without any deliberation or hesitation.[14]

Ayatullah Mutahhiri, the third *mujtahid* under consideration, agrees with the psychological differences between men and women cited by Nuri but calls them "natural" differences. He uses these natural differences in a more subtle manner than Nuri but justifies the same end—that women are not qualified to have the right to divorce. He starts his argument from the nature of marriage, which is considered to be a natural bond rather than a contractual bilateral relationship. In this natural bond, his view is that the man attempts to possess the woman while she coquettishly tries to charm and ensnare him. The emotions of the man are based upon the full possession of the woman, but she is set on capturing his emotions. Marriage is based on affection, which cannot be enforced through legislation. The affection of each partner has different effects on the marriage.

> The natural mechanism of marriage upon which Islam has based its laws is that the woman should be loved and respected within the family, that is to say, if she is no longer desired and loved by the man, then the foundation of the family is shaken . . . From the point of view of Islam, the greatest insult to a woman is for her husband to say: I do not love you; I hate you; and then through legislation being kept in that man's house.[15]

It is not stated why in such a case she should not be able to initiate divorce proceedings. Divorce laws giving the woman the right to divorce, however, are depicted in such a way as to force unwilling partners to live together.

Matahhiri poses the question as to what would be the consequences if the woman stopped loving the man. Would the foundations of the marriage be shaken in such a case? He answers in the negative, as it is the man who sustains the relationship and nurtures the affection. It would be impossible for a woman not to love a man who loves her.

> Nature has given the key of the natural dissolution of marriage to the man. It is the man who by being unloving and unfaithful makes her cold and unloving, contrary to the woman, whose indifference has no effect on the man, and even increases his desire. Therefore, man's lack of love results in both sides not loving each other, but woman's lack of love does not have any effect. The extinction of man's love results in the death and end of marriage, whereas extinction of a woman's love simply turns the marriage into a sick being who is curable.[16]

ʿAllamah Nuri uses the alleged psychological and emotional differences to support his argument as to who is most qualified to be responsible for the family and to have guardianship in general. The justification is based on Koran IV:34, discussed above, and the argument is as follows: "There can be no discussion of the fact that giving the reins of guardianship into man's intellect and wisdom is better than letting loose the ship of life into the storm of woman's emotions."[17]

Aside from the general question of man's superiority over woman, the first practical step in the subjugation of women within Islamic society begins with the veiling of women (*hijab*). This practice, most common in upper-class society as a sign of status, is based upon the interpretation of Koran XXIV:31, which in translation reads as follows: "And say to the believing women that they lower their gaze and restrain their sexual passions and do not display their adornment [*zinah*] except to their husbands or fathers . . ."

In the interpretation of this verse, there is a difference of opinion as to what the term "adornment" (*zinah*) exactly means. Some interpreters maintain that it includes the beauty of the body, while according to some others it is exclusively applied to external adornments. Ayatullah Mutahhiri contends that the *zinah* in Arabic not only means ornaments that are separate from the body but also includes those that are part of the body.[18] According to him, the injunction is that women should not display their adornments and ornaments with two exceptions, the first exception being those adornments that are manifest. He concludes from this that women possess two kinds of ornaments, those that are self-evident and those that are hidden unless a woman displays them purposely. He then treats the question as to which ornaments are self-evident and which hidden. By taking various interpretations of the Koran he holds the view that manifest ornaments are either outward garments, kohl on the eyes, or rings or henna on the fingers. He then concludes with the second exception: the only parts of a woman's body that do not need to be covered are the two hands and the oval of the face.[19]

ʿAllamah Nuri, without quoting any of the Koran interpreters, also reaches the conclusion that Koran XXIV:31 only allows the hands and the face to be uncovered.[20] Both Mutahhiri and Nuri agree in their justification of veiling (*hijab*), that lack of it would lead to the breakdown of the family, adultery, prostitution, and sexual corruption of all kinds. The basic assumption is that, although the Koran enjoins believing men to lower their gaze and restrain their sexual passions (Koran XXX:24), man's sexuality in the face of temptation is uncontrollable.

The westernized female's preoccupation with clothes and makeup is made into a parody by Mutahhiri, who contends that these women devote most of the day to such activity and are therefore unable to function as useful members of society.[21]

Turning now to the question of polygamy (*ta'addud-i zawjat*), it is generally asserted that in Islam marriage is given preference over celibacy. This preference and the interpretations of Koran IV:3 are the basis of multiple marriages in Islam. The verse reads as follows: "And if you fear that you cannot do justice to orphans, marry such women as seem good to you, two or three or four, but if you fear that you will not do justice [*ta'dilu*], then [marry] only one or that which your right hand possesses." An interesting aspect of this verse is that the only condition limiting a man's right to polygamy is fear of injustice, which is legally indefinable. There is no justification for polygamy in the Koran, but the interpreters do so in terms of shortage of men, orphans, and the female's need for sex. Another justification of polygamy is that it is better to formalize the male's polygamous desires than to force him to have extramarital sex as in other societies.

Matahhiri and Nuri give as the primary justification for polygamy the population ratio of men to women.[22] They claim that in most societies there are more women than men, often using European population statistics that go back to the period after the Second World War, and that if each man married one woman then many women would be deprived of the pleasure of marriage. It would then lead these women to have affairs with married men and would encourage prostitution.

The differences in the nature of men and women are emphasized as one of the social causes for the historic appearance of polygamy. Mutahhiri says, "Man is the slave of his passions, and woman is desirous of affection."[23] According to both Nuri and Mutahhiri, this passionate male cannot restrain his passions during the woman's monthly period or during childbearing. He would be forced, they answer, to go to prostitutes. This, they add, would be further encouragement of prostitution. The basic assumption is that there is no need for prostitution in countries where polygamy is practiced. Another cause for polygamy is that women reach menopause, and that their childbearing years are limited, whereas a man may be desirous of having more children than one woman can produce.[24] Finally, having brought out many social, economic, and demographic justifications for polygamy, the *mujtahid*s reach the qualifying clause in the Koranic verse: ". . . but if you fear that you will not do justice [*ta'dilu*], then [marry] only one . . ." Here both Nuri and Mutahhiri agree that justice (*'adl*) is an important qualification and limitation to polygamy and, although difficult to fulfill if precise prescriptions are followed, its fulfillment is possible.[25] Another *mujtahid* is more explicit in this respect when he argues that since by justice equality of love, affection, and emotion is implied, then polygamy in Islam is possible only in theory and virtually impossible in practice.[26]

Another form of marriage, known as *mut'ah* or temporary marriage, is practiced by Shi'a Muslims. As the name indicates, *mut'ah* (or *sighah*, the term more often used in Iran) is exactly like any other contractual marriage (*nikah*) with the added stipulation that here a time limitation is agreed upon between the two parties. The practice of this type of marriage is based upon certain interpretations of Koran IV:24, the relevant lines being "Then as to whose whom you profit by [marrying] [*istamta'tum*], give them their dowries as appointed." There is a great difference of opinion over this verse, as some Shi'a interpreters actually read or add words to the verse that the standard Sunni interpreters do not accept. The issue revolves partly around the meaning of the Koranic word *istamta'tum* (from which the term *mut'ah* is derived), whose connotation is related to the idea of "seeking pleasure." After this word, an expression denoting time (*ila ajal musamma*, "for a specified period") is sometimes added as a variant reading of the Koranic verse.

The Shi'a *mujtahid*s face great difficulty in the justification of *mut'ah*, as it is neither practiced nor accepted by the Sunnis since it was banned by the Prophet's first successor, the caliph Abu Bakr, and is considered illegal. The justification for *mut'ah* once again centers on the male's uncontrollable sexuality and the prevention of prostitution. This view is echoed by the well-known modern Iranian scholar Sayed Hossein Nasr in the following words:

> Islam is a universal religion and its legislation takes all types of human beings into consideration. Considering the fact that permanent marriage does not satisfy the instinctive sexual urge of certain men and that adultery and fornication are according to Islam among the most deadly poisons, destroying the order and purity of human life, Islam has legitimized temporary marriage under special conditions of which it becomes distinct from adultery and fornication and free of their evils and corruption.[27]

'Allamah Nuri also justifies temporary marriage by saying that adultery and fornication are the worst sins in Islam. Due to this, they have to be legalized. He states its origin as the time of the conquest of Mecca (during the last year of the Prophet's life) and the great need of the Muslim soldiers for women. *Mut'ah* is for occasions when men and women would not be able to enter into permanent marriage, and is a great preventive measure against prostitution.[28]

Mutahhiri, on the other hand, touches on the "modernistic" aspects of this institution, and argues that "one of the brilliant rules of Islam from the point of view of the Ja'fari *mazhab*, which is the official religion of our country, is that marriage can be contracted in two ways—

permanent and temporary."[29] He adds that since it is a contract between two parties, they are free from any kind of obligation toward each other other than that stated in the contract, with the added advantage that, should there be any children, they are recognized as legitimate.

The advantages of temporary marriage are emphasized for young men who have not finished their education, who are unable to undertake the obligations of permanent marriage, and who have sexual needs that must be fulfilled.[30] This is seen as a preventive measure against homosexuality, fornication, and adultery. Both Nuri and Mutahhiri quote Bertrand Russell in support of their argument for the advantages of temporary marriage for young people. They do not mention that Bertrand Russell advocates this type of marriage only for young people as an experiment so that they would not inadvertently enter into a mistaken permanent marriage.[31] They also fail to mention that, in theory and according to the rule, it is possible for a man of eighty with four permanent wives to enter into any number of temporary marriages. Finally, although ʿAllamah Nuri states that under certain conditions and in order to fulfill specific needs temporary marriage is admissible, he does not state who is to be the arbiter of those conditions and needs, and, in their absence, who is to prevent the marriage. The justifications by the *mujtahid*s of this type of marriage are never conclusive. In a sense, however, the position expressed by Dr. Nasr mentioned above appears to be the most realistic and straightforward, as he simply bases his argument on the male's sexual urge.

Since the most well-known Shiʿa *mujtahid* in the world today is Ayatullah Khomeini, the present leader of the Islamic Republic of Iran, this discussion would be incomplete without a cursory glance at some of his views. Khomeini has not specifically written on women, but his views are well known if not set out in detail by him personally.

Khomeini's early protests against the reforms of Muhammad Riza Shah Pahlavi, which finally led to his exile, are generally known for their anti–land reform content. But he protested women's right to vote very early, before the shah did in 1963, when a Council of Ministers' directive proclaimed that women should be allowed to vote in elections for provincial councils. The protests led by Khomeini were so strong that the government had to give in. Women did not vote.

Imam Khomeini is essentially in line with the standard Shiʿa position both in its theory or ideology and in its actual practice. In *Tawzih al-masaʾil* (further described as a *risalah*, "treatise"), Khomeini touches on some points concerning family law.[32] The rights and duties of a husband and wife are considered to be so different from each other that they are set out in different paragraphs. For example:

A woman who has entered into a permanent marriage is not allowed to leave the house without her husband's permission. She must submit herself to any pleasure he desires. She may not refuse herself on any ground other than religiously accepted ones . . .

And again:

If a woman does not obey her husband according to the manner set out in the previous cases [masa'il], she is then sinful and is not entitled to food, clothes, housing, or intercourse. But she is entitled to her *mahr* [marriage portion].[33]

In his *Tawzih al-masa'il*, Khomeini devotes an entire section to temporary marriage (*mut'ah*), which he begins, "Entering into a temporary marriage with a woman is correct even though it may not be for pleasure."[34] As far as veiling (*hijab*) is concerned, Khomeini devotes ten sections of his *Tawzih* to rules regarding looking at women. These set out in detail specific points as to who may look at whom and which parts of the body may be seen by whom. The only parts of a woman's body permitted to be seen are the oval of her face and her hands. Even this injunction is further qualified by the stipulation that the onlooker must not regard these parts of the female anatomy with sexual desire.[35] Finally, the section on divorce gives the male power to divorce his wife at will, the only qualifications being related to the last date of sexual intercourse and the woman's menstrual period. There are no restrictions, however, on divorcing menopausal women and nine-year-old girls.

These interpretations of the Koran have led to woman's unequal position in Iranian society. It must, however, be pointed out that the subject is much more complex and needs more detailed analysis than has been possible within the scope of this paper. For every word of the Koran there are pages of interpretations. The *mujtahids* whose ideas on the position of women in Iran have been examined and who are representative of Shi'a ideology and practice tend to follow a traditional, conservative line of argument. Between the difficulty of understanding the exact meaning of Koranic revelation as an expression of God's will and the attempts by the *'ulama* or *mujtahids* to go beyond the meaning of the revealed word, the exact position of women and their role in Iranian society will continue to suffer from an obscurantism that is almost impossible to sort out either in the sources themselves or in the interpretations of the authorities.

The roots of the Shi'a position on women lie in centuries of tradition. 'Allamah Muhammad Baqir Majlisi in the seventeenth century, the high Safavid period, says, "A woman must obey all that her husband commands and, when in private, submit willingly to all his demands."[36] This injunction is identical to that of Khomeini. Baydawi and Tabataba'i are in agreement that women cannot participate in government, judgeship, or holy war (jihad). Through the centuries up to the present, the Shi'a 'ulama have been generally in accord in their views on the position of women. For the moment this view prevails in Iran under the regime of the Islamic Republic, but the future may hold a different promise for the women of Iran.

NOTE: *I am indebted to Professor Michel M. Mazzaoui of the University of Utah for his comments on an earlier draft of this paper.*

Notes

1. For a useful account on early Shiism, see E. G. Browne, *A Literary History of Persia* (1924; reprinted Cambridge: Cambridge University Press, 1930), chap. 8, "The Orthodox Shi'a Faith and Its Exponents, the Mujtahids and Mullas," pp. 353–411. See also M. M. Mazzaoui, "Shi'ism in the Medieval, Safavid and Qajar Periods: A Study in Ithna'ashari Continuity," in P. J. Chelkowski (ed.), *Iran, Continuity and Variety* (New York: New York University Press, 1971), pp. 39–57.

2. See Muhammad Baqir Majlisi, *Hulyat al-muttaqin* (Tehran: 'Ilmi, 1379/1959).

3. See *Encyclopedia of Islam*, 2nd ed., "Ijtihad."

4. For some work on Shiism, see Shahrough Akhavi, *Religion and Politics in Contemporary Iran: Clergy-State Relations in the Pahlavi Period* (Albany: State University of New York Press, 1980); Hamid Algar, *Religion and State in Iran: 1785–1906* (Berkeley and Los Angeles: University of California Press, 1969); D. M. Donaldson, *The Shi'ite Religion* (London, 1933); Joseph Eliash, "Some Misconceptions Concerning Shi'i Political Theory," *International Journal of Middle East Studies* 9 (1979): 9–25; Marshall Hodgson, "How Did the Early Shi'i Become Sectarian?" *Journal of the American Oriental Society* 75 (1955): 1–13; Nikkie R. Keddie (ed.), *Scholars, Saints and Sufis* (Berkeley: University of California Press, 1972); A. K. S. Lambton, "A Reconsideration of the Position of the Marja' al-Taqlid and the Religious Institution," *Studia Islamica* 20 (1964): 115–135; and 'Allamah Sayyid Muhammad Husayn Tabataba'i, *Shi'ite Islam* (Albany: State University of New York Press, 1975).

5. Allamah Sayyid Muhammad Husayn Tabataba'i (1903–1982) was born in Tabriz into a family that claims descent from the Prophet. He studied classical Islamic subjects at Najaf (in Iraq) and read *Usul al fiqh* (The Principles of Islamic Jurisprudence) with two great masters: Mirza Muhammad Husayn Na'ini and Sheikh Muhammad Husayn Isfahani. He also studied Islamic philosophy and the "acquired sciences," also under distinguished scholars. For more on his life and background, see the preface by Sayed Hossein Nasr in Tabataba'i, *Shi'ite Islam*, pp. 22–25. This is an English

translation of the author's *Shiʿah dar Islam*. The present Islamic republican regime in Iran recently issued a commemorative stamp with Tabatabaʾi's picture on it.

6. ʿAllamah Yahya Nuri was born in 1311/1932 in Baladah, a village in the district of Nur. He left his birthplace in early childhood and went through the different stages of classical Islamic education until he reached the rank of *mujtahid*. During his studies he also graduated from the College of Theology of the University of Tehran, where he later taught. His publications include *Islam va ʿaqaʾid va araʾ-i bashari, ya jahiliyyat va Islam* (a work in comparative religion) and *Hukumat dar Islam* (Government in Islam).

7. Ayatullah Sheikh Murtaza Mutahhiri was assassinated by a group called Furqan on May 1, 1979 shortly after the revolution in Iran. He was professor of theology at the University of Tehran and among the reformist ʿulama dealing with social problems within an Islamic context, and he was conscious of the need for a redefinition of the Shiite position in the modern world. His publications include many articles in *Guftar-i mah*, a series of public lectures initiated by Mutahhiri in 1960 lasting two and a half years and published in three volumes under that title. He also participated with Tabatabaʾi and others in *Bahthi dar barahʾ-yi marjaʿiyyat va ruhaniyyat* (Tehran: Intishar, 1341/1962). For more on Mutahhiri, see Akhavi, *Religion and Politics*.

8. All the translations of the Koranic verses have been taken from a translation of the Koran by Maulana Muhammad ʿAli (Lahore, 1951).

9. For example, in Marmaduke Pickthall's translation, *The Glorious Koran*, the words "maintainers of women" are rendered "in charge of women," the word "desertion" is translated as "rebellion," and "chastise them" is translated "scourge them." Actually the word *udrubuhunna*, which is rendered "chastise them" by one translator and "scourge them" by the other, could very well mean simply "hit them" or "beat them up." The Arabic verbal root *daraba* means "to strike."

10. As quoted in Reuben Levy, *The Social Structure of Islam* (Cambridge: Cambridge University Press, 1957), p. 99.

11. ʿAllamah Sayyid Muhammad Husayn Tabatabaʾi, "Zan dar Islam" (Woman in Islam), *Maktab-i tashayyuʿ* 1 (1338/1959): 29.

12. Yahya Nuri, *Huquq-i zan dar Islam va jahan* (Women's rights in Islam and the world) (Tehran: Muʾassasah-yi Matbuʿati-yi Farahani, 1343/1964), pp. 68–73.

13. Ibid., pp. 73–76.

14. Ibid., p. 229.

15. Murtaza Mutahhiri, *Nizam huquq-i zan dar Islam* (Legislation of women's rights in Islam) (Qum: Inthisharat-i Sadra, 1357/1979), pp. 279–285.

16. Ibid.

17. Nuri, *Huquq-i zan dar Islam*, pp. 132–133.

18. Murtaza Mutahhiri, *Masʾalah-yi hijab* (The question of veiling) (Tehran: Anjuman-i Islami-yi Pizishkan, 1353/1974), p. 128.

19. Ibid., p. 135.

20. Nuri, *Huquq-i zan dar Islam*, p. 91.

21. Mutahhiri, *Mas³alah-yi hijab*, p. 91.

22. Murtaza Mutahhiri, *Ta'addud-i zawjat, izdivaj-i muvaqqat* (Polygamy, temporary marriage) (Shirkat-i Sihami-yi Siman-i Fars va Khuzistan, n.d.), p. 92; Nuri, *Huquq-i zan dar Islam*, pp. 182–189.

23. Mutahhiri, *Ta'addud-i zawjat*, p. 45.

24. Ibid., pp. 90–91.

25. Nuri, *Huquq-i zan dar Islam*, p. 192; Mutahhiri, *Ta'addud-i zawjat*, pp. 140–147.

26. Hasan Sadr, *Huquq-i zan dar Islam va Urupa* (The rights of women in Islam and Europe) (Tehran: ³Ilmi, 1357/1978), p. 206.

27. 'Allamah Sayyid Muhammad Husayn Tabataba³i and Sayed Hossein Nasr, "Mutah or Temporary Marriage," in Tabataba³i, *Shi'ite Islam*, appendix 2, pp. 227–230.

28. Nuri, *Huquq-i zan dar Islam*, p. 202.

29. Mutahhiri, *Ta'addud-i zawjat*, p. 152.

30. Ibid., p. 155.

31. Bertrand Russell, *Marriage and Morals* (London: George Allen and Unwin, Ltd., 1972), pp. 81–86.

32. Ayatullah Khomeini, *Risalah-yi tawzih al-masa³il* (Tehran: Saziman-i Chap va Intisharat Javidan, 1357/1978). The word *masa³il* (plural of *mas³alah*) in the title is a technical term. It may be translated as "question" or better as "answer to a question." However, perhaps the rendering "case, cases" retains its legal force.

33. Ibid., p. 490.

34. Ibid., p. 491.

35. Ibid., p. 493.

36. Majlisi, *Hulyat*, p. 74.

PART VI
Work

A basic shift has taken place in the lives of Middle Eastern women in the past generation. Economic conditions are changing women's place. Instead of solely fulfilling the traditional role of wife and mother who labors at home to make life possible for husband, children, and probably in-laws, a rapidly growing number of women are going outside the home to work for wages.

The change has taken place as the Arab world has shifted from a predominantly agricultural to a mixed industrial economy. People in the area also face new pressures of consumer capitalism and a higher cost of living as inflation rises. Traditional patterns of family earning power and family life are shaken, as men can often no longer comfortably support even a nuclear family, let alone a large extended kin group. Many men and, increasingly, women now migrate to Europe or to oil-rich Arab countries in search of work. The 1976 Egyptian census reported nearly 1.25 million men as officially not present and presumed working abroad (the figure was much larger by 1981); Algeria, Morocco, and Tunisia have been sending hundreds of thousands of workers to France since the late 1950s; and West Germany's "Economic Miracle" was made possible through the labor of a flood of Turkish migrants.

The absence of men from the household means that many women must function as heads of households as well as breadwinners to supplement wages sent home from abroad. Women may also keep the family business going or supervise farming. In rural areas women have always worked in the fields beside men, raised livestock, and sold eggs, butter, and milk; they continue to do so today where possible. Others toiled in groups of migrant workers, part of a growing rural proletariat. Specialists, such as midwives and beauticians and religious functionaries, worked and continue to work in both city and country today. But today the majority of uneducated urban women who need to work outside the home for the first time are seldom trained for specific vocations. They can only find poorly paying, low-status jobs as servants or washerwomen. In the past, lower-class urban women were forced to accept such jobs, but any claim to higher social status required that they be avoided at all cost. A woman working outside the home, in public with strange men, was seen as shameful in the very recent past, as it indicated a man's inability to support his family and to control the actions of his women relatives. Today this is changing for all classes.

However, even a generation ago some recognition of women's needs and responsibilities was evident in the measures adopted by governments and private organizations throughout the Middle East, measures to help women earn extra money and yet remain at home to care for the family. Following independence from colonial rule in the 1950s, training programs were undertaken. The women's *nadi* (club) movement in Morocco, for example, was an effort to teach women skills such as sewing, embroidery, and basic literacy so that they might work at home, combining both new and old worlds. Similar workshops and literacy classes can be found in Egypt, Sudan, Algeria, Iraq, Tunisia, Jordan, Lebanon, and Libya, sometimes under the aegis of the government ministries, sometimes under the supervision of women's cooperatives. Markets for their products have also been organized. This experience might be compared with that of our own grandmothers who, in the early years of industrial development in the West, earned extra income or even supported entire families with similar labor at home.

However, piecework at home (or even for hospitals and schools on a regular basis) is not enough to make ends meet in most Middle Eastern families today. Many women must work full-time outside the home, even if their husbands have a good job. A thirty-one-year-old woman says, "I work so that when I put eggs on the table and one child asks for more, I'll have a second egg to give."

Women work in shops, banks, schools, hospitals, and most recently in industry. In the 1960s, according to Nadia Youssef, Egyptian women constituted only 3.5 percent of the total public work force.[1] But by 1981 Egyptian women in the industrial work force alone constituted 18 percent of the total. The 18 percent is an official figure, again probably lower than the actual unofficial totals, for in many cases women's work is unreported.

For married women with children, a factory job or any job eight hours a day in addition to family duties means double responsibility. As one married worker says, "Without a college degree, it would be better to stay home and care for one's children. But I have no choice. I must work." For single women, a job outside the home offers new areas of social involvement and benefits. In industry, for example, there are guaranteed wages and health and pension benefits, things not available to women (nor to men) in Egypt a generation ago. Barbara Lethem Ibrahim's interviews with women factory workers in Cairo and Andrea Rugh's analysis of strategies for coping give a sense of the ways in which women are adjusting to the new work pressures. "The Shoes," a short story by the Egyptian woman writer Iqbal Barakah, chronicles some of the new problems of working women.

Some women are beginning to see virtues in the new necessity for outside work and are insisting on their freedom to exercise that right. Algerian women, like Egyptian women, are campaigning for more state support to facilitate wage labor day-care centers in the factories and provide better bus service and more labor-saving appliances. Thus, for better or for worse, in the Middle East as in the Western world women are taking positions in the public work force as wage earners outside the home. In most cases, economic necessity is the motivation. Since the fifties, a small percentage of Middle Eastern women who have been able to obtain a higher education have entered the professions, jobs in government bureaucracies, and positions in engineering and architectural firms, banks, businesses, universities, and even in the foreign service of their countries. But the great majority of working women in the Middle East, like women in America, work outside the home at routine and even menial jobs to help themselves and their families survive in a world radically different from that of their mothers.[2]

Notes

1. Nadia Youssef, *Women and Work in Developing Societies* (Berkeley, 1974).

2. A conservative estimate of married American women with children in the full-time public work force is 52 percent. Of that total, 2 percent are estimated to hold professional-level jobs (Lucia Gilbert, unpublished manuscript, 1981).

Women and Work: Strategies and Choices in a Lower-Class Quarter of Cairo

ANDREA B. RUGH

Scholars who study women's roles often assume that given a free choice women will elect to work outside the home for wages or salaries, if not just for economic rewards, at least for the increase in respect and status they will earn. In this paper I will examine the factors involved in women's choices about employment—how they conceive of work, what their strategies are to obtain more income, and how they choose appropriate kinds of work. I will look at the consequences of employment, both negative and positive, as they are perceived by women in a lower-class study sample and attempt to discern the changing attitudes of lower-class people to the question of what is appropriate work for women. First, not all classes accord prestige to women as a direct result of outside employment. Second, although employment may become an economic necessity for some women and may even pave the way for the social mobility of later generations, women themselves may feel the quality of family life suffers to such an extent that the decision to work becomes a last and not favored resort. Third, the data tend to substantiate the view that higher levels of education permit women to compete for jobs with higher status, but the lengthy periods of education required before a real difference is made discourages the vast majority of lower-class people from choosing this alternative. I do not attempt to assess whether women's employment leads to better social development.

This paper is based on long-term participant observation in Bulaq, a lower-class neighborhood of Cairo. The data were collected over a five-year period from 1976 to 1981 through intensive involvement in the activities of a social welfare center.

Working Women in Bulaq

In 1976 Um A. stored her small heap of belongings in the ground floor central hallway of a three-story apartment building. Two families lived in the other three rooms leading off of the hall, one being the family of her married sister. Um A. slept with her two children on a cotton mattress in one corner under the stairwell and accepted handouts of food from her sister. Frequently the sister's husband, furious over the drain on his income from feeding two families, would beat the women mercilessly. Um A. was a young woman in her thirties, recently widowed and unusually active in trying to find some means of supporting herself and her children. She found a middleman supplier of baggage tags to airlines who was willing to let her attach the strings to the cardboard tags. He paid her a few piasters for every six hundred finished tags. At that time, the product of a day's work earned her enough to buy eight flat Arab loaves of bread. Next she approached a charitable center and was given table cloths to embroider. Though the money earned was proportionately better it was difficult to wait the week or so it took her to finish the work before getting paid. She next tried another piecework project that paid better and lent her the money to tide her over until payday. For several months she worked hard at this work, earning enough to rent her own small room, make down payments on some furniture, and buy a kerosene cooker for food. As soon as she could afford it she bought chickens to raise under the bed so her children could have fresh eggs and meat at feast days. Soon she organized a network of women for whom she would bring piecework, return the finished products, and collect a percentage of the profits. This along with an occasional cleaning job and continuation of the baggage tag work kept her going. But with more money in her hands she soon discovered new expenses. For example, as her children grew older she wanted to bring them the customary tutors so they could pass end-of-the-year exams and stay in school. Her work was soon not adequate to take care of her expanded needs and she set out to find a job with more regular and higher pay. By 1980 she had found a permanent job cleaning in homes, and that along with embroidery work in the evening gave her a relatively substantial income for Bulaq. It meant, however, that almost all her waking hours were occupied with her income-earning projects.

Um N. lived in a relatively large apartment of three rooms and a long hallway. Living with her were her elderly mother-in-law, her father, her husband, and five children. Um N. as a girl had learned from nuns in a charitable institution to do very delicate smocking work that was much in demand not only by her neighbors but also by elite clients that bought from a store to which she sold her finished products. The store owner brought her the material and gave her fifty piasters (seventy-five cents) for the finished product. He then sold the item for twenty times what he paid her. Later she increased her production by selling to the project of a welfare center and earned three times what she earned selling to the store. Nevertheless she continued to work for the store in order to keep her options open. Her husband all during this period brought in a moderate wage that barely sustained the household and her children took over a number of the household tasks. Um N. was able over the years to earn enough to buy a number of things for her house—a refrigerator, a washing machine, a *butagaz* stove, and a television set. Part of the money also went for clothing and books that her eldest daughter needed in her schooling. This daughter, the brightest of the children, eventually finished her university degree and after waiting a year received a teaching position in a government school. Her mother ruefully commented that the daughter would be earning less in her new position than she did with her embroidery work. Nevertheless, the family was very proud of the daughter's accomplishments and the community always talked about the family as "you know, Um N., the one with the daughter who finished university."

H. was a young divorced woman with a small baby in 1976. After her husband divorced her when she was six months pregnant to marry another woman she moved in with her mother and a young brother into one room with no furnishings. An older brother who was a peddler and very poor himself helped them out from time to time though his own wife and children needed every cent he could earn. H. was young and strong and soon took up water carrying for her sympathetic neighbors at one piaster a canister. She spent most of every morning carrying the canisters back and forth from the public well. Her mother cared for the baby and accomplished the few household chores their limited existence required. A year later H.'s baby died from what was probably meningitis. Because she had so little money she had procrastinated about taking the baby to an expensive doctor and when she finally went the baby died in the doctor's office.[1] The death of the baby freed H. to seek better-paying work, a necessity now that her elder brother had been caught as a draft evader and had entered the army. At a pay level that at that time was three pounds (about five dollars) a month he could not support his own family, much less H. and her mother. The mother took over H.'s water-carrying jobs and H. appealed to a charitable center to find her work. They eventually found her janitorial/cleaning work in the offices of a private institution where she received a salary of fifteen pounds (about twenty-two dollars) a month at first and later was raised to twenty pounds and then twenty-five. During this period the mother of a young man seeking a bride made inquiries about marriage to H. Because of her vulnerable position and obvious disadvantages the bridegroom's mother felt certain she would accept his offer gladly. The bridegroom's previous offers to other young women had failed because of his reputation for having an unpleasant temperament, for having no skill or secure work (he was the assistant to a vegetable seller), and because he was a heavy drinker and hashish smoker. H. was anxious to marry any man and stop work but her mother and brother refused to accept her marriage to this candidate. Next she "fell in love" with a male janitor at her work who had been recently widowed but, though he liked her, his family urged him to marry a candidate from a better family.

Women's Roles

In Bulaq, women's primary responsibilities are household tasks and child care, and these responsibilities have become synonymous with femininity. Financial support is a man's responsibility and is synonymous with masculinity. Deviation from these responsibilities threatens the femininity or masculinity of the individual. The fundamental difference between sex roles pervades the whole fabric of Egyptian society and is echoed in important institutions such as inheritance, where a man, because of his greater financial responsibilities, receives twice the amount of a woman.

Behavior that deviates from the norm (such as the employment of women) is rationalized as somehow enhancing that norm. A mother with no male supporter works "for the sake of her child"; the unmarried woman works "temporarily" to afford the costs of marriage; the young married woman works "to buy a few more appliances" for her home; the mother works "to give her children more opportunities." In Bulaq a woman's concept of self is fully involved in her sense of her womanly responsibilities. She gains more respect from her family and neighbors by performing her responsibilities as a woman well than she does through employment. Employment in effect threatens her ability to perform these roles well and may subject her and her family to outside criticism. Further, no one holds her responsible for supporting the family.

Resource-Saving and Income-Generating Work

Women in Bulaq find acceptable ways of increasing the resource level of households without risking the disapproval of the community by considering the context in which they contribute. They gain approval if they can save resources (without sacrificing generosity) by, for example, knowing where to find bargains and by developing dressmaking, handwork, and cooking skills. They aid the income-producing work of their husbands by washing vegetables and fruits that are sold from carts, cooking foods or making handicrafted goods, cleaning shops, or helping out with the sales of a street corner stand or small shop. They can raise chickens, pigeons, or goats for household consumption or to sell. They can regularly visit the villages of their relatives and bring back cheese, bread, or fruits and vegetables that they can then sell to neighbors. They can buy clothing or dry goods at wholesale prices and sell at retail in their homes. They can act as pawnbrokers for neighbors who need money, earning interest on the money before the goods are returned. All these ways of increasing the resource base of the household are accepted as compatible with women's supportive roles and generally are not considered to carry the onus of certain kinds of outside employment. They are not in effect formally defined as work in the sense that men's attempts to earn income, no matter how ad hoc, are defined as work.

When does income-producing work become "real" work for a Bulaq woman? Usually people perceive it as real when it interrupts the natural rhythm of the day or takes the woman for long periods on a regular basis away from the domestic context in which her responsibilities are centered. A woman can sew dresses on an occasional basis for her neighbors and still not be "working." If she spends several hours a day sewing in her own home, she becomes a professional seamstress (*khayyata*). If she goes out three mornings a week to clean in homes she is working.

Qualitative Changes Resulting from Employment

Household tasks can be scheduled with a certain flexibility but efficiency demands that they be patterned in ways that take advantage of proximity, compatibility, and certain kinds of natural sequences. Women wash floors and straighten rooms when the other household members are at school or work; women need to do their marketing before cooking; food needs to be ready when the other family members return; laundry is consolidated into one or two mornings because of the difficulty in bringing and heating extra water. Many houses do not have their own private water taps, so women regularly fill water vessels (*zir*) from community faucets. Even with scheduling the housewife normally tolerates well, even looks forward to, interruptions that offer social interaction with neighbors.

The working woman in Bulaq cannot tolerate such interruptions as well since she has less time in which to perform household tasks. Working requires her to sacrifice scheduling and reduces quality in the performance of housework. Working does not usually reduce the housework load unless children can assume some tasks. Men normally do not do this; in fact, they may be less inclined to assume feminine tasks if women are challenging their masculinity by assuming financially supportive roles in the family. A working woman usually shops on her way home from work when produce is not so fresh; she must cook in the evening for the next day; she must wake up early to clean her house and get her family off to their activities; she spends her one day of holiday doing the laundry. Short-cutting conveniences are not readily available in Bulaq, and poor families cannot afford them.

Though a woman's responsibilities continue nonstop over a twenty-four-hour period, a Bulaq housewife still has time for leisure. She measures her work, stopping for tea with a friend, cleaning rice on her doorstep with a neighbor, joining the family for conversation or television in the evening. She would find it difficult to make a qualitative distinction between leisure and labor. By contrast, the husband's activities are recognized as divided between a work period and a leisure period. For the lower-class male, work is considered time spent fulfilling responsibilities, doing something he would rather not do, and leisure is a time spent doing what he prefers. Full-time employment forces women to make similar distinctions. Work is the period away from home activities for which she is paid; after work is the time for her "true" responsibilities. Most working opportunities available to the lower-class woman are arduous and do not provide work she enjoys. An exception may be found in the factory, where literate lower-class women have jobs with lenient performance quotas. Women in these jobs sometimes express pleasure at the company of their factory companions and the leisurely pace of work. Egyptian middle-class women report that office work is relaxing and restful, and sometimes work hours can be spent organizing their housework by shopping during tea breaks and by performing small housework tasks in the office. For the most part, however, lower-class women see employment as draining their energies; they recognize that they give up the measured way of doing housework and their moments of leisure. Many women, including those in the poorest households, when asked why they do not work simply say, "I don't have the time to work," meaning they do not want the frantic pace of the employed woman's life.

Real work as defined by women, therefore, implicitly requires a qualitative change in life-style, one that demands organization around its requirements and not around what a lower-class Bulaq woman views as her primary concerns. It also changes the quality of her day from an integrated fabric of labor and leisure into distinctively sectioned-off blocks of time; from what "she should be doing" into what "interferes with what she should be doing." The woman loses control over the organization of her own day.

Status

Another reason the distinction between "real" work and a woman's normal responsibilities becomes important involves family status in the

Bulaq community. A family with a strong financial position is viewed positively by the community, all other factors begin favorable. Part of this image includes the fact that the women of the family do not work outside the home. A family that permits its women to work risks appearing needy. A husband in such a family is viewed as a poor provider and, since support is so heavily equated with masculinity, his self-image consequently suffers. Lower-class women can succcessfully fulfill their roles by producing many children, caring well for them, and managing the housework skillfully. Lower-class men often have difficulty supporting rapidly increasing families. Unskilled laborers and self-employed peddlers have little job stability, few wage increases, and few connections to better themselves. At the bottom of the employment hierarchy, they suffer the daily abuse of their "betters." Thus many men return home, frustrated by their failures, to hear their wives complain of not having enough money. Women's employment piles one more offense on a man's sense of masculine pride by broadcasting his failures to the community.

The woman by her employment often creates conditions for possible community criticism. The neighbors tend to assume impropriety. Women who work try to forestall such criticisms by making sure they are escorted to and from work or public transportation by male family members, they say they are working in a factory when in reality they are working as servants, or they may conceal the fact of their employment altogether. Some dress more conservatively for work, or they may assume middle-class dress to indicate a life-style that accepts women's employment. Women's precautions, in short, are not those suggesting an expectation of increase in status. The opposite is the case. Many women refuse to work rather than face a possible decrease in respect/ prestige for themselves or their families. They say, "My husband would never let me work" or, with scorn, "Me, work! I would never do that!" much as if one was asking them to go out and become prostitutes.

Most Bulaq women who admit they work say they do so because their family needs money. Most agree they would not work if their family's financial situation improved. Higher family status is correlated with a lower rate of female employment. However, by working a woman may hope for greater future achievements for her children: longer education and training and good marriage partners. Family standing in the community is critical when children's marriages are involved.

Critical decisions about employment that are forced upon families sometimes reveal their sensitivities to certain issues. In one Bulaq family, the daughter worked in her elderly father's small store. When her father died, she could easily have taken over the store, but instead the family closed the shop. If the store had been left open, the girl's work would have had to be redefined as "work that supported the family" and would have reflected poorly on her brothers (who should support her) and on the whole family.

This case illustrates the importance of appearances and the disapproval felt by some families for demonstrating blatant financial need. A Bulaq woman can quietly take piecework into her home, go out and wash clothes in homes, carry water from the public taps for families, or sit on a street corner and sell food she has cooked. In all these activities she employs skills learned within the scope of her womanly roles to earn income outside the family, but each activity carries a different degree of appropriateness as conceived by herself and her community. The last (selling food in public) is the least and the first (piecework at home) the most accepted way for a woman to earn income. Going out to clean, carrying water, and selling food are considered too public a demonstration of the family's economic problems. The first two are usually performed by young or middle-aged women who feel themselves strong enough for such taxing work and have clear-cut financial needs. It is sometimes possible to conceal the fact that a woman is working in this way for payment. Cooking and selling food, because they are less arduous, are more the province of elderly widowed women. In general, all jobs that blatantly display need are performed by women whose husbands are either dead or have abandoned them and therefore are not present to incur shame, or they are performed by women whose husbands' inability to earn sufficient income is so devastatingly apparent that the point of shame has been passed. Such women have little community status left to lose. Even then some families do not relinquish what little pride is left.

> In one of the families in Bulaq, a young husband, with wife and two children, was unable to hold a job and remained constantly at home. The irritated wife, unable to see any alternative, finally went out and found work cleaning in the home of a Kuwaiti family living in Cairo. Her husband, infuriated partly by what he saw as the insult to himself of her going out to work, and partly as a result of his active imagination about what might be going on in the Kuwaiti house, poured kerosene over himself and burnt himself to death. His family blamed the wife for his death and tried to track her down to take revenge for exposing him to such shame.

In a lower-class neighborhood like Bulaq, therefore, a woman's decision to work is determined to a large extent by the extremity of her need. Need in any society tends to disrupt the realization of community norms. In Bulaq, despite respectable models of middle-class women's employment, resistance to women assuming work outside the home is still strong.

Changing Patterns of Work

Historically in Egypt working-class women's rates of employment have tended to rise and fall in relation to labor market demands and the availability (or sometimes willingness) of male workers to fill that demand. This has certainly been true in agricultural and industrial production and also in construction work. In the first quarter of the century and intermittently during war time when labor was scarce,[2] women in Egypt worked in industries and on construction sites in poorly paid jobs that males would not take. In many agricultural areas, they are still paid only half the wage of a man for the same work. While men gravitated in times of labor scarcity to higher paying jobs, women filled in where need arose. Because they were considered to be earning "supplementary" income they were compensated proportionately. Lacking active organizational means, lower-class women did not claim their rights to equal pay guaranteed them under the Egyptian constitution.

In the second and third quarters of the century a stagnant economy and a burgeoning urban population created severe unemployment and underemployment among male laborers. The result was more limited opportunities for women, who had nothing to offer but physical labor and homemaking skills. In the last four decades the Economic Activity Rate[3] of women in the labor force has declined from 7.9 in 1937 to 3.5 in 1970. Males suffered a comparable decline from 65.1 in 1937 to 49.5 in 1970.[4] This overabundance of manual laborers probably contributed to the tightening of social restrictions on lower-class women's employment at the same time that middle-class women were taking jobs in government bureaucracies without risk of undermining their social positions. In recent years the trend has reversed itself again, as large numbers of male laborers traveled to other Arab countries where they could command high wages compared with Egypt. By 1976, the Economic Activity Rate of women had dramatically increased from 3.5 in 1970 to 9.2 while men's rates rose more slowly from 49.5 to 52.9.[5] Now lower-class women appear more frequently on construction sites, as street sweepers, and as peddlers. The large number of employed middle-class women has also created a strong demand for household servants and a subsequent large increase in their wages. Other severe labor shortages have appeared in construction skills: electricians, plumbers, mechanics, carpenters, plasterers, concrete pourers. As yet social and cultural obstacles have prevented women from assuming such occupations, but demand may eventually break down social resistance.

Historically, then, opportunities for lower-class women have been predicated to a large extent on a satisfactory level of male employment. Few jobs outside the home have consistently been defined in the past as women's work. Men, for example, work as servants, sew clothing, carry water, or work in laundries. The main distinction between men's and women's work seems to lie in its ad hoc nature. Where work becomes professional (as in a laundry compared with washing at home), large scale (involving machine work embroidery as opposed to piecework), or managerial (directing the output of others), it becomes men's work. What is defined as men's work in times of job scarcity, however, often becomes redefined as women's work in times of labor shortage. No persistent cultural tradition in Egypt appears to oppose certain kinds of work for women; rather, opposition to women working comes from changing definitions of what is modest, what is appropriate, and what are the implications of the woman's employment. And these factors in large part are determined by the social and economic conditions of the moment.

Changing Perceptions of Work

Even in the short period of time between 1978 and 1980, there is evidence that families in Bulaq were responding to changing conditions in the Egyptian economy and that woman's employment was directly affected. In 1976, among 175 families who frequented a social welfare center in Bulaq, few women worked outside their homes and most consistently expressed their desire not to work. By 1978 these households averaged 2.2 sources of income (income including wages of more than one family member, charitable donations, and pensions). Seventy percent earned combined incomes of less than twenty pounds (about thirty dollars) a month. In 1978 many women still publicly rejected work, but a careful survey indicated that a number were earning income. Principal females in 173 limited-income households were asked if they contributed to the family's income. After excluding sixty-six "ineligible" females (those whom no one expected to work; that is, the physically handicapped, the aged, and those defined by the community as "rich"), researchers found only about 107 cases of principal women working in 1978.

There appeared to be five critical factors by which women and their families judged the appropriateness of work for women: (1) how protected (in terms of the opportunities for moral indiscretion) the work area is, (2) how public the display of family need is, (3) how much status is connected with the work, (4) how much income is earned, and (5) the extent to which the work interferes with a woman's other responsibilities. Each factor had a positive and negative value. In general, in 1978 the higher the woman's economic need the more likely she would accept work evaluated negatively.

Work can be divided into five categories based on combinations of the factors above.

1. Incidental work such as chicken and pigeon raising. The work takes place in the seclusion of the home, does not display family need, has no significant status value, and does not compete with household responsibilities. In 1978, 12 percent (thirteen) of the eligible women claimed to contribute income in this way. Another large but unreported number raise poultry and animals for home consumption, thereby saving family resources.

2. Part- or full-time work such as sewing, piecework, washing, child care, or selling items bought at wholesale in a woman's own home. Even when these tasks are paid for in money or return exchanges, they are often considered as helpful favors rather than work. They take place in the protection of the home, wages are usually higher than those for incidental work, the work does not reflect poorly on the family, and the women may be considered "clever," both because the work requires a low-level skill or entrepreneurial ability and because she enhances her housewifely role by means of a valuable exchange service. How the public views her work depends ultimately on a complex of factors, not least of which is the amount of time she spends on the activity and the extent of her need. One who "works for a living because she has to" is held in less esteem than one who "works because she is clever at something and is in demand." In 1978, 7 percent (seven) of the eligible women occupied themselves with this kind of work.

3. Service work such as cleaning or washing clothes in other people's homes. This work demonstrates clear need, has low status, and is carried on in private homes where a woman's reputation may be compromised. In 1978, 9 percent (ten) of the eligible women were engaged in this kind of work but most were trying to conceal that fact from their neighbors.

4. "Professional" work such as selling *ta'miyya* (fried bean patties) in her own shop, factory work, janitorial service, or a *daya* (midwife). This work either requires a specialized skill or takes place in an impersonal institutional setting that is less compromising to a woman's reputation. Higher status is associated with these jobs because of their regular and sometimes higher pay and the more specialized talents they require. In 1978 only 2 percent (two) of the eligible women were occupied in positions of this kind.

5. Street corner work such as selling prepared food, nuts, sweets, vegetables, or kerosene or carrying water for neighbors. Only the poorest engage in such work. It produces little income and is publicly humiliating to the families of such women. In 1978, 5 percent (five) of the women made their living in this way.

In 1980 the income-generating activities of the same families were surveyed again to confirm what was already an obvious trend: a tendency to move toward more lucrative types of employment whether or not these kinds of employment were considered "status enhancing." People were complaining more bitterly about the high cost of living even though evidence suggested that materially at least they were better off in 1980 than in 1978. Many more had television sets, *butagaz* stoves, and washing machines. Low wages had denied them such consumer items before and indeed such items had been beyond most people's expectations. By 1980, however, they were buying such goods and feeling their need for higher income more pressing as monthly credit payments came due.

Between 1978 and 1980 the number of women working doubled. The number who claimed to contribute income from incidental sales to neighbors remained relatively stable at 14 percent (compared with 12 percent in 1978), as did the low return work of street corner peddling and water carrying (7 percent in 1980 compared with 5 percent in 1978). The rate of those engaged in home industries rose from 7 percent in 1978 to 21 percent (twenty-two) in 1980, a threefold increase. This increase was largely due to new activity in a center-sponsored handicraft project.[6] Service jobs in private homes made a similar threefold leap from 9 percent to 27 percent (twenty-nine). "Professional" jobs also showed a threefold increase from 2 to 6 percent, but because the numbers are so small the tendency is only noted. Overall, a clear trend toward higher paying and more regular work activities for women was seen. And, indeed, more and more women were articulating the general axiom that it is not "shameful" for a woman to work.[*]

In general the factors that were probably the strongest in influencing the change of attitude among women and their families were (1) the rising inflation rate that put ever-increasing strains on subsistence-level incomes, (2) rising expectations about what the basic needs of the household were, generated out of watching the rest of society's growing affluence and neighbors returning with large sums from work in the other Arab states, and (3) observation of middle-class women working without any reduction in family status or personal respect. With a continually increasing number, still small but growing, of young lower-class women finishing university degrees and moving into what is, for the lower classes, the high-status occupation of government employee, a disjunction began to be created in the perception of women's employment. While it was still shameful for many illiterate mothers to work, it became highly prestigious for their young educated daughters to do so. The difference lay at least partially in the kinds of work each was qualified to do and demonstrates the importance of education level to women's entrance into the employment market.

Because education (or lack of education) features so prominently in the future trends of women's employment, it is important to look briefly at whether parents in Bulaq are presently encouraging their daughters to continue their education.

Parental Strategies in Educating Children

Education is compulsory in Egypt for both boys and girls until the ninth grade or to around the age of fifteen. Since compulsory rules have not been enforced parents (and more indirectly children) have retained some choice in whether and how long children go to school. Middle- and upper-class urban parents universally send their children to school, but lower-class urban parents often are forced out of economic necessity to choose from among a number of less costly alternatives when providing training for their children. They are more likely to recognize the training ground of the home or the workshop as equal to or in some ways superior to formal education programs, because they prepare children in a shorter time period to earn larger incomes.

Parents generally regard the early years of adolescence as a time of special preparation for a child's adulthood. In the case of boys it is preparation for an occupation and in the case of girls it is preparation for marriage. Family investment in longer and more intensive training for boys brings returns to parents who expect their sons to help in supporting other family members before marriage and later to help with support as the parents grow old. Investment in girls is viewed as primarily benefiting the households of their husbands.

In 1980, in interviews with parents in 228 Bulaq households, 177 families had 617 children living at home. At that time, of the children six years and above (437), only 56 percent (245) were enrolled in school. Twenty-four percent (107) of the children six years and above had never gone to school and 19 percent (eighty-five) had dropped out of school. The survey in effect summarizes the educational strategies of parents in the past decade. However, individual interviews with Bulaq families suggest that in recent years almost all parents sent children to school at an early age when their contributions to the family work efforts had not yet become significant.

Evidence in this sample group suggests that there are significant differences in how parents approach choices about educating their sons and daughters. For example, the ratio of girls who never enter school is twice that of boys. But boys on the other hand have higher attrition rates (59 percent of all dropouts were boys). Overall this means that there is a smaller discrepancy in the balance of sex ratio in elementary school than one would expect—out of 172 cases, 52 percent (ninety) are boys and 48 percent (eighty-two) are girls. At the intermediate level, out of thirty-eight cases the ratio of girls (53 percent, or twenty cases) to boys (47 percent, or eighteen cases) reversed to show a majority of girls, a surprising fact given the generally lower number of the girls in the system as a whole. By secondary (57 percent, or twelve cases out of a total of twenty-one) and university (100 percent, or four cases in this sample) levels, the boys again have reasserted their majority. The rapid attrition rates between educational levels for both boys and girls becomes apparent in the figures.

There are several reasons why this pattern shows up in lower-class neighborhoods and not affluent neighborhoods. First, the burden of family financial insufficiency falls more heavily on boys than girls. By age thirteen when a boy theoretically enters intermediate school, he has reached the age when he can effectively contribute income to a family. Parents recognize that formal educational programs offer two qualitatively different levels of career preparation: a level useful to any job where the child is equipped with basic functional literacy (by about the sixth year) and a university-level diploma that guarantees a job in the government bureaucracy. In between, with the occasional exception of a secondary diploma, there are few concrete benefits parents can see that derive from extending the years of education. Parents therefore tend to remove male children from school at the intermediate level, particularly if the boys are showing little aptitude for school, if family resources are strained, and if attractive competing opportunities are available such as jobs or apprenticeships.

Further supporting evidence was found for these points when the families were divided into a three-category scale according to qualitative assessments of their economic circumstances. Of the total number of school-age children (172) in "poor" families, 61 percent were enrolled in school. Of similar children (108) in "self-sufficient" families, 76 percent were enrolled in school, a predictable increase under the assumption that where there is greater economic margin in the household children will remain longer in school. However, in the third category among those families who were "doing well" economically (forty-eight cases), there was a surprising drop in enrollment of school-age children to 42 percent, mostly through attrition at the intermediate level. Interviews with parents revealed that many of these families could provide attractive opportunities for sons in their own business establishment or with well-connected friends, opportunities more promising and financially more secure than the bureaucratic positions that come from remaining in the educational system. Such families could also attract sons-in-law who could support a family without their wives working.

While these factors influence the low enrollment rates of boys in intermediate school, other factors affected the tendency toward greater participation of girls at this level and bring into focus the dilemmas faced by parents in a time of changing conditions and perceptions about women's employment. Without exception parents appear to be more concerned about marrying off their daughters than they are about preparing them for an occupation. One group of parents feels that girls learn what they need to know better by staying home and learning from their mothers. A growing group of other parents, however, believes that young men are beginning to seek wives who work. But even for this latter group there is a strong reluctance to let girls work outside the home in manual forms of labor. They would rather see their daughters in less well paid but more prestigious clerical or bureaucratic government jobs that require prolonged education. As a result of such perceptions, these parents often urge their daughters to continue their education. In short, boys and their parents in the lower classes make career decisions at intermediate school level, weighing the factors of academic talent, future income, available opportunities, and status. Girls and their parents are less concerned with long-term career goals and more interested in enhancing their qualifications as marriage partners, whether they see this as requiring home training from a mother or gaining a marketable skill in school.

Conclusion

A number of complicated changes are in progress in lower-class Egyptians' perceptions of women's employment. Beyond the monetary reward of work little else recommends this choice for a woman. People in the reported sample view the employment of women as having certain negative aspects: women are taken away from their true responsibilities in the home, work threatens the husband's sense of masculine pride, it may compromise the women's reputations, and in many cases it changes the quality of their measured daily family lives. Part of the problem lies in the nature of the work available to women of this class and their level of education. But with the importance placed on women's housewifely roles many parents feel little inclination to press the advantages of long-term education that would increase girls' levels of skills. Parents with this perspective see education as interfering with the mother's training of a girl and fear a reduction in suitors who will not want a wife more educated than themselves.

What has recently encouraged a re-evaluation of some of these views by a minority of the population is a rapidly growing inflation rate and a rise in the general level of expectation about what constitutes the minimum needs of a family. Because of the inelasticity of unskilled laborors' wages, satisfying these expectations requires that families generate income in new ways even if that means allowing daughters and wives to work. The perceived need for money, in effect, has increased sufficiently as an incentive to overcome some of the resistance toward women working. One consequence is that women increasingly seek jobs that pay more, even when these jobs are objectionable for other reasons. Another is that parents are beginning to feel the advantages of educating girls for an occupation as a means of better attracting a marriage partner. Little has changed with regard to the basic perception of sex roles as involving household responsibilities for women and economic support functions for a man. What has happened is that now, as in the past, women are being asked to step in and fill the gap between the actual household income and what is needed to meet family members' expectations. Many step into the breach with considerable reluctance.

Notes

1. Public medical care is free in Egypt but to obtain it usually requires long waits at public hospitals and then the cursory attention of overburdened doctors. Even the poorest try to obtain the medical services of private doctors whenever possible if the case is serious.

2. R. Mabro, *The Egyptian Economy 1952–1972* (Oxford: Clarendon Press, 1974), pinpoints the middle 1930s as the time when general shortages were replaced by labor surpluses.

3. Economic Activity Rate refers to the people aged six and over who are active in the labor force.

4. Population censuses for 1937 and 1970 and Labor Force Sample Surveys from the Central Agency for Mobilization and Statistics as found in *ARE Economic Management in Periods of Transition VI* (World Bank, Statistical Annex, May 8, 1978), p. 5.

5. Population census for 1976 and Labor Force Sample Survey as found in ibid.

6. The handicraft project employed about one hundred women at its peak. The project turned out to be a useful transitional stage between strictly housewifely roles and worker roles. Women became used to the additional income and sought ways to regularize modes of obtaining it.

The Shoes (a short story)

IQBAL BARAKAH

Translated from the Arabic by Mohammad Khazali

We pulled back the curtains of the office where we worked and opened the windows. The morning greeted us, beautiful and dazzling. We each went to our desks and sat down.

Su'ad sighed.

"This negligence is unbelievable," she said. "Every morning the dust is thick on the desks. . . . 'Abd Mun'im must clean early in the morning and never come back in the afternoon."

A ray of sunlight shone on her hair and a cold feeling that I could not explain overwhelmed me. So I moved quickly to the window and crossed my arms across my chest while looking out. . . .

People, cars of every kind, crowds . . . crowds . . . crowds . . . Cairo.

Steam rose from the full cups of tea, and the same remarks were exchanged that are exchanged every morning, about the sleeplessness that is always with me and the headache that does not leave Su'ad's head. We swallowed the *ful* and ta'*miyya* sandwiches and gobbled quantities of pickles and hot peppers. . . . My mind wandered to the thought of ten o'clock. After an hour and a half, I would have a pass to leave for half an hour. Su'ad was talking about something, and suddenly I said, "I will buy the shoes today."

She stopped drinking tea, put the cup on the desk, and said, "I think you should forget about those shoes, really."

I said to myself, Of course she would say that. She's jealous.

I looked intently at the paper, as if I were reading an important news item, and my thoughts raced fast.

Su'ad has a deep-seated jealousy of me. Yes, she does. True, she is more chic and more attractive than me, but I far exceed her in beauty and ability. Everyone admits that. It's natural that Su'ad disagrees with me. It's because she is unsure of herself.

We saw the shoes yesterday when we were walking together toward the al-'Atabah, and when she saw how I admired the shoes and how much I wanted to buy them, she could only disapprove. Now, as she drank her tea, she had decided to enumerate her objections.

"First of all, the silver color does not go with your dark feet," she said spitefully. "Second, the high heels will make your legs look thin like goat's legs. Third . . ."

A rush of anger, of warm blood, filled me, and I cut her off quickly. "I suppose you think that your legs are the most beautiful legs in the whole world!"

Suᶜad took a big bite of the *taᶜmiyya* sandwich and said, "Not at all, but I know how to choose suitable shoes that are comfortable for my feet."

My appetite for the good food disappeared. I pushed the pickles aside and went on drinking tea quietly. After I finished my cup I settled in my chair, opened the desk drawer, took out a few handwritten pages, and started typing. Sometimes I feel that mechanical work relaxes my nerves and calms my temper a bit. Therefore I perform this work very well and am considered one of the fastest typists in the company. . . . True, words dance before my eyes and sometimes a line escapes. . . . But ultimately, while I am working at the typewriter, I feel total isolation from all the world: I do not answer questions that are posed to me, I do not talk to anyone, and hence I am not exposed to the harsh criticism and endless discussions of Suᶜad.

I found suddenly that I had finished typing a whole set of papers and it was only 9:15 when I looked at my wristwatch. So fast!

Maybe I made too much noise when I stood up quickly, closed my desk drawers, and left. I felt Suᶜad's astonished, ridiculing looks following me. But I moved ahead with stubborn, quick steps toward the director's room.

"Sir, I need a half-hour pass."

Mr. ᶜAbd al-Munsif looked up from the piles of papers that he was reviewing and signing. He took off his glasses. Without them, he looked strange, even laughable. He wiped his eyes with his handkerchief and then said, "Only half an hour?"

"Yes."

"You're sure, Miss Amal?"

"Yes, I might need even less time."

This sentence popped out of my mouth involuntarily. He signed the paper for me. Then he sunk once again into the piles of papers that were arranged before him. . . . I felt as though I had picked up the deed to my freedom. I ran quickly down the stairs without waiting for the elevator.

I thought about going along Suleiman Pasha Street, but decided against it. The stores there are packed with beautiful shoes, purses, scarves, and ready-made clothes that make me dizzy and nauseous; even my chest flares harshly with bitterness and a sense of deprivation.

But ʿAbd al-Khaliq al-Tharwat Street is relatively pleasant and quiet. My favorite place is the store that sells multicolored birds. I can never go past without stopping for a moment in front of it to admire the birds, bright, beautiful, trilling sad melodies to pass the time and dispel their boredom. Sometimes they fly from one side of the cage to another . . . in worry and nervousness? . . . waiting for a buyer?

Often I have wished to open the cages and set them free so they can choose their own fates.

But today I did not watch the birds as long as I usually do because I remembered that my pass was only for half an hour. I was coming from Azbakiyyah on my way toward Fouad Street. I quickened my steps and I felt a sense of enthusiasm course through my veins. I ran as if I were following something . . . something I was not sure about!

I suddenly became aware that the traffic light had changed to "Go." I crossed quickly and headed for Muhammad Farid Street. All my friends bought silver and gold shoes, so why should I be deprived of the same pleasure? Suʿad says I will not wear them often because they are only good for going out at night and I do not go out often in the evenings. This is true, but who knows . . . ? Maybe these shoes will be a first step toward my going out again and again.

I found myself in front of the shoe store. I went in quickly and stopped thinking about everything else. I pointed to the silver shoes.

"What size, ma'am?" asked the salesman.

"Thirty-nine."

He shook his head sadly. "Sorry, we're out of that particular size."

I screamed at him in disbelief, "That can't be!"

In my imagination Suʿad appeared, smiling with pleasure at her victory.

"Please," I said to the clerk. "Are you sure? Then give me size thirty-eight with the nine-centimeter heel."

He went away to look and came back carrying my dream shoes. I put them on my feet with happiness . . . They were very tight, but they would stretch after a few days, I told myself. I walked proudly and vainly around on the carpet in the shoe store, looking at my silver-shod feet in all the mirrors.

I turned to the salesman. "What do you think?"

"Magnificent," he said. "Congratulations."

I paid the high price and left the store, clutching the narrow white box. I felt that I was carrying a treasure from heaven. A tumultuous sea of joy carried me along waves of heads, arms, and legs . . . and the breeze carried to me the high voices of the crowds around me and other voices whispering, the sounds of rough laughter, of tender and gentle words. A mixture of screams, curses, words of love and admiration carried me back down Muhammad Farid Street and into ʿAbd al-Khaliq al-Tharwat Street.

I looked at my watch and my heart jumped. What could I say to the director? I was late. How could I justify it? How could I possibly excuse myself?

In the elevator a mixture of feelings—victory and regret, desire and surrender—overwhelmed me. I did not know exactly what I was feeling at that moment. I carried in my hands what I had dreamed of . . . what now would I do with them? I found the silver shoes emerging into my rational mind, and I asked myself, Was I reckless in buying them? Wouldn't it have been better if I had bought a practical pair of shoes for work, as Suʿad had suggested? Wouldn't it have made more sense to defer the wish that possessed my mind, to push it down to the depths of my consciousness as I had done with many other wishes over the years? Wouldn't it have been better if I had bought school shoes for my little sister Samira, as my mother had suggested? I couldn't decide. All that counted was that the silver shoes were in my hands. They were now my own private property, and no more thinking was needed.

I found Suʿad engrossed in conversation with ʿUlayyah, who works in the accounting section of the company. They saw me come in and stopped talking. Suʿad laughed sarcastically and said, "So you did it after all!"

ʿUlayyah rushed to the white box, pulling off its cover eagerly to see what was inside. She examined the shoes for a moment and said, "Wow! . . . splendid! . . . great! . . . magnificent! . . ." Then she turned back to me. "But they look too small. This can't be your size, Amal."

And she hurried to try one on her right foot, and then the left. She took a few conceited steps forward, imitating the seductresses of the movies. Then she took the silver shoes off and put them back in the box, covering them carefully. I took her aside and whispered in her ear. "Would you like to buy them, ʿUlayyah?"

She rushed toward Suʿad, laughing loudly. "Imagine, Suʿad, she barely bought them and now she wants to sell them to me already!"

Suʿad giggled happily, and tears of laughter came into her eyes. I ignored their rising laughter, wrapped the paper tightly around my narrow white box, and turned to ʿUlayyah.

"You didn't really believe me, did you? I was just kidding."

I put the box close to me on the desk and began to look for more pages to type . . . and as I began to type, a mysterious feeling came over me that I would never again open the narrow white box containing the silver shoes—never.

Cairo's Factory Women

BARBARA LETHEM IBRAHIM

You ask why I work and I will tell you: I work so that when I put eggs
on the table and one child asks for more, I will have a second egg to
give. We could get by without my income but it would not be really
living. I want to walk not crawl along in life. *—Fardous, age thirty-one.*
Twelve years assembling gear boxes.

Statistical trends reveal that Egyptian women are expanding their participation in the formal workforce. Not only are more women employed, but the range of jobs open to women has been slowly increasing
in recent years. Official surveys found 540,000 women in non-
agricultural employment in 1979.[1] By 1982, the government was reporting a million women in the labor force.[2] Missing from the statistical picture, however, is a way of gauging the impact of these changes on
women's lives. How does factory employment, for example, differ in its
effects from the more traditional ways in which urban women have contributed to household income as self-employed seamstresses or small
traders? What patterns can be identified in the reasons for coming to
work, the ways wages are spent, and the accommodations families
make to a working mother or wife?

In search of answers to these questions, life histories were solicited
from a group of twenty married women who worked on the assembly
line at a large Cairo electrical firm in 1978.[3] By sitting alongside the
women as they worked over a period of several months, it was possible
to record topics of conversation among workmates and to listen as they
talked together about common problems. Interviews with factory man-
agers and industry officials provided their perspectives as well on the
organization of production work and national labor policies as they have
evolved in recent years.

The picture that emerged was one of important shifts over the past
twenty-five years in the employment strategies of working-class families. Child labor has declined as families choose to take advantage of
free education. In urban areas, many men have assumed two or three

different jobs in order to support their families. But when male earners are either unable to keep up with inflation or they are absent or incapacitated, then older daughters and wives are increasingly likely to seek employment. The expansion of industry beginning in the late 1950s provided most of the new jobs for women who had less than a secondary education.

It is unusual for women to begin work in both large- and small-scale industry after they have married. The exceptions tend to be divorced or widowed women, who must take up factory work to support their children. These women constituted 15 percent of all female production workers in Egypt at the time of the 1976 census.[4] By far the most common pattern is for single girls to join the factory after failing or being pressured by family members to leave school. Among the women interviewed for this study, most had come to work at age eighteen while still single. All were then living in their parent's household and contributing something to the monthly family budget. After a year or two at the factory they married, often preferring a man who was a fellow worker rather than a relative or family acquaintance. When children came along they continued to work, sometimes against strong objections from husbands, because they felt that their income was essential for the welfare of their expanding families. Most had been working continuously for ten to fifteen years at the time of the interviews.

The work experiences of these women are set in a context far different from that of earlier generations of factory workers in Egypt or the industrialized West. They are among the first groups of women to be drawn into factory production as it expanded in the 1960s. By that time nearly all large- and medium-scale industry was under public sector administration in Egypt. This created a protected environment for female workers, with generous health benefits, maternity leaves, transportation, and child care services. The new legislation did more than expand women's opportunities to work under favorable circumstances. Perhaps of equal importance, it served to redefine factory work as respectable, even desirable employment for working-class girls. This went a long way toward undermining the old cultural barriers surrounding work for Egyptian women.

In practice, factories today vary widely in the degree to which they live up to the standards set for worker benefits. This in turn affects the costs of hiring women as well as the ultimate satisfaction of workers. At the electrical factory, a conscientious staff of social workers grants leaves of absence to women with pressing family problems. Workers are referred to free maternity health and family planning centers. Sexual harassment on the job is rarely a problem in this system where legal protections reinforce the informal consensus regarding respect for women. And yet the factory administration has avoided complying with laws requiring them to provide on-site child care despite workers' demands over many years. Transportation is provided to workers on sex-segregated buses; but service for men is more extensive, since they are greater in number and consequently have more routes. Women workers complain that health clinic doctors prescribe only the cheapest medicines and refuse to order lab tests in order to keep company costs low.

Many of these factors are reflected in the ambivalence women express about their jobs. They know that public sector factories provide relatively good wages and benefits despite some of the drawbacks. Yet they feel locked in by an inflationary economy that ties them to jobs. These economic strains heighten the conflict between home responsibilities and work; for example, they create pressures for women to work overtime in order to earn extra pay.

But let the women speak for themselves. Through their voices we hear a collective message from strong women struggling to cope with a modern workplace while maintaining images of traditional female respectability. Long hours of their day are given to the job in the hope that the monthly remuneration (averaging thirty-five Egyptian pounds; equivalent to about fifty dollars in 1978) will bring improved life chances for their families, especially their children. In return, they call on employers and society to seek remedies for the current hardships faced by women in Egypt's factories.

Hadiya

My parents were not old-fashioned. They thought it was a natural thing for girls to work if the job was a respectable one. My husband was known by my father at work; they are together at the plant next to this one. When we married it was easy to continue working since our house is close by—a ten-minute walk. The difficult times began when my son was born. At first my mother-in-law came to stay with us and she took over everything at home. But she is old and not in good health, and she left behind responsibilities in her own house. So when the boy became two we looked for a *hadana* (a nursery or day-care center, literally "embracer").

The closest one is in Helwan (a distance of ten miles); our neighborhood doesn't yet have schools or clinics. . . . But the factory has land in front of the gate. They could build us a nursery and solve this problem. At least fifty workers here live in the area and suffer from this problem. But we are not organized, we don't cooperate. Each one is running to keep ahead of her own situation. And from the administration we get promises. For sixteen years now the workers have been asking for a nursery but nothing happens.

Now my son is four and I take him every day by train to the nursery in Helwan. It's OK except when the train is so crowded that we get pushed apart and then he cries. It keeps me away from home an extra two hours each day. Since I've been pregnant it seems that I'm tired all the time.

Our Egyptian men are all the same; they leave the work of the house to women. Sometimes my husband will shop or take the boy out if he sees me tired. But all of this is a matter of whim. If I complain, he tells me to leave work and get along without my pay. But he knows we couldn't do that, not in today's conditions. Not with another baby coming, by the will of God. No, I won't leave work as long as I can stand on two feet.

Work strengthens a woman's position. The woman who works doesn't have to beg her husband for every piaster she needs. She can command respect in her home and can raise her voice in any decision. . . . At the end of the day I'm exhausted. Sometimes I sit down in a chair and think I'll never get up again. But at 5:00 A.M. you'll find me up, running to prepare breakfast and lunch before leaving. Not like housewives who sleep whenever it pleases them. . . . Look at us. Our hands are rough like a man's from work at the factory. Still a woman is a woman, no matter what her manner of work. Factory work can sometimes make one forget. But then I look in the mirror: I see myself as a woman and I remember my femininity.

The following are two rather atypical cases of women who came to work after marriage or the birth of children. Soraya's story illustrates the difficulties faced by working women who are part of nonurban, traditional households (her decision to continue working may in fact be a way of escaping from problems at home). Fatma is a case of someone initially reluctant to take up factory employment because her aspirations had been set higher for finishing school and finding an office job.

Soraya

I married an Arab (the colloquial term for bedouin; in this case, settled farmers)—not really Egyptian—whose clan is across the river in Giza. Our fathers are distant relations. When my husband first came to our house to ask for me (in marriage) I could see no objection and so I agreed. He owned land and impressed me with his generosity. At first we lived in Helwan in a nice apartment. I came to work because my husband was in the army earning nothing and rent was expensive. Now we have sublet the apartment and moved to his family's compound in their village across the Nile. Their ways are different: my father-in-law has three wives, each living in one room of the house. Next to us is an uncle with twenty children.

I have three. The oldest is four and a half and I am tired. All of his relatives speak to me about having more children, even him . . . but I am secretly taking the pill.

His family finds fault with me. The women do not approve that I leave every day on a bus for work. They do not approve of my clothes— they all wear the black head veil. Each of them works in the fields helping her husband. . . . My younger sister has come to stay with us and take care of the children while I am at work. She is unhappy there and wants to get married.

A long time ago I tried a nursery school in Helwan, but I found it not well run; a bad place to take children. Last year the government built a nursery school in our village to help rural women. It was to be free and they would provide a good lunch. But none of the women except me are interested. The others take their children to the field and don't trust government workers. It never opened, but the nursery worker is living in the empty building.

Now my husband is working in #54 (a nearby factory) and he is trying to get me a transfer there. . . . Working is hard, but not to work would be worse. The young girls here, they dream of getting married and brag that they will be able to quit. Of course, all of us would prefer to stay home. They will find it the same as the rest of us. Salaries they can waste on new dresses and outings now will be needed for food and rent once they have families of their own. Quitting work is easy to talk about, hardly anyone can do it.

Fatma

I did well in school and had the idea to continue until I qualified as a teacher or a secretary. Then it was arranged that I should marry my cousin, and we moved in with his parents. When it was time for the final exams the school director told me, "Married women are forbidden to sit for exams." This was a new rule—I knew others who had married and then finished school—but all my pleading could not change it. So for one year I sat at home. My husband is reasonable and good-hearted. When he saw my disappointment he suggested that I come to the factory.

In the first weeks I hated it here, the loud machines and some of the people—I tell you I went home crying every day. But then I saw that the work here is pleasant and it is respectable. The women I work with are good people, even though not very educated. I became resigned to work and now I am happy here.

Everything about the work is fine except our schedules. The hours are too long for mothers like us. My children beg me to take them out of the apartment, but usually I'm too tired. Then on my day off I have the week's cleaning and cooking to do. Everyone here will tell you that the worst thing about working is how impatient and nervous it makes us.

My husband works two jobs now so he is never home before eight or nine o'clock at night. He comes home too tired to give me any help, but, anyway, that's the way with Egyptian men. I try to teach my two sons to be helpful. I tell them it's not shameful to work in the house, but, of course, they follow the example of their father. . . . It would be nice to have a daughter. My husband is always saying we should have another child. But two is enough for a woman who works.

While we still lived with my mother-in-law everything was easier. She took care of the babies and I would come home each day to a freshly cooked meal. Then my husband received a company flat near his work and everything changed. The area we live in is new—I must walk a long way or take the bus to do our shopping. . . . When my son was younger there was only one nursery close by. It opened during the hours of office workers, not factory workers. The teachers came to open the doors at 7:30, but I must catch my bus for work at 6:30, so what can be done? So I paid some money to the watchman to look after my son at the gate until the teachers came. Then my husband would pick him up on his way home. The whole day at work I used to worry about him. Now he is in school, thanks be to God. We manage.

Attiat

I left school before the secondary level, even though my mother is from Alexandria and had modern ideas about girls. But my father has the restrictive ideas of Upper Egypt, and besides he had recently fallen ill. When I told them later that I would not sit at home, I would go to the factory, they left the decision to me. We needed money to feed the younger ones, so even my father said nothing. . . .

But everything is ordained by God. Do you know that my younger sister was allowed to finish school and she married very well? Now my father gives *us* money each month because we can't seem to cover our expenses. . . . My sister is a housewife. She cares for my children in the afternoon. They have no need of her salary so she has never gone to work.

My husband is a guard at the main gate, so he has me constantly under his gaze! There has never been an argument over my work. . . . He never asked me to leave work until after the babies were born. He saw how tired I was and then he worried about my health. I refused to quit, but the social worker arranged a six-month leave for me. Sometimes we joke that we are married to the factory, not to each other. . . .

But no one can convince me to give up my salary. We want to bring our girls up with all of the advantages I never had. The oldest is going to a private nursery school for four pounds per month where everything is clean and the children learn their ABC's. . . . Even with two incomes I have trouble budgeting our money. My father has to help us by paying the rent (6.50 pounds) and utilities. Maybe you should do a study of husbands' mismanagement of money: one month my husband took charge of the budget and by the seventh day he had spent it all. Men let money slip through their fingers like water.

We are closer than sisters or relatives (at the factory). Why? There is jealousy and envy in the family. But at work there are fewer comparisons. . . . Friendship here is stronger than outside. We talk about nearly everything that occupies our minds, especially problems with bringing up children, problems with husbands. When you can joke about problems with someone who understands you go home feeling lighter. We have a term for the last demand that husbands are likely to make on us at the end of the day—we call it "working overtime." We tease each other about it being voluntary or mandatory. Little things to laugh about and the day moves faster.

We are a tight group. We keep together and on most subjects we think alike. We defend each other's rights. If we see a fellow worker poorly dressed whose husband is taking her salary, we show her the unfairness of it and encourage her to ask for her rights. All of us work hard, we have earned these rights. You see us all with strong personalities. Aren't our eyes opened wider than housewives'?

Notes

1. 1979 Labor Force Sample Survey (Cairo: Central Agency for Moblization and Statistics, 1981).

2. Al-Ahram newspaper, January 16, 1982.

3. This formed the preliminary stage in a broader research project on women in Egyptian industry (see Barbara Ibrahim, "Social Change and the Industrial Experience" [Ph.D. dissertation, Indiana University, 1980]).

4. Population census for 1976 (Cairo: Central Agency for Mobilization and Statistics).

PART VII
Identity

Middle Eastern women have never had any doubts about their own identities: they were mothers, sisters, daughters, grandmothers, aunts, cousins; they were Muslims, Christians, Jews; they were Armenians, Kurds, Nubians, Berbers. They were Arabs, women. The search for identity has been a Western search, arising as it does out of philosophical ideas about the individual, the single human being, fulfilling itself outside the contexts of family, religion, or ethnic group.

The poems, stories, and essays in this section are about identity but should not be seen as reflections of a turn to Western thought. Not at all. The exciting thing about these materials is their testimony to a new mode in the Islamic Middle East; women like Hoda al-Namani in Lebanon, Forugh Farrokhzod of Iran, Assia Djebar in Algeria see themselves not as isolated individuals in an alien wilderness, but as women forging new connections with their groups, with their origins, finding themselves in new relationships to the past, the present, to men, and to other women. The Palestinian poet Salma al-Jayyusi poses an old problem in a new light in her poem about mother and son; Hoda al-Namani uses the Sufi creative tools of her great-uncle to new ends in her poems; Forugh Farrokhzod sees the role of the artist in Iran as one of confrontation; Tahereh Saffar-Zadeh sees it as one of conformity; Lami'a 'Imarah looks for new roles. Assia Djebar points to falsehoods in the old Western view of Middle Eastern women as Delacroix saw them: clois-

tered, exotic, imprisoned. But she also recognizes
the ugly truth of that vision. And having thus destroyed the West as scapegoat, she sees her society as now freed to make its own vision, it is to
be hoped a better one. Storytellers in Tunisia are
changing their form and style to adapt to new
events. All, as women and as artists, are speaking
about identity, but in their own context—an identity combining old patterns with new experience.

I Remember I Was a Point, I Was a Circle

HODA AL-NAMANI
Translated from the Arabic by Tim Mitchell

I remember
I was
a point, I was a circle,
I walked
The swords are porous green. I fell, to the edge of a whitened
eyelash, I laughed, to the edge of death I laughed.
I remember I was glass that breaks the water, stretched out across
a cloud,
I remember I was a butterfly,
despair began to spread like darkness, bullets began
to make shadows, pointed shadows.

He is your blue-colored shirt, my cup and fork, my
balcony, the din of silence in the void, my closed eyelids,
the bird that shall bear me to the grave, he is the grave.

How often they have wrangled with mountains on my lips. Hands
that burn are extinguished in wine, rivers that run dry are pinned
to the walls, parched earth tries to imprison
your voice, your voice.

I have not been dreaming that I would have courage one
day and kill myself. A feather, fields, handkerchiefs.
I shall kill myself! Like a sun throwing itself into a sea.
Have you the courage to dance on a mirror? Have you more
strength than the brilliance of a bee upon its knees, than
the kiss of pearls shoulder to shoulder? Have you the
courage for blood?
   Do you spell out tears as I set forth a tree?

From the ledge of each well, pots of hyacinth fly
in all directions. As though temples exploding, they
cross the marble to the final star, like the grasses that
glitter in a pebble. I watch her veiling herself,
I strangle her asleep at my cheek, in vain I pluck her
    at the shoot.
                                        Pots of hyacinth.
    On my clothes I write God, I write heaven.
        This is me. And this is you.
    I open my eyes. I open my hands. I see my fingers
cut off.
                                        Cut off.

    The sun's valleys have no color. Children's nails
have no color.
        Bracelets of fire have no color.
                        Screaming has no color.
                        Beirut . . . you are screaming.

    Like one who lives on a seesaw, I live in the
pupil of your eye.
Come morning you destroy me like an arrow, come evening
I yield to you, without a struggle I turn to dust. I
say he is a mountain that bears a city, I say he is
a horse that gallops in the sun.
    Like one who lives in deceit, I stone myself
and call for help

Is there a terror greater than veiled fear, than
a deserted evening, than feet that tread on heaven,
than waves sketched like rainfall, than signs of thunder,
than a cage without a bird, a bird without wings, wings
without love, without love?

    From your two hands I gather tenderness at night,
from your two hands I grant a smile to each star, from
your two hands I bury my head on your breast, from your
two hands I search for my prayer.

    I draw halos around you, as if you are the foe, as
if you are the Messiah. If you were alone, I tell you, I would

prostrate myself to you. If just ten, I would hide you
in my lungs. Since you are a thousand, I shall give you
to drink from my blood. Your wound grows and grows,
it slits my throat from vein to vein. I put sand in your
wound, I put in your wound a giant, and around myself I
light the fire.

—Who are you, that I should love you in the space I love you, in
the wound?

The stones are whispering:

There is no myth save in a wrestling goddess, a moon fragmenting. The
statues are countless, beyond all computation. The poison is a single
dose placed in a cup.

I pluck suns from between your eyes, I pluck thorns. I kindle the
twigs of the dream alight, melt the years and the bloodgroups, the
necessities of war and necessities of peace. I cordon off a blue volcano
to right and left, watching me with its white fangs.

—Twilight, is it some calamity that brings you, or a flood?

The desert is turning black, the desert is turning green.

—Orbits, be scattered beyond time, beyond weapons, beyond vipers. Be
in harmony with the strength of gods, with mercy like the gods, with
optimism like the gods. Upon the trackless sand each teardrop has a
garden, the birds a small handful of honey.

We die, oh, how many we die!

In death I find none but you,

in the breeze too, and the scythe and the drizzle, the barricades and
handguns and men in hoods, in live broadcasts and telephones cut dead,
in bulletins of news, the safe roads and the unsafe, interrogations,
delays, prayerbooks and beads, chess pieces, tranquilizers, pine and
saffron, weddings, births and spare time, and arguments, arguments,
arguments,

I find none but you.

Here am I bending down to drink and I lose my memory.

I have not let my face leap like a bat, I have not kicked my foot
against the place of my exile, I did not move like phantoms over the

rooftops, I did not try child hunting, I did not steal the sea's wings,
I did not break glass over a breast, I did not eat my flesh that burns,
I have not withdrawn into despair, I did not go mad in gathering honey,
    I did not go mad, I did not go mad, I did not go mad.

No need for my corpse.

No need for the flanks of suffering, for my armor.

No need for my charred body. A ship carries us to the end of the world.
Rivers push us seaward. A destiny in which I dress. Nets by which I am
woven. Statues that I destroy. A debt I pay. Flocks of birds.

A disaster. An earthquake. Travel. Return.

Return. Return. Return.

O Jerusalem! From thou . . . we shall ascend!

Forgive me O Lord,

    Plains accepting no death, a shore gathering pearls, a white
horse enfolding me and taking wing, a bird that immolates me as I am
warmed by its eyes, eyes in which I pray and weep, my ribs that are
translucent, trees of emerald, the rose of compassion above unity,
the dissension of daybreak's crown, the willfulness of nightly grandeur,
the sanctity of pain, roses raining down,

    him, him, him.

I grasp the wave and I tumble

A divine vigilance in my eyes?

I leave at your door the burnt moments of time, the sunset, the harvest
of error, an endless slipping, the gasp of truth, ingots of gold, faces
of those who have died, faces of those who will die, footsteps of the
prophets, shadows of the priests, the thinness of words, the misfortune
of the world, the secrets of the fields,

    my love for you, your hatred for me,
        and the white lilies
        and the white lilies.

I grasp the wave and I tumble . . .
I remember I was a point, I was a circle.

She is a voice . . . any voice.
He is a land . . . not every land.

An Interview with Hoda al-Namani

AMIN AL-RIHANI

The fourth and most recent collection of poetry by Hoda al-Namani is her work *I Remember I Was a Point, I Was a Circle*. This book can be considered as a single long poem, divided into separate sections or scenes, each independent of one another yet at the same time complementary.

The poem is a work that springs up from within the earth and from the ruins, determined to search for a new hope, for resurrection amid the specters of destruction and loss. The sections of the poem turn, in a rhythmic succession of episodes, from the lover whispering to her loved one, to the rebellious revolutionary youth, to those in despair turning toward God, to the restive wanderer across the stars.

The lover's words, moreover, are a movement through perplexing questions on paths that lead to the doors of questions that cause pain, to return and end in surrender to divine will, or to the will of fate, whose remorselessness is conveyed by the verses. Thus the whispered conversation of the lover is transformed into a whispered conversation of life.

The following discussion of the poem between its author and the critic Amin al-Rihani took place on Lebanese radio on the program "Book of the Week."

Question by Amin al-Rihani: What is the symbolic dimension of the ideas of the point and the circle in your latest poem?

Hoda al-Namani: If we must make explicit the symbolic dimension of these two ideas, the first thing is to get away from the identification of the two words that come from textbooks of grammar and style, and even from books of mathematics and astronomy . . .

Amin al-Rihani: The abstract in the poetic imagery, while totally separated from actuality, changes from metaphor into constructive fantasy. How do you explain this kind of abstraction in your poetry, especially in this particular poem?

Hoda al-Namani: Abstraction should never be separated from reality. However much the metaphor exceeds the limits of literary style, rises high, and hovers, there are always invisible lines connecting the image to the object. The connection is embedded in the roots and in the subconscious.

Constructive fantasy is inevitably based upon experience and reality. How do we distinguish between our dreams and reality? There's no difference! They're distinguished only among other people. All experience, any experience, is tangible. How and why do we distinguish between the material world and the spiritual? How can you imprison a poet? You can't. Thought is a bird. Prevent me now from ascending to heaven— can you? Poetry is a part of us. The poet remains above the poetry, around the poetry, within the poetry, grasping with it whatever appears to be escaping from him.

In the same way, misunderstanding can arise from the ambiguity of the symbols. I sometimes use mystic symbols, and these should be comprehended with the heart. I saw them with the heart, because they often penetrate, and they must be apprehended with compassion.

The wing, the bird, the ship, the woman, are all indicators of the soul. The bird might be love, for example, and likewise death, which in its turn is life. The poet is a child playing with words, as a child would play with seashells and with stars. This, in my opinion, is the one great delight of life.

Women's Folk Narratives and Social Change

SABRA WEBBER

Middle Eastern culture is often characterized as sharply distinguishing between the worlds of men and of women. Traditionally, groups of men and women do not mingle publicly or privately. In Kelibia, Tunisia, a coastal town where I have conducted research intermittently for fifteen years, home is the province of the women for work and socializing, and the cafés, the fields, and the shops are meeting places where men work and socialize.

To the extent that men and women have different concerns, it is likely in any society that they will draw on divergent forms of expressive culture to comment upon and explore those concerns. Some kinds of folklore may be accessible to, if not used by, both sexes, while other forms may be private to or reserved for one sex. Even when the two sexes draw on the same genres of verbal art—riddles, jokes, folk poetry, and so on—the subject matter and appropriateness of time, place, and style of presentation may be significantly different.

In Kelibia, storytelling is still an everyday activity. A distinction is made between *khurafah*s (fantasy stories) and *hikayah*s (true stories). Typically, women tell *khurafah*s to each other and to boys and girls. Men tell *hikayah*s—narratives about their younger days, past experiences of other townsmen, or significant episodes in local history. I rarely hear women telling *hikayah*s. A Tunisian folk-culture specialist affirmed that, indeed, all over Tunisia women are known for their *khurafah*s, not *hikayah*s, because, he said, women traditionally have not gotten out in the world and have not had adventures to tell about.

But in Kelibia women's lives have changed drastically in regard to their access to the outside world—the world outside of their home and even outside of their town. Now most little girls attend school, whereas twenty years ago few little girls attended school. Now more and more women are leaving home for a university education and/or a career in another city. More and more women go together on shopping expeditions or handle business formerly dealt with by men. If one accepts the idea of verbal art as an expressive culture mode that individuals and groups use to define and comment upon or criticize their situation, then, as situations change, different artistic strategies may be appropriated or devised to deal with them. In Kelibia, the verbal art forms women draw upon have been changing over the last fifteen years. Women are now telling more *hikayah*s, personal experience narratives once the province of men, in order to objectify and evaluate their new experiences in the world outside the home.

In the first half of the twentieth century during colonial rule and the French presence, "respectable" women in Kelibia did not even go into the hall of their father's house. Should a woman go out of her home, she was bundled within the cocoon of her heavy, blanket-like veil, watched over and protected by father, brother, or husband. Today even women in their late thirties remember those days when they saw the world through a veil, from the shadows behind the intricate latticework covering an upstairs window, or from the rooftop of a house.

Of course, in their imaginations women were not confined but traveled by means of the *khurafah*s they told each other. The heroines went on fantastic voyages to search for love. They had adventures. They were sometimes poor girls who escaped from impossible situations and married princes. Or they were scholarly princesses refusing to marry any but a man more clever than they. These fantastic *khurafah*s gave scope for adventure into the world of imaginative possibilities since actual exploration of the real world was so curtailed.

An example of the strong imaginative resources of women is this excerpt from Lella Halima's "all lies" story. In this story, the youngest of three brothers is required to tell a story that is all lies in order to save himself and his two older brothers. Though the story is about men, it is artistically constructed and presented by a woman. Through *khurafah*s women symbolically intruded into, manipulated, and explored the world of men.

After a lengthy introduction, the young man begins his lying.

> A man had three pieces of money. Two were no good and the other couldn't be used. And with that that couldn't be used, he bought three gazelles. Two ran away and one he couldn't catch. And the one he couldn't catch he cooked in three big pans. Two were empty and the other had nothing in it. He brought two one-eyed youths and the other who couldn't see. They took the pan and ran away. He searched far and wide and didn't find them. He ran and ran.
>
> He said, "I ran and I came upon a river full of honey. Oh, incomparable river." He said, "What will I do? Where will I put the honey?" He said, "I'm like that and lots of gazelles were passing. I told them, 'Take off your skins, take off your skins.'"
>
> He took off all their skins and put them down. Filled up the skins with honey but didn't find anything to tie them with—the skins with

the honey. He said, "I was like that and a lot of cats passed by—wild. I told them, 'Take out your whiskers. Take out your whiskers.'" Each one took out its whiskers and threw them to him. Threw them all. He said, "I made a rope, lots of ropes and tied the skins." Yes, and sat pondering how he was going to carry them. He said, "I was like that so I scratched my head and out fell a male louse and a female louse from my head. The female louse became a donkey and the male louse became a camel. I filled up the skins with honey.

"I looked for the donkey and the camel and didn't find them." He said, "I had a piece of needle in my head. I placed it in the ground, and shimmied up it." He said, "I saw the donkey selling the honey and the camel taking money. I caught up with them and took the money and sold the camel and mounted the donkey and bought a few olives and bought bread." He said, "I went along eating bread and olives." He said, "The pits from the olives were being put in the ear of the donkey. Out came an olive tree, a magnificent olive tree from the ear of the donkey."[1]

The story continues with more and more outrageous impossibilities as the young man meets the challenge to tell all lies and thus frees himself and his brothers along with their horse, saddle, and bridle. In her imagination Lella Halima has transported us out of the ordered home and into the world of men (the three brothers). From there we are lifted into a topsy-turvy world where lice become beasts of burden, where gazelles remove their skins upon request, and where rivers of honey flow. Anything, in short, can happen as long as it doesn't happen in real life. We witness the power of the imagination to overcome not simply social barriers but the laws of nature as well.

Sometimes the town did intrude into the secluded world of women in the person of dervishes. Dervishes could cross the male-female boundary. They could move from the street world of men to the center-of-the-house informal world of women just as little boys and girls could. Be they men or women, dervishes were considered immune from certain social, religious, and even natural laws. Naive, asexual, vulnerable, they are protected by God or by a *wali* (friend of God). Women often refer to male dervishes as *khal*, the attribution for maternal uncle with whom one usually has a more informal, joking relationship than with a paternal uncle (*ʾamm*). The few lively, typical, first-hand *hikayah*s I heard from women were accounts of their experiences with dervishes. A neighborhood dervish, for example, used to come into Lella Fafani's home in the morning while she was working (not an appropriate time for visits of any sort), disrupt the work routine, play with the baby girl, and even take the baby outside—unfed and improperly dressed for the elements. "She's going to die [if you take her out like that]," Fafani laments. "Let her die then," the dervish replies gruffly. (But of course a baby girl in the hands of a dervish is safer than she would be bundled in her cradle.) One opposed or was rude to a dervish at one's own peril, as we see from the following *hikayah* by Fafani.

> [Soft voice] Your Uncle Mustafa was crazy [he was a dervish].
> Listener: Um huh.
> The morning . . . I was tying cloth over the churn (we were churning) and Uncle Mustafa comes in. (If God moved me I'd sometimes give him a little yogurt or milk or old buttermilk.)
> [Louder] That day, I was angry with your Uncle Mahmud [her husband]. It was March like now. [Laughter] So he said, "Good morning!" And I replied, "Good *morning*! And if I weren't seeing your face, it would be a better *morning*!" [Laughter] And I kept on churning, the *kanun* by my side.
> Just then, by God, the churn broke in two [exclamations], by God on high in two, the churn! He said [deep monotone], "There now, it broke." [Laughter]
> [Speaking quickly] I ran . . . I jumped up, grabbed the churn thus [holding the crack together so the liquid wouldn't spill out], and left it leaning [against the wall]. I brought in a pail, washed it, and poured [the liquid] in. I ordered him, "Well, go on then and buy me a churn!" And he repeated [deep monotone], "And why are you angry at me? [Loud normal voice] Why are you angry!?" He came and sat [by the *kanun*] and said [deep, slow, man's voice], "By God that's shameful. By God, shame on you. Why are you angry?" To this day my daughter Mufida laughs about it. My daughter Mufida remembers the churn story.
> [Low voice] Ahh . . . those dervishes are . . .
> Frightening.

The storyteller is recounting an episode from her young adulthood but in the style of the male *hikayah*s. She imitates the voice of the dervish, speaks very quietly and in a high voice while she describes her fluster when the churn breaks, and speaks in an angry, loud voice accenting the rhyming words when she shouts out her rhymed insult to the dervish. Altogether, the story is quite similar to those told by men. It relates one incident where someone slighting a dervish is "unlucky." Compare the following account by a man:

> You've got Shadli. Shadli, also. He doesn't look the type [to be a dervish]. [When] Shadli was still a bit young, see, they were working with drilling equipment on their farm and he was a devil—wanted to play, see. He wanted to put [the drill] down, wanted to sink it. And the drill was down about sixteen, seventeen, eighteen meters to the floor of the well. Workers were working on it. When they didn't want to let him interfere he said, "May God prevent you from succeeding!" He finished his phrase and the drill broke. Til' now it's still there because they made him mad not letting him . . .

*Hikayah*s about dervishes are still more often told by men. This is quite understandable for the stories as told in Kelibia are most often stories about men interacting with the nonfamilial world: the community world, the spirit world, the world of the "friends of God" (*walis*), or the world (countryside or city) outside the town. Traditionally (at least from the onset of colonial domination), Kelibian women remained within the family. As in Lella Fafani's story, *hikayah*s women do tell touch on those brief moments when a figure from outside the family is met. Most often, of course, this figure is a marginal one, like the dervish—one for whom contact with women is acceptable or at least tolerated. Thus, women also may tell *hikayah*s about spirit possession or encounters with spirits (genies).

As women interact more with nonfamily and even noncommunity members and as they are born into a culture where it is taken for granted that women belong in the world outside the home, they may tell more *hikayah*s. Three years ago I heard two stories that may be a clue to one new way in which *hikayah*s might be used by women to comment on outside experiences. In the first story a woman in her thirties had to deal with a gold merchant. She laughed as she recounted how she persuaded the man three times with three different arguments to increase the price he would pay her for a gold bracelet she was selling for another woman. The second *hikayah* is told by a woman in her sixties, Lella Fafa, who is very traditional. She wears old-fashioned Tunisian dress rather than Western clothing and the thick blanket-like veil that most women have discarded in favor of a light silky one. A follower of old-fashioned customs, she never has a visitor even in early afternoon for whom she doesn't prepare dinner. She likes to retire to the countryside from time to time with some of her women relatives, yet she rarely goes about town although she could do so since she is an older woman. She is a confident, forceful woman, very aware of town interaction and politics. She is also a woman known for skill in storytelling. Young adults remember that she even made up riddles for them when they were young. What happens when a woman such as this is confronted with the need to deal with the outside world?

A group of us women of various ages was waiting together one day to welcome Lella Fafa's brother and sister-in-law home from Mecca. She told us a story about her trip to the doctor in Tunis. Interestingly, the story came after an argument between her and another, younger woman over who does the most housework. Lella Fafa without preamble transported us in her story out of the house and out of the town to Tunis where she had persuaded her grown son to take her to a kidney specialist.

The story commences with the arrival at the doctor's office and the nurse demanding whether Lella Fafa has an appointment. (Fafa calls it "rendez-vous" to show that she considers this an example of French officiousness and an affectation by the Tunisian nurse and doctor.) In great gasping breaths (amid much laughter from the listeners), Fafa informs the nurse that she doesn't know anything about an appointment but if she doesn't see a doctor she will die.

Next she imitates her embarrassed son as he tried to talk her out of her "inappropriate" dramatic behavior. "Now there Mama that's not the way to act, now Mama . . ." The nurse, now properly intimidated (or perhaps harassed?) leads Lella Fafa into the waiting room but admonishes her that she will have to wait until the patients *with* "rendez-vous" have seen the doctor.

Two male patients are waiting in the room. In very audible tones Lella Fafa then begins moaning to her embarrassed son, "My son, better if I had died at home. Better if I were dying in my own bed rather than far away in Tunis." To her son's chagrin, this continues until the nurse comes in to call the next patient, at which time the suitably unnerved man says, "No, no, let this woman in—quickly."

Finally she is sent to get X-rays. Again she is told she will have to make an appointment for another day, and again she assumes a false naiveté to persuade the medical personnel to complete the procedure while she waits.

All the women in the room—young and unmarried to postmenopausal —were listening and laughing. What was so taking about the story was that Lella Fafa was deliberately playing an "old, naive countrywoman not aware of proper public behavior" role to manipulate her son and the "city slickers" as well. Women understand the stereotypes used against them and are not averse to turning them to their advantage.

Looking at this last story, we can speculate that women may be beginning to tell *hikayah*s that incorporate some elements of the more familiar *khurafah* tradition. This *hikayah*, unlike the one told by Fafani, is not exactly like men's *hikayah*s. *Khurafah*s (fantasy stories) in many cultures use the number three (three brothers, three bears, three tasks, and so on). Lella Fafa's story seems to draw on the *khurafah* tradition in its reliance on three episodes or incidents. (The "all lies" story, for example, had three brothers and three challenges to tell a lying story.) All of the one hundred men's *hikayah*s that I recorded, on the other hand, revolved around a single problem and its resolution or comment.

Other differences are that men's *hikayah*s are historically more remote than those of women. The men's stories are of themselves as younger men, twenty or thirty years earlier. Perhaps as women reach a time when they are more able to spend time out of the house and talk about outside events, men will become more inclined to stay home and reminisce.

More studies of women's expressive culture will have to be made and more time will have to pass before we are able to see just how women will cope artistically with their new access to the world outside the home. Certainly, verbal art forms will be manipulated to suit their changing status. Will younger women's stories, then, resemble those of Lella Fafa, an amalgam of *hikayah-* and *khurafah*-telling techniques? Or will younger women, telling *hikayah*s to men and women rather than to women only, fashion *hikayah*s more nearly like the men's? One thing is evident: in appropriating and restructuring what traditionally have been men's stories, women are symbolically asserting their right to a significant place in the male world—outside the house.

Note

1. Stith Thompson, *Motif-Index of Folk Literature* (Copenhagen and Bloomington, Ind., 1955–58). See Motif H509.5 Test, telling skillful lie, and Motifs X900–X1899, humor of lies and exaggerations. Two examples are X1130.2, fruit tree grows from head of deer shot with fruit pits, and X1547.2, river of honey.

Conformity and Confrontation: A Comparison of Two Iranian Women Poets

FARZANEH MILANI

Although the tradition of women's poetry in modern Iran is a rich and diversified field, at its very core lies a sense of division between seeing life as an opportunity and seeing it as a stifling discipline. And stifling discipline there has been, it seems, in the life of these women hungering for real freedom and consistently refusing to be posed as mere subordinates to men, cogs in the social structure. Often their work is a fervent protest against their fated condition and is used as an effective public forum, a politically potent form.

In fact, the issue of women's emancipation became a focus of increasing attention and broader concern by the middle of the nineteenth century. As early as 1848, a woman, also a poet, voluntarily threw off her veil before a crowd to demonstrate, as a member of the Babi faith, her religious conviction of the equality of men and women.[1] The gathering was set in commotion, and yet Qorratol'Ayn delivered her lecture, concluding with these words: "This is the day on which the fetters of the past are burst asunder. Let those who have shared in this great achievement arise and embrace each other."[2] Embrace each other they did not. One slit his throat, and many others left the ranks of Bab's followers, pronouncing her a heretic. Yet the liberation of women was not to be stopped. Veiled women marched in the streets, organized strikes, carried arms, and fought alongside men. Women poets, at the forefront of many of these movements, used their works as a platform for involvement in the social currents of the day.[3] Their poetry, for the most part topical and issue oriented, is to be valued more as a contribution to women's political awakening than for its intrinsic literary merit. These poems also provided the soil from which later works grew, works that will ultimately rank among the foremost and most valuable products of modern Persian poetry.

Two such important bodies of work are those of Forugh Farrokhzod (1935–1967) and Tahereh Saffar-Zadeh (born 1939). Rated as two of the most important figures of modern poetry in Iran, they both started their poetic careers with the awareness that they were writing as members of a poetic tradition lacking in feminine concerns and orientations. Yet their poetry evolved in completely different ways. While Forugh continued to confront her experiences as a woman directly, Tahereh, after a revitalized interest in Shiism, turned her poetry into a clearly genderless vehicle with a distanced, asexual voice.

When these two poets deliberately chose to challenge, reject, and transcend accepted mores and assumptions about "femininity" in life or in literature, they were misunderstood, abused, or avoided by an unresponsive and at times hostile literary structure. But while Forugh was to work throughout her short literary career in an atmosphere of contempt, denunciation, and disdain, Tahereh has finally achieved both popularity and public recognition. Her poems are printed on the front pages of the most widely circulated papers. While Forugh, after her death, turned into a (safely dead) cultural hero (a trend that has been reversing for the last three years), Tahereh enjoys fame and praise.

Did the one have to die and the other submerge her femininity, one wonders, in order to be redeemed from critical abuse and misunderstanding? Is "fame," as opposed to notoriety or obscurity, the reward for conformity in life or in poetry? Are women poets tolerated and acclaimed as long as they confine themselves within prescribed social boundaries? The fact that Tahereh in her growth as a poet took her imaginative cues from sources outside herself, while Forugh followed her more spontaneous inner promptings, surely has had a profound effect both on the ultimate ethos each attained in her poetry and on society's assessment of that ethos.

Born in Tehran in January 1935, Forugh never finished high school.[4] She was sixteen when she married and seventeen when her first poetry collection, *Asir* (Captive), appeared in 1952. Forugh's only child was born the following year. His birth, however, did not regenerate a decaying marriage and in 1954 she decided to leave her husband. Enduring much pain and grief, she not only lost custody of her son but was also denied occasional visits with him. Her second poetry collection, *Divar* (Wall) was published in 1957, and *Osian* (Rebellion) less than a year later. By then Forugh was well established as a notorious yet promising poet. After several years of silence, *Tavalodi dighar* (Another birth) was published in 1964. On February 14, 1967, at the height of her creativity, Forugh was killed in an automobile accident. *Iman biavarim be aghaz-e fasle sard* (Let's believe in the dawning of the cold season) was published posthumously in 1974.

Tahereh was born in Syrjan in 1939 and enjoyed a more scholarly education. She earned a bachelor's degree in English literature from Pahlavi University (Shiraz) in 1958. Like Forugh, her married life did not last long, and in 1968 she left Iran to work for a master's degree in creative writing at the University of Iowa. After a little over a year in America, she returned to teach at the National University of Iran. Before long her Western-influenced poetry turned into religiously oriented poetry. After the establishment of the Islamic Republic she ran unsuccessfully for parliament, and today she is among the very few prominent writers to consistently support the new regime.

In Tahereh's work we witness the development of feminist concerns in *Peyvand-haye talkh* (Bitter unions, 1963) and *Rahghozar-e mahtab* (Moonlight's passerby, 1963); their flowering in *Red Umbrella* (published in America by Windhover Press, 1969), *Tanin dar delta* (Resonance in the bay, 1971), and *Sad va bazovan* (Dam and arms, 1972); their diffusion in *Safar-e panjom* (Fifth journey, 1978); and their total disappearance in *Bey'at ba bidari* (Allegiance with wakefulness, 1980).

Growth and change are the hallmarks of both of these prolific poets. Daring in their use of taboo subjects, they challenged the dominant value systems of their society in order to assert their own sense of authenticity and autonomy. Even their technical and imaginative development is linked to their attempt to transcend traditional limitations. Indeed, their gradual break away from more traditional forms and their tenacious search for new avenues of expression are emblems of their desire to liberate themselves from the tyranny of "established" forms. Adventurers in life, they are adventurers in language as well.

The body of Forugh's work and Tahereh's prerevolutionary poetry are significant feminist achievements, not only in their consciousness of and attention to the fact that women have been and continue to be the "other" and the "underprivileged," but also in their attempt to expose the double standard and perpetual prejudices of masculine perceptions and masculine values. These two poets depict "reality" in terms of the perspective of a woman imprisoned in her femininity. They resent the structure of male dominance, which has pushed them to live on the outskirts of society. Although the feminine character that emerges from this early poetry can hardly be called a "traditional" woman, she is still manipulated by cultural expectations and experiences herself in terms of and in response to masculine-centered values and definitions. She thus becomes the embodiment not of wholeness but of separateness, not of integrity but of alienation. Confused and unable to operate properly within the patriarchal framework, Forugh writes in *Captive*:

I am the cause of my own sorrows
there is no easing of this self-inflicted pain
my feet in chains still I lament
I have no affinity with their links.[5]

The poet finds herself in collision with existing moral and social codes, but the dominant values of the society, although deliberately disregarded, nonetheless hold sway over her. Unable to express her anger clearly or to direct it at the appropriate target, she turns her rage inward, where it becomes a nagging desire for isolation.

I run away from these people
who seem so sincere and friendly
but who at heart, in an excess of contempt,
charge me with countless accusations

These people, who, listening to my poems,
bloom like sweet-smelling flowers,
but in private
call me a "notorious fool"[6]

The inner experience conveyed through Tahereh's early collection of short stories, *Bitter Unions*, and through *Moonlight's Passerby* is also one of doubt, loneliness, and frustration. The poem entitled "Stranger" expresses this feeling of dislocation. The poet, who has crawled out from under traditions and conventions, condemns the man who proves to be deeply rooted in all that is static, outgrown, and obsolete. To find real, fully developed human relationships, he has to go beyond the confining regions of tradition.

I am a pantheon of feelings,
and I will not hold you—deep snowdrift of hypocrisy—
I am afraid you will freeze the remembrance I cherish,
                    remembrance of humanity.

I am that lonely one who understands
the agony of loneliness,
the silence of the tolerant,
the wrath of the inflamed.
But I never understand you—all insouciance and silly cheer—
I love more the bitter smile of the self-made man
who works with mind and muscles for tomorrow,
more handsome than the glare of your wealth,
more precious than your legacy of riches,
which you guard like a dragon,
                    day in and day out,
                        ceaselessly.

I am unfettered by desire
or the clanking chains of fame.
I have no need of people
the companions of my life are God and poetry.
You will never taste the freedom I taste
as you join without a thought your destined peers,

loaded with jewelry,
colored with deceit,
drained of human passion.
Go, marry the bride you have never met
and follow in the footsteps of your countless ancestors.[7]

If both Forugh and Tahereh, in their first poetry collections, begin by creating an eloquent reality out of the prison of their femininity and by chronicling the trials of a woman's search for an independent identity, they soon move to an attack on the structure, institutions, and customs that in their view have led to women's oppression. If in their early poetry they explore femininity, they now want to transform it. Their sense of frustration and dissatisfaction urges them to demand and advocate basic changes. Expressing resentment against the unequal treatment of men and women, they both repudiate all forces that prevent the full blossoming of women's potentialities. Certainly, a sense of outrage provides the impetus for the writing of many poems of this period. In the following poem from *Wall*, Forugh reveals not only her bitter realization of women's oppressive condition but also her open rebellion against the crippling constrictions placed on them.

My sister, take your rights
from those who keep you weak,
from those who through a thousand ploys
keep you seated in a house.

Your angry complaining
must become shouting, screaming.
You must break this heavy chain
to liberate your life.

Rise, uproot oppression,
revive the heart drenched in blood.
Struggle, struggle to transform laws
for the sake of your own freedom.[8]

Infused with a sense of outrage and a will to change, "My Birthplace," from *Resonance in the Bay*, portrays Tahereh's acute sensitivity to sexual politics.

I have not seen my birthplace,
where my mother deposited the heavy
　　　　　　　　　　　load of her inside

under a low ceiling.
It is still alive,
the first tick-tick of my small heart,
in the stovepipe
and in the crevices between crumbling bricks.

It is still alive in the door and walls
                              of the room
my mother's look of shame
at my father,
at my grandfather,
after a muffled voice announced,
"It's a girl."
The midwife cringed, fearing no tip
for cutting the umbilical cord,
knowing there'd be none
for circumcision.

On my first pilgrimage to my birthplace
I will wash from the walls
my mother's look of shame,
and where my heart began to pound,
I will begin to tell the world
that my luminous hands have no lust
to clench in fists,
nor to beat and pound
I do not yell,
I do not feel proud to kill,
I've not been fattened
at the table of male supremacy.[9]

Written out of reflexive, retrospective perception, this poem not only reaffirms the bonds between two victims, the mother and the daughter, it carries with it a sense of power and strength. It is not a poem bemoaning the injustices of a patriarchal culture, but a forceful and vindictive attack on that culture. The anger, however controlled, speaks of the rebelliousness of the poet. Far from perpetuating a lonely desolation or endurance, it reinforces the urgency of action.

The poet's pilgrimage to her birthplace is a metaphorical journey into the past. It is a second visit to a place where a woman continues to suffer silently the "shame" of having given birth to a girl. It is an attempt to first revive and then revise the past—a valiant effort to be a psychological and emotional survivor. If the first part of the poem is a descriptive rendering of an all-too-common scene, the second portion is a vigorous struggle against its lingering aftermath. Thus, the earlier objective and representational tone turns quickly into one of anger and militancy. Just as the daughter refuses now to be a mere observer, the poet, too, refuses to merely record. If change is to be effected she has to become a participator, one with a personal sense of identity and strength. She can thus develop her own personal context for strength and power and as a victor witness her rebirth.

Anger and mutiny are part of the self-affirmation of these two poets, and they both experience at this point a dilemma in its crudest form. Traditional codes of manners and established commitments clash bitterly with the demands of a new and basically revised order of beliefs and desires. Past solutions and modes of expression prove to be no longer adequate, and both poets feel an urgent need for growth and change.

However, the agents of change differ for the two. For Tahereh the journey starts mainly through an outer motive or inducement. It is determined, intended. It is a reaction to circumstances rather than an independent initiation. The innermost predispositions need a certain justification, rationalization, or catalytic agent. In Forugh, too, circumstances inevitably determine the course of her actions, yet she seems ultimately to respond to her inner self rather than to outside forces. This allows her the privilege of a unique voice and keeps her from submerging herself in someone else's vision or aspiration. In short, it makes her more spontaneous, more instinctive.

The exploration of sexuality in the work of these two poets best illustrates their differences. Although sex is explored beyond the boundaries of tradition in both works, although both poets' expressions of sexual desire represent sincere attempts to integrate sex with love, work, and social consciousness, although both try to gracefully reconcile the sensuous, spiritual, and social dimensions of a female self, each poet's treatment of love and sexuality is finally quite different.

Forugh is both possessed by and possesses prodigious powers of love that create far-reaching changes in her. Sexuality is central in her psycho-intellectual development, a symbolic self-creation. Her sexual adventures are a spontaneous response to ebullient, rousing desire. The poem "I Sinned," from *Wall*, best epitomizes this feeling of overpowering lust. Checked by conventions and yet sanctioned by passion, this poem is exhilarating in its candor and lustfulness. It heralds the awakening of a woman's sensuality, an unmediated, impulsive passion.

> I sinned—I voluptuously sinned—
> beside a tremulous, intoxicated body.
> O God! How could I have known what I had done
> in that dark retreat of silence?
>
> In that dark retreat of silence
> I looked into his mysterious eyes
> in my breast, my heart trembled restlessly
> at the pleading in his eyes
>
> In that dark retreat of silence,
> disheveled I sat beside him,
> freed from the agony of a maddened heart,
> passion poured from his lips to mine

I whispered the tale of love in his ears:
I want you, my love!
I want you, my life-giving embrace!
you, my mad lover![10]

For Tahereh, on the other hand, sexual adventures and activities have their raison d'être beyond themselves. Azar, the heroine in one of the short stories of *Bitter Unions*, writes: "Like a magic key, every one of her [Bilitis'] songs unlatched the sturdy lock of my parents' advice. Gradually, I was being delivered from all the ludicrous fear and terror they had instilled in me."[11]

Clearly, the same fear and terror were instilled in Forugh. However, she finds herself liberated from their tyranny in response to an ardent desire. She needs no model to emulate, no Bilitis to rescue her from the impediments of moral proprieties. Furthermore, although sexuality undergoes a basic metamorphosis in Forugh's writing, its direct and clear expression remains a tantalizing facet of her poetry to her last days. In Tahereh's work, however, passion seems to be transfigured, moving from the personal to the religious. In fact, in her later poetry she courts admiration more than intimacy. The proper sphere of emotions for her proves to be no longer the private and lyrical metaphors of love and sexuality, but religious passion. Gone is the free flow of emotions and with it her previous unique and personal vision.

Indeed, perspectives change for both poets in their later poetry. They move toward broader concerns and preoccupations and convey a keen awareness of political responsibility. A heightened perception, a capacity for seeing beyond the female self, is the hallmark of this poetry, poetry expressing distaste for and hatred of decay and corruption and all their attendant implications, poetry reflecting disdain for all forms of social injustice.

Tahereh, after a series of unsuccessful social, political, and spiritual journeys, finds the sole way to salvation in traditional Islamic values. Obviously, there is no instantaneous conversion and surely her ardent interest in Islam is not only tactical but motivated by and deeply rooted in the subjective needs of her personality. But while in the early poetry religion has an individual, personal function, in her later poetry it is an institutionalized, politicized product, a most potent weapon to create a just society on the ruins of a decayed, corrupt one.[12] Religious beliefs, while not totally absent in the early poetry, do not have the vigor of their later expression. They exist on the edges of her work, which is centrally occupied with different themes. In an interview with Mohammad Ali Esfahani, Tahereh clearly connects her interest in Islam with "the justice-seeking, uncompromising nature of Shiism."[13] The following passage from the later poem, "Passageway of Torture and Silence," epitomizes this militant view of Islam.

> We were sound asleep
> so fast asleep
> that the footsteps of thieves
> —internal and external thieves—
> couldn't wake us up
> God itself visited us
> and woke us up
> and a mountain of a man
> sustained us
> and the height of faith
> directed us toward
> struggle and martyrdom [14]

Forugh's view of Islam was completely different. In the poem "I Feel Sorry for the Garden," religion is viewed as a hindrance to change. The poet subtly yet forcefully portrays the failings of the members of her family—and by extension all the members of society at large—in curing the present social problems. She brings into focus the political apathy of each member of her family and cunningly challenges them to reveal their impotence and passivity, for each in his or her own special way proves to be chained actually and metaphorically to a system of belief that obstinately refuses change. The mother, for instance, believes conveniently that the blasphemy of some plant has wilted the garden (society). She passively awaits the blessing and forgiveness of a divine savior and finds solace in prayer.

> Laid out at the threshold of a dreaded hell
> mother's whole life
> is a prayer rug
> mother traces the footsteps of sin
> at the core of everything
> and believes the transgression of some plant
> has blighted the garden
> mother is a natural sinner
> and prays for all the flowers
> and prays for all the fishes
> and prays for herself
> mother is waiting for a second coming
> and a descending grace. [15]

In another poem titled "Mechanical Doll," religion is viewed once again as a possible excuse for inertia, passivity, and quiescence.

One can prostrate oneself for a lifetime
at a saint's crypt—head bowed—
one can see God in a certain tomb
one can find faith with a certain coin
one can rot in the chambers of a mosque
like an old prayer reader.[16]

Not only do Forugh and Tahereh differ noticeably in their views of the political role of Islam, they also adopt different roles as women. Tahereh virtually submerges her female self, but Forugh continues to use, throughout her life, an identifiable woman's voice. *Another Birth* heralds Forugh's emancipation from her initial sense of victimization and her subsequent anger and exasperation, but it depicts a woman who continues to confront her innermost feelings and experiences. The speaker in the later poetry always has a distinctive voice—her gender is never in question. In an interview with Iraj Gorghin, Forugh clearly elaborates on the issue. "It is only natural that a woman, due to her physical, psychological, and emotional characteristics might perceive things differently from a man. She might have a point of view that is different from a man."[17] In Tahereh's later poetry, on the other hand, the female voice is suppressed. The earlier lingering resentment totally disappears; one no longer hears from the emotional and intellectual woman who bitterly senses her social limitations and restrictive roles. *Allegiance with Wakefulness* contains not a single image that might have emerged from a woman's experience. The poet submerges her femininity in a neuter persona, if not discounting, then at least hiding her sex behind an asexual facade. In these gender-indistinguishable poems, the poetic persona is not only linked to but submerged in a collective self. The peculiarities of the self as portrayed in the early poetry are transformed, harnessed into the new social system, a system where issues are "human" and solely defined by men. Thus, one no longer finds any concern over the fate of women, let alone protest. What one sees instead is a series of political statements and a paucity of personal experiences, a deductive rather than inductive presentation. If earlier the poetic persona was presented from within, she is now revealed solely from without through her actions, this mask (veil) created and imposed on the natural self by sociopolitical exigencies. If earlier the self was at the center of the perceived world, it now has moved to the periphery. Inevitably, the original quest for inner growth is supplanted by superimposed feelings, wishes, and thoughts. And certainly it proves to be easier to submit than to rebel. The poetic persona depicted in these poems seems now to have been saved from the burden of responsibility for her life, saved from making decisions, saved from doubts and contradictions. The clouds of frustration and alienation that hung over her previous books seem to have lifted. Inner pain is transformed into something more objective and less personally threatening. Loneliness, a nodal point at which many previous images converged, vanishes altogether.

As for the volcanic energy of the previous rebelliousness, it finds a specific directional thrust against the Pahlavi regime and the West. Tahereh's earlier admiration and imitation of the West changes to rejection and denunciation. Time and again she condemns its unjust exploitation of Iran's major resources, associating it with secularism and corruption. The West becomes chief villain, symbol of destructive outside force. And as the problems are more concrete and tangible, so are the victories more definable, more definite. If her earlier poetry traces gradually the breakdown of the loci of authority, *Allegiance with Wakefulness* witnesses the emergence of another. In a poem offered to Ayatullah Khomeini she writes:

> Never was night followed by such awakening
> never did night see so many keeping vigil
> Enemy of sleep
> Soul of God spreading justice
> you are the ancestor of all heroes
> the hero among prophets
> in an era of ubiquitous murder
> an era of conniving imposters
> of bribe-givers and night-seekers
> in the darkest night of history
> you are the east in every universe
> with nothing between you and the sun
> your movement
>   is the movement of sun's hours
> with freedom and power
>   and no leave from anyone.[18]

The earlier self-regulated behavior and moral code were obviously exhilarating. Nonetheless they also caused anxiety and loneliness, feelings that are absent in her religious poetry. If she relied earlier on idiosyncratic and private rules, depending mainly on her individual temperament, she can now rely on socially validated codes of conduct, shared beliefs, and principles. Freed from the independence that both limited her and gave her individuality, she finds a comfortable refuge from the heavy burden of her autonomy. The adventurous Tahereh needs no longer to search or reassess. Believing she no longer stands outside, she loses the virtues of the "outsider" who struggles for rights.

The religious metamorphosis in Tahereh's poetry not only influences

the subject, persona, and poetics of the poem, but also the very relationship of the poet to her art and to herself. Indeed, her concept of her
value and function as a poet, her notion of her intended relationship with
her audience, even the very techniques she uses all point toward a trans-
mogrification. The poet who did not want to "eliminate poetic imagination" from her poetry and debase it to the level of mere "reporting and
journalism"[19] is now producing hastily put together issue-oriented poetry, poetry where poetic imagination suffers. *Allegiance with Wakefulness* is replete with clear-cut statement of intent. The poet's desire to be
readily comprehensible makes her rely on the familiar, the unambiguous, the cliché. By pushing her work into political events she actually
pushes political poetry out of her poems. Amazingly, this is a book by a
poet who emphatically maintained that

> pure poetry is as fallible for me as some of the didactic poems of Saʾdi
> and Milton or the socially oriented poetry of the Constitutional era. Be-
> cause none of these three categories encompasses life in an inclusive
> and natural fashion. One busies itself with language, texture, and the
> sound of words, the other with ethics and theology and the last with
> superficial social issues.[20]

Both Forugh and Tahereh, through a long process of growth and
change, challenged the dominant value systems of their culture in their
work, yet their animating influences always came by different paths.
That Tahereh put an end to her own search for freedom and identity in
exchange for the comforts of espousing an almost utopian feeling and
partisan zeal about Shiism perhaps points to the intensity of her need to
identify in some way with her culture, submerging her female self in the
collective. This may have been her way of overcoming the painful conflicts so often expressed in her early poetry. Forugh's corresponding
search ended with her early death, yet one gets the impression from the
intensely inner-directed nature of her poetic quest that no need to find
an external directorship would have developed.

The significance of these two women's parallel yet divergent developments is that both have achieved some measure of acceptance by society. Forugh's desire for personal autonomy, self-understanding, and
growth was always a strong force in her poetry, and this freedom-loving
source could only be safely assimilated by the society once it had been
ossified by her death. In a like manner, Tahereh's poetry is now welcome in the society because she has transformed those forces of personal liberation into impersonal political forces suitable to the needs of
the current regime. If both poets expressed their private feelings with an
explosive effect, that explosion was muffled—at the very height of their
poetic career—by forces either within or from outside themselves.

Notes

1. For many other writers and poets—male and female—the veil became an indication of the oppressive condition of women in Iran and a
token of their social deprivation. In ironic yet simple language, Iraj Mirza
(1874–1925) satirizes the custom of the veil.

On the door of an inn
in chalk was drawn a woman's face.
From a reliable source
the turban-wearers heard the news.
"Woe to our faith," they said,
"people have seen a woman unveiled."
Religion and order were indeed in danger
when the pious arrived in haste.
One brought dirt, another water
with a veil of mud they covered the face
and thus reassured returned to their homes
religion and order were once more in order.

Eshgi (1894–1924), with characteristic openness, rails against the imprisonment of women in the veil.

What are these graceless cloaks and veils?
Nothing but shrouds for the dead
Death to all who bury women alive
If but two or three poets join me,
soon our sound would grow,
women would throw off their vile masks,
and joy dawn on us
but while they remain in shrouds,
half our nation is dead.

2. H. M. Balyuzi, *Baha'u'llah the King of Glory* (Oxford: George Ronald,
1980), p. 45.

3. Many such poems are published in women's magazines and peri-
odicals, the first of which was called *Danesh* (Knowledge) and was published in 1910.

4. For the poet's biography, see Michael C. Hillmann, "Furugh Farrukh-
zad, Modern Iranian Poet," in Elizabeth W. Fernea and Basima Q. Bezirgan
(eds.), *Middle Eastern Muslim Women Speak* (Austin: University of Texas
Press, 1977), pp. 291–317.

5. Forugh Farrokhzod, *Asir* (Captive) (Tehran: Amir Kabir, 1975), p. 129.

6. Ibid., p. 20.

7. Tahereh Saffar-Zadeh, *Harekat va dirooz* (Motion and yesterday)
(Tehran: Ravagh Publishing, 1978), p. 9.

8. Seid Abdol-Hamid Kalkali, *Tazkareye sho'araye mo'aser-e Iran*
(Memories of modern Iranian poets), 2 vols. (Tehran: Zahouri Publishing,
1978), p. 250. It is interesting to note that this poem has been suppressed
from new printings of Forugh's poetry collection.

9. Saffar-Zadeh, *Harekat va dirooz*, p. 23.

10. Forugh Farrokhzod, *Divar* (Wall) (Tehran: Amir Kabir, 1976), p. 13.

11. Tahereh Saffar-Zadeh, *Peyvand-haye talkh* (Bitter unions) (Tehran: E'tela'at Printing, 1963), p. 217.

12. As early as 1947, Fakhr-al-Din Shadman, in *Taskhir-e tammadun-e faranghi* (Rapt with Western culture), called attention to what was later labeled as "westoxication" by Jalal al-Ahmad. "Westoxication" is the effect of the West upon the life, culture, and way of thinking of Iranians without the necessary traditional base, evolutionary process, or historical continuity. Shadman believed the way to salvation was through revival and reassertion of traditional, especially Islamic, values.

13. Saffar-Zadeh, *Harekat va dirooz*, p. 162.

14. Tahereh Saffar-Zadeh, "Passageway of Torture and Silence," *E'tela'at* 16,461 (1360/1981): 2.

15. Forugh Farrokhzod, *Iman biavarim be aghaz-e fasle sard* (Let's believe in the dawning of the cold season) (Tehran: Morvarid Publishing, 1974), p. 54.

16. Forugh Farrokhzod, *Tavalodi dighar* (Another birth) (Tehran: Morvarid Publishing, 1977), p. 73.

17. "Iraj Gorghin: An Interview with Forugh Farrokhzod," in Syrus Tahbaz (ed.), *Arash* (Tehran: Darakhshan Publishing Co., 1967), p. 33.

18. Tahereh Saffar-Zadeh, *Bey'at ba bidari* (Allegiance with wakefulness) (Tehran: Hamdami Publishing, 1980), p. 25.

19. Saffar-Zadeh, *Harekat va dirooz*, p. 158.

20. Ibid., p. 145.

Poems

LAMIᶜA ABBAS AL-ᶜIMARAH
Translated from the Arabic by Basima Bezirgan
and Elizabeth Fernea

THE FORTUNE-TELLER

If the fortune-teller had said
That you would be my love
I would not have written love poems
For any other man
But prayed in silence
That you would be with me always.

If the fortune-teller had said
That I would touch the moon's face,
I would never have played
With the pebbles in the river
Or strung my hopes
On beads.

If the fortune-teller had said
That my love would be a prince
Riding a horse of rubies,
I would never have dreamed
Of death
For earth would have held me
With its golden ropes of light.

If the fortune-teller had said
That my love would come to me
On snowy nights, with the sun in his hands
My breath would not have frozen,
And old sorrows
Would not have welled up in my heart.

If the fortune-teller had said
That I would meet you in this wilderness
I would never have wept for anything on earth
But collected my tears
All my tears
For the day you might leave me.

(1977)[1]

THE PATH OF SILENCE

I warned you
Don't ask for explanations
When you walk with me,
And you agreed.
But we haven't gone far,
You said

"Didn't you kill a young man yesterday?
He was gentle, weak and loving . . ."

My son.
Don't dwell on it.
This, this death was a separation.
He was gentle, weak, loving
But after all, what do the dead need?

And we walked . . .
I warned you
Not to curse the people of yesterday
When you walk with me,
And you cursed.

And we walked . . .
Your eyes shifted back and forth
Whenever a girl passed by.
You were close to me
And far from me.
You were arrogant

And we walked . . .
And we became thirsty

And we stopped to drink
I swear that I have never drunk before
The way I drank yesterday.
I was the cup
And you were the wine.

And we walked . . .
And you were content.
I said, Come in, Adam.
Here are the trees of heaven
Strip them, bough by bough
Except the sorrow trees . . .
For I fear, I fear the sorrow trees.

You bypassed the permitted boughs.
You disobeyed.

The sorrow trees darkened like clouds
Before my eyes.
And I cried.

You left, Adam, you were expelled.
Go back to wherever you came from.

BUT I . . .

Across the rivers that have no bridges
Are lovers I do not know.
The thought of me excites them to rapture.
But I . . .
I am only a body
Buried beneath the snow.
Beautiful and beloved
Forever.

(1978)

Note

1. In *Law anba'ani al-'arraf* (Beirut: Al-Mu'assasah al-'Arabiyah Lil-Dirasat Wa al-Nashr, 1980).

PART VIII
Postscript

A Forbidden Glimpse, a Broken Sound
(from *Women of Algiers in Their Apartment*)

ASSIA DJEBAR
Translated from the French by J. M. McDougal

On the 25th of June 1832, Delacroix left for Algiers for a short stay. He had just spent a month in Morocco immersed in a world of extreme visual richness—the splendor of costumes, the fury of fantasias, the feasts of a royal court, the quaintness of Jewish weddings and of musicians in the streets, the nobility of the royal cats (lions, tigers, and so on).

This Orient of the mid nineteenth century appeared to Delacroix, in all its excess, as a new vision. It was an Orient exactly like the one he had dreamed of for his work *The Death of Sardanapolis*, but here it was cleansed of any idea of sin. Moreover, it was an Orient in which only Morocco had escaped the abominable authority of the Turk since the Scenes of the Massacres of Scio.

Morocco, then, was the place where the dream and the aesthetic ideal intersected, a place of visual revolution. Thus, Delacroix could write later, "Men and things appear to me in a new light since my journey."

In Algiers, Delacroix stayed only three days. This brief passage through the capital recently conquered by the French oriented him, thanks to a fortunate series of circumstances, toward a world from which he had remained an outsider during his long Moroccan tour. In Algiers for the first time he penetrated into a special world, the world of women.

The world he had discovered in Morocco and illustrated in his sketches was essentially masculine and warlike. In a word, it was virile. It was concerned with the outside spectacle of feasts, noises, cavalcades, and rapid movement. It was these spectacles that were revealed to him. But crossing the border from Morocco to Algeria, Delacroix also crossed a vague frontier that would invert all the signs, and that frontier crossing would be the origin of what posterity would see as the result of this singular "voyage to the Orient."

Delacroix's adventure is well known. The chief engineer of the Port of Algiers, M. Poirel, an amateur painter, had in his service a *chaouch*, a

former merchant, who had been the captain (ra'is) of a trading ship before 1830. This man agreed, after long discussions, to let Delacroix enter
his house.

Fournault, friend of a friend, reports the details of the intrusion. The
house stood on the old Duquesne Street. Delacroix, accompanied by the
husband and, surely, by Poirel, crossed through "a dark hall" at the end
of which was, unexpectedly, the harem, bathed in an almost supernatural light. There women and children awaited them "in the middle of a
heap of silk and gold." The wife of the former ra'is, young and pretty,
was sitting next to a *narghile*, or water pipe. As for Delacroix, Poirel
reported to Cournault, who wrote, "Delacroix was drunk on the spectacle he was witnessing."

Entering into the room in conversation with the husband-interpreter,
Delacroix wanted to know everything about "this new and mysterious
life." On the numerous sketches that he made (various poses of the
seated women) he wrote what he thought most important, what not to
forget: precise colors ("black lines of gold, lacquered violets, deep India
reds . . .") along with details of the costumes. It was a strange and varied
mixture that met his eyes.

In his brief, graphic, handwritten notes, there is a sort of fever of the
hand, an inebriation in his vision. For a fleeting instant of evanescent
revelation within this moving frontier, reality and dream stood side by
side. And Cournault notes, "This fever was scarcely calmed by fruits
and sherbets."

The vision, completely new, was seen as pure image. And even though
this almost too new brilliance seemed about to confuse reality totally
for Delacroix, he did force himself to also note on his sketches the first
and last names of the women. There are watercolors with the names of
Bayah, Mouni, and Zorba bint Sultan, Zora, and Khadoudja Tarboridji.
Crayoned figures emerging from their exotic anonymity.

Abundance of rare colors, names with new sounds. Is this what
troubled and exalted the painter? Is this what made him write, "It's
beautiful. It's like being at the time of Homer!"

There, in a visit of a couple of hours to the secluded women, what
shock or, at the very least, what ambiguous feelings seized the painter?
A harem, partly open—was that really what he saw?

In his mind, Delacroix took away from this partly open place certain
objects: images of slippers, a scarf, a blouse, a pair of pants. Not the
banal tourist trophies, but rather tangible proof of a unique, fleeting experience. Ironic traces.

He had to touch his dream, to give it life beyond his remembrance of
it, to complete what his notebooks had trapped in sketches and draw-
ings. Within those notebooks was a fetishlike compulsion that was ag-

gravated by his certainty of the irrevocable uniqueness of that lived moment. A moment that would never be repeated.

Upon his return to Paris, the painter worked two years on the image of his memory. It is an image well documented and supported by local, indigenous objects, but around which still moves an air of mute and unformulated uncertainty. He created a masterpiece that has always made us question ourselves.

Femmes d'Alger dans leur appartement. Three women, two of them seated in front of a *narghile*. In the first rendition the third woman is semi-reclining, leaning on cushions on her elbow. A maidservant, three-quarters turned away from us, is raising an arm as if she were drawing aside the heavy drape that conceals this closed world. The maidservant, an almost accessory character, is barely touched by the sheen of colors that radiates from the other three women. All the messages of the painting play themselves out in the painter's depiction of these women— their relationship with their bodies and with the site of their incarceration. They are prisoners resigned to a closed space who are illuminated by a sort of dreamlike light coming from nowhere, like the light of a greenhouse or an aquarium. The genius of Delacroix is in rendering them at the same moment both present and faraway. They are very enigmatic figures.

Fifteen years after his days in Algiers, Delacroix remembered his dream again, set to work once more, and presented to the Salon of 1849 another version of his *Femmes d'Alger*.

This new composition was almost identical, but several changes in the painting allow the latent meaning of the work to emerge more clearly.

In this second canvas, where the characteristics of the figures are less precise and the elements of decor less exact, the angle of vision has been enlarged. This framing effect has triple results: it removes us from the three women and puts them further into their retreat; it uncovers and denudes the walls of their room, thereby increasing the weight of their solitude; and, finally, it accentuates the unreal nature of the light. The light appears to come more directly out of the concealing darkness, which is like an invisible menace, omnipresent thanks to the presence of the maidservant, who is now hardly distinguishable but who is still there, attending.

The figures are still women, waiting women. But suddenly they appear less like female sultans and more like prisoners. They have no link with us, the viewers of the painting. No relation. They neither acknowledge nor hide from our stares. They appear strange but terribly present to us in this rarified atmosphere of confinement.

Elie Faure recounts that the elderly Renoir could not keep from weeping when he recalled again and again the special light in *Femmes d'Alger*.

Should we also weep like the aged Renoir, but perhaps for other than artistic reasons? Should we not then evoke, a century and a half later, Bayah, Zora, Mouni, and Khadoudja, these women whom Delacroix (maybe in spite of himself) knew how to look at as no one had done before? These women who still have something unbearable to tell us about the present day?

Delacroix's painting can be seen as an approach to the feminine Orient—the first in European painting, which had been so accustomed to treating and retreating the odalisque theme or to depicting only the cruelty and nudity of the seraglio.

The dream in the lost eyes of those three is so distant from us and yet so near. If we were to try to define its nature, we might say it is nostalgic, soft, sweet, or vague. Or we might say it is a dream of sensuality. It is as if behind these figures, and before the maidservant lets the curtain fall again, a whole world is spread out before us, a world in which they live and have lived, both before and after their appearance before us.

For, actually, we are only spectators. And in reality, our act of watching them is forbidden. If Delacroix's painting unconsciously fascinates, it is not because of this superficial Orient that he proposes, this penumbra of luxury and silence, but because we are placed in front of these women as spectators, while the painter reminds us that normally we don't have the right to look. The painting itself is a stolen glance.

I believe that what Delacroix remembered, more than fifteen years later, what he remembered above all, was that "dark hall" at the end of which, in a room without exit, the prisoners were kept in secret like monks. We cannot guess the remote drama of these women except through this unexpected glimpse that the painting offers.

These women. Is it because they are dreaming that they don't look back at us? Or is it because, locked away like that without recourse, they can no longer even see us? There is no way for us to probe the souls of these dolorous women who seem as though they are drowned in their surroundings. They seem to live at another level, absent from themselves, from their bodies, from their sensuality, from their happiness.

Between these women and us, the spectators, a brief unveiling has taken place; we have for a moment crossed over the threshold of intimacy. Like the thief, the spy, the voyeur. Only two years previously, if he had attempted such an action, the French painter would have risked his life. . . .

Water, then, lies between these Algerian women and us, we who are forbidden, neuter, anonymous, omnipresent—spectators.

For a long time, this glimpse of the women of Algiers was thought to have been a stolen glimpse because it was the look of a foreigner from outside the harem and the community.

But for several decades now, in the wake of the triumphs of nationalism, we have come to realize that inside the new Orient, which is now left to itself, the image of an Algerian woman is not really perceived any differently by her father, her husband, and, in even a more troubling way, by her brother and son.

In principle, only these men can look upon the woman. To the other men of the tribe (since every cousin who might have shared games of infancy becomes a powerful voyeur-thief) the woman, if she has been allowed to follow the first step of the softening of the code of dress, will show only her face and hands.

The second step of this dress code relaxation paradoxically depends on the veil. By totally enveloping her body and her extremities, the veil permits the wearer to move around outside under its protection. But, in turn, the veiled woman becomes a possible thief within the men's space. She appears in that space like a fugitive silhouette—blinded in one eye when she uses two. But in certain cases the largess of "liberalism" allows her to use her other eye, thus integrating her vision. In other words, her two eyes, thanks to the new veil, the *voilette*, are now opened to the world.

Thus, another eye is present: the feminine view. But this liberated eye, which can be seen as a way to conquer the light of others, becomes a menace outside of confinement. Such is the vicious circle of reform.

In times past, the master made his authority over the female cloister felt through his unique power of being the only male to look upon the women. He eliminated the glances of others. In turn, today when the female "eye" moves about, it seems to be feared by the men who sit in the cafés of today's *medina*. They sit immobilized while that white-clad phantom passes by enigmatically.

The eye of the one who dominates looks for the eye of the dominated before taking possession of the body. In those glimpses of the female eye and body that are permitted (that is to say, those of the father, brother, son, and husband) there is an unforeseen risk, unforeseen because it can be accidental.

An accidental or unintentional movement, the parting of a curtain that covers a secret corner—such accidents may expose the other eyes of the body (breasts, genitalia, navel). If that happens, it is all over for the men, vulnerable guardians that they are. Their night, their misfortune, their dishonor, has arrived, by means of . . .

A forbidden look.

For it is absolutely forbidden to gaze on the female body, incarcerated as it is behind walls, or at best behind veils, from the age of ten to forty, or forty-five. But there is a danger that the woman's glance, now that it has been liberated and moves freely in the world outside the home, may at any moment disrobe other bodies. It is as if suddenly the woman's entire body was beginning to dare to look around, or at least the men see it that way. A woman, moving around outside and therefore "nude," who is herself looking around—isn't she a new threat to the man, to his formerly exclusive prerogative of "scoping out" the world?

The most visible sign of the evolution of Arab women, at least in the cities, was the lifting of their veils. Many women, often after a cloistered adolescence, have lived through the experience of unveiling.

When the women went out of the house for the first time unveiled, they said they felt they were exposed and everyone was looking at them: the woman's gait was stiff, her step hasty, her expression contracted.

Dialectical Arabic relates this experience in a significant way: "I no longer go out protected," says a woman who has stopped wearing the veil. She feels she is going out "undressed" or even "naked." The veil, which diverts the stares, the looks, is actually sensed to be an article of "self-clothing." Not to have it on is to be totally exposed.

And as for any man who consented to share, in even a most timid fashion, the evolution of his sisters or wife, he may feel condemned to live in malaise and uncertainty. He imagines first just an eye, and then the body without its wrap . . . and then without the veil itself. His woman then passes to the stage of the ultimate risk: she may uncover the other eye, the eye of her sex. Halfway through this journey comes the one halt in this "belly dance," the one that draws grimaces in cabarets. The other eye, the navel, is exposed.

Such is the body of the woman. As soon as she leaves her patient waiting within the cloistered interior of the house, her body conceals the danger of nature. As soon as it moves about in open space, this wandering multitude of eyes in it and on it is suddenly perceived.

Around this evolution of the woman is crystallized the paranoid obsession of the dispossessed man. (After all, the only man in the Algiers of 1832 who let a foreign painter into his harem was precisely that kind of dispossessed person, a former small-time independent corsair and merchant who had become a *chaouch* in obedience to a French bureaucrat.)

It was precisely in the Algeria of 1830, when the foreign intrusion (maintained whatever the cost at the doorsteps of the impoverished seraglios) began with the progressive enclosing of outside space, that a progressively silent freezing of internal communication started to take place between generations, and even more so between the sexes.

These women of Algiers. These figures that have remained immobile on Delacroix's canvas since 1832. If once, long ago, it was possible to see in their steady gaze an expression of nostalgic happiness or the softness of submission, today when we look at them we feel only a sense of their hopeless bitterness.

In the heroic past of our people, the women stood by and shouted during battles; they witnessed the entire battle and kept up their ululations, cries that reached to the horizon like deep gurglings from the center of their beings, sexual calls to encourage the warriors.

But the battles in the nineteenth century that took place farther and farther south in Algeria were lost one after the other. The heroes finished only by biting the dust. And in this final act of failure they continued to see and hear, in the distance, the stares and voices of the women.

For those men who lived and died during that age of surrender, whether they were feudal or proletarian, sons or lovers, the spectacle was the same: the women spectators stood there, they did not move, and it is in retrospective fear then that men still dream of those accusatory looks.

Thus, as an entire society was dividing itself between conquered and conquerer, native and invader, in the harem, now reduced to a shack or cave, a dialogue almost surely began between men and women. Men perhaps wished to "hem in" the woman, the remaining spectator, or, better yet, besieged this last fort in order to forget the defeat they were incurring in the world outside, redoubling the immobility that made a woman a prisoner. But every move they made to fight back with the fury of their ancestors was pushed back, to curdle in itself, and these failures increased their powerlessness and this made the woman a prisoner.

In the oral culture of Algeria, principally in the small walled towns, in poems, songs, even dances about male-female relations, the almost unique theme of the bruise or "the wound" developed, a theme that replaced the spontaneity of ironic desire in other societies.

The fact that the first encounter between the sexes happens only during the rites of marriage sheds light on an obsession that deeply marks our sociocultural being. A living wound is cut into the body of the woman on the assumption that a virgin should be violently deflowered and that marriage is somewhat of a martyrdom for the woman. The wedding night actually becomes a night of blood. Not a night of mutual learning and pleasure, but one of blood and silent staring. A night when the shrill chorus of cries let loose by other women (a sisterly cry that tries to flee into the dark of the night) makes a din in order to cover that silent staring.

This bloody sexual vision of marriage can be traced to that first image of woman: the mother in childbirth. The ambivalent image of the mother in the throes of pain, weeping, totally veiled, yet nude, her legs smeared with blood.

The Koran contains the oft-repeated verse: "Paradise is located at the feet of mothers." If Christianity is the adoration of the Virgin Mother, Islam, more brutal, understands by "mother" a woman without sensual gratification, even before she becomes the source of tenderness. The hope is that the sex-eye that has given birth is no longer menacing. Only the mother, then, can be allowed to look.

At the time of Abdel Kadir, some nomadic tribes that were his followers, the Arbas and the Harazelias, found themselves besieged at the fort of Ksar el-Hayran by their traditional enemy, the Tedjini. That was in 1839. On the fortieth day of the siege, the attackers had scaled the walls when a young girl of the Harazelias named Messaouda (the happy one) saw her tribe turning their backs to the enemy. She cried out,

> Where are you running to? The enemy is on the other side.
> Must a young girl show you how men should behave?
> Well, then, so be it.

She climbed the rampart, slid to the ground outside, and faced the enemy, declaring all the while,

> O where are the men of my tribe?
> Where are my brothers?
> Where are those men who sang me songs of love?

Hearing this, the Harazelias threw themselves into the battle again and rushed to her aid, shouting a cry of battle and love: "Rejoice, Messaouda. Here we are, your brothers, and your lovers!" Stung into action by the young girl, they pushed back the attackers.

Messaouda was returned to the fort in triumph, and since that time the tribes of southern Algeria sing the "Song of Messaouda" to recount these deeds. The song ends with this exaltation of the heroic girl who goaded them into action: "Messaouda, you'll always be a pincer for tearing out teeth!"

Many episodes in the history of nineteenth-century Algerian resistance cite women who left their traditional roles as spectators and became warriors. The women's redoubtable looks goaded the men to courage, but also, at the last hopeless moment, their very presence in the middle of the tumult of combat often decided the battles.

Other chronicles of female heroism mention the tradition of the feudal queen-mother (intelligent, possessing a sense of organization and great courage), as in the example of the ancient Berber queen Kahina.

But the more modest story of Messaouda seems to me to present a newer aspect: it is a variant, of course, on the classic tale of heroism and tribal solidarity, but this time the heroism belongs to someone in danger who, in a single moment, calls out to, defies, and shames the men. Through Messaouda's action, the men are cured of potential cowardice and come back to achieve a victory.

"Be happy, Messaouda. Here we are, your brothers, your lovers . . ." These brothers-lovers, were they more mortified at seeing the female body totally exposed in public or was it the sound of the female voice that electrified them? The sound from deep inside her, that smeared the blood of death with the blood of love. And then there is that last line: "Be happy, Messaouda."

The song of Messaouda commemorates a particular happiness of the woman, a happiness that is at the same time improvised and dangerous. This is the happiness of the woman as creator.

Alas, there were few Messaoudas in our recent history of anticolonial resistance. Before the war of liberation, the search for a national identity (when it included female participation) took pleasure in portraying even the exceptional and renowned women warriors of our history as symbols of motherhood, devoid of flesh and blood. At the end of seven years of a struggle for national liberation, the theme of the heroine came into play again, centering around a group of young girls whom I term the bomb-carriers and whom the enemy jailed for their actions. And so for a time there were harems in prisons like that of Barberousse. The Messaoudas of the Battle of Algiers were called Djamilas.

Since the time of Messaouda's call to arms and the response of her brothers-lovers, since the beginning of our march toward liberation and female pride, what have we said about our women in terms of their speech?

Delacroix's painting shows us two women seemingly surprised at conversing, but their silence does not reach us. It is only the broken speech of those who communicate by lowering their eyes, or by staring into thin air. It is as if the women's speech were a secret over which the servant keeps watch. As for the servant, we cannot tell whether she is spy or accomplice.

From early childhood, the young girl is taught "the cult of silence, which is one of the greatest powers of Arab society." This silence, which a French general, a "friend of the Arabs," calls "power," seems to me to be more like a second mutilation.

Even the woman's "yes," which must follow the beginning of the marriage process and for which a father must ask his daughter (the Koran obliges him to do so), is smothered almost everywhere in the Muslim world. The fact that the young girl cannot be seen uncovered to utter her agreement (or disagreement) makes her speak through male intermediaries. This substitution of one person's word for another is a terrible thing, and it opens the way to the illegal practice of forced marriage. It is as if the violent deflowering of one's word precedes that other deflowering, that other violence.

Moreover, even without an intermediary (*ouali*), it is commonly accepted that the woman's "yes" (which is expected of her) can because of her modesty be expressed by silence or by her tears. We know in ancient Persia of another practice even more indicative of this female powerlessness: in order to consecrate a marriage, the male made his agreement clearly heard, while the fiancée was placed in an adjoining room in the middle of other women near a curtained doorway. To make the necessary "yes" heard, the women would knock the bride's head against the doorway, drawing from her a loud sigh.

Thus, the only word that the woman has to pronounce, this "yes" of submission that takes place under the cover of propriety, is exhaled with great difficulty in response to pain, or through the ambiguity of silent tears.

It is said that in 1911 in various Algerian military campaigns the women (mothers and sisters) would appear at the camps where the native conscripts were incarcerated and would wail and tear at their faces. The image of the woman in tears, lacerating her cheeks in hysteria, became the only current female image for the ethnologists of the time. No more warriors, no more female poetesses. When they weren't invisible and mute, the women, if they remained members of their tribes, appeared only as impotent furies. There was only silence even from the dancer-prostitutes of the Oualed Nail tribes, their bodies completely covered, their idollike faces laden with jewelry, their ankle bracelets tinkling in rhythm.

In Algeria between 1900 and 1954, the native society, more and more dispossessed of its land and even of its tribal structures, began to turn inward, to close in on itself. The Orientalist view, presented first by French military interpreters and then by its photographers and movie makers, revolves around this closed society, especially around the mystery of its women. This hid from general notice the hostility of the entire Algerian community, which knew it was endangered.

Moreover, during the first half of the twentieth century, the constriction of space led to a tightening in parental relations between cousins, brothers, and so on. In relations between brothers and sisters, the women were often disinherited for the benefit of the males of the family (still thanks to that silent "yes" of tears). The alienation of the body from its physical property was another step along the road of abuse of mutual trust.

Doubly imprisoned, then, the woman no longer had the right to anything but a sorrowfully restricted space. The only relationship that was reinforced during this period was that between mother and son, to the point that this relationship stifled all others. It seemed that, among these new proletarians without land (and soon to be without culture), one could find one's roots by means of the umbilical cord.

Beyond this tightening of the family, in which only the males enjoyed tangible benefits, a reconnection with the oral roots of history took place.

Songs, poems. We heard the sound of the mother, a woman without body or an individual voice, but who speaks eloquently in the asexual tone of a collective voice. In this time when defeat seemed to be frozen tragically, a search for models of rebirth began. Some could be traced to this sort of huge nourishing womb where mothers and grandmothers, in the shade of patios and huts, preserved the cultural memory . . .

Illiterate narrators recounted battles lost in the last century, details of colors worthy of a Delacroix; the whispered voices of these forgotten women helped to weave our sense of Algerian history.

In the same way, the larger presence of the mother (woman without body or, on the contrary, with multiple bodies) became the most stabilizing factor in the almost total breakdown of communication between the sexes. At the same time, in her transmission of oral history and literature the mother seems to have become the single authentic expression of cultural identity. Her descriptions were limited, certainly, to the homeland, to the village, to the local popular saint, sometimes to the clan; but they were always concrete and specific as well as full of emotion.

It is as if the mother, recoiling from constant procreation, hid her body in order to take on the voice of an indefinite ancestor, a timeless chorus to retell history. But this is a history from which the archetypal female body has been omitted.

A trace of this chorus can be faintly heard today, the remains of a culture of women who are slowly smothering themselves: the songs of young girls on terraces, the love quatrains of the women of Tlemcen, the magnificent funeral lamentations of the women of Laghouat—an entire literature that is becoming more and more rare, soon to resemble these rivers without mouths that disappear into the sands. It is to the detriment of our folklore that these Jewish and Arab female singers of Algerian wedding rites, this ancient sweetness, this amorous nostalgia, is transmitted only from women to young girls, as if the songs close in on themselves. This is our loss, and that of our cultural future.

We, children on the patios where our mothers appear to us to be still young, serene, dressed in jewelry that doesn't crush them—not yet—but adorns them with an inoffensive vanity, we in the weakened rustlings of the lost female voices, we still perceive the ancient warmth . . . but rarely its dissipation. From these small islands of peace, this intermission that surrounds our memory, are they not reminiscent of the cataleptic autonomy of the Algerian women in the painting? Of a world of women completely separate from men?

This is a world that the boy leaves as he matures, but from which the young girl escapes today only if she liberates herself. For her, this removal takes the place of her former silence: she exhanges the harem and the old community of women for a face-to-face, often false relationship with a man.

Thus, the world of women, when it is no longer full of complicit tender whispers and lost complaints, of a romanticism of vanished enchantment—this world is suddenly becoming an arid and autistic world.

The present reality deveils itself plainly, without a longing for the past: the sound is broken.

Today reality is unveiling itself: it is a plain unvarnished reality, devoid of romanticism; the sound of the past is interrupted, broken.

As the Algerian war of liberation was beginning, from December 1954 to February 1955, Pablo Picasso was living daily in the world of Delacroix's *Femmes d'Alger*. He constructed around them, with them, a universe completely transformed: fifteen canvases and two lithographs with the same title.

It seems to me that with this work the genial Spaniard painter was presiding over a change in the weather.

For the beginning of our "colonial night," Delacroix presented a vision of the women of Algiers that, as Baudelaire remarked admiringly, "emitted a strong perfume, the aroma of a bad place that quickly leads us toward the fathomless extremities of sadness." This "aroma of a bad place" came from a long distance and would become more concentrated the closer one came to it.

But Picasso turned this curse upside-down, dispelled the ill humor, drew from his bold strokes a totally new canvas of happiness. His foresightedness should guide us, even today.

"Picasso always liked to liberate beauties from the harem," says Pierre Daix. And in the new canvases we find a glorious space, a freedom, an awakening of the body in dance, in energy, in free-form movement. But, also, there is the preservation of one of the women as hermetic and olympian (aloof). It is like a proposed moral here, as if a relation was needed between ancient and adorned serenity (the woman, frozen previously in her sudden sadness, is now still motionless, but like a rock of internal strength) and the spontaneous bursting-out into open space.

Because there is no more harem in these works of Picasso. The door is wide open and the light is streaming in. There is no longer even a maidservant-spy, but simply another woman, dancing and mischievous. And finally, except for the queen who only has her breasts visible, the heroines themselves are totally nude. It is as if Picasso found the requisite visual language to translate the Arabic word "unveiled" as "unclothed." This denuding he saw not only as a sign of "emancipation" but also as a sign of rebirth for women in relation to their bodies.

Two years after Picasso presented his new artistic vision, the generation of the women bomb-carriers appeared in the Battle of Algiers. Were these women just the sister-companions of the national heroes? Certainly not. The way things happened was that first the men, isolated and outside of the clan, had to travel a long way, from 1920 almost to 1960, to recover their "sisters-lovers." And the men had to do it in the shadow of the prisons and the cruelty of the French soldiers.

The heroes dead at the hand of the guillotine, those first sacrifices in the cold dawn, caused the young girls to tremble for their blood brothers, and they said so. Until then, the traditional response had been only a cry, an ululation of triumph and death.

But then . . . and here the crux of the matter is whether the women bomb-carriers, the Djamilas chose to leave the harem by chance; for in exposing their bodies to the outside world they were themselves attacking other bodies. Actually, the women threw out these bombs as if they were removing their own breasts. These grenades backfired against them, for later some were tortured with electric shocks applied to their genitalia.

Rape as a traditional act of war may have become a horribly banal thing in the long years of human history since war began. But when our heroines were the victims of such acts, the effect was traumatic for the entire Algerian community. Public denunciation of the act in newspapers and in the courts certainly contributed to greater public knowledge of the scandal; the words that named the dreadful act were unanimously reproachful. In this way a word barrier was breached, a veil was rent before a menaced reality; but the event was too forceful and traumatic for people not to notice. Afterward, after independence, the solidarity of discontent that had been momentarily efficacious (against the enemy) dissolved. What words had uncovered during war became taboo subjects in time of peace. The revelation was reversed. That heavy silence that puts an end to the momentary resurgence of sound returned. The sound was once again muted. It was as if the fathers, brothers, and cousins were saying, "We have already paid enough for this uncovering of words!" They forgot that women had inscribed in their murdered flesh this new assertion of independence upon which silence once more descended.

This sound is broken once more, this look is forbidden again, the ancestral barriers are being rebuilt. "The aroma of a bad place," said Baudelaire. In the modern era there are no more seraglios. But the "structure of the seraglio" still tries to impose itself by its laws: the law of invisibility, the law of silence.

From the fragments of ancient songs I can see how we might search for the restoration of a real conversation among women, those women that Delacroix put into his painting. I only hope that with the door open in bright sunlight, as Picasso painted it, we can search for and find a concrete and permanent liberation of women.

Notes on the Contributors

Malika Abdelaziz and **Fatiha Akeb** are regular staff members of *Algerie Actualité*, one of the major newspapers in Algeria. They have both been concerned with issues of women's position for many years.

Leila Abouzeid is a writer and free-lance journalist based in Rabat, Morocco. She has been a columnist for *Al Alam* (Rabat) and an anchor woman for Moroccan TV. She has also produced a daily program of interviews and music for Moroccan Radio and worked at the press section of the Ministry of Information and the prime minister's office. She is the author of several books, including *The Year of the Elephant*, a novel set in present-day Morocco. She has studied at the Mohammed V University in Rabat.

Daisy al-Amir, an Iraqi writer, has to date four collections of short stories: *Al-Balad al-Baᶜid al-Ladhi Nuhib* (The Far Away Country Which We Love), 1964; *Thumma Taᶜud al-Mauja* (Then Returns the Wave), 1969; *Al-Bait al-ᶜArabiyy al-Saᶜid* (The Happy Arab Home), 1975; and *Fi Dawwamat al-Hub wa ʾl-Karahiya* (In the Whirlpool of Love and Hate), 1979. She is currently director of the Iraqi Cultural Center in Beirut.

Fathiyyah ᶜAwada is a young Egyptian short-story writer. This is her first appearance in English.

Mustafa O. Attir is a well-known sociologist, both in the Arab world and in the West. He received his Ph.D. degree from the University of Minnesota and has conducted cross-cultural research in cooperation with social scientists from several nations working at the University Center for Urban Research at the University of Pittsburgh. His publications in English and Arabic are concerned with problems of social change and modernization; among them is *Attitudes toward Modernization in Libya*. At present he is professor of sociology at al-Fatah University, Tripoli, Libya.

Maroun Baghdadi and **Nayla de Freige** live in Beirut, where they work as journalists for *L'Orient de Jour*, one of the most widely read newspapers in Lebanon. Their series of articles on the Kalashnikov Generation appeared in 1980, received a great deal of critical attention, and served as a focus for discussion in both academic and popular circles.

Halim Barakat was born in Syria and raised in Lebanon. He studied at the American University of Beirut and received his Ph.D. degree in social psychology from the University of Michigan in 1966. He is well known as both a sociologist and a novelist in the Arab world and in the West. One of his four novels, *Days of Dust*, has been translated into English, French, and Japanese. His sociological studies in English include *Lebanon in Strife: Student Preludes to the Civil War* and *Visions of Social Reality in the Contemporary Arab Novel*. He is currently research professor at the Center for Contemporary Arab Studies, Washington, D.C.

Iqbal Barakah is a young Egyptian short-story writer. This is her first appearance in English.

Donna Lee Bowen is assistant professor of political science at Brigham Young University. A graduate of the University of Utah, she received M.A. and Ph.D. degrees from the Department of Near Eastern Languages and Civilizations, University of Chicago. She has studied and conducted research in the Middle East for nearly five years, principally in Morocco but also in Tunisia, Egypt, and Iran. Her major research concerns religious and political attitudes toward demographic problems in North Africa.

Assia Djebar is one of the best-known novelists and writers in North Africa. Her first novel, *Thirst*, appeared in 1957 in Paris; since then she has published three other novels and many short stories in French and most recently produced a film about women's lives in Algeria. This selection is from her most recent work, *Femmes d'Alger dans leur Appartement*.

Evelyn Early received her Ph.D. degree in social anthropology from the University of Chicago. She is finishing a book on the subject of her research, the everyday life and narratives of Baladi women of Cairo. She has served as a public health consultant in Egypt and has researched everyday expressive life in Syria. At present she is assistant professor of anthropology at the University of Houston.

Valerie J. Hoffman is visiting lecturer in the Religious Studies Program and the African Studies Program at the University of Illinois at Urbana-Champaign. She holds an M.A. degree and is completing her Ph.D. degree in Arabic and Islamic studies at the University of Chicago. Her dissertation topic focuses on the participation of women in the Islamic religious life of contemporary Egypt.

Aziza Hussein, a graduate of the American University in Cairo, was one of the founders of the Cairo Family Planning Association. She has spent many years working and researching in the area of family planning and served as president of the International Planned Parenthood Association. From 1962 to 1977 she served as Egyptian delegate to the United Nations Committee on the Status of Women. She has been honored by Egypt and by the Food and Agricultural Organization of the United Nations for her work on behalf of women.

Barbara Lethem Ibrahim is an urban sociologist who has lived and worked in the Arab world since 1973. She holds an M.A. degree from the American University of Beirut and a Ph.D. degree from Indiana University, where her topic was the changing role of women in the industrial labor force in Egypt. She has taught at the American University in Cairo and is currently working with the Ford Foundation in Egypt, developing projects for urban working women in the area.

Ilfat Idilbi was born in Damascus, Syria, where she lives today. She is considered a pioneer in depicting the lives of women in traditional Damascene society. She has published four collections of short stories from which many stories have been translated into German, Russian, and other languages. They are *Qisas Shamiyya* (Damascene Stories), 1960; *Wa Yadhak al-Shaitan* (And Laughs the Devil), 1970; *Wadaʿn Ya Dimashq* (Goodbye Damascus), 1963; and *ʿAssyya al-Damʿ* (Stingy in Tears). Her novel, *Dimashq, Ya Basmat al-Huzn* (Damascus, Smile of Sorrow), 1981, is currently being made into a film by the Syrian Cinema Institute. This is her first appearance in English.

Lamiʿa Abbas al-ʿImarah published her first book in 1959. Since then she has published four other collections, the most recent in 1979. She lives in Baghdad.

Salma Khadra Jayyusi is a well-known Palestinian critic and poet who has been publishing poetry and critical articles since 1959. She graduated from the American University in Beirut and received a Ph.D. degree in Arabic literature from the University of London. Her dissertation, *Trends and Movements in Modern Arabic Poetry*, was published in two volumes in 1977. She has taught in Jerusalem, Baghdad, Khartoum, and Algiers as well as at several American universities. She lives in Cambridge, Massachusetts, where she directs PROTA, a project of translating Arabic literature into English.

Ann Bragdon al-Kadhi has spent seven years in the Middle East, where she taught school and conducted research in anthropology. She received her Ph.D. degree from the State University of New York at Buffalo and currently teaches at the University of Houston.

Shireen Mahdavi was born in Tehran, Iran. She received a B.Sc. degree in social anthropology from the London School of Economics and Political Science. She then worked as a civil servant in Iran for eighteen years, where she served as special adviser to the minister of budget and planning. During that period, she was active in women's movements seeking reform of Islamic laws and improvement in women's position in Iran. After the Revolution she moved to Salt Lake City, Utah, where she has been awarded an M.A. degree in history and is currently working on a Ph.D. degree.

Farzaneh Milani, a native of Iran, lives in Los Angeles, where she writes and teaches. She received a Ph.D. degree from the University of California, Los Angeles, and has published several articles in the field of modern Persian literary criticism.

Safia K. Mohsen received her law degree from Ain Shams University in Cairo and her Ph.D. degree in social anthropology from Michigan State University. Her field research resulted in her work, *Aspects of the Legal Status of Women among the Awlid Ali of the Western Desert of Egypt*. She has been a consultant for many educational projects and is currently involved in research on the lives of women in prison in Egypt. She is professor of anthropology at the State University of New York at Binghamton.

Eric Mueller studied for one year at the Islamic University in Madina, Saudi Arabia. He received an M.A. degree in government from the University of Texas at Austin. He has worked as translator and consultant and is currently finishing a dissertation in Islamic history at the University of Texas at Austin.

Hoda al-Namani was born in Damascus, lived in Egypt for many years, and now resides in Beirut. She has published four books of poetry, including the critically acclaimed *I Remember I Was a Point, I Was a Circle*, from which the title poem was translated. She writes regularly for *Al-Nahar*, Beirut's leading Arabic-language newspaper.

Emily Nasrallah is one of Lebanon's best-known and best-loved novelists. In addition to writing six highly acclaimed novels, two collections of short stories, and a book for children, she has served as delegate to the United Nations Woman's Forum on Population and Development in New York, has taught school, has worked as a journalist, and is currently on the editorial board of the monthly magazine *Fayruz*, published in Beirut. Her first novel, *September Birds*, brought immediate acclaim and in 1983 she was honored for a generation of "outstanding literary work." This is her first appearance in English.

Amin al-Rihani is a well-known literary critic and author in the Arab world. He lives in Beirut.

Andrea B. Rugh received her B.A. degree from Oberlin College and a Ph.D. degree in social anthropology from American University. She has lived in the Middle East for fifteen years, in Lebanon, Saudi Arabia, Egypt, and, presently, Syria. Her book *The Family in Egypt* has just been published by Syracuse University Press. Currently she is senior associate of Creative Associates, a women-owned-and-run consulting firm in Washington, D.C., working on contract in Egypt.

Nawal al-Saʿdawi, Egypt's best-known contemporary feminist, received her medical training in Egypt and has practiced there in the areas of gynecology, family medicine, thoracic surgery, and psychiatry. This experience formed the basis for her first, best-selling book in the Arab world, *Women and Sex*. She has since published several books and many short stories and articles; *The Hidden Face of Eve* has been translated into English. She has also worked for the United Nations in Beirut. In 1980 she was imprisoned by President Anwar Sadat on the basis of her controversial views on women's condition in Egypt. Today she lives in Cairo and lectures regularly in the West.

Nagat al-Sanabary holds a B.A. degree from Cairo University, two education diplomas from Ain Shams University, and M.A. and Ph.D. degrees in educational administration from the University of California, Berkeley. She has taught in high school, worked as radio broadcaster in

Cairo, and taught in college in the United States. Since 1977 she has been associate director of the Women's Center, University of California, Berkeley.

Rosemary Sayigh is the author of the book *Palestinians, from Peasants to Revolutionaries*. English by birth, she has lived for many years in the Arab world, where she has worked as a teacher, an editor, and a journalist (Middle East correspondent for various papers, including the *Economist*). She now teaches at the American University in Beirut and is conducting research among Palestinian women.

Fadwa Tuqan lives in Nablus on the West Bank, where she was born, but her poetry is read all over the Arab world. She published three volumes of love poems, beginning in 1955. After the 1967 war, her work became more politically centered and she has published five collections of poetry dealing with the situation of the Palestinians. Her most recent work was *Nightmare in Daylight* (1974).

Nahid F. Toubia became, in 1981, the first Sudanese woman surgeon. She received her basic medical education at Cairo University, practiced for two years in the Sudan, and did her surgery specialization in the United Kingdom. She is currently consultant pediatric surgeon at Khartoum Teaching Hospital and a member of the editorial board of the *Sudan Medical Journal*. She is active in the Sudanese feminist movement and is currently in charge of the Female Circumcision Information and Resource Centre being established at the Traditional Medicine Research Institute of the Sudan National Council for Research.

Sabra Webber spent more than five years in Tunisia, first teaching in the Peace Corps, then doing research for her M.A. degree in folklore from the University of California, Berkeley, and her Ph.D. degree in anthropology and folklore from the University of Texas at Austin. Her Ph.D. dissertation focused on male storytelling in a Tunisian Mediterranean town, and her M.A. thesis on Tunisian riddles. A volume of Tunisian verbal art collected by Webber (nursery rhymes, lullabies, children's games) was published in Tunisia in 1969.